PRIVACY LAW

A COMPARATIVE STUDY

S.K. SHARMA

ATLANTIC PUBLISHERS & DISTRIBUTORS

Published by
ATLANTIC PUBLISHERS & DISTRIBUTORS
B-2, Vishal Enclave, New Delhi-27
Phone: 5413460

Sales Office
4346/4C, Ansari Road, Darya Ganj,
New Delhi-110 002
Phone: 3273880

ISBN 81-7156-385-6

Typeset at
APD Computer Graphics
B-2, Vishal Enclave, New Delhi-110 027
Printed in India at
Print India, Maya Puri
New Delhi

DEDICATED

To

Justice Suba Rao, (Judge of the Supreme Court of India) for his minority view in *Kharak Singh* Vs. *State of U.P.*

PREFACE

"Privacy Law–A Comparative Study" is the comparative analysis of the privacy law prevailing all over the world. The leading decisions of various courts from *Griswold* to *Govind* have been judicially analysed. The book divided into 17 Chapters has been made comparative. Freedom of Information Act of U.S.A. has been critically commented upon. The Younger Committee Report of U.K. and the Morrison Report of Australia have also been briefed. Constitutional position of privacy in U.S.A., U.K., India, West Germany, Australia, Canada and other countries has been emphasised. United Nations provisions relating to privacy have been cited. Role of European Convention on Human Rights and the Covenant on Civil and Political Rights has been evaluated.

This is a systematic study of a small part of a big chapter on Fundamental Rights. An effort has been made to cover every relevent aspect of the subject. I hope that the book will interest the readers all the world over. All suggestions for future editions are welcome.

S. K. SHARMA
Advocate

CONTENTS

I

INTRODUCTION

> **"Over the Years, legal scholars have attempted to define privacy – one of the earliest is Lewis D. Brandeis's formulation of it in 1890 as "the right to be let alone".**

CONSTANCE HOLDEN OF SCIENCE MAGAZINE

The word privacy never appears in the constitution. It is only in the last century that this word has been used as a legal concept to describe the state's duty to let people alone. A later formulation by Alan F. Westin of Columbia University is that privacy is "the claim of individuals, groups or institutions to determine for themselves when, how and to what extent information about themselves is communicated to others". Privacy is not defined by the constitution although the preponderance of legal opinion has it that the right to privacy is implicit in the Bill of Rights.

(1) *Privacy not an abstract Concept*

Privacy is not an abstract concept. It has meaning only in relation to a national culture a particular political system and a specific period of time. It has become an issue in modern democratic societies which are characterised by large scale sophisticated bureaucratic structures and advanced Technology in communications and information systems. Technological development has been permitted to evolve without regard for its impact on our democratic political system. Ongoing social revolution threatens to make privacy impossible.

(2) *Privacy in different political systems*

A major factor of the privacy problem is the absence of legislation and organisational rules ensuring privacy, confidentiality and due process to the subjects of computerised information. Data banks have been established at all levels of govt., business and the military services without any real knowledge or concern for their potential impact over individual rights. The privacy issue is all the more urgent because of the widespread use of information systems to administer services which are considered essential to their well being. Along with the values of a democratic system people have constantly rising expectations in terms of medical services, health insurance, credit, family assistance and education. Those in search of jobs, credit, housing, welfare and other services must disclose extensive information of a particular nature in order to obtain these benefits. This information further accumulates into the files maintained by various private and public institutions. Postponing attention to this problem has led to believe that an encroachment into their personal privacy is the price they have to pay to enjoy these services. Many people support the concept of privacy with a sense that it is somehow related to other values, such as individual freedom or the pursuit of happiness. So important is the value of privacy that one can use it to distinguish between different types of political systems. In authoritarian systems, such as the Soviet Union, privacy is enjoyed by the politburo, the highest organ of the Communist Party and the source of all policy in that society, on the other hand, the Soviet citizenry is subjected to thorough surveillance. In liberal democratic societies, individuals enjoy privacy in order to pursue their happiness and interest groups enjoy privacy in order to form public consensus, resolve conflicts and promote the expression of independent ideas. The partial autonomy of individual, family, religious and corporate groups in a liberal society prevents total politicising of life.

Every democratic society develops particular privacy balances between the need of the governmental agencies for privacy and the need of the free press and interest groups for knowledge of government operations. At any time in an open society there are conflicts between values, such as national security (which requires a certain amount of secrecy), freedom of the press, the right to know and the right to privacy. Compromise between these conflicts of interest vary according to time and place. Fundamental values of individual and group autonomy cannot be compromised without transforming the entire political system.

(3) *Privacy at the basis of man's claim for human dignity*

Privacy is the guarantor of individual moral autonomy, a basic value in a democratic system of government. Privacy can be defined as the right to control one's physical being and one's information system. Both rights are closely related to the principle of respect for persons. Both must be reinterpreted in the light of changing technological and social contexts. Privacy, the control of one's own person and of the extension of one's person in the form of information, is at the basis of man's claim for human dignity. Information about a person is an extension of selfhood, for him to communicate or withhold as he sees fit. Even when an individual divulges personal information to receive certain benefits, such as credit or insurance, or to win a law-suit, he has a continuing interest in retaining control over that information beyond the original disclosure, and especially the right to decide whether this information should be communicated to third parties.

(4) *Place of the individual in a technological society*

If the facts about a person are freely disclosed with the knowledge and consent that they may be shared with others, there has been no violation of privacy. A person's control over personal information and access to and dissemination of that information are at the heart of individual autonomy. The privacy issue involves other concerns often emotionally associated with, but not actually included in the concept of privacy. People may feel threatened by the very existence of massive and efficient information systems even though the privacy has not actually been invaded. They are often concerned about the endless search for personal data by social scientists, market researchers, opinion pollsters, and the institutions that use this data. When the institutions seeking information also control funds, the threat appears much greater. Although people may change institutions that operate information systems with invasion of privacy, their real complaint is often about institutional power and its linkage to possession of informaion. An issue frequently associated with privacy is the relationship of the individual to any large institution operating a data bank.

These concerns focus on the place of the individual in a technological society and reveal that not too much power is held by too few, but that so little is held by so many. In the relationship between individuals and organisations, scales are balanced in favour of the latter. The information process is one way in which institutions learn more about individuals, but individuals learn no more about institutions or even what institutions learn about them. Concern for privacy is caught up in the more general debate regarding the effect of Technology on society. Some contemporary thinkers share a pessimistic view of this relationship and conclude that what is technically feasible is allowed to occur without regard for the consequences. Hannab Arendlt, Herbert Marcuse and Lewis Mumford share this attitude. At the other end of the spectrum are those who argue with Alvin Toffler that technology has allowed the individual a greater range of choice than he has ever enjoyed before, one that may even be bewilderingly broad. They argue further that problems resulting from modern technology can be shared by the use of more technology. The privacy issue, however, will suffer from being embroiled in this debate. Since technology is here to stay, the privacy discussion should ,not focus on its desirability, but rather on finding ways to protect humanistic values and goals. Given the ease and speed with which information passes from one organisation to another, it could become the basis for unjust discrimination.

(5) *Social and Psychological Bases for the desire for Privacy*

Privacy has always been high on the hierarchy of values of the people. Privacy should not be sacrificed for the sake of governmental efficiency any more than other basic freedoms. Privacy, should not be viewed in isolation from other preferences of people, when it conflicts with other values, chiefly economic well being, it likely will give way. If people have to make choices, probably they would rather give up some or much prıvacy in order to gain what to them is the greater goal. For some reasons, social and behavioural scientists have made few inquiries into the social or psychological bases for the desire for privacy.

(6) *Desire for Privacy*

It is by no means a self-evident proposition that people, beset by the loneliness of living on a dying cinder in the midst of limitless space, prefer privacy over, say, the solace to be gained from the warmth of human associations. The tendency of the people to form groups, noticed as far back as the Tocqueville, is testimony to a pervasive wish not to be alone. Furthermore, as......[Dostoievsky's) Grand Inquisitor well knew, man cannot stand the intolerable burden of freedom. Few–only a few–would choose a Robinson Crusoe existence, either on a remote island or as hermits. Man is conformist, rather than individualist. The fear of freedom is greater than the desire for it. The Inquisitor said that man requires three things :

miracles, mystery and authority. It is these, rather than atomistic individualism, that drive man, particularly man in a mass society. Freedom and that includes privacy are of less consequence. Attainment of privacy means loneliness – precisely what most people likely avoid (if they can).

(7) *Legal interest in privacy*

Legal, including judicial interest in privacy coincides roughly in time with the closing of the American frontier. The seminal law journal article on privacy, by Warren and Brandeis, was published in 1890 precisely the time that Frederick Jackson Turner said that the frontier had vanished. But concomitantly with increasing legal recognition of privacy, there has developed a Technological ability to invade it by a number of means heretofore not known. Data on individuals is easily collected and as easily stored. What is Technologically possible will be done. Privacy tends to get recognition and protection in the law when the interests of the state are considered to be furthered – or, at least, are not considered to be endangered. The desire for companionship, the fear of loneliness far outweigh individual interests in privacy. Professor Miller asserts that people are essentially in effect, not loners but herd animals, not individualists but conformists. Privacy, he says, means loneliness a condition intolerable to most people.

(8) *The Civil Liberties Concept of Privacy*

The values of privacy that are the concern of Civil Libertarians do not deny and are not inconsistent with the social values of companionship, mutual dependency within families, love, team, sports, political activity and all the other things that people do, by their own choice, within other people. To value one's privacy enough to litigate over it, as in *Wyman* vs. *James* or the *Abortion* cases, one need not be an actual or potential hermit, nor even an admirer of hermits (Wyman involved warrantless searches of welfare recipients' homes).

The Civil Liberties concept of privacy embraces that area within the life of a person to which he can say to an intruder, "This is none of your business. Keep out." It becomes a true Civil Liberties issue where the intruder is the government, or where the government licences the intruder in some way, against the will of the person intruded upon.

(9) *Need of people for privacy*

The need of people for privacy is not limited to the middle or upper classes, as shown by *Wyman* vs. *James*. The need is perhaps most acute where the ability to achieve privacy is least, at the interface between the law enforcement arms of society and persons accused of crime. The whole law of search and seizure expressed the never-ending efforts of members of these classes to safeguard to themselves a small personal enclave into which the minions of the law cannot pear. That people ask the courts to protect their right of privacy is as significant as that the right is hard to defend, and is a sufficient proof that there is a human need for privacy as fundamental and as real as the social needs that Professor Miller puts first.

The purpose of any same political ideology should be freedom for all human beings. In psychological terms, we want all people to experience the feeling of freedom. In many instances Candor yields a wonderous sensation of being free. Unquestionably, people must be able to free themselves of ideas and emotions that trouble them and upset their relationships with others, and which in many cases confuse and damage institutions. Children should be allowed to safely reveal their problems to school personnel, workers their inner worlds to one another and their bosses, family members to each other. People do have a need to confess or let others know bits and pieces of their private lives. But if there is a need to reveal, there is also a need to protect and withhold.

(10) *Privacy* Versus *the Press*

The right to privacy – perhaps the most cherished right of all – is guaranteed, but more and more lately it is coming into conflict in the courts with the press right to report freely news. How much privacy does a person who is not a public figure have when his privacy collides with the rights of the press. The person's right to disseminate information was explicitly guaranteed in the constitution, and an individual's right to privacy has been obtained through a series of judicial rulings, each one put atop the other like so many bricks in a wall, since the beginning of the century. The reality of the law is such that lawyers who defend newspapers in privacy cases will now bring appeals based on the broader words of the ruling, hoping finally to inch the court toward absolutely guaranteeing the press the right to print whatever information it wants. Do private people who are connected to events of a public interest have a buffer of privacy against reporting and, if so, how wide a buffer? Most legal experts think it will be a slow process to define the distinction between private facts and public news, and to determine precisely when the printing of a private fact is offensive.

(11) ***On Balancing Rights***

The presentation of privacy seems to be one of the main legitimate passions of the moment. This concern for privacy is welcome – as long as it is not used as an excuse to strengthen the opportunities for secrecy in the government. Edward Shills, a sociologist, political scientist and a student of the American, British and German systems of government has written of the balance we seek. Reviewing the history of western man's struggle for freedom in *The Torment of Secrecy*, he writes:

> The struggle for constitutional government, for the extension of the franchise and particularly for the freedom of the press.... was directed against privacy in government. Almost as much as the extension of the franchise and constitutional restraint on monarchical absolutism, publicity regarding political and administrative affairs was a fundamental aim of the modern liberal democratic movement. The demand for the publicity of governmental affairs was attended by a demand for the protection and reinforcement of privacy in other spheres – a demand which was itself the child of the aspiration for individual liberty.

The result Shills says was a balancing of rights. The traditions of liberal and individualistic democracy maintained an equilibrium of publicity, privacy and secrecy. The equilibrium was enabled to exist as long as the beneficiaries and protagonists of each spector .... respected the legitimacy of the other two and were confident that they would not use their power and opportunities to disrupt the equilibrium. The principles of privacy, secrecy and publicity are not harmonious, among themselves. The existence of each rests on a self-restrictive tendency in each of the others.

*

II

DEVELOPMENT

> **"The accelerating development of technology and the almost exponential expansion of the ability to manipulate personal information in variegated ways may be altering the balance between the individual citizen and those institutions in society that seek to exercise control over him. The individual has little ability to protect himself against governmental and private snoopers who can employ sophisticated electronic surveillance to monitor his activities and to obtain information about him. More substantial legal safeguards than those currently available are required merely to maintain the *status quo* in the privacy field."**
>
> *Miller, Computers and Privacy (1969)*
> *67 Michigan L.R. 10 91 at 1176-77*

The excesses of media publicity in the aftermath of the assassination of President Kennedy in Nov. 1963 were seen by the Warren Commission as "a dramatic affirmation of the need for steps to bring about a proper balance between the right of the public to be kept informed and the right of the individual to a fair and impartial trial."

(1) *Warren and Brandeis View*

The right to privacy goes far beyond a claim to be protected from the unjustifiable intrusions of the press and the other media. A rapidly developing technology which makes it easily possible to exercise surveillance over the activities and conduct of individual by the use and exploration of a variety of devices, has become a matter of increasing and anxious concern. Almost forty years after the publication of the Warren and Brandeis article, Brandeis, by this time a distinguished judge of the Supreme Court of the United States wrote in *Olmstead* vs. *United States* (1928) 277 U.S. 438, case which raised the issue of the admissibility of evidence obtained by eavesdropping (specifically by Telephone tapping) against a man charged with crime. Brandeis at the time in dissent, declared that it was not admissible. In a famous and prophetic passage he wrote:

> "Discovery and invention have made it possible for the Government by means far more effective than stretching upon the rack to obtain disclosure in court of what is whispered in the closet... The progress of Science in furnishing the Government with means of espionage is not likely to stop wire-tapping. Ways may some day be developed by which the Government without removing papers from secret drawers, can reproduce them in court, and by which time it will be enabled to expose to a jury the most ultimate occurrences of the home. Advances in the psychic and related sciences may bring means of exploring unexposed beliefs, thoughts and emotions. The makers of the constitution.... sought to protect Americans in their beliefs, their thoughts, their emotions and their sensations. They conferred as against the Government, the right to be let alone ...... the most comprehensive of rights and the rights most valued by civilised man."

In the course of time, Brandeis' view, expressed in ***Olmstead*** in dissent, became the law. Brandeis spoke of surveillance by government, which has special dangers. Such devices are not only available to, and have not been used exclusively by governmental instrumentalities. They are part of the armoury of an army of snooper. Computer technology makes a special and formidable contribution to the problem. The capacity of the computers to assimilate and store and print out a mass of information provides the possibility of comprehensive surveillance by dossier over individuals with an ease and to an extent never before comprehended. Whatever the present dimensions of the threat, the possibilities of far-reaching surveillance are very real.

(2) *The lead by the United States*

The United States has given leadership in the common law world in exploring the complex issues involved in the protection of privacy. Committees in the United Kingdom have made substantial reports on privacy (Report of the Committee on Privacy of 1972; Younger Report), on contempt of court, bearing *inter alia*, on issues of publicity and fair trial and on defamation. Over the past decade and a half private members' bills have been introduced into the United Kingdom Parliament to deal with various aspects of privacy starting with Lord Mancroft's Right of Privacy Bill of 1961 which attracted distinguished and thoughtful participation in the debate in the House of Lords and which purported to give a right of action to an individual for unauthorised publication in the mass media of the words "relating to his personal affairs or conduct" if such publication is calculated to cause him distress or embarrassment. During the sixties, other bills introduced in the United Kingdom Parliament dealt with various aspects of the matter with industrial espionage, with computer data banks, with electronic surveillance and with family generally. The comprehensive *Walden Bill* of 1969 was inspired by the Report and Proposals of a Committee of Justice, the United Kingdom section of the International Commission of Jurists, and the *Walden Bill* in turn led the United Kingdom Government to appoint the *Younger Committee* whose substantial report on privacy appeared in 1972. In Canada broadly framed Acts dealing with privacy issues have been enacted in British Columbia and Manitoba. In Australia, there has been considerable activity in the area of defamation and privacy.

(3) *Concern with problems of privacy in Australia*

There has been growing and active concern with problems of privacy in Australia. Legislation in two states in the latter 1960's dealt with surveillance devices. In 1971 legislation was enacted in Queensland which tackled a variety of privacy issues including credit reporting and data banks; in South Australia in 1972, legislation dealt with surveillance devices and more recently there has been sensitive and acrimonious debate on proposed legislation in South Australia and Tasmania designed to provide more comprehensive protection for privacy. One of the most significant and comprehensive surveys of the privacy issue in Australia has been the Report on the Reform of the Law concerning Privacy by Professor W.L. Morrison which was commissioned by the conference of Attorney-General of the Commonwealth and the Australian States and was published in 1973. This very able study canvassed many issues and aspects of privacy and it critically examined the recommendations of the Younger Committee published in the United Kingdom in the previous year. Recommendations in the Morrison report have been translated into law in New South Wales (Privacy Act, 1975). In the juristic literature there has been a burgeoning interest in privacy in recent years.

(4) *Position in United Kingdom*

The Younger Committee which reported on privacy in the United Kingdom in 1972 observed that while privacy is widely recognised as a legally defensible right in the United States, it is not established as a coherent principle of law and it has not significantly contributed to Respect for Privacy in everyday life, especially by the mass publicity media. It is generally agreed that, to this point, the Common Law of England and many other commonwealth Common Law Jurisdictions knows no generalised right to privacy. In the parliamentary debate on the first of the private members' Bills on privacy introduced in the United Kingdom during the 1960's, *Lord Mancroft's Right of Privacy Bill, 1961*, Lord Denning said that the law on privacy in the United States had evolved from the English Common Law and that in England "the judges may well do it". The Younger Committee commented that Great Britain has less in its law aimed specifically at the invasion of privacy than any other country whose law it had examined. Lord Denning's statement in the debate on the *Mancroft's Bill* was very much in character, but it is very doubtful if the Common Law of England would, at this time, recognise or announce a general right of privacy.

As in England, so elsewhere in The Commonwealth, there has been no common law development of a generalised right to privacy. In the Australian High Court in *Victoria Park Racing Co*. Vs. *Taylor* (1937) 58 C.L.R. 479, Latham C.J. said that however desirable some "limitation upon invasion of privacy might be, no authority shows that any general right of privacy exists". There is no mention of privacy and the reason is surely that *Indian law*, had, to that point, developed no general right to privacy. At the international level, Art. 12 of the *Universal Declaration of Human Rights* and Art. 17 of the *Covenant on Civil and Political Rights* affirm a general right to privacy.

(5) *Composite Picture of the Development*

Series of private members' Bills were introduced in the United Kingdom Parliament during the 1960's, which dealt with privacy issues, *Lord Mancroft's Bill* was concerned with privacy in the context of the media. Other Bills have defined the right to privacy in very broad and general terms while others have listed specific diverse areas of conduct which are said to constitute breaches of privacy for example industrial espionage, electronic surveillance and data banks. In the United States there has been a great volume of writing and substantive legislative investigation and enactment of which Title III of the omnibus *Crime Control and Safe Streets Act, 1968*, dealing particularly with wiretapping and electronic surveillance is the most conspicuous recent example. In Canada, at least two provinces have enacted Privacy Acts, in Australia at Commonwealth and State levels, there is legislation relating to wiretapping to electronic surveillances, data banks and there is a tendency on the part of the State Legislatures providing for more general right to privacy. In the United Kingdom, the debate on *Mr. Walden's Bill* in 1970 led to the appointment of the *Younger Committee* whose terms of reference were to consider whether legislation was needed to give further protection to the individual citizen and to commercial and industrial interests against intrusions into privacy by private persons and organisations or by companies but the committee was not authorised to enquire into intrusions into privacy by public authorities. The Committee reported in 1972. In that year, the Attorney-General of the Commonwealth of the Australian States commissioned a report by *Prof. W.L. Morrison* of the University of Sydney, with particular reference to the question of the protection of the privacy of the individuals having regard to the increased means of collecting, storing, retrieving and disseminating information.

(6) *Concern for the Protection of Privacy*

Advancing technology has enabled the media to make even more searching intrusions into individual privacy and the reach of the television, with the assist of the satellite, is formidable. The Younger Committee spoke of a growing tendency on the part of the media to engage in "investigative journalism" and devoted a substantial part of its report to problems associated with the media. Edward Shills has written of the growth of a "new sector of the profession of journalism that regarded the penetration of the private spheres as its media occupational task. It justified this penetration by reference to the satisfaction of popular desire and the freedom of the press to enlighten the public." The Younger Committee noted that from a wider point of view, concern for the protection of the privacy has been stimulated by the growing pressures exerted by modern industrial society upon the home and daily life including such factors as the density of urban housing and the consequent difficulty of escaping from the observation of neighbours.

(7) *Threats to Privacy*

It is also likely that the threats to privacy represented by the assembly of massive computerised data banks are potential, rather than actual. The Younger Committee noted that "the computer problem as it affects privacy in Great Britain is one of apprehensions and fears and not so far, one of facts and figures, and Professor Morrison's estimate of the Australian situation was in substantial accord with this. He noted further that computer organisations displayed the greater sensitivity to the possible effects on privacy of what they were doing, and the utmost anxiety to see that privacy was fully protected. There are seriously and deeply felt fears concerning the use to which such computer data banks may be put, especially in such fields as credit, medical and police records. There is certainly deep concern at the use of the battery of sophisticated devices available and constantly becoming available for surveillance and information gathering. Spectacular and widely publicized events add to the unease, the revelations of wiretapping, bugging and break-ins associated with *watergate* have brought to many a new or renewal awareness of the scale and character of intrusions into individual privacy.

(8) *Privacy Not Absolute*

No one can claim that privacy can or should be absolute; the very fact of living in society involves some sacrifice of it, and there is often a head-long collision between the individual's claim to privacy and highly prized social values such as freedom of expression and the media and the socially desirable objectives such as enforcement of the Criminal Law; efficient government and national security. Most constitutional Civil Rights would be details of the one true civil right, the right to privacy. There is, however, a support for a very broad definition of privacy in modern American cases. It seems that the court in these cases has been using the term privacy in a strained sense, and that what is in issue in cases like *Griswold* and *Roe* Vs. *Wade* is individual's autonomy or his interest in self-determination rather than his privacy.

(9) *Right to Be Let Alone Not Synonymous with Privacy*

The Younger Committee argued that it was appropriate to narrow the definition of privacy, that while there was an element of privacy in the state of being let alone, it was not synonymous with privacy. An unqualified right of this kind would be an unrealistic concept, incompatible with the concept of society, which implies willingness not to be let entirely alone and a recognition that other people may be interested and consequently concerned about us. The committee proposed a narrower definition of privacy which it saw as having two main aspects: one, one's home, family and relationships, the other, privacy of information, the right to be determined for oneself how and to what extent information about oneself is communicated to others.

(10) *Breach of Privacy*

In the German Legal System, defamation has lost its identity as a separate tort and has become fused into the broader tort of the infringement of the right of personality, but this has not occurred, thus far, in the common law. The press has consistently attacked proposals designed to provide a general tort action for privacy. It is at best doubtful whether the public disclosures of family life and celebrations which outraged Mr. Samuel Warren and which were said to be the catalyst of the famous Warren & Brandeis article of 1890 would have given rise to a modern action for breach of privacy.

Both the majority in the *Younger Committee* & Professor Morrison in his Australian Report are major contributors to the study of privacy problem and both opposed the enactment of a general tort provision for the protection of privacy. In such an unchartered area, there would be formidable problems in striking acceptable balances between values implicit in the respect for privacy and other values of at least equal importance to the well-being of society. The recommendations of the *Younger Committee*, were cautiously progressive and that they were very gentle with the press. Morrison approach was similar in that he favoured an examination of specific aspects of privacy problems and central to his recommendations was the establishment of a continuing privacy committee which would receive submissions and conduct research so as to provide the necessary background information for the task of drafting appropriate legislation and for taking appropriate action to assure due protection for privacy. The burden of guarding privacy in a free society should not be on its citizens, it is the government that must justify its need to electrically eavesdrop. Almost any form of invasion of privacy can be and indeed is defended on grounds of public interest, but the onus of justification must always rest on the person or authority claiming to exercise surveillance. The annihilation of all privacy might perhaps bring organised crime to an end. In the police state of George Orwell's imagination, the commission of a private crime was practically impossible but the price paid was an all-embracing public crime of such magnitude that freedom was totally destroyed.

(11) *Human Rights & Privacy*

Professor Rene Marcic was an original and interesting theoretician of the Neo-Catholic conception of natural law. Until his tragic death several years ago in an airplane crash he lived in the lovely Austrian city of Salzburg. Marcic wrote a good deal about human rights. He believed, however, that pre-eminent among all of man's God-given rights, the culmination of his freedoms, is the freedom to die. Marcic's religio-social pessimism led him to a gloomy, apocalytic view of the limits of human freedom. "Death, although it is our end, is the meaning of existence", he wrote. Marcic believed that the "culmination, consummation, and end" of life is to be found in the single moment of death. We read in *Man-Law-Cosmos*, the last book Marcic wrote before his death, that the ultimate freedom and ultimate equality of mankind appear in death.

Equality in Death : Every body is equal in the face of death. But why hymn equality in the strains of a requiem? Perhaps there was a time when he thought of equality in death could console the slave who had no rights in life. But people who are truly free strive above all to realise that freedom – and its necessary condition, equality – in life and through life.

Right to Life : First, among the rights of man which the official doctrine of the Catholic church affirms is the "right to life". Many commentators attempt to justify the prohibition of artificial birth control and of the voluntary termination of pregnancy through abortion by attributing absolute rights, above all the right to life, to the unborn.

Legal Protection of Unborn Child : On May 24, 1978 a Liverpool Court heard the suit brought by one Bill Paton against his wife. The plaintiff asked the court to issue a decision requiring his wife to relinquish her intention of having an abortion. Paton based his argument on the "right of his unborn child." The court denied the plaintiff's petition. Thereupon the *Society for the Protection of*

Unborn Children (London) began a campaign whose slogan was "Help the unborn child to obtain legal protection."

There are a number of positions that might be taken on the question of abortion, but to restrict the freedom of a woman to terminate her pregnancy on the basis of the "right to life" of a newly conceived child is from the point of view of materialist philosophy, unjustifiable.

Ecological Rights of Man : The noted French dramatist, author of absurdist plays, and member of the Academy of Letters *Eugene Ionesco* sees the entire question of human rights through the prism of homosexuality. If, in a given society, a man's right to have intimate relations with a member of his own sex is acknowledged then human rights are respected there. *Manfred Siebker* of the Federal Republic of Germany, made the curious suggestion in the Frankfurter Hefte that we return to the last paradise of mutual equilibrium by global recognition of the four basic "ecological rights of man". The system of human rights consists, according to Siebker, of the right to live without work, the right to poverty, the "right to a non-smokers' section", and the right to truth. These examples are manifestations of peripheral positions in the controversy about human rights. They represent extreme points of view as to what constitutes human rights.

John Paul II Address : The idea of a deideologized approach to the problem of human rights was expressed with considerable clarity by Pope John Paul II in an address that he gave in January 1979, during a conference of Latin American bishops in Puebla (Mexico). Having condemned violations of basic human rights as universally tolerated, the Pope declared that "the church has no need to resort to systems and ideologies in order to love, defend man, and attribute to his liberation". As Le Monde commented with a certain degree of surprise, "For John Paul II human rights are not connected with any ideology."

Peace and Human Rights : The relationship between international co-operation for peace, security and respect for human rights is embodied in the United Nations Charter, the basic constitutional instrument of the world organisation. Paragraph 3 of Article I stresses the need for "promoting and encouraging respect for human rights and fundamental freedoms for all without distinction as to race, sex, language, or religion". United Nations documents have repeatedly stressed that "peace is the underlying condition for the full observance of human rights and war is their negation" (This quote is from a resolution adopted by the UN-sponsored International Conference on Human Rights in 1968).

The Right to live in peace : The right to live in peace is a basic and essential right binding together the entire system of human rights and freedoms. The right to live in peace is in fact the right to life itself; it tops the scale of values of human rights since it is the prerequisite of all other rights. The supreme expression of the right to live is the right to live in the totally emancipated and genuinely free environment. The supreme expression of the synthesis of the right to peace and of justice is the right to live in a world of international security and social justice. The right to live in peace is a right of man as an individual. It also belongs to nations and should be extended to the entire human race. War is a denial of this right, of the supreme human value – life – and the paramount human right to live in peace and security. More and more people around the world realize that peace and human rights are organically linked. They raise their voices to demand that the right to peace be recognised as a basic human right. The growing acceptance of this approach was evident at the Peace and Human Rights – Human Rights and Peace Conference named after Dr. Armand Hammer, prominent U.S. industralist and public figure. In its Final Document the conference solemnly reaffirmed that "the right to peace should be recognised as a human right." It will take time and effort to fit the right to peace into the key international legal instruments. The important thing is that today the right to peace as a human right is already beginning to emerge as a juridical norm.

Protection of Human Rights : Protection of human rights must be viewed in close association with the other fundamental principles of international relations. This was reflected in the Final Act of the Helsinki Conference on Security and Cooperation in Europe. Significantly, among the ten basic principles listed in the Final Act, the following two are found side by side: the sixth, "non-intervention in internal affairs;" and the seventh: "respect for human rights and fundamental freedoms, including the freedom of thought, conscience, religion or belief." Joint elaboration and adoption of international agreements on human rights and, most importantly, international obligations under these agreeements, are the most significant form of international cooperation in the field of human rights. The United Nations has drafted and adopted about 20 such international instruments. The principal agreements are:

(a) International Covenant on Civil and Political Rights.
(b) International Covenant on Economic, Social and Cultural Rights.
(c) International Convention on the Elimination of All Forms of Racial Discrimination
(d) Convention on the Prevention and Punishment of the Crime of Genocide.
(e) Convention on the Suppression and Punishment of the Crime of Apartheid.
(f) Convention on the Suppression of the Traffic in Persons and of the Exploitation of the Prostitution of others.
(g) Convention on the Political Rights of Women.
(h) Convention on the Non-Applicability of Statutory Limitations to War Crimes and Crimes Against Humanity.

Protection in United States: The Terms "open" and "closed" can hardly be of any use for a serious analysis and objective comparison of socially different political systems. There is an aspect of western society that is indeed open. Perhaps "Transparent" would be a better word, since it is increasingly open to covert government surveillance. Sophisticated technology and computer data processing make this surveillance particularly widespread and dangerous. Various public organisations in the United States, West Germany and Great Britain have recently drawn public attention to the growing threat of police surveillance. In the United States over 40 organisations and activist groups are now campaigning vigorously, including the Los Angeles Citizens' Commission of Police Repression, the Program on Government Surveillance and Citizens' Rights, the Coalition Against Government Spying of Philadelphia, and the National Organising Conference of the Campaign to stop Government spying. The U.S. administration was compelled to respond to the public outcry against civil rights violations. Special government bodies were established to draft guarantees of personal inviolability against "excessive" police surveillance. One such body is the *Advisory Committee on Automated Data Systems*, established by the Department of Health, Education and Welfare. The Committee has published a report entitled *Records, Computers and the Rights of Citizens* [DHEW Publication No. (OS) 73-94]. Among other things, the report admits that "the public fear of.... a pervasive network of intelligence dossiers focuses on the computer, but it includes other marvels of twentieth century engineering such as the telephone tap, the wireless microphone, the automatic surveillance camera, and the rest of the modern investigator's espionage". The Committee notes hypocritically that "such worries seem naive" to a data processing specialist. To appease public opinion, several directives have been issued. These, however, merely create on illusion of guarantees against police surveillance that pervades public and private life. Besides, their language is so complex and specialised that citizens are practically unable to resort to them. Section 205 (C) (2) (B) (i) (II) of the *Social Security Act* as amended by section 137 of Public Law 92 – 603 is a good example. A curious thing happened in this connection. In 1979 there were calls in the United States to begin preparations for the Bicentennial of the United States Constitution, to be held in 1987. There was talk of updating the constitution. Experienced law experts justifiably stressed that "changed time have presented wholly new situations calling for constitutional protection of individual and group rights." Typically, the right to privacy of personal and public life was foremost among recommendations of new human rights provisions to be included in the constitution. Ironically, the demand for constitutional guarantees against "undue governmental ... curiosity" that appeared in the *American Bar Association Journal*, was raised by none other than William Colby, CIA Director from 1973 to 1976. Mr. Colby is indeed an authority on violations of privacy and on invading the personal, professional and political life of people.

Protection of Human Rights in United Kingdom:– Art. 12: No one shall be subjected to arbitrary interference with his privacy, family, home or correspondence, nor to attack upon his honour and reputation. Everyone has the right to the protection of the law against such interference or attacks.

Liberty for the individual in his private life is secured by the ordinary law of the land, enforced by the courts. It is illegal to molest a fellow citizen because his views do not conform to those held by the majority or because his way of life is different from that of the rest of the community. The common law allows the individual to speak and act in his own home as he pleases and to carry on his daily business, provided that in so doing he does not infringe the rights of others, or behave in such a way as is likely to cause a breach of the peace, or commit an offence. Parents are free to bring up their children as they wish, provided that they do not infringe various statutes aimed at preventing cruelty and exposure to moral and physical danger, and that they observe the law regarding compulsory education.

The law does not include a general right to privacy but a number of provisions apply in particular circumstances to protect privacy. Certain forms of intrusion may involve criminal offences – for example, interference with the mail or with telephoning systems, the use of unlicenced radio transmitters for 'bugging', the harassing of tenants to make them quit, or the sending of indecent or obscene matter through the post. Other attempts to obtain private information might involve offences of breaking and entering. In some instances of intrusion on privacy, the civil law of trespass, of contract and copyright, or of breach of confidence may provide a right of action leading to pecuniary damage.

Some protection to privacy is given by the law in court proceedings, notably (in England and Wales) in Criminal proceedings, proceedings in juvenile courts (children's hearings in Scotland), rape cases and in certain aspects of domestic proceeding. In England, Scotland and Wales the Right to privacy of some convicted offenders is safeguarded by legislation under which a person convicted of a criminal offence in general need not admit or reveal it after a rehabilitation period of from six months to ten years depending upon the nature or length of the sentence given. It does not apply to people who have received prison sentence of more than two and a half years. Protection against attacks on a person's honour and reputation is given by the laws on libel and slander (defamation), injurious falsehood and passing off (appropriation of a person's business or professional reputation at his expense).

The report of the Younger Committee on Privacy, published in 1972, contains the results of the committee's detailed examination of the whole question of the right of privacy. It contains proposals for the restatement of the law of breach of confidence, the creation of–

(a) a new criminal and civil offence of unlawful surveillance by technical devices, and

(b) a new civil offence of publication of information obtained by unlawful means; and the establishment of administrative controls over certain activities involving a possible threat to privacy.

The majority of the Committee rejected the idea of a general enforceable right of privacy on the ground that it could inhibit freedom of speech and communication. Specific proposals were more likely to be effective in the main areas of complaints than any general declaration. The Government is still considering many of the recommendations, but has published proposals on computers and privacy.

The need for legislation to protect the privacy of personal information held in computer, and to set up machinery to ensure that all existing and future computer system in which personal information is stored are operated with appropriate safeguards, was the main theme of Government proposals published in 1975 in a white paper, *Computers and Privacy*.

As promised in the white paper, the Government set up a *Data Protection Committee* to advise on the powers and functions of a statutory authority which would maintain suitable safeguards of privacy and confidentiality in relation to personal information held on computers. In the meantime the Government is continuing to ensure that the administrative rules, under which its own computer systems operate, will provide safeguards for the accuracy and relevance of personal information and for the privacy of the subjects of that information. Respect for the individual freedom and for the citizen's right against the state is embodied in the constitutional traditions of the United Kingdom. British people attach great importance to the exercise of human rights and the ways in which they are preserved and enlarged through political and legal institutions.

One of the most important forums for discussion of human rights is the United Nations whose General Assembly adopted the Universal Declaration of Human Rights in 1948. The rights authorised in the Universal Declaration have been included in the legally binding *International Covenants on Human Rights* which came into force early in 1976. The covenants – one of *Civil and Political Rights & The other on Economic, Social and Cultural Rights* – have been ratified by the United Kingdom. The *European Convention on Human Rights and Fundamental Freedoms* has been ratified by the United Kingdom and other member states of the Council of Europe.

A New Conception of Human Rights : The demand that individual privacy be respected is becoming more common and more insistent in our age. This probably reflects a rapidly increasing need for privacy arising from converging ecological, cultural, technical and social changes. The population explosion together with modern urbanisation, have made it much more difficult for the individual to get away physically & psychologically, from the crowd of strangers around him. The growing allegiance to political individualism and moral autonomy have caused the individual to resent and resist legal regulation and social interference more intensely. At a time when bugging and other techniques of surveillance have been perfected to an alarming degree, the development of computers enables us to store and retrieve vastly increased amounts of information about any specified individual in even very large populations. Finally, as organisations have grown larger in size and more bureaucratic in structure, their tendency to invade the life of the individual has grown apace.

Political freedoms are not recognised in an absolute fashion. The recognition of a higher good that must not suffer detriment from the free exercise of individual rights encroaches on the interests of the individual, reducing him to a condition in which he is virtually without rights. What can limit the freedom to exercise one's rights? only one thing: the interests of the aggregate of citizens, the interests of society. But does this mean that the question comes down to a simple dilemma: either the interests of society or those of the citizen; either the absolute, self interested exercise of rights or no freedom, no rights? As early as 1789, the *Declartion des droits de Thomme et du citoyen* declared that freedom must not extend to the right to commit actions harmful to others. *The Universal Declaration of Human Rights of 1948* proclaims the basic rights of the individual, but also speaks of the limits on these rights set by duties to the individual, but also speaks of the limits on these rights set by duties to the community (Article 29). Rights and freedoms can be enjoyed only within a concrete social milieu. Freedom is not an abstraction — it does not exist in a social vacuum. Can there be absolute freedom for even the enemies of freedom? No, of course not. Freedom of speech implies no "right" to promote war, aggression, and the arms race; or to spread racism and hatred of other nations. That would be not a right, but, in essence, a denial of rights, a sort of right in reverse, or anti-right.

The question of the balance of the exercise of freedom with the protection of the interests of society immediately comes to mind when one recalls a shocking case which occurred towards the end of

1978 in France. The magazine *L'Express* published, without any comment whatever, an interview with the former Commissioner on the Jewish Question of the Vichy government ***Louis Darquier de Pellepoix*** in which he declared that the Nazi extermination of six million Jews was "a fiction, pure and simple." Darquier, who took refuse in Spain at the end of the war, was condemned to death for his crimes by a French court in 1947. At the trial Darquier's guilt in the deportation of seventy-five thousand Jews, most of whom perished in the gas chambers of Auschwitz, was demonstrated. Thirty years later, Darquier declared in print that the death of a million persons in Auschwitz alone was "a pure fiction, a Jewish fiction"! In the Auschwitz camp "gas was used, certainly, but against lice, for the disinfestation of clothing". Photos of the Nazi extermination camps were called "montages". The remarks of this Nazi criminal, published in the name of "freedom of speech", brought a storm of protest from right-minded Frenchmen. Once again the question arose in all its poignancy: How can such abuses of liberty be permitted for the sake of freedom of speech? President of France Valery Giscard d'Estaing gave this answer: "The freedom of the press must be kept in balance with decency."

Thus the law formulates with complete clarity the limits of freedom of expression in the name of and "in accordance with the interests of the people." The criteria for determining what is beneficial and what is harmful are universally accepted. And the democratic nature of social relations appears in the fact that the ultimate judge of what injures "the interests of society and the state" is not a Tsar, a band of oligarchs, or the owners of the capital, but the society itself, which follows democratic procedures for the formation of public opinion and an established order for making known the will of the people and for the expression and fixation of that will in law. Political freedom is manifested and expressed in the guaranteed right to participate in the formation (according to the interest of the majority, the interest of the people) of the state will, which is expressed in laws, and in conscious and voluntary obedience to those laws.

In carrying out the functions the citizen exercises his freedom of speech, of assembly, of meetings, of demonstration. These freedoms are a means for participation in the solution of concrete problems of the management of social and government affairs, a means for formulating and expressing the "interests of the people". The concept "interests" has more than one level. It implies first of all fundamental, vital interests, strategic or global interests and together with these private, particular interests. Fundamental interests express those ideas, ideals and values which permeate the entire political organisation of society, the entire political system.

Discrimination Against those who Hold Certain Views, Opinions, and Convictions: Discrimination is the antipode of equal rights. In our times discrimination is rarely officially acknowledged or fixed in laws. Everyone recognised the apartheid system as a direct, overt form of racial discrimination. Discrimination on the basis of race, of skin, colour or ethnic origin, represents an infringement of human dignity, and is condemned as a violation of human rights and basic freedoms. In our times, this kind of discrimination is seen as a social and historical anomaly. Nevertheless, it existed and was backed up by all the punitive might of the South African government, despite opprobrium, despite boycotts, embargoes, and all the other measures adopted by the United Nations. Discrimination as a political institution is decidedly out of style, however. Anti-discrimination declarations are the rule in contemporary constitutional law. Violations of anti-discrimination declarations, non-recognition in practice of the idea of equality, and flouting of citizens' right to equality nullifies in fact, a broad spectrum of legal guarantees, and voids many constitutional declarations. This holds true of concrete rights and freedoms, from the freedoms of speech, of thought, opinions, convictions, and views to the right to work, to employment in accordance with one's qualifications and free choice.

The constitution of the Federal Republic of Germany, for instance contains a high-flown anti-discrimination declaration: "No one may be prejudiced or privileged because of his.... faith or his religion and political opinions". (Article 3, paragraph 3). The system of political discrimination is found in a country that western political commentators have long cited as a model of a political system embodying social justice and the rule of law. (The authors of the constitution of the Federal Republic of Germany even introduced a special new term: "*Socialer Rechtsstaat*": Socio-legal government.) And this system of discrimination is a typical example of the way in which impressive and liberal-sounding constitutional declarations are abrogated as soon as citizens make a serious, large-scale attempt to actually use their proclaimed rights and freedoms, as soon as people of democratic convictions, anti-fascists, communists, persistent opponents of revanchism and militarism, and true friends of social progress come forward to claim their rights.

(12) *A Philosophical Prelude*

When Justice Douglas wrote for the Supreme Court, in *Griswold* vs. *Connecticut* that various constitutional guarantees create "Zones of Privacy" he was quite right in pointing out that the court was dealing "with a right of privacy older than the Bill of Rights". Indeed "Zones of Privacy" can be found marked off, hinted at, or groped for in some of our oldest legal codes and in the most influential philosophical writings and traditions.

Almost the first page of the Bible introduces us to the feeling of shame as a violation of privacy. After Adam and Eve had eaten the fruit of the tree of knowledge, "the eyes of both were opened, and they knew that they were naked, and they sewed fig leaves together and made themselves aporous". [Thus, mythically, we have been taught that our very knowledge of good and evil – our moral nature, our nature as man – is somehow – by divine ordinance, linked with a sense and a realm of privacy]. [Helen M. Lyod, ON SHAME AND THE SEARCH FOR IDENTITY Ch.2 (1958)]. When after the flood, Noah became drunk he "lay uncovered in his tent", and Ham violated his father's privacy by looking upon his father's nakedness and by telling his brothers about it. His brothers took a garment, "laid it upon their shoulders, and walked backward and covered the nakedness of their father. Their faces were turned away and they did not see their father's nakedness". [Genesis 9: 20-27 (Revised standard version)].

The distance from the biblical garden to the statutory wilderness may have taken thousands of years to traverse; but surely that distance and the distance between the "Zone of Privacy which two of Noah's three sons respected and the sacred precincts of marital bedrooms", which the Supreme Court sought to protect in *Griswold* cannot conceptually be great.

Once a civilisation has made a distinction between the "outer" and the "inner" man, between the life of the soul and the life of the body, between the spiritual and the material, between the sacred and the profane, between the realm of God and the realm of Caesar, between church and state, between rights inherent and inalienable and rights that are in the power of the government to give and take away, between public and private, between society and solitude, it becomes impossible to avoid the idea of privacy by whatever name it may be called, the idea of private space in which man may become and remain "himself". [Herbert Marcuse, One Dimensional Man 10 (1964)]. Western Man's interest in our subject is thus accounted for.

It is against a view of the nature of man that one can best understand the court's opinion by Justice Douglas in *Griswold* vs. *Connecticut*. First comes the re-interpretation of certain constitutional guarantees in the U.S. constitution as "emanations", "penumbras", "zones" or "facets of privacy". This is true of the First Amendment freedom, of the prohibition in the Third Amendment against the quartering of soldiers "in any house" in times of peace without the consent of the owner, of the affirmation of the Fourth Amendment of the "right of the people to be secure in their persons, houses, papers and effects, against unreasonable searches and seizures", of the self-incrimination clause of the Fifth Amendment, and of the Ninth Amendment, which provides that "the enumeration in the constitution of certain rights shall not be construed to deny or disparage others retained by the people."

Second, comes the notion that just as man needs the zones of privacy that are recognised by those express constitutional provisions, so, too, the constitutional guarantees themselves generate sub-guarantees. The process of transcedence cannot be arbitrarily contained. So – to go back to Justice Douglas' opinion – the first amendment has "a penumbra" in which "freedom to associate and privacy in one's associations" are to be found. So, the right to educate one's children as one chooses, and the right to study a foreign language in a private school, flow out of the first amendment. So freedom of speech and press includes also the right to distribute, to receive, to read, to teach, and to pursue inquiry. So, the constitutional amendments mentioned protect the intimate relations of husband and wife and their relations to their physician – a "Zone of Privacy" created by several fundamental constitutional guarantees". These zones of privacy are nowhere expressly situated in the constitution, but the express provisions "create zones of privacy".

Breathing Space: The conception of constitutional emanations or penumbras probably flows out of Justice Brenan's notion of "breathing space". In *NAACP* Vs. *Button*, 371 U.S. 415 (1963), Justice Brenan said for the court that the first amendment freedoms are "delicate" and "vulnerable", they need, he said "breathing space to survive". In that case, the exercise of the first amendment rights was held to need the right to enforce constitutional rights through litigation assisted by an association. This was the "breathing space" that the first amendment freedoms needed.

In *New York Times* vs. *Sullivan*, 376 U.S. 254 (1964), Justice Brenan, again writing for the court said that freedom of the press needed "breathing space" in order "to survive". In that case the court held that the exercise of the first amendment freedom of the press needed the legal immunity to publish libelous misstatements of facts about public officials, provided there is no actual malice – this is a needed "breathing space".

It is, of course, man who in the first instance needs the "breathing space", and it is his needs that guarantee the penumbras and emanations are so essential to him that they must become a part of the very definition of the "life" or "liberty" that makes up his own person. There is no definite answer to such questions since man himself can never be fully delineated. His nature changes as it emerges, as it is created. Property is no longer a supreme value in our constitutional scheme. But surely a man's home is his property and his bedroom is his property, and these certainly came close to his very skin and bones.

Superior Decisive Value : It was Justice Douglas who, in a sit-in case [*Bell* vs. *Maryland* 378 U.S. 226 (1964)], involving a restatement, said:

The problem with which we deal has no relation to opening or closing the door of one's home. The home, of course, is the essence of privacy, in no way dedicated to public use, in no way extending an invitation to the public. The facts of these sit-in cases have little resemblance to any institution of property which we customarily associate with privacy.

In the same case, Justice Goldberg pointed out that "constitutional protection extended to privacy and private association" is an assurance against "the imposition of social equality". He said.:

> Prejudice and bigotry in any form are regretable, but it is the constitutional right of every person to close his home or club to any person or to choose his social intimates and business partners solely on the basis of

> personal prejudices involving race. These and other rights pertaining to privacy and private association are themselves constitutional protected liberties."

But these words of Justices Douglas and Goldberg may not be acceptable in all their reach. Our anti-discrimination housing laws by no means absolutize the term "home" in such a way as to assure a person full enjoyment of his "social intimates" solely on the basis of his personal prejudices including race. Questions of privacy may touch vital issues of justice and public order which cannot be answered by mere verbal definitions. Such questions call for delicate judgement–judgement that will reflect our changing views of the nature of man and that in turn will contribute to emerging views of man's natures.

There can be no fixed inventory of things, acts and values that pertain to the inner man and those that pertain to the outer man; for inner and outer, like soul and body, are terms that describe living processes. In passing the *Civil Rights Act of 1964*, Congress was compelled to move man, acts, and values from the inner to the outer realm, and even when it comes to what may be admitted to belong to the inner realm, values may be in conflict there, *e.g.*, the Roman Catholic Church must consider whether in the marital bedroom privacy or scruples over the use of contraceptives shall work out the superior decisive value.

Contribution By Cooley: Warren and Brandeis took the phrase, the "right to be let alone," from Cooley's treatise on torts. But it was the Supreme Court in *Adair* vs. *United States* 208 U.S. 161 (1908), rather than Warren and Brandeis, that conveyed the spirit of what Judge Cooley meant by this right "to be let alone". Declaring a federal anti-yellow dog statute unconstitutional as "an invasion of personal liberty" guaranteed by the fifth amendment, the court quoted with approval from the treatise by Cooley:

> It is a part of every man's civil rights that he be left at liberty to refuse business relations with any person whomsover, whether the refusal rests upon reason, or is the result of whim, caprice, prejudice or malice. With his reasons neither the public nor third persons have any legal concern.

What to Cooley was a civil right, a right "to be let alone" has now become a denial of a civil right. And the humiliation becomes more powerful as we note that the court's opinion in Adair was by the first Justice Harlen whose (dissenting) views on Civil Rights have become the law of the land.

The great contribution made by Cooley, however, should be gladly acknowledged; for his phrase, "the right to be let alone", is preferable to the Warren-Brandeis phrase, "the right to privacy". For the latter is too restrictive in its implications, it suggests what has been withdrawn from public view–like the marital bedroom in *Griswold* or a respectable married woman's past immoral life. It suggests darkness and secrecy. But the opinion of Justice Douglas and Goldberg in *Griswold* rightly imply that "privacy" may also be the character of acts performed in public view – for example, joining the National Association for the advancement of coloured people or performing an act of public worship in a church. A person may be asserting his right of "privacy" when he dresses in an unorthodox way or when he "loafs" in a public park. A person may claim the right to be let alone when he acts publicly as when he acts privately. Its essence is the claim that there is a sphere of space that has not been dedicated to public use or control. It is a kind of space that a man may carry with him, into his bedroom or into the street. Even when public, it is part of the inner man; it is part of his "property" as Locke would say, the kind of "property" with respect to which its owner has delegated no power to the state.

(13) *Conclusion*

It has been said that the modern claim to privacy has been based on "science, the secularization of Government and political democracy". Undoubtedly scientific advancement has made much of our personal privacy possible, but science has also taken its toll in making possible severe invasions into privacy. An example is the use of electronic devices to overhear and record what is said without the knowledge of those speaking. Individual differences in outlook and development of personality can be attributed in part at least to the separation of church and state. And guarantees of basic freedoms and a respect for the dignity of man stem from the strength of political democracy.

*

III

SOURCES

> "The broad and general maxims of liberty and justice applied in England only as guards against executive usurpation and tyranny; here they have become bulwarks also against arbitrary legislation, but, in that application, as it would be incongrous to measure and restrict them by the ancient customary English law, they must be held to guaranty not particular forms of procedure, but the very substance of individual rights to life, liberty and property."
>
> *(1884) 110 US 516 (531): 28 Law Ed 232 (237)*

(1) *Natural Law and Natural Rights*

It is widely believed that the concept of human rights emerged from the notion of natural law. It is not even uncommon to find "natural law" used as a rough synonym for "natural rights". In fact, though the two concepts are largely unrelated: Natural law represents an approach to questions of political order quite different from that of natural or human rights. This is particularly clear in Aquinas' theory of natural law and right, perhaps the best developed and best known of the classic natural law theories.

For Acquinas, a law is an ordinance of reason for the common good, made by him who has care of the community and promulgated. All law is encompassed within what Acquinas calls the eternal law of God. However, this eternal law is specified in the main branches, which are largely independent of one another; the 'divine law', the inspired revelations of the Bible, which deals primarily with questions of spiritual salvation; and the 'natural and human laws'. Politics is regulated by the second branch.

Man has special access to the eternal law 'through understanding the Divine commandment'. The participation of the eternal law, in the rational creature is called the 'natural law'. But since human reason is able to grasp only certain general principles of the perfect divine reason, natural law is restricted to general precepts. Therefore, it must be supplemented by what Acquinas calls human laws, roughly the laws of political life and practice – which are particular specifications of the general precepts of natural law.

Natural law, which is prior to and above merely human ordinances, is the only major directly accessible restraint on abuses of power that Aquinas recognises; natural law from which the human law flows, serves as a check on the ruler and a guarantee to the ruled that justice will be observed. Therefore, Aquinas claims that human laws are merely acts of violence. Yet, because of the absence of natural or human rights in Aquinas theory, the political consequences of this are not what the modern reader is likely to imagine.

Although all laws ought to be consistent with one another – they are just reflections of the eternal law – fallible and corrupt men are likely to make human laws which conflict with both natural and divine law. When human and higher laws diverge, which ought to be obeyed? Aquinas' general position is that human laws are binding in conscience if the law in question is just. Since right (*jus*) is the object of justice, and law is the written expression of right, this is equivalent to saying that human laws are binding in conscience in so far as they are truly laws, which in turn means that they are binding in so far as they do not diverge from the natural (or divine) law. However, Acquinas' actual discussion of what we can call 'unjust laws' laws not in accord with higher justice as expressed in natural or divine law, does not follow the line of reasoning.

Laws that contravene divine law 'must in unwise be observed' for to obey them would risk the loss of eternal beatitude. But laws that are unjust by way of their end (they do not aim at the common good), author (they exceed the authority of the law-giver) or form (they do not distribute burdens proportionately) do not bind in conscience except in order to avoid scandal or disturbance, for which cause a man should even yield his right. This exception leaves us with 'laws' that are both binding and not binding. The requirements of natural and human law conflict, yet the priority of natural law is not unambiguously maintained. Aquinas view that there are laws which are just only with regard to specific regimes adds a further, and quite large, set of such problematic laws.

Tyranny, which can be viewed as rule through systematically

unjust laws, presents the problem of unjust laws in the most acute form. In his most sustained discussion of tyranny, Aquinas' advice is simple, practical and cautious; if the tyrant is not too terrible, it is best not to seek to depose him, for if one fails, he is likely to become more harsh, while success risks tearing society into factions or attaching the masses to a deceitful leader who will set himself up as a new, and even more harsh, tyrant.

But intolerable tyranny does not in itself justify resistance. If explicit legal authority is present and if the natural law provides sufficient moral grounds, resistance would be legitimate public action (although prudential considerations might still counsel obedience) if explicit public authority is lacking, however, resistence is unjustifiable private rebellion. Due deliberations and substantive justice alone are not sufficient justification for acting against a tyrant.

Whereas human rights warrant direct remedial action when they are violated, natural law alone provides no such warrant. In the absence of explicit authority to depose the tyrant, he must be endured; recourse must be had to God alone. Unauthorised resistance is not only no better in kind than the acts of the tyrant, it is actually more dangerous, according to Aquinas, for it is likely to produce faction, sedition and even civil war, thereby forfeiting all the benefit of political society in the attempt to remedy a few of its contingent defects in the end, for Aquinas, the tyrant's unjust laws oblige, while the obligation of the natural law is effectively cancelled.

From a human rights perspective, we might say that the subject are entitled to expect that the natural law will be obeyed by their rulers; the priority of natural law over human law is their guarantee that their interests under the natural law will be protected. When Aquinas requires obedience to the tyrant, he deprives them of the protection of the natural law by abrogating its binding force and its priority over human law. Such a reading, however, is anachronistic and seriously misleading in its claim that the subjects are entitled to a just rule and have rights under the natural law. In fact, such ideas are totally absent from Aquinas' political thought in general, and from his notion of natural law in particular.

Right (*jus*) is, for Aquinas, the good at which justice aims, and the law is the written expression of right, of the just. Thus right and law are inseperably linked. Right and law, *jus and lex*, are not merely correlative. Right and law, for Aquinas, are two ways of looking at the same thing: they are two ways of stating a duty under which one is placed, by right in the sense of 'what is right'. Acquinas' *jus* encompasses only 'what is right' in its entirety. In particular, it does not include the notion of right in the sense of 'having a right'. Natural law does not give rise to rights, but only states what is right. Thus Acquinas considers tyranny and resistance solely in terms of what is right (*i.e.* in accord with natural law and justice). This is completely independent of the rights of the people.

The tyrant, like all men, is obliged to obey the natural law, which states what is right. In ruling as a tyrant, he fails to fulfil this obligation, but the natural law in itself, provides insufficient grounds for political action against him. Natural law is only a standard of judgement, not a warrant to act. Natural law gives the people no right to charge their rulers; the claims and appeals they may make to the tyrant lack the special force of rights/titles.

Even if a people has the right to remove a tyrant, for Acquinas this is not a natural right. Furthermore, natural law is not the moral foundation for the action of the people against the tyrant: self-government is consistent with, but not demanded by the natural law and 'natural right'. And even if self-government were demanded, this would provide no natural or human rights, given the disjunction of rights and righteousness in Acquinas' system. The foundation of a right to self-government is human and contingent rather than natural or necessary: such a right is a political right, perhaps even an entrenched constitutional right, but most definitely a right resting on human, not natural law.

Compare this with parallel modern conceptions of rights to national self-determination, political participation or revolution. Such rights generally are held to be natural and universally valid. They belong to man *qua* man, and their violations warrant remedial action by the people. Such rights simply do not exist for Acquinas, neither individuals nor groups are naturally endowed with rights on the basis of which they make entitlement-based claims against others, let alone their rulers. Thus, the requirement to endure a tyrant is not simply the result of Acquinas' views on monarchy or peculiarities introduced by his religious perspectives. Rather it rests on a view of political right formulated almost entirely in terms of 'what is right', lacking the idea of natural or human rights. Any deontological system of ethics would be likely to produce such results if applied directly to politics.

The demands of natural law may be considerable but the position of the people in a political system based on natural law, and the operation of that system, would be quite different from one based on natural or human rights. Natural law and human rights theorists may pursue similar goals, but they rely on quite different strategies for regarding relations between citizens and the state. The social and political precepts of Islam do reflect a strong concern for human good and human dignity. The precepts of Islam, much like Acquinas' natural law, are concerned only with right in the sense of 'what is right'.

There are many bases on which a government might be limited– divine commandment, natural law, human rights, legal rights, extralegal checks such as the balance of power, etc. Therefore, the simple fact that a people enjoys rule by a limited government says nothing about human rights. Traditional societies, wherever located seem to have had no place for human rights. To reduce the question to one of traditional *versus* modern world, however, be misleading, the concept and practice of human rights is no more uniquely modern than, say, totalitarianism – universal rights/titles held equally by all simply because they are human beings – is one distinctive approach to securing human dignity. When applied to the foundation, and regulations of the state, utility, like natural law – and like prescription as well – has a strong tendency towards paternalism.

(2) *Dworkin's Thesis*

Natural rights came into prominence with the rise of individualism. Each person was thought of as enjoying as area of sanctity. "Natural rights" are abstract versions of claims, liberties and immunities and at this level of generalisation are akin to principles, standards and doctrines. It is in this sense that they have been embodied in sundry Bills of Rights, charters of Fundamental Freedoms and Constitutions; they are called 'natural' perhaps because they are thought to be essential to social existence. Rules of law crystalise out of them and it is a mistake to equate them with specific claims, liberties and immunities expressed in rules of positive law. Principles etc. exert pressure on the law to develop according to them, but such pressure may be overriden by other pressures in particular instances.

A modern case for fundamental rights has been argued by Professor Dworkin. Although he dislikes the description of his 'rights' as 'natural', his thesis is not dissimilar to 'natural rights' as traditionally conceived. He distinguishes between 'background rights, which are rights that hold in an abstract way against decisions taken by the community or the society as a whole, and more specific institutional rights that hold against a decision made by a specific institution'. Legal rights are institutional rights to decisions in courts. Intuitions about justice presuppose a fundamental right, namely, 'the right to equality' (*i.e.* the right to equal concern and respect). The utilitarian approach to justice is rejected on the ground that the individual has 'rights' against the government, from which it follows that justice cannot lie in the subordination of the individual simply because doing so would, on balance, benefit the common weal. Now, the 'right of free speech' of one individual can indeed be limited by the 'right' of another individual to the integrity of his reputation; and another major qualification is that the 'right' of the individual may be overriden even by government 'to prevent a catastrophe, or even to obtain a clear and major public benefit.' What is not permissible is for government to act on no more than a judgement that its act is likely to produce, overall, a benefit to the community.

Dworkin also rejects the positivist conception of law as consisting solely of rules. These are not enough in themselves since justice and obligations have a moral dimension: Individual 'rights' are principles, which are required by justice or fairness or some other dimension of morality; and law as a whole incorporates rules and principles. Positivists maintain that in 'hard cases' judges have a discretion to decide on 'policy' grounds. Dworkin disputes this on the ground that there is always a right answer, which entitles one party to the decision on principle. Decisions that look like policy decisions are decisions about existing 'rights' of individuals.

The law has of necessity to reflect the majority view of the common good. 'Fundamental rights' represent the promise by the majority to minorities that their views on this will be respected. Such 'rights' are against government and enjoy authority superior to and independent of government (unlike, *e.g.* the 'right' to drive both ways down a street, which is created only by government; and can be restricted by it) and they are usually found in guarantees of due process and equal protection, which call for respect for fairness and equality. Where there is a 'fundamental right' a person has the 'right' to do something even though it is forbidden by law. Therefore, with regard to civil disobedience it follows that, subject to the qualification referred to above, the individual has a 'right to follow conscience'. There is, however, distinction between a person having 'right to do something' when it would be wrong for government to punish him and something being 'the right thing for him to do'; and if the majority break it on this ground, respect for law requires its repeal. On the other hand, when the 'right to do something' interferes with another's fundamental right'; it is no longer 'the right thing to do'.

Dworkin's demonstration of the law-quality of principles and the shortcoming of positivism in failing to accommodate them is acceptable, so too is his contention that, unlike rules, they have a dimension of weight, which exert pressure on the development of rules. The point, however, is that pressure of any kind may be outweighed by others, which does give judges discretion to decide on policy or other grounds. All this falls short of the contention that the choice is only between competing 'rights' so that there is always a correct answer in principle, that policy considertions do not come in, and that such 'rights' have superior weight, which makes it wrong to condemn people for exercising them against government. The issue boils down to whether these 'rights' carry with them in addition to the duty to accept them as 'law' (which is acceptable), a further duty to apply them, or at least to choose only between them, as opposed to a liberty to apply them or not. A mental leap is required from the acceptable part of his argument to these further contentions, which he does not appear to have bridged.

As regards reservations that might be felt about the practicalities of his 'fundamental rights', while the sincerity of some dissidents cannot be doubted, it would be unwise to trust the sincerity of others who often join in 'fundamental rights' actions for motives such as the overthrow of the system, or to gain positions of power which will enable them eventually to deny equal 'rights' to those disagreeing with them. The presence, or even the justified suspicion of the presence of the latter under the banner of 'fundamental rights' weakens the appeal of the 'right to follow conscience'. The thrust of the Dworkinian thesis is anti-government, which in itself is no bad thing; but in the real world of today the naivety of this kind of attack on authority is like sawing away at the branch on which one is safely ensconced, so far.

(3) *Meaning of Source of Law*

The courts of every country accept some medium, or media, as capable of imparting the quality of 'law' to propositions. The usual designation for such medium is 'criterion (criteria) of validity' because if a proposition has filtered through it, then it is a valid proposition of law, if it has not done so, it is not valid proposition of law. In Great Britain the label 'English law' is regulated by legislation, judicial precedents, immemorial customs and after Britain's accession to the European Economic Community, its Regulations and Decisions. The mere fact that a proposition is embodied, or even applied in a judgement does not *ipso facto* make it 'law'; it has to be enunciated and applied as such. Thus, judges constantly employ rules of arithmetic, but these do not thereby become 'English law' since they are not being applied as such.

The expression 'source of law' is sometimes used in this connection. 'Source' has more than one meaning. It may refer to the source of information of a rule (*e.g.* a textbook); or the origin of the material content of a rule, or the formal stamp of authority as 'law'. It is the last sense which is relevant in identifying legal material. Failure to bear the distinction in mind, especially between the second and third meanings, introduces an element of confusion.

(4) *Essence and Existence*

The use of "essence" and "existence" by Sartre is partly derived from phenomenology and partly from scholasticism. The latter influence is apparent in the way in which Sartre uses the formula that existence precedes essence in order to deny that men are created by God. Sartre identifies such a conception of creation with the notion of God creating beings with fixed already determinate natures who would therefore be unfree. Nothing of this appears to be entailed by Acquinas use of "essence" and "existence", but Heibentz and Wolf could be more convincingly convicted on this charge, Smith wishes to convey by his formula that men do not have determinate natures fixed in advance of their choices.

What then is Sartre assisting? The contention that existence precedes essence may be interpreted as entailing various consequences, not all of which were necessarily intended by Sartre. Sartre does clearly believe that his contention not only constitutes the denial of one species of determinism, but also involves the invalidity of any version of the ontological argument whether Anselmian, Cartesian or Hegelian that is, no essence is such that it is a necessary truth that there must exist some individual embodying that essence. But unfortunately, the Sartrian contention is so loosely stated that he might also be taken to imply–what he certainly would not want to imply – that there are no essences, that is no meanings, apart from existences. That is plainly false. Many meaningful expressions do not name or denote anything that exists, many descriptions do not characterise anything that exists as the common examples of "unicorn" and "glass mountain" make clear. The chief difficulty with the Sartrian thesis, however, is not that it plainly entails absurd consequences. It is, rather, that the thesis is stated so generally, and is so inadequately developed that it is not at all clear what does or does not follow from Sartre's contention.

(5) *God, Concepts of*

It is very difficult – perhaps impossible – to give a definition of God that will cover all usages of the word and of equivalent words in other languages. Even to define God generally as a superhuman or supernatural being that controls the world is inadequate. "Super human" is contradicted by the worship of divinized Roman emperors, "supernatural" by Spinoza's equation of God with Nature, and "control" by the epicurean denial that gods influence the lives of men. Therefore, while the above definition satisfies a wide range of usages, it is not universally applicable.There are four things which may be said mainly of concepts of God namely.

(1) God as final cause.

(2) World as emanation from God (mind, soul and the material world flow from the one without impairing its self-sufficiency).

(3) World as pre-existent matter set in order (Plato said: God is bounded on the one hand by the world of Forms and on the other by the pre-existent matter. His task is to impose the Forms on matter, and so construct a rationally ordered whole. Being wholly good and therefore free from jealousus, he wished everything to be like himself. Since an intelligent being is superior to an unintelligent one, and since intelligence cannot be present in anything that is devoid of soul, he puts intelligence in soul and soul in body, that he might be creator of a work which was by nature best.)

(4) Creation "*ex nihilo*": In contrast with all the previous views, Christian theists since Augustine have held the doctrine of

> creation out of nothing. This phrase is meant to exclude both the idea that the world is a necessary emanition from God's nature and the idea that matter pre-exists his creative act. God brings the whole world into being by an undetermined choice. He does not need the world to complete his nature, for he is wholly self-sufficient. He is not confronted with an alien Necessity for he is the efficient cause of all that is.

This conception of the relation between the creator and the creature can be elucidated through the contrast between necessary and contingent being God exists necessarily. In him essence and existence are identical. He is self existent in a unique and incomprehensible way. Creatures, on the other hand, are contingent. Their essence, while pre-existing ideally in the mind of God, would not have achieved independent being if he had not chosen to grant it by a free act of love. Therefore, while they participate in him both by nature and by grace, they never lose their created status. They can be defined within their finite limits, but they cannot become divine in the sense of sharing God's aseity.

The full Christian doctrine does not restrict God's creative act to an initial moment in the cosmic process. All things owe their being continuously to his power. He is a first cause in the order of existence, not of time, for he himself is supernatural. Hence it is irrelevant to theology whether the world did or did not have a temporal beginning. Acquinas held that while such a beginning was revealed through scripture, it could not be rationally proved. All reason knows is that God is eternal, ever-present, and creative source of anything that does (or can) exist. Creation and preservation are identical. However, while no creature exists from itself (*a se*) every creature exists by itself (*per se*) or in itself (*in se*). Created substances have a relative independence, or derived autonomy. The paradoxical expressions are required in order to affirm the God as their first cause, they also act according to secondary causes that are appropriate to their natures.

(6) *Indian Position*

A right recognised by law which is enforceable is a legal right as against a moral right which has no sanction behind it. According to *Warton's Law Lexicon* right is described as "the liberty of doing or possessing something for the infringement of which there is a legal sanction". The enforceability of a right on the basis of a recognised remedy readily available is the most distinguishing characteristic of a legal right. *Manusmriti* which represents one of the earliest attempts of codification of human law, has emphasized this all important aspect of enforceability as follows:

> The sanction of authority (*danda*) behind the law (*dharma*) including the rights enshrined in law is a factor priceless and at once victorious throughout the universe of man since it is on account of factum of that sanction (*danda*) that law (*dharma*) is duly observed and everyone's rights are safeguarded which in turn enables mankind to enjoy the fruits of the world in peace with all.

This ancient verse of *Manu* thus pinpoints the distinguishing characteristic of a legal right which in its enforceability having the necessary sanction of *danda* behind it as against a mere moral precept which at best sets an ideal to live upto. Again, the distinction between a legal right as against a non-legal right is embodied in the well known legal maxim *ubi jus ibi remedium* described as one of the fundamental principles of English law. In *Ashby* vs. *White* (2 Raym. Ld. 938 p. 953) C.J. Holt observed that if a man has a right he must have a means to vindicate and maintain it, a remedy if he is injured in the exercise and enjoyment of it; and indeed it is a vain thing to imagine a right without a remedy, for want of right and want of remedy are reciprocal. In short, if there is a right, there must be a remedy but in spite of the fact that there is a recognised right if there is no remedy available to the aggrieved when that right is violated, such a right unenforceable in character becomes a mere shadow without substance and ceases to be a legal right.

(a) *Fundamental Rights Under the Indian Constitution*: Even prior to the present constitution of India, the idea of Fundamental Rights was present in a tenuous form, in the Indian polity. The provision in Section 293 (1) of Government of India Act, 1935, in regard to the capacity to hold office had been on the statute book ever since 1833. It was Section 87 of the Government of India Act, 1833 and Section 96 of the Government of India Act, 1915. The above provisions constituted a statutory recognition of the fundamental principles of British Jurisprudence.

Art. 15 of the Draft Constitution was Art.21 of the present Constitution. Given below are the statements made by members of the Constituent Assembly quoted in *Constituent Assembly Debates Vol.7 1948-49, page 842.*

(I) KAZ. SYED KAMMUDIN:

Sir, if the proposed amendment by the Drafting Committee is accepted and the Article is allowed to stand as it is:

> "No person shall be deprived of his life or personal liberty except according to procedure established by law..."

Then in my opinion, it will open a sad Chapter in the history of constitutional law. Sir, the Advisory Committee on Fundamental Rights appointed by the Constituent Assembly had suggested that no person shall be deprived of his life or liberty without due process of law and I really do not understand how the words "personal" and "according to procedure established by law" have been brought into Art. 15 by the Drafting Committee.

Sir, if the words "according to procedure established by law" are enacted there will be very great injustice to the law courts in the country because as soon as a procedure according to law is complied with by a court; there will be an end to the duties of the court and if the court is satisfied that the procedure has been complied with, then the judges cannot interfere with any law which might have been capricious, unjust or iniquitous. The clause, as it stands, can do great mischief in a country which is the storm centre of political parties and where discipline is unknown. Sir, let us guarantee to individuals inalienable rights in such a way that the political parties that come into power cannot extend their jurisdiction in curtailing and invading the Fundamental Rights laid down in this Constitution.

Sir, there is an instance in the American Constitutional law in a case reported in *Chambers* vs. *Florida*, where an Act was challenged in a court of law on the ground that the law was not sound and that it was capricious and unjust. Therefore, my submission is that if the words "according to procedure established by law" are kept then it will not be open to the courts to look into the injustice of a law or into a capricious provision in a law. As soon as the procedure is complied with there will an end to everything and the judges will be only "spectators". Therefore, my submission is, first, that the words "except according to procedure established by law" be deleted, and then that the words "without due process of law be inserted.

(II) MAHBOOB ALI BAIG SAHIB BAHADUR:

Sir, I beg to move:

That in Article 15 for the words "except according to the procedure established by law" the words "save in accordance with law" be substituted.

In the note given by the Drafting Committee, it is stated that they made two changes from the proposition or article passed by his Assembly in the month of August, April or May of 1947. The first is the insertion of the word "personal" before liberty and the reason given is that unless this word 'personal' finds a place there, the clause may be construed very widely so as to include even the freedoms already dealt with in Article 13.

As regards why the original words "without due process of law" were omitted and the present words "except according to procedure established by law" are inserted, the reason is stated to be that the expression is more definite and such a provision finds place in Article 31 of The Japanese Constitution of 1946.

It is no doubt true that in the Japanese Constitution, Art. 31 reads like this: but if the other articles find place in the Japanese Constitution (*viz.* Article 32, 34 and 35) had also been incorporated in this Draft Constitution that would have been a complete safeguarding of the personal liberty of the citizen. This Draft Constitution has conveniently omitted these provisions.

Article 32 of the Japanese Constitution provides that "no person shall be denied the right of access to the court". According to the present expression it may be argued that the legislature might pass a law that a person will have no right to go to a court of law to establish his innocence. But according to the Japanese Constitution Art. 32 clearly says that "no person shall be denied the right of access to the court". Is there such a corresponding provision in this Draft Constitution? It does not find any place at all.

Article 34 of the Japanese Constitution provides that "no person shall be arrested or detained without being at once informed of the charges against him or without the immediate privilege of counsel, nor shall be detained without adequate cause and upon demand of any such person such cause should be immediately shown in open court in his presence and in the presence of his counsel". Such a clear right has not been given in these draft provisions.

Further, Art. 35 provides that the right of all persons to be secured in their homes and against entry, search etc. shall not be impaired, except upon warrant issued only for probable cause and so on. If for the sake of clarity and definiteness you have imported into this Draft Constitution, Art. 31 of the Japanese Constitution you should in fairness have incorporated the other articles of the Japanese Constitution, which are relevant and which were enacted for safeguarding the personal liberty of the honest citizen.

The only extent to which the courts can go is to find out whether there is bona fides or mala fides for the action of the government and the burden is laid upon the person to prove that there is mala fides on the part of the Government in having issued a warrant of detention or arrest. Therefore, the words, except according to procedure laid down by law "would mean that the future legislature might pass a law by which the right of citizen to be tried by a court to establish his innocence could be taken away. I do not by this mean to convey that under certain circumstances it may not be necessary for Government or prevent a person from committing an offence and to take the precaution of arresting him and thus prevent him from committing an offence. But I submit that there must be the right of the citizen to go to a court to prove that the ground on which he has been arrested is wrong and he is innocent. That is the elementary right of the citizen as against the executive which might be clothed with power by a party legislature, which might pass a law saying that the executive is empowered to take away the liberty of a person under certain circumstances and he will have no right to go to court and prove his innocence.

We must understand that the words "without due process of law" have been held in England and other countries to convey the meaning that every citizen has got the right, when an action has been taken against him depriving him of his personal liberty to go before the court to say that he is innocent. That right is given under the expression "without due process of law" or "save in accordance with law". In England the law of the land does not deprive a man of this fundamental and elementary right. All laws that may be made are subject to the relevant principle that no person shall be convicted and no man shall be deprived of his liberty without a chance being given to him to provide that he is innocent. Therefore, it must be a law which will hear, before it condemns a man.

(III) PANDIT THAKUR DASS BHARGAVA:

The section as it is, with this amendment namely the substitution of the words "without due process of law" is the one which I wish to support. By using these words "without due process of law" we want that the courts may be authorised to go into the question whether a particular law enacted by Parliament is just or not, whether it is good or not, whether as a matter of fact it protects the liberties of the people or not.

(IV) SH. CHIMANLAL CHAKUBHAI SHAH:

Sir, the right conferred by Art. 15 is the most fundamental of the Fundamental Rights in this chapter, because it is the right which relate to life and personal liberty without which all other rights will be meaningful. Therefore, it is necessary that in defining this right we must make it clear and explicit as to what it is that we want to confer and not put in restrictions upon the exercise of that right which makes it useless or nugatory. I, therefore, support the amendment which says that the words 'without due process of law' should be substituted for the words "except in accordance with the procedure established by law". Sir, the words, "without due process of law" have been taken from the American Constitution and they have come to acquire a particular connotation. The contention is that in reviewing legislation the court will have the power to see not only that the procedure is followed, namely, that the warrant is in accordance with law or that the signatures and the seal are there, but it has also the power to see that the substantive provisions of law are fair and just and not unreasonable or oppressive or capricious or arbitrary. This means that the judiciary is given power to review legislation.

Secondly, sir, in the word "liberty" that we have used, we have added the word "personal" and made it "personal liberty" to make it clear that the article does not refer to any kind of liberty of contract or anything of that kind, but refers only to life and liberty of person. Therefore, it would be wrong to say that the words "due process of law" are likely to lead to any uncertainty in legislation or unnecessary interference by the judiciary in reviewing legislation.

(V) SH. KRISHNA CHANDRA SHARMA:

The term "without due process of law" has a necessary limitation on the powers of the state, both executive and legislative. The doctrine implied by "without due process of law" has a long history in Anglo-American law. It does not lay down a specific rule of law but it implies a fundamental principle of justice. These words have nowhere been defined either in the English Constitution or in the American Constitution but we can find that meaning through sending the various antecedents of this expression. As a matter of fact, it can be traced back to the days of King John when the barons wrung their charter from him *i.e.*, the *Magna Carta*. The expression "*Per Legum Terrea*" in the *Magna Carta* have come to mean "*without due process of law*". Chapter 39 of the charter says:

> "No free man shall be taken or imprisoned, or outlawed, exiled, or in any way destroyed, nor shall we go upon him, nor send upon him, but by the lawful judgement of his peers or by the law of the land.

These words were used again in 1331, 1351 and 1355. Statute No. 28 during the reign of Edward III says:

> "No man of what state or condition so ever he be, shall be put out of his lands or tenements, nor taken nor imprisoned, nor indicted, nor put to death, without he be brought to answer by due process of law."

Sir, in the American Constitution these words were first used in 1791:

> "Nor shall any person ... be deprived of life, liberty or property, without due process of law.

What this phrase means is to guarantee a fair trial both in procedure as well as in substance. This procedure should be in accordance with law and should be appealable to the civilised consequence of the community. It also ensures a fair trial in substance that is to say, that substantive law itself should be just and appealable to the civilised conscience of the community.

(VII) SH. K.M. MUNSHI:

If the clause stood as it is, it would have no meaning at all. We want to set up a democracy and the essence of democracy is that a balance must be struck between individual liberty on the one hand and social control on the other.

(VIII) MR. Z.H. LARI:

It is necessary not only in the interest of individual liberty but in the interest of proper working of the legislatures that a clause as due process of law clause should find a place in the constitution. If you have the words in this clause, as they stand at present, namely "procedure established by law" it means that the legislature in all-powerful and whatever procedure is deemed proper under the circumstances will be binding upon the court. We should profit by the experience of other countries and by what has been observed for centuries. If this clause is accepted, then the whole constitution becomes lifeless. The article, as it stands is lifeless and it also makes the whole constitution lifeless.

(b) ***Right to Personal Liberty and Property***: The Constituent Assembly has deliberately departed from the British conception and adopted a formal declaration of Fundamental Rights in the Constitution. In so far as India has adopted in its Constitution a formal declaration of Fundamental Rights which are to be beyond the conscience of any Legislature to affect except to the extent and under the conditions laid down by the Constitution; the Indian Constitution has made a departure from the British model and has adopted the American model. Some of the rights granted by Part III are limited to citizens while in the case of others such a limitation does not exist.

A clear distinction has been made between 'persons' and 'citizens' in Part III. The right to property under Article 31 is not restricted only to the citizens of India, but it is conferred on non-citizens as well. Foreign nationals as such are not excluded from fundamental rights. Government servants as such are not excluded from fundamental rights (Except as provided in Article 33). For a prisoner all fundamental rights are an enforceable reality though restricted by fact of imprisonment. The right to move Supreme Court for the enforcement of Fundamental Rights is itself a guaranteed Fundamental Right. There is no similar provision in the American Constitution. The rights which are guaranteed under Part III of the Constitution as Fundamental Rights are not merely natural rights recognised by the Constitution but are rights conferred by the Constitution.

It is open to President to suspend the enforcement of any of the fundamental rights conferred by Part III by an order under Article 359 and this Article shows that whenever such suspension is made, it is in the interest of security of India and no further proof of it is necessary.

There can be no loss of fundamental rights merely on the ground of non-exercise. If an act constitutes an infringement of a fundamental right, it cannot be justified on the plea that a similar act was done in the past. The fundamental rights have been enacted as a matter of public and constitutional policy and the doctrine of waiver cannot apply to them. The laws, which were in force before the commencement of the Constitution, will become void only from the date of the Constitution, if they conflict with the fundamental rights and not *ab initio* from the date of their enactment. Any action already taken under such laws before the coming into force of the Constitution will, therefore not be affected by the fundamental rights. All Articles including those relating to fundamental rights can be amended provided that the basic structure of the Constitution and its framework are not altered.

While the restriction of personal freedom under Article 19 is made a matter in respect of which the reasonableness of any law that may be made by the state may be scrutinised by the court with a view to seeing whether the restriction keeps within the limits permitted by the Constitution, the courts have no jurisdiction to consider the reasonableness or otherwise of a law relating to the deprivation of life or total deprivation of property or liberty. In such cases, the Constitution in effect provides that deprivation may take place if it is in accordance with law. Under Articles 21 and 31 the deprivation of a person of his life or personal liberty or property will be constitutional, if it is in accordance with "law" which has been authoritatively held to mean only a law made by Legislature and not principles of natural justice. The term "law" in Articles 21 and 31 refers to a positive legislative enactment and not principles of natural justice.

The duty of courts begins and ends with ensuring that the authority concerned does not transgress the bounds set for it by the instrument conferring power and that it does not trespass, upon the hollowed ground enclosed by Part III and by other provisions of Constitution. For legislative enactment within the bounds of authority conferred courts hold no sanction. Our Constitution contains express provisions for judicial review of legislation as to its conformity with the Constitution. As regards the Fundamental Rights the Supreme Court has been assigned the role of sentinal on the *qui vive*. While the court naturally attaches great weight to the legislative judgement, it cannot desert its own duty to determine finally the constitutionality of an impugned statute.

Where the question is only of deprivation of certain freedoms specified in Article 19, the courts have the power to consider the reasonableness or otherwise of legislative provisions affecting such freedoms. Constitution of India has struck a balance between the British theory of parliamentary supremacy and the Aamerican theory of judicial supremacy and has evolved a principle of its own combining both the elements.

The established principle of British jurisprudence which may be regarded as also forming part of our legal system is that the personal liberty of any person cannot be affected by mere executive action of the Government in the absence of some provision of law to sustain such action.

There cannot be any such thing as absolute or uncontrolled liberty wholly free from restraint for that would lead to anarchy and disorder. The possession and "enjoyment of all rights" as was observed by the Supreme Court of America in (1905) 197 U.S. 11 (26, 27); 49 Law Ed. 643 (650) are subject to such reasonable conditions as may be deemed by the governing authority of the country essential to the safety, health, peace, general order and morals of the community. What the Constitution, attempts to do in declaring the rights of the people is to strike a balance between individual liberty and social control.

Fundamental Rights are not absolute but are limited. Parliament has been given the power to impose further restrictions and in doing so to confer authority on the Executive to carry its purpose into effect. But in every case it is the rights which are fundamental, not the limitations, and it is the duty of this court and of all courts in the land to guard and defend these rights jealously. It is our duty and privilege to see that rights which were intended to be fundamental are kept fundamental and to see that neither Parliament nor the Executive exceed the bounds within which they are confined by the Constitution when given the power to impose a restricted set of fetters on these freedoms and in the case of the Executive to see further that it does not travel beyond the powers conferred by Parliament.

The object of these Fundamental Rights was not merely to provide security to and equality of citizenship of the people living in this land and thereby helping the process of nation-building, but also, and not less importantly to provide certain standards of conduct citizenship, justice and fair play. In the background of the Indian

Constitution, they were intended to make all citizens and persons appreciate that the paramount law of the land has swept away privilege and has laid down that there is to be perfect equality between one section of the community and another in the matter of all those rights which are essential for the material and moral perfection of man. The guarantee of Fundamental Rights may be regarded as part of the method adopted to achieve the high ideal of establishing a society founded on the principle of justice, liberty, equality and fraternity proclaimed in the preamble.

Article 13(2) and Art. 359 stand on an equal footing and have to be read harmoniously. In order that the intention behind Art. 359 is carried out and is not destroyed altogether by Art. 13 (2). An order passed under Article 359 (1) cannot by law within the meaning of Art. 13 (2) and it cannot be tested under the very fundamental right the enforcement of which it suspends. Notwithstanding the difference in the language employed in the various classes of Articles occurring in Part III entitled Fundamental Rights they confer rights on persons either positively or by prohibiting the state from taking certain legislative or executive action in violation of those articles. They cannot be construed as mere injunctions. They are the most valuable rights. The difference in the language employed in conferring the rights under the various Articles in Part III is one of form and does not affect the contents of right.

Art. 13 makes it clear that the fundamental Rights guaranteed by the constitution are not meant merely to be pious enumerations of certain principles supposed to be at the basis of the constitution. Certainly all those who have framed written constitutions, contemplate them as forming the fundamental and paramount law of the nation, and consequently the theory of every such Government must be that an Act of Legislature, repugnant to the Constitution is *void*. The insertion of a declaration of Fundamental Rights in the forefront of the Constitution coupled with an express prohibition against legislative interference with the rights (Article 13) and the provision of a constitutional sanction for the enforcement of such non-interference by means of a judicial review (Article 32) is a clear and emphatic indication that these rights are to be paramount to ordinary state made law. The Fundamental Rights constitute express constitutional provisions limiting legislative power and controlling the Temporary will of a majority by a permanent and paramount law settled by the deliberate wisdom of the nation. The part on Fundamental Rights is sacrosanct and not liable to be abridged by any legislative or executive orders except to the extent provided in the appropriate article in Part III. It is not to be supposed that the legislative powers are absolute and despotic and that the Amendment prescribing due process of law is too vague and indefinite to operate as a practical restraint. It is not every Act legislative in form that is law. Law is something more than mere will exerted as an act of power. It must be not a special rule for a particular person or a particular case.

The view that the strict rule enjoined by the *Smriti* writers as a result of which the *sudras* were considered incapable of entering the order of Yati or Sanyasi has ceased to be valid because of the fundamental rights guaranteed under the Constitution is not correct. Part III of the Constitution does not touch upon the personal laws of the parties. It is emphatically the province and duty of the judicial department to say what the law is. Those who apply the rule to particular cases must of necessity expound and interpret that rule. An Act passed by the Legislature cannot be declared to be *void* merely on the ground of its being opposed to what the court conceives to be the spirit of the Constitution, when there is nothing express in the Constitution against a piece of legislation on the basis of which it can be declared *void*.

While the court must always be vigilant to prevent any encroachment by the Legislature upon Fundamental Rights which have been guaranteed, it must also remember that it is not a third chamber sitting in judgement on the policy laid down by the Legislature and which has been embodied in the legisation which it is considering. The line to be drawn between the powers of the Legislature and the powers of the court may sometimes be indistinct and uncertain but that a line exists must never be forgotten. The powers conferred upon the courts of law by our Constitution are immense but the very immensity of those powers must require of us a wise and unfailing restraint.

Under the American Constitution, although there is no express limitation in the Constitution, an act contrary to the first principles of the social contract is *void*. No one except those whose rights are directly affected by a law can raise the question of the constitutionality of that law. In the realm of constitutional law, especially, this court has perceived the embarrassment which is likely to result from an attempt to formulate rules or decide questions beyond the necessities of the immediate issue. It has preferred to follow the method of a gradual approach to the general by a systematically guarded application and extension of constitutional principles to particular cases as they arise, rather than by out of hard attempts to establish general rules to which future cases must be fitted. In determining the constitutional validity of a measure or a provision therein regard must be had to the real effect and impact thereof on the fundamental right. Names, forms and appearances are not material and the court must look behind them to discover the true character and nature of the legislation.

The pith and substance doctrine looks only at the object and subject-matter of the State action, but in testing the validity of the State-action with reference to fundamental rights what the court must consider is the direct and inevitable consequence of the State action, otherwise the protection of the Fundamental rights would be eroded. The provisions relating to fundamental rights must be construed broadly and liberally in favour of those on whom they have been conferred. There is a presumption in favour of the constitutionality of statutes. Legislation though enacted for the purpose of implementing the Directive Principles of State Policy contained in Part IV of the Constitution cannot transgress the provisions as to fundamental rights.

In general the invalidity of a procedural enactment cannot be held to affect the validity of a substantive provision. Where the invalid and the valid parts are not separable, the whole enactment will be *void*. Where law is judicially declared to be *void* as contravening a fundamental right, the law ceases to be enforceable, not only with regard to the actual parties to the litigation but with regard to all persons whose fundamental rights may be affected by such law. In considering whether an enactment adversely affects a fundamental right, it is only the direct aim of the legislation, that should be taken into consideration and not its possible and indirect effects. A person who has himself derived advantages from an Act cannot question its validity as contravening the provisions of Part III of the Constitution. The constitutionality of a Statute cannot be questioned by the State.

Constitutional safeguards are as a rule directed against the State and its organs and not against private individuals. Civil rights, such as are guaranteed by the American Constitution against State aggression, it has been held, cannot be impaired by the wrongful acts of individuals unsupported by state authority in the shape of laws, customs or judicial or executive proceedings. Although under Art. 19 (1) (g) of the Indian Constitution, a citizen has the fundamental right to carry on any occupation, trade or business he cannot do so as to create what, in law, would amount to a private nuisance affecting other citizens and if he does so, the person whose rights are affected can sue him for damages and injunction and he will not be entitled to plead in defence, his right under Art. 19 (1) (g).

Where any Fundamental Right is infringed by an order of the Executive, it is the duty of the High Court or the Supreme Court to set it aside. Although Art. 13 only provides that any law which contravenes the fundamental right will be *void*, this Article has only been interested *ex abundi cautela* and does not imply that the executive action of the state is immune from challenge on the ground of contravention of fundamental rights.

Even though there may be no express limitation on the power of the Legislature imposed by the (American) Constitution an Act of the Legislature which is contrary to first principles of social contract will be *ultra vires*. There are Acts which the Federal or State Legislature cannot do without exceeding their authority. There are certain vital principles in our free republican Government, which will determine and overrule an apparent and flagrant abuse of legislative power. An act of the Legislature contrary to the great first principles of the social contract cannot be considered a rightful exercise of legislative authority. The obligation of a law in Governments established on express contract, and on republican principles must be determined by the nature of the power, on which it is founded. The genus, the nature and the spirit of our State Governments amount to a prohibition of such acts of legislation and the general principles of law and reason forbid them. The Legislature cannot change innocence into guilt or punish innocence as a crime or violate the right of an antecedent lawful private contract; or the right of private property. To maintain that our Federal or State Legislature possesses such powers, if they had not been expressly restrained, would be a political heresy altogether inadmissible in our free republican Governments.

Under the Indian Constitution, the Supreme Court has authoritatively laid down that unless there is an express provision in the Constitution with which the Act of a Legislature conflicts, it cannot be held to be *void* merely on the ground of its being inconsistent with what the court considers to be the spirit of the Constitution.

A right which has not been expressly declared to be a fundamental right in Part III is not a Fundamental Right. Although Art. 265 gives rise to a constitutional right, the right is not a Fundamental Right and so cannot be enforced by the Supreme Court under Art. 32. An electoral right is a Fundamental Right to which the special remedy of moving the Supreme Court might apply although the right was not expressly mentioned as a Fundamental Right in chapter II of the Burma Constitution. Under the Indian Constitution it must be taken as settled law that no right can be regarded as a Fundamental Right unless it is expressly included in Part III of The Constitution.

It is an established principle of British jurisprudence which may be treated as constituting a part of the Indian law also, that no member of the executive can interfere with the liberty or property of a subject except on the condition that he can support the legality of his action before a Court of Justice. Although the Executive cannot infringe civil rights whether amounting to Fundamental Rights or not where there is no question of infringement of civil right, the Executive is not debarred from acting as for instance running a State bus service merely because there is no legislative enactment authorising it to do so.

A right of appeal is purely a creature of statute and is not a fundamental right. In interpreting the Fundamental Rights, American precedents relating to what may appear to be analogous provisions should not be blindly followed. The jurisdiction of civil courts to entertain suits against the state would not be barred merely because the act impeached was done in the exercise of sovereign power unless the act amounted to an act of State. A distinction is drawn between acts done by the State in the exercise of sovereign power and acts done in the exercise of powers which cannot be regarded as "sovereign".

Art. 19 refers to the rights of citizens in their free State and is not concerned with the question of taking away their basic freedom itself and putting a citizen in confinement. This latter question is the subject matter of Article 20, 21 and 22. Article 19 is not applicable to the question of detention of a person–preventive, punitive or otherwise. Where a person is totally deprived of his personal liberty and detained in confinement, Article 21 and not Art. 19 will only apply where the legislation hits a citizen's liberties as enumerated in Art. 19, directly and not where the restriction on or the deprivation of those liberties results from the application of some other law.

Where a person's personal liberty is not totally taken away by his being kept in confinement, and only certain restrictions are placed upon the freedom of his movement and as for instance, by means of an externment order, Art. 19 will apply and not Art. 21. Art. 19 does not contain the entire substantive law on the question of personal liberty and Art. 21 does not deal merely with procedure and is not merely complementary to this Article. Article 21 itself is a substantive provision with a distinct and individual scope. While Art. 19 enacts that a citizen shall have the various rights enumerated and proceeds to lay down the extent to which these rights may be curtailed by the State by means of laws, Articles 21 and 22 are couched in a negative form and purport to enact restrictions on the power of the State.

Where personal liberty is restricted by a particular law and the law does not relate to topics mentioned in Article 19, the examination of its reasonableness is an exclusive legislative function. Our Constitution does not maintain a provision corresponding to the due process clause of the American Constitution. There are five distinct lines of thought in the matter of reconciling Article 21 with Article 19, namely:

(1) If one loses his freedom by detention, he loses all the other attributes of freedom enshrined in Art. 19.

(2) Personal liberty in Article 21 is the rectitude of personal liberty after excluding the attributes of that liberty embodied in Article 19.

(3) The personal liberty included in Article 21 is wide enough to include some or all of the freedoms mentioned in Art. 19 but they are two distinct fundamental rights – a law to be valid shall not infringe both the rights.

(4) The expression "law" in Article 21 means a valid law and, therefore, even if a person's liberty is deprived by law of detention, the said law shall not infringe Art. 19.

(5) Article 21 applies to procedural law, whereas Article 19 to substantive law relating to personal liberty.

Unless a right comes within the four corners of Part III it will not be a fundamental right. A right may be both a common law right and a fundamental right. In such cases, although the act complained of by the citizen might give rise to a suit for damages for tort, this does not mean that the same act cannot also amount to infringement of a fundamental right, for which an application under Art. 32 can be preferred. There is no fundamental right in a litigant that any adjudication in his favour should have an attribute of finality. It is, therefore, competent, for the legislature to give a right of appeal to any party, be it Government or a private individual. A merely contractual right against the Government is not a fundamental right. A *right of privacy* is not a guaranteed right under the Constitution. Hence, an attempt to ascertain the movements of an individual, which is only a manner in which *privacy* is invaded, does amount to any infringement of any fundamental right.

A state may consider the relation of fundamental rights; and accommodate their co-existence and in the interests of the community, limit one right that others may be enjoyed. It is constitutionally impermissible to any one to contract out of fundamental rights. It is not the object of the Constitution of India to enable the citizens of India to break obligations arising under the guise of that obligation being something that is repugnant to the recognition of a Fundamental Right. Such an idea is foreign to the Constitution of India.

Art. 19 does not contain any guarantee against infringement of rights by private individuals. The article was intended to protect the fundamental freedoms assured to the citizen by clause (1) against State action other than the legitimate exercise of its powers to regulate private rights in the public interest. Article 19 is not directed against the infringement by private individuals for which remedies should be sought under the ordinary law. Where a petition under Article 32 is directed to questioning the validity of a legislative enactment which creates certain rights against the petitioners, the gravemen of the complaint is against the imagined Act and the petition is aimed against State action and not against private individuals merely because persons in whose favour the enactment has created the impugned rights are joined as respondents. Laws restricting fundamental rights should be strictly construed. In order to determine whether any enactment amounts to an interference with any of the rights conferred by Art. 19, it is the direct effect of an enactment and not its indirect or incidental effect that should be considered.

Where a statute is impugned on the ground that it adversely affects rights guaranteed by Art. 19 the courts would first have to ascertain whether the right claimed is one of the rights guaranteed by the Constitution and secondly whether the right is affected in a manner not warranted by the Constitution. The presumption is always in favour of the constitutionality of the enactment and this principle also applies when an Act is impugned on the ground of its infringement of any of the fundamental rights under Article 19. In order to decide whether a particular legislative measure contravenes any of the fundamental rights it is necessary to examine with some strictness the substance and the true nature of the legislation. In order to sustain the presumption of constitutionality the court may take into consideration matters of common knowledge, history of the times and may assume every state of facts which can be conceived as existing at the time of the legislation.

A judicial decision purports to decide a controversy brought before it and nothing more. A judicial verdict pronounced by court in or in relation to a matter brought before it for its decision cannot be said to affect fundamental rights of citizen under Art. 19 (1). Art. 19 only applies to the rights of citizen of India. Non-citizens cannot claim fundamental right under Art. 19 but can claim right under Arts. 20, 21 and 22. A corporation or a company is not a citizen for the purpose of this Constitution and therefore, cannot claim the rights mentioned in Art. 19. A foreign company cannot claim any of the rights under Art. 19 as fundamental rights. A citizen of India although coming within the definition of an evacuee is entitled to the full rights of citizenship under Art. 19. A State cannot claim any fundamental right under Art. 19. Hence when the State purports to exercise its own right of property, the ordinary law applies and the remedy of a high prerogative writ is not available. Since a corporation is not entitled to the fundamental rights under Art. 19, it cannot apply under Art. 32, for the enforcement of any right under Art. 19.

(7) *British Position*

In the Constitution of England, there are no guarantees or absolute rights. The safeguard of British liberty is in the good sense of the people and in the system of representation and responsible Government which has been evolved. The liberty of a subject in England "is a liberty confined and controlled by law, whether common law or statute. In America written Constitutions were intended to act as limitations on the power of the Legislature as well as of the Executive while in England the maxims of liberty are only applied as guards against Executive usurpation and tyranny.

The actual and practical security for English liberty against legislative tyranny was the power of a free public opinion represented by the commons. In this country written Constitutions were deemed essential to protect the rights and liberties of the people against encroachments of power delegated to their Governments and the provisions of *Magna Carta* were incorporated into *Bills of Rights*. They were limitations upon all the powers of Government, legislative as well as executive and judicial..... "these broad and general maxims of liberty and justice applied in England only as guards against arbitrary legislation, but in that application as it would be incongruous to measure and restrict them by the ancient customary English law, they must be held to guaranty not particular forms of procedure but the very susbtance of individual rights to life, liberty and property."

In accordance with British jurisprudence no member of the executive can interfere with the liberty or property of a British subject except on the condition that he can support the legality of his action before a Court of Justice. And it is the tradition of British Justice that judges should not shrink from deciding such issues in the face of the executive. If an Act of Parliament were to create a man judge in his own case, the court might disregard it. That dictum, however, stands as a warning rather than an authority to be followed. If an Act of Parliament has been obtained improperly, it is for the Legislature to correct it by repealing it but, so long as it exists as law, the courts are bound to obey it. The proceedings in the courts are judicial and autocratic which they would be if the courts could make laws instead of administering them. The term "unconstitutional" as applied to a parliamentary statute in England means merely contrary to general principles which are supposed to lie at the basis of the British Constitution and does not signify that the Act is *void*.

Even if an Act of Parliament is in contravention of the *Magna Carta* or *Petition of Right*, it will not be *void*. The *Magna Carta* and the common law were the supreme law of the land and controlled both the King and Parliament. In many cases, the common law will control Acts of Parliament, and sometimes adjudge them to be utterly *void*; for, when an Act of Parliament is against common rights or reason, or repugnant, or impossible to be performed, the Common Law will control it, and adjudge such Act to be *void*.

The sovereignty of Parliament was affirmed and established by the Revolution of 1688 with legal consequence that the validity of any law passed by the Parliament could not be questioned by any person or body on any ground. But the views expressed by Coke profoundly affected public opinion in United States and the Colonists adopted in their Constitution the doctrine that a statute which is opposed to common right and reason is *void*, and that it is the duty of the judges to declare it to be so.

The fact that an Act has not been adopted under Art. 372 (2) of the Indian Constitution by the President does not affect the question whether it continued in force after the commencement of the Constitution. The adaptation of a pre-existing law by President's order under Article 372 (2) does not ensure the validity of the Act if it offends any of the articles of the Constitution. The law made by the Legislature under Article 194 (3) relating to powers and privileges of the Legislature of a State is "*law*" within the meaning of Art. 13. So also the privilege claimable by the Legislature under Art. 194 (3) on the ground of their being privileges of the House of Commons are also subject to fundamental rights. The resolution of a House of the Legislature (*e.g.* suspending a member) is not '*Law*'.

The *British North America (B.N.A.)* Act contains no Bills of Rights guaranteeing the individual civil liberties of Canadian citizens. The absence of a Bill of Rights probably resulted from the view held by the Fathers of confederation that Canada inherited the English Constitutional Law. The preamble to the B.N.A. Act states that the Constitution is to be "similar in principle to that of the United Kingdom". If asked how Civil Liberties were to be insured, the Fathers of the confederation probably would have answered as Dicey did some twenty years later.

Freedom from arbitrary arrest, the right to express one's opinion on all matters subject to the liability to pay compensation for libellous or to suffer punishment of seditions or blasphemous statements and the right to enjoy one's own property seem to Englishman all to rest on the same basis, namely on the law of the land. To say that the Constitution guaranteed one class of rights more than the other would be to an Englishman an unnatural or senseless form of speech.

Until the enactment of the Canadian Bill of Rights in 1960, therefore, the principles of the English Constitutional Law, the Fathers of confederation placed their constitutional principles, the

Rule of Law and Parliamentary supremacy. The Rule of Law expresses the citizens' right to perform any act not expressly prohibited by law. Each citizen enjoys the freedom to speak, write, worship and assemble in any fashion not expressly prohibited by law. Concern for fundamental rights and freedoms affected by Parliamentary action are placed beyond the competence of the courts.

In interpreting section 19 of the Jamaican Constitution, which provided that "no person shall be subjected to the search of his person or his property or the entry by others on his premises, Lord Hodson stated in *King* vs. *The Queen* (1969) 1 AC 304:

> This constitutional right may or may not be enshrined in a written Constitution, but it seems to their Lordships that it matters not whether it depends on such enshrinement or simply upon the common law as it would do in this country. In either event the discretion of the court must be exercised and has not been taken away by the declaration of the right in written form.

The Canadian Bill of Rights appears as Part I of the "Act for the Recognition and Protection of Human Rights and Fundamental Freedoms". Section I is the declaratory section. It recognises and declares the political civil liberties of speech, religion, assembly, association and the press. It also contains the "due process" and "equality before the law", clauses. However, section I goes beyond simply listing the protected civil liberties. It describes these rights and freedoms as existing prior to and continuing after the adoption of the *Bill of Rights*.

It should be noted that with respect to the "legal rights", the main lacunae which are proposed to be filled by the charter are the rights to be free from "unreasonable search and seizure" [Section 8 (1)].

It is the function of the state in order that human liberty might be preserved a human personality developed to give recognition and free play to rights of man. Fundamental Rights were practically to be found in every constitution that came into existence after World War I. After World War II as a result of the discussions on the proposed United Nations Charter of Human Rights, they have become even more visibly important in most Constitutions framed after that war.

The limitations imposed by constitutional law upon the action of the Governments, both state and national, are essential in the preservation of public and private rights notwithstanding the representative character of our political institutions. The enforcement of these limitations by judicial process is the device of self-governing communities to protect the rights of individuals and minorities. In India written constitutions were deemed essential to protect the rights and liberties of the people against the encroachments of power delegated to their Governments, and the provisions of *Magna Carta* were incorporated into Bills of Rights. They were limitations upon all the powers of Government, legislative as well as executive and judicial.

Paramountcy to state-made laws is the hallmark of a Fundamental Right. The aim of having a declaration of Fundamental Rights is that certain elementary rights of the individual such as the right to life, liberty, freedom of speech, freedom of faith and so on should be regarded as inviolable under all conditions and that the shifting majorities in the Legislature of the country should not be able to temper with them.

The very purpose of a *Bill of Rights* was to withdraw certain subjects from the vicissitudes of political controversy, to place them beyond the reach of majorities and officials and to establish them as legal principles to be applied by the courts. Fundamental Rights may not be submitted to votes they depend on the outcome of no elections.

The word "liberty" is given a very wide connotation by American decisions as including not only freedom from bodily restraint but also the right of the individual to contract to engage in any of the common occupations of life, to acquire useful knowledge, to marry, establish a home and bring up children, to worship God according to the dictates of his own conscience, and generally to enjoy those privileges long recognised at common law as essential to the orderly pursuit of happiness by freeman.

(8) *American Position*

The leading feature of the conception of Fundamental Rights as developed under the American Constitution may be said to be the doctrine of *"due process of law"*. Under Amendment V in the Constitution which is directed against the Federal Government, it is provided *inter alia* that "no person shall be deprived of his life, liberty or property without due process of law". A similar provision is contained in Amendment XIV which relates to the powers of the states (1873) 21 Law Ed. 394 (408), 16 Wall 36, *Slaughter House Case* (Under the U.S. Constitution 14th Amendment, Section I, a distinction is made between "privileges and immunities" of citizens of the United States and it is only the former that are protected by the above amendment). The framers of the American Constitution did not attempt to define the expression with the result that it has a vague and indefinite content. Evidently, the framers of the American Constitution preferred flexibility to certainty when they chose the phrase "*due process of law*". It is not possible therefore to give an exhaustive definition of the phrase.

The phrase '*due process of law*" does not refer to a law enacted by the legislature. The very opposite is the construction placed on the expression "procedure established by law" in Art. 21 of Constitution of India "that the distress warrant issued under Act of May, 1820 is legal process is not denied. It was issued in conformity with an Act of Congress. The court must examine the Constitution itself to see whether this process is in conflict with any of its provisions. If not found to be so, the court must look to those settled usages and modes of proceeding existing in the common and statute law of England before the emigration of our ancestors and which are shown not to have been unsuited to their civil and political condition by having been acted on by them after the settlement of this country."

It is easy to see that when the great Barons of England wrung from King John, at the point of the sword, the concession that neither their lives nor their property should be disposed of by the Crown, except as provided by the law of the land, they meant by law of the land the ancient and customary laws of the English people or the laws enacted by the Parliament of which those Barons were a controlling element. It was not in their minds, therefore, to protect themselves against the enactment of laws by the Parliament of England. By 'the law of the land' is most clearly intended the general law; a law which hears before it condemns; which proceeds upon inquiry and renders judgement only after trial. The meaning is that every citizen shall hold his life, liberty, property and immunities, under the protection of the general rules which govern society. Everything which may pass under the form of an enactment, is not, therefore, to be considered the law of the land. If this were so... it would tend directly to establish the

Union of all powers in the Legislature. There would be no general permanent law for courts to administer for men to live under. The administration of justice would be an empty form and idle ceremony.

The expression "*due process of law*" was in the earlier stages treated as referring to the English Common Law. The words "*due process of law*" it was held were intended to convey the same meaning as the words "by the law of the land" in *Magna Carta*. Lord Coke in his commentary on the words "by the law of the land" (2 Ins. 50) says they mean due process of laws. "In many cases, the common law will control Acts of Parliament, and sometimes adjudge them to be utterly *void*, for when an Act of Parliament is against common rights or reason, or repugnant, or impossible to be performed, the common law will control it, and adjudge such Act to be *void*." *(1610) 8 Cokes' Rep 107 (a) at p. 118 (a)*.

The courts evolved the principle that new procedures were due process if they served the ends of substantial justice. The argument that a process of law which was not sanctioned by the settled usage of law is not tenable. There is nothing in *Magna Carta* rightly construed as a broad charter of public right and law which ought to exclude the best ideas of all systems and of every age. The doctrine of *due process* guarantees not only particular forms of procedure but the very substance of individual rights to life, liberty and property.

"The broad and general maxims of liberty and justice applied in England only as guards against executive usurpation and tyranny, here they have become bulwarks also against arbitrary legislation, but in that application, as it would be incongruous to measure and restrict them by the ancient customary English law, they must be held to guaranty not particular forms of procedure, but the very substance of individual rights to life, liberty and property."

Courts began to examine the constitutionality of all legislative measures in the light of their own political, social and economic ideas. By virtue of the due process clause, the courts exercised the power of examining legislative enactments with a view to determine whether they formed an undue, arbitrary or unreasonable invasion of individual liberty and rights.

While the meaning of constitutional guarantees never varies, the scope of their application must expand or contract to meet the new and different conditions which are constantly coming within the field of their operation. In a changing world it is impossible that it should be otherwise. But although a degree of elasticity is thus imparted not to the meaning but to the application of constitutional principles, statutes and ordinances, which after giving due weight to the new conditions, are found clearly not to conform to the Constitution, of course, must fail...." The line which in this field separates the legitimate from the illegitimate assumption of power is not capable of precise delimitation. It varies with circumstances and conditions. In solving doubts, the maxim *sic uteri tuo ut alienum non laedas*, which lies at the foundation of so much of the common law of nuisances, ordinarily will furnish a fairly helpful clue....." (1926) 17 Law Ed. 303 (310); 272 U.S. 365.

The Bill of Rights gurantees to each American protections which we equate with specific rights of citizenship in a free society. The Privacy Act of 1974 is a major first step in a continuing effort to define the "penumbra" of privacy which emanates from specific guarantees in the Bill of Rights and which helps to give them life and substance as recognised in *Griswold* Vs. *Connecticut*. The Constitution creates a right to privacy which is designed to assure that the minds and hearts of Americans remain free. The bulwark of this constitutional principle is the first amendment. The first amendment was designed to protect the sanctity of the individual's private thoughts and beliefs. It protects the individual's right to free exercise of conscience, his right to assemble to petition the Government for redress of grievances, his right to associate peaceably with others of like mind in pursuit of a common goal; his right to speak freely what he believes; and his right to try to pursuade others of the worth of his ideas.

The fourth amendment guarantees the right of the people to be secure in their persons, houses, papers and effects against unreasonable searches and seizures. In addition to the privacy of one's home and personal effects, the privacy of his person – or bodily integrity – and even his private telephone conversations are protected by the fourth amendment. The fifth amendment guarantees that an individual shall not be forced to divulge private information which might incriminate him. It also protects individual privacy by preventing unwarranted governmental interference with the individual's person, personality and property without *due process of law*. The Ninth Amendment's reservation that "the enumeration in the Constitution of certain rights shall not be construed to deny or disparage others retained by the people clearly shows that the Founding Fathers contemplated that certain basic individual rights not specifically mentioned in the Constitution – such as privacy should nevertheless be safe from governmental interference.

The premise underlying the *Privacy Act of 1974* is that good government and efficient management requires that basic principles of privacy, confidentiality and due process must apply to all personal information programs and practices of the Federal Government and should apply to those of state and local government as well as to those of the organisations, agencies and instruments of the private sector.

The broad principles involved in what is conveniently called "the individual right of privacy" are deeply rooted in our history and derived from the Bill of Rights of the United States Constitution. The Fourth Amendment to the Constitution was written as the result of the American Colonial experience with warrants and writs issued under King George III of England which often gave his officers an excuse to search anyone, anywhere any time. In their famous 1890 Harward Law Review Article "*The right to privacy*" Samuel Warren & Louis D. Brandeis concluded:

> It would doubtless be desirable that the privacy of the individual should receive the added protection of the Criminal Law, but for this, legislation would be required.... The Common Law has always recognised a man's house as his castle, impregnable, often even to its own officers engaged in the execution of its commands. Shall the courts thus close the front entrance to continued authority, and open wide the back door to idle or prurient curiosity?

Almost 40 years later, Justice Brandeis, in his famous dissent in the case of *Olmstead* Vs. *United States* set forth the basic constitutional principles of individual privacy. The makers of American Constitution undertook to secure conditions favourable to the pursuit of happiness. They recognised the significance of man's spiritual nature of his feelings and of his intellect..... They conferred, as against the Government, the right to be let alone – the most comprehensive of rights and the right most valued by civilised men. To protect that right, every unjustifiable intrusion by the Government upon the privacy of the individual, whatever the means employed must be deemed a violation of the fourth amendment.

He went on to say further in his dissent even more reluctant in these days of wholesale abuses of governmental power in our modern computerized society. Experience should teach us to be most on our gurad to protect liberty when the government's purposes are beneficient. Men born to freedom are naturally alert to repel invasions to their liberty by evil-minded rulers. The greatest dangers to liberty lurk in insidious encroachment by men of zeal, well-meaning, but without understanding.

While there can be no right of absolute privacy in our complex civilisation, there is an urgent need today to assert the fundamental right of privacy for all Americans to the maximum extent consistent with the overall welfare of our Nation. The Federal Government can and must take the lead to achieve this important objective. On August 13, 1974 in his first address to the Congress as Chief Executive, President Ford pledged his personal and official dedication to the individual right of privacy. He declared, "There will be put pursuit of tough laws to prevent illegal invasion of privacy in both government and private activities.

The Privacy Act created a right of access for individuals to their own files, a right to correct mistakes contained in those files, and a responsibility on the part of the Government to protect personal information from misuse and disclosure which constituted an invasion of the privacy of the subject of that information. The *Freedom of Information Act* amendments speeded access by the public to Government records, strengthened the rights of the public to obtain disclosure of public information and limited the scope of the Government's authority to withhold certain kind of information.

The Freedom of Information Act had always recognised the Government's authority to withhold information whose disclosure would constitute a clearly unwarranted invasion of personal privacy. And the *Privacy Act* was drafted to avoid interference with the free flow of information to the public required to be released by the *Freedom of Information Act*. They were enacted but a few weeks apart by a Congress dedicated both to an opening of the Federal Government – so recently tainted by the effects of the Watergate Scandal – and a protecting of the rights to personal privacy of each citizen who became subject of a government file.

Nonetheless, with the need to enact the Freedom of Information Act and with the need to complete work on the Privacy Act, the two laws do not appear to mesh as easily as might have been desired. Two different committees in the Senate worked on the different Bills, and while the office of the management and Budget was pressing hard for enactment of privacy legislation, the Justice Department was pressing equally hard to defeat of Freedom of Information legislation. The forces seeking greater disclosure of govt. operations and information often are found in opposition to forces seeking protection of individual privacy. Some of the leading cases interpreting the Freedom of Information Act deal with the kinds of information about individual citizens which can be released without invading their privacy. If information about an individual would be released under an FOI Act request, it could be released under b (2) of the Privacy Act. The standard for release under the FOI Act is in section b (6) which permits the withholding of information, the release of which would constitute a "clearly unwarranted invasion of personal privacy".

The Freedom of Information Act states generally that each Federal agency shall make available to the public certain specified information. Section 552 (b) of Title 5 represents a recognition by Congress that "Certain information in Government files" should be exempt from disclosure while the cases involving exemption (6), are numerous, every effort was made to include only those cases which construe by definite analysis the provisions of the exemption. Exemption (6) protects from disclosure "personal and medical files" and similar files the disclosure of which would constitute a clearly unwarranted invasion of personal privacy.

Congressional awareness of possible conflicts between the right of the public to know and the intrusion into individual privacy would appear to be the reason for the creation of exemption (6) as the privacy balancing machinery. A general exemption for the category of information is much more practical than separate statutes protecting each type of personal record. The limitation of a clearly unwarranted invasion of personal privacy provides a proper balance between the protection of an individual's right of privacy and the preservation of the public's right to government information by excluding those kinds of files the disclosure of which might harm the individual. The exemption is also intended to cover detailed Government records on an individual which can be identified as applying to that individual and not the facts concerning the award of a pension or benefit or the compilation of unidentified statistical information from personal records.

At the same time, a broad philosophy of freedom of information is enacted into law. It is necessary to protect certain equally important rights of privacy with respect to certain information in Government files, such as medical and personal records. It is also necessary for the very operation of our Government to allow it to keep confidential certain material, such as the investigatory files of the Federal Bureau of Investigation.

(9) *Meaning of Expression "Law"*

Clause (3) (a) of Article 13 of the Indian Constitution defines "*Law*" and Clause (3) (b) defines "*laws in force*". But the definitions are not intended to be applicable only to the respective clauses in which the expressions "*laws*" and "*laws in force*" have been used. Thus, although clause (1) uses the expression "laws in force", the definition of "*law*" in clause (3) (a) is also applicable to the "*laws in force*".

The principle analogous to the principle that the King can do no wrong continues to apply after the Constitution and the State is not bound by a statute unless it is so provided in express terms or by necessary implication. Custom or usage which is included in the definition of "*law*" in clause (3) (a), will be covered by the expression "*laws in force*" in clause (1) and to the extent that a custom or usage may be inconsistent with any of the fundamental rights, it will be *void* under that clause.

The definition of *"law"* refers to the concept of law for the purpose of the whole Article and not only to the particular expression "*law*" used in clause (2). An Act of the Legislature will obviously be a "*law*" within clause (3) (a) although it is not expressly mentioned in it. The word "*law*" in Article 366 (10) will include a notification having the force of law. The definition of "law" in Art. 13 as specifically including an ordinance is limited for the purpose of that Article. But in Article 366 the term "existing law" is defined to include an ordinance. Even on general jurisprudential ground an ordinance will pass as law.

The expression "*existing law*" in Art. 366 (10) includes an Act or other law which has been passed but has not yet been brought into actual operation. This expression and the expression "*laws in force*" have the same meaning in this respect, notwithstanding the difference in the definition. The expression "*existing law*" as defined in Art. 366

(10) and occurring in Art. 254 can be equated with "*law in force*" as defined in Art. 13 (3) (b) and Art. 372 (3), Explanation I. Thus an "existing law" as used in Art. 254 may be a law imperative and not in force when the Constitution came into force. The words law occurring in Art. 254 with reference to enactments other than "existing laws" do not have a different scope and are not confined to enactments when enforced. The definition of "law in force" in Art. 13 is not its ordinary grammatical meaning. The same is the case with its definition in Art. 372. These definitions are of no avail in construing the expression in Art. 31-A (1).

A temporary Act passed before the Constitution was due to expire after the coming into force of the Constitution. It contained the provision for extension by the State Government by notification for a further specified period. The duration of the Act was extended by another Act passed after the Constitution instead of by Government Notification. It was held that the later Act does not constitute a new Act and is covered by the expression "*laws in force*". Hence, such an Act falls within the scope of clause (1) and not Clause (2). Even the local laws are subject to Art. 13. Under section 18 (3) of the Indian Independence Act, 1947, the laws passed by the British Parliament and which were applicable to India continued in force till 21.1.1950.

Law includes not only the law passed by the Legislature but also law in all other forms. The word "law" as used in Art. 13 bears the same meaning as under Art. 21 and 31, under which the word has been used in the sense of a legislative measure and not a mere executive order. When a statute creates a right for the first time and imposes certain conditions for the enjoyment of that right these conditions should be such as would not infringe the provisions contained in Art. 13. Term "*law*" includes even rules, bye-laws, regulations, notifications or orders issued under power conferred on Government to issue same. Most statutes creating statutory bodies and corporations, consist of two kinds of provisions *viz*.: (i) provisions authorising administrative action such as section 6 and 26 of Life Insurance Corporation Act and (ii) provisions empowering the Central Government to make rules and the corporation or other bodies to make regulation such as sections 48 and 49 of the Act. The exercise of the former authority results in administrative actions or instructions. It is only the exercise of the latter power which results in the making of legislation or subordinate legislation. An administrative scheme framed by the corporation is not law because there it has no authority to make such law. Law in Art. 13 (2) refers to the exercise of an ordinary legislative power and does not include constitutional amendments under Art. 368.

*

IV

NATURE

> "Once a civilisation has made a distinction between the "outer" and the "inner" man between the life of the soul and the life of the body, between the spiritual and the material, between the sacred and the profane, between the realm of God and the realm of Caesar, between church and state, between rights inherent and inalienable and rights that are in the power of government to give and take away, between public and private, between society and solitude, it becomes impossible to avoid the idea of privacy by whatever name it may be called—the idea of a private sphere in which man may become and remain himself.
>
> —*Charles Warren and Louis D. Brandeis* :
> *Harward Law Review* 193

In his dissenting opinion in *Griswold* Vs. *Connecticut* Mr. Justice Black berated the majority for discovering and applying a constitutional right to privacy. His reading of the Constitution failed to uncover any provision or provisions forbidding the passage of any law that might abridge the "privacy" of individuals. Therefore, he would have upheld a Connecticut Act prohibiting the use of, or the giving advice concerning the use of contraceptive devices. If Justice Black had examined state constitutions, he would have found them similarly devoid of specific reference to a "*right to privacy*".

In private law, there are statutes and court decisions that protect various aspects of privacy and human dignity frequently under property or contract concepts, but until very recent times, these have not been viewed by the public or most legal commentators as spelling out a comprehensive "*right to privacy*". The only explicit recognition of a "right to privacy" has been found in certain tort cases, dating from the first decade of this century and following the suggestion of the famous Warren and Brandeis article.

(1) *Three Categories of Claims*

We must examine privacy as a series of legal claims with respect to desired or unwanted relationships with others, some of which have received protection in law while many others are pressing for but have not yet achieved legal recognition. One can readily discern at least three categories of claims that inhere in the legal concept of privacy at this time and must be given a place in any working definition of a right to privacy. Therefore, a right to privacy as a legal concept can be defined as the legally recognised freedom or power of an individual (group, association or class) to determine the extent to which another individual (group, class, association or government) may

(a) obtain or make use of his ideas, writings, means, likeness, or other indicia of identity, or

(b) obtain or reveal information about him or those for whom he is personally responsible, or

(c) intrude physically or in more subtle ways into his life, space and his choosen activities.

The concept "right to privacy" represents essentially an effort to define some reasonable rules for governing the behaviour of active people whose work, play and interactions are part of a highly complex independent society. The right is an affirmation of the importance of certain aspects of the individual person and his desired freedom unreasonable intrusive conduct by others.

(2) *German Law*

A right to personality is recognised in German law. The German Courts construed the right to privacy on the basis of two extremely general substantive attitudes in the 1949 West German Constitution. Article 1 (1) "The Dignity of man shall be inviolable". To respect and protect it shall be the duty of all State authority and Art. 2(1). "Everyone shall have the right to the free development of his personality insofar as he does not infringe the rights of others or offered against the constitutional order or the moral code."

(3) *American Position*

Whether one welcomes or despises the propensity of Americans to regard the Constitution as the embodiment of our most cherished values, it is a fact of our political life that a constitutional right is more dearly prized than one proclaimed solely by legislative Act, and, as we know any novel or doubtful piece of legislation must inevitably run the gauntlet of judicial scrutiny of its constitutionality.

Interpreting and applying an 18th century document to problems and situations that were unforeseeable in 1787. Apart from the warning of Madison and others that the enumeration of certain rights would tend to disparage claims to others, an argument rejected by those supporting a "*Bill of Rights*" it is hard to see how several of the specific rights can be given meaningful scope without necessarily safeguarding a right to privacy. It would be indeed ironic if this were not so in a constitutional system designed to protect the integrity of the individual in an age that laid stress on the necessity of recognising both the rational and irrational elements in man but which, above all, wanted to protect the integrity of the individual in an age that laid stress on the necessity of recognising both the rational and irrational elements in man but which, above all, wanted to protect his dignity and status as an individual.

The great contribution of Brandeis in his famous *Olmstead* dissent was his drawing of the distinction between the interest to be protected and particular forms of invasion of that interest. In his view, the devising and ingenuity of man in substituting new scientific techniques for the older, heavy-handed secret observation of the thoughts, words and acts of others should not be allowed to succeed in outflawing the law.

One of the most interesting of constitutional developments has been the search for a suitable rationale for protecting the privacy of groups, against state efforts to identify members and through various other strategems to make hazardous the enjoyment of a right to association clearly, there cannot be an unlimited right to the privacy of association that seek undesirable social objectives or whose methods of operation run afoul of reasonably applied conspiracy doctrines. In undertaking this very ticklish process of separating permissible from prohibitable associational activity, the Supreme Court has taken a long step toward bringing constitutional guarantees into closer alignment with social realities.

For better and for worse, individuals today frequently find meaningful avenues for asserting personal and social claims only through associational activity. But some form of associational activity may threaten the freedom including the right to privacy of other individuals and groups. A weighing of ends and means is clearly required, and, as in so many other situations where we seek to use law to shape conduct, resolution of issues in individual cases is difficult and any rule of law other than a rule of reason is virtually unthinkable, whether or not one agrees with the court's performance in balancing interests to protect the NAACP while allowing harassment of the Ku Klux Klan and the Communist party, U.S.A., there are sufficient differences between both means and ends to make plausible a different treatment in law of these associations.

With respect to privacy values, which have often been viewed as a privacy concern only of higher status individuals, the effort through law to enhance the privacy and dignity of disadvantaged individuals and groups, whether criminal suspects, religious or ràcial minorities or welfare clients, tends to strengthen the claims to privacy and dignity of all citizens.

Privacy is an outcome of a person's wish to withhold from others certain knowledge as to his past and present experience and action and his intentions for the future. The wish for privacy expresses a desire to be an enigma to others, or more generally, a desire to control others' perceptions and beliefs *vis-a-vis*, the self conceding person. Privacy is essential for that disclosure which illumines a man's being-for-himself, changes his being for others, and potentiates desirable growth of his personality. Privacy is experienced as "room to grow in" as freedom from interference, and as freedom to explore, to pursue experimental projects in science, art, work, play and living. In the name of the *status quo* and others, even more attractive goals, privacy may be eroded. But without privacy and its concomitant, freedom, the cost far to be paid for the ends achieved in terms of lost health, weak commitment to the society and social stagnation may be too great.

(4) *Need to Reveal and Need to Protect and Withhold*

The purpose of any same political ideology should be freedom for all human beings. In psychological terms, we want all people to experience the feeling of freedom. In many instances Candor yields a wonderous sensation of being free. Unquestionably, people must be able to free themselves of ideas and emotions that trouble them and upset their relationships with others, and which in many cases confuse and damage institutions. Children should be allowed to safely reveal their problems to school personnel, workers their inner worlds to one another and their bosses, family members to each other. People do have a need to confess or let others know bits and pieces of their personal lives. But if there is a need to reveal there is also a need to protect and withhold.

When considering the issue of the right of privacy it is particularly important to be reminded that this is not a new idea. In fact this right lies at the roots of American heritage. Incensed reaction to the continuous infringement on the personal liberty of our early Colonists gave birth to this nation – and it has been the protection of our hard-won rights that has sustained this republic through nearly two centuries.

To guarantee tranquility for all, freedom must be regulated. Total freedom would be chaotic. Therefore, for the good of all, rules must be established and laws must be enforced. It is in this area of maintaining the peace that problems have arisen regarding the methods of enforcing the law and concerning the retention of criminal records. At the core of the problem lies the issue of the right of privacy.

(5) *Privacy The Balance of Individual and Societal Rights*

Interestingly enough, this right is not defined nor specified in the American or of the Constitutions of the world. Yet, the principle of privacy permeates this document. Though privacy is not specifically mentioned, it is certainly a factor in the First Amendment (religion, speech, press, assembly); Third Amendment (quartering troops); Fourth Amendment (unreasonable search and seizure); Fifth Amendment (self-incrimination); and Ninth Amendment (rights enumerated in the Constitution not to be construed to deny or disparage others retained by the people). Therefore, privacy is what freedom is all about.

The right of privacy does not mean that shackles must be thrown around the legitimate operations of the law enforcement officer. It also does not mean that a citizen can freely declare that his activities are free from scrutiny. No person in our society is above the law.

Historically, freedom has meant a balance of individual and societal rights. Never, is it a question of one or the other but both. The moment we lose this balance, our free society will be jeopardized. Any criminal justice information system must give equal concern to protecting the rights of all individuals and to the necessity for law enforcement agencies to have all pertinent information to meet their responsibilities. This represents quite a delicate balance, but a balance that has to be maintained.

Just as each of us treasures his personal privacy, it is our obligation to respect the privacy of others. Likewise, because of our professional responsibilities, it is essential that we have access to all information that will aid us in providing criminal justice. The challenge of combating crime while giving utmost concern to personal privacy is certainly complex, but it is a challenge that must be successfully handled for the good of all.

The thin line between intelligence and surveillance, between the public's right to know and the citizen's right to privacy, is the foundation of much current American soul searching. Both principles, the right to knowledge and the right to privacy are finally entrenched in the constitutional traditions. Thus, the existence of investigatory agencies are troublesome to the extent that they involve us in a legal double-bind-a veritable contradiction between competing needs in a modern society. The limits of privacy come full force against the limits of knowledge. And choices are made in terms of shifts in the moral sentiment more than new legal foundations of the social order. What balance is needed regarding secrecy, privacy and publicity in the presser?

"It's not the number that's the evil, and it's not the information that's the evil, it's the decision to collect and use the information" says Hope Eastman, a lawyer for the American Civil Liberties Union.

The ultimate thing will be that citizens can be tracked by the government from cradle to grave. It wipes out the possibility of making a clean start. It is also a mechanism of social control. The more information they have, the less creative, less adventurous, less politically active, you are for fear of offending "someone". When people fear surveillance, whether it exists or not, when they grow afraid to speak their minds and hearts freely to their government or to anyone else, then we shall cease to be a free society.

There is presently no coherent body of "privacy law" but rather an amalgam of legal concepts deriving from the constitution and various interests recognised by the common law. The confidentiality of personal information is perhaps the central privacy issue. The burden of legislating in this field requires a delicate balancing of the interests of each individual to control the gathering and use of information about him and the interests of government in obtaining the information needed to administer its services and enforce its law.

Nothing can be more sacred to our democratic society than the security of the citizen in his home, and the privacy of the individual in the conduct of his personal affairs. The issue of the right to privacy is at a crossroads. The policy choices to be made in the next few years will determine whether our nation will leash technology to prevent its stampede over the rights to privacy or whether enormous interconnected data systems carrying information above all of us will grow unchecked.

Until recently, the available technology made difficult the automatic transfer of information gathered by one agency for one purpose to another agency for another purpose without the knowledge of the individual. Suddenly people have become intensely aware that the situation has changed. Now, they are faced with an erosion of their privacy, for which they will receive no benefit or right in exchange. In fact the entire process of collection and transfer of information can and does occur without the individual's knowledge, let alone his or her consent. What is lost, as much as the right to privacy, is the right to contract one's life.

By living in a diffuse society, certain rights to privacy are automatically surrendered by everyone. There are other rights to privacy that some citizens choose to give up voluntarily when a person wants a privilege that others do not have – whether it is a government job, a credit card or an educational scholarship – there is an implicit understanding that the goal is important enough to warrant giving out some relevant personal information. In that case, since it is a conscious decision made with the knowledge of how it will be used, the individual retains his or her free choice.

The right of privacy has been said to be the right of the individual to be left alone. It is without doubt a right inherent in our liberation system. While it is said that this right is not explicitly asserted in our constitution, it does however find expression in certain related provisions and in the basic philosophy which prompted the adoption of the Constitution itself. By that instrument those freedoms and liberties were reserved to the individual which were not deemed essential to the co-existence of man in society. Hence, like other rights, the right of privacy is not deemed an absolute right.

Logically, the absolute right of privacy could be fully asserted only in a state of anarchy. But even in such a state, if extended to its outer and extreme limits the exercise of any such absolute right must necessarily collide with the rights of other individuals. The resulting conflict would consequently result in the destruction of the rights asserted by each. It necessarily follows that if the right of privacy is to be recognised as a legitimate claim in an ordered society, it must be subject to limitations and must be conditioned upon the rights of others and exercised consistently also with the rights of the public.

*

V

BASIS

> "Where pity and mercy and humanitarianism are subordinated to utilitarian considerations and the power of the state is employed to destroy the virility of unfortunate human beings rather than their segregation and treatment toward recovery or amelioration, we as a people invite atavism to the state of mind evidenced in separate ancient Rome and the dark ages where individuality counted for naught against the mere animal breeding of human beings for purpose of state or Tribe. There is a limit even to the power of the state over the bodies of men and women."
>
> –*Smith* Vs. *Wayne Probate* Judge [1925] 231 Mich. 409

In early times, the law gave remedy only for physical interference with life and property for trespass *vi et armis*. Then the right to life served only to protect life from battery in its various forms; liberty meant freedom from actual restraint and the right to property secured to the individual, his land and cattle; later there came a recognition of spiritual nature of his feelings and his intellect. Gradually, the scope of these legal rights has come to mean the right to enjoy the life, the *right to be let alone*.

(1) *Concept of Life*

Generally speaking, a civilised man has a different concept of life and consequently of his home. The danger of not having a private zone for every individual was indicated by Douglas J. He said, "that a time may come when no one can be sure whether his words are being recorded for use at some future time. When everyone will be in fear that his most sacred thoughts are no longer his own but belong to the Government, when the most confidential conversations are open to eager, prying ears; when that time comes privacy and with it liberty is gone. If a man's privacy is invaded at will, who can say that he is free? If his every word is taken down and evaluated or if he is afraid of every word he says, who can say he enjoys freedom of speech? If every association of man is known and recorded; if his conversation with his associates are purloined, who can say that he enjoys the freedom of association". [*Mass Media and the Law*, 187 at 195)

The demand that individual privacy be respected is becoming more common and more instant in our age. This probably reflects a rapidly increasing need for privacy arising from converging ecological, cultural, technical and social changes. The population explosion together with modern urbanisation have made it much more difficult for the individual to get away physically and psychologically, from the crowd of strangers around him. The growing allegiance to political individualism and moral autonomy have caused the individual to resent and resist legal regulation and social interference more intensely. At a time when bugging and other techniques of surveillance have been perfected to an alarming degree, the development of computers enables us to store and retrieve vastly increased amounts of information about any specified individual in even very large populations. Finally, as organisations have grown larger in size and more bureaucratic in structure, their tendency to invade the life of the individual has grown apace. In the United States, whatever may be the case in other societies, the legal system has responded to these changes by relying mainly on statutory safeguards.

That the individual shall have full protection in person and in property is a principle as old as the common law; but it has been found necessary from time to time to define anew the exact nature and extent of such protection. Political, social and economic changes entail the recognition of new rights, and the common law, in its eternal youth, grows to meet the demands of society. Thus in very early times, the law gave a remedy only for physical interference with life and property. There the "right to life" served only to protect the subject from battery, in its various forms; liberty means freedom from actual restraint. Later, there came a recognition of man's spiritual nature, of his feelings and his intellect. Gradually the scope of these rights broadened, and now the right to life has come to mean the right to enjoy life, – the ***right to be let alone***, the right to liberty secures the exercise of extensive civil privileges.

The intense intellectual and emotional life and the heightening of sensations which came with the advance of civilisation, made it clear to man that only a part of the pain, pleasure and profit of life lay in physical things. Thoughts, emotions and sensations demanded legal recognition and the beautiful capacity for growth which characterizes the common law enabled the judges to afford the requisite protection, without the interposition of the legislature.

(2) *Illustrations of Invasion*

Recent inventions and business methods call attention to the next step which must be taken for the protection of the person, and for securing to the individual what Judge Cooley calls the "*right to be let alone*". Instantaneous photographs and newspaper enterprise have invaded the sacred precincts of private and domestic life; and numerous mechanical devices threaten to make good the prediction that "what is whispered in the closet shall be proclaimed from the house tops". For years there has been a feeling that the law must afford some remedy for the unauthorised circulation of portraits of private citizens and the evil of the invasion of the privacy by the newspaper is long keenly felt.

The press is overstepping in every direction the obvious bounds of propriety and of decency. Gossip is no longer the resource of the idle and of the vicious, but has become a trade, which is pursued with industry as well as effrontary. To satisfy a prurient taste the details of sexual relations are spread broadcast in the columns of the daily papers. To occupy the indolent, column upon column is filled with idle gossip, which can only be procured by intrusion upon the domestic circle. The intensity and complexity of life, attendant upon advancing civilization, have rendered necessary some retreat from the world, and man, under the refining influence of culture, has become more sensitive to publicity, so that solitude and privacy have become more essential to the individual, but modern enterprise and inventions have, through invasions upon his privacy, subjected him to mental pain and distress, far greater than could be inflicted by mere bodily injury. Nor is the harm wrought by such invasions confined to the suffering of those who may be made the subjects of journalistic or other enterprise.

It is our purpose to consider whether the existing law affords a principle which can properly be invoked to protect the privacy of the individual, and if it does, what the nature and extent of such protection is. It is certain every man has a right to keep his own sentiments, if he pleases. He has certainly a right to judge whether he will make them public, or commit them only to the sight of his friends.

Owing to the nature of the instruments by which privacy is invaded, the injury inflicted bears a superficial resemblance to the wrongs dealt with by the law of slander and libel. The wrongs and correlative rights recognised by the law of slander and libel are in their nature material rather than spiritual. Our law recognises no principle upon which compensation can be granted for mere injury to the feelings. However, painful, the mental effects upon another of an act though purely wanton or even malicious, yet if the act itself is otherwise lawful, the suffering inflicted is ***damnum absque injuria***. The common law secures to each individual the right of determining, ordinarily. To what extent his thoughts, emotions and sentiments shall be communicated to others. Under our system of government, he can never be compelled to express them (except when upon the witness stand); and even if he has chosen to give them expression, he generally retains the power to fix the limits of the publicity which shall be given them. The existence of this right does not depend upon the particular method of expression adopted. It is immaterial whether it be by word or by signs, in painting by sculpture, or in music. Neither does the existence of the right depend upon the nature or value of the thought or emotion. The same protection is accorded to a casual letter or an entry in a diary and to the most valuable poem or essay, to a botch or damb and to a masterpiece. In every such case the individual is entitled to decide whether that which is his shall be given to the public. No other has the right to publish his productions in any form, without his consent. The right is wholly independent of the material on which, or the means by which, the thought, sentiment or emotion is expressed. It may exist independently of any corporeal being, as in words spoken, song sung, a drama acted, or if expressed on any material as a poem in writing, the author may have parted with the paper, without forfeiting any proprietory right in the composition itself. The right is lost when the author himself communicates his production to the public, – in other words, published it.

It may now be considered settled that the protection afforded by the common law to the author of any writing is entirely independent of its pecuniary value, its intrinsic merit or of any intention to publish the same, and, of course, also wholly independent of the material, if any upon which, or the mode in which, the thought or sentiment was expressed. If privacy is once recognised as a right entitled to legal protection the interposition of the courts cannot depend on the particular nature of the injuries resulting. The protection afforded to thoughts, sentiments and emotions expressed through the medium of writing or of the acts, so far as it consists in preventing publication, is merely an instance of the enforcement of the more general right of the individual to be let alone. It is the right not to be assaulted or beaten, the right not to be imprisoned, the right not to be maliciously prosecuted, the right not to be defamed. The principle, which protects personal writings and all other personal productions, not against theft and physical appropriation, but against publication in any form, is in reality not the principle of private property, but that of an inviolate personality.

If then, the decisions indicate a general right to privacy for thoughts, emotions and sensations, these would receive the same protection, whether expressed in writing, or in conduct, in conversation, in attitudes, or in facial expression. The principle which protects personal writings and any other productions of the intellect or of the emotions, is the right to privacy, and the law has no new principle to formulate when it extends this protection to the personal appearance, sayings, acts, and to personal relations, domestic or otherwise.

If the invasion of privacy constitute a legal *injuria*, the elements for demanding redress exist since already the value of mental suffering caused by an act wrongful in itself, is recognised as a basis for compensation. The right of one who has remained a private individual, to prevent his public portraiture, presents the simplest case for such extension the right to protect one's self from pen portraiture, from a discussion by the press of one's private affairs, would be a more important and far reaching one. If casual and unimportant statements in a letter, if handiwork however intrinsic, and valueless, if possessions of all sorts are protected not only against reproduction, but against description and enumeration how much more should the acts and sayings of a man in his social and domestic relations be guarded from ruthless publicity. If you may not reproduce a woman's face photographically without her consent, how much less should be tolerated the reproduction of her face, her form and her actions, by graphic descriptions colored to suit a gross and depraved imagination. The right to privacy, limited as such right must necessarily be, has already found expression in the law of France. The application of an existing principle to a new state of facts is not judicial legislation. To call it such is to assert that the existing body of law consists practically of the statutes and decided cases and to deny that the principles exist at all.

(3) *Austin's Jurisprudence, p. 224*

"I cannot understand how any person who has considered the subject can suppose that society could possibly have gone if judges had not legislated, or that there is any danger whatever in allowing them that power which they have in fact exercised, to make up for the negligence or the incapacity of the avowed legislator. That part of the law of every country which was made by judges has been far better made them that part which consists of statutes enacted by the legislature."

(4) *Protection under Common Law*

The common law has for a century and a half protected privacy in certain cases, and to grant the further protection would be merely another application of an existing rule. It is the unwarranted invasion of individual privacy which is reprehended and to be, so far as possible, prevented. The general object in view is to protect the privacy of private life, and to whatever degree and in whatever connection a man's life has ceased to be private before the publication under consideration has been made, to that extent the protection is to be withdrawn.

(5) *Privacy in other democratic societies*

In democratic societies, there is a fundamental belief in the uniqueness of the individual, his basic dignity, his worth as a human being. Psychologists and sociologists have linked the development and maintenance of the sense of individuality to the human need for autonomy, one of the accepted ways of representing the individual's need for an ultimate core of autonomy has been to describe the individual's relations with others in terms of a series of zones or regions of privacy leading to a "*core self*". This core self is pictured as surrounded by a series of layer consecutive circles. The inner circle shelters the individual's ultimate secrets, those hopes, fears and aspirations that are beyond sharing with anyone unless the individual comes under such stress, that he must pour out these ultimate secrets to secure emotional relief. The most serious threat to individual autonomy is that some will penetrate this inner zone and learn the ultimate secrets either by physical or other means. This deliberate protection of an individual's protection shells his psychological armour will leave him naked to ridicule and will put him under the control of those who know his secrets.

There is a school of thought of which Dean Prosser is the most outstanding spokesman that privacy is not an independent value at all but a composite of interest in reputation, emotional tranquillity and intangible property. The view of Dean Prosser has been adopted by Salmond in his "The Law of Torts" 15th Edition (pages 44 and 46), although English Common Law does not recognise invasion of privacy as a tort in all cases in which the American Courts do. According to Dean Prosser, the four distinct torts, which are discovered in these cases are:

(1) Intrusion upon a person's solitude or seclusion or into his affairs;
(2) Public disclosure of embarrassing facts of a person's private life;
(3) Publicity which places an individual in false light in public eyes.
(4) Appropriation to a person's advantage of another's name or likeness.

The interests protected in these cases are interests in freedom from mental distress, in public disclosure and in false light cases, the interest in reputation and in appropriation cases, proprietary interest in name and likeness; from this angle the prized right of privacy shrinks in its stature so that it becomes a mere application to novel circumstances of the traditional legal rights to protect well identified and established social values. In this view, privacy is not an independent legal right protecting a fundamental human value. Assaults on privacy are transmuted into a species of defamation, infliction of invasions of mental distress and misappropriation. Accordingly, there is no new tort of invasion of privacy but only new ways of committing old torts. In other words, the social value or the interest in privacy is not an independent one but only a composite of the value society places on protecting mental tranquillity, reputation or intangible forms of property.

When scientific and technological developments have raised the spectre of new and frightening invasion of privacy, it is all the more necessary to have conceptual basis of the elements of the wrong and the nature of the remedy. Confusion here will have disastrous effect on the development of this new but important branch of the law. Moreover, any conceptual disarray will offend the primary canon of all science; that a single general theory is to be preferred to a congeries of disparate rules. Privacy has psychological, social and political dimensions. This means that it has overtones beyond the legal orbit.

Whereas Warren and Brandeis thought that privacy is exclusively a remedy for a single tort, Dean Prosser thinks that what is involved is not one tort but a complex of at least four torts violating four different interests none of which would seem to pertain distinctively to any interest in privacy. Now, is it possible to discover a common principle in the tort cases, in the testimonial compulsion cases of accused under Art. 20(3) of the Constitution of India or in the law prohibiting peeping, wiretapping, eavesdropping and prohibiting publication of confidential information collected by Government agencies.

(6) *Legal Notion of Privacy*

The difficulty is to find words to express adequately the value involved in the legal notion of privacy. The value is more spiritual than mundane. Owing to the nature of instruments by which privacy is invaded, the injury inflicted bears superficial resemblance to wrongs dealt with by the law of the libel and slander. The principle on which the law of defamation rests is radically different from that on which the law of privacy is based. The law recognises no principle upon which compensation can be granted for mere injury to feelings.

Warren and Brandeis said in their famous article that the object of privacy is to protect "*inviolate personality*". They elaborated the proposition as follows:

> Thus in early times, the law gave remedy only for physical interference with life and property, for trespass *vi et armis*. Then the right to life served only to protect life from battery in its various forms; liberty meant freedom from actual restraint and the right to property secured to the individual, his land and cattle, later there came a recognition of spiritual nature of his feelings and his intellect. Gradually, the scope of these legal rights

has come to mean the right to enjoy the life – the right to be let alone.

The Supreme Court of America has described the general right of privacy as "the right to be let alone". *Seekalz* Vs. *United States* (389 U.S. 347) and *Olmstead* Vs. *United States 277 U.S. 438*. Justice Brandeis had the vision to comprehend the significance of man's spiritual nature, of his feelings and intellect, that only a part of the pain, pleasure and satisfaction of life are to be found in material things and the necessity of law to protect his beliefs, thoughts, emotion and sensation for a meaningful pursuit towards the goal of happiness (His opinion in *Olmstead* case).

Clinton Rossiter has said that privacy is a special kind of independence which can be understood as an attempt to secure autonomy in at least a few personal and spiritual concerns, if necessary in defiance of all pressures of modern society. Privacy, according to him, seeks to erect an unbreakable wall of dignity and reserve against the entire world. The free man is the private man, who keeps some of his thoughts and judgements entirely to himself, who feels no overriding compulsion to share everything of value with others, not even with those he loves and trusts.

The right of privacy attempts to preserve individuality by placing sanction upon outrageous or unreasonable violations of conditions for its sustenance. This then is the social value to be served by the law of privacy. It is served not only in the law of tort but in other areas. Protection of privacy is the central purpose of the privilege against self-incrimination in Art. 20 (3) of the Constitution of India. The privilege reflects the respect which we accord to the inviolability of human personality and the right of each individual to a private zone where he may have his private life. It reflects the private inner sanctions of the individual feeling and thought and prescribes state intrusion to extract self-condemnation.

We are all of necessity subject to some minimum amount of scrutiny by our neighbours as a condition of civilised life in a society. Man has always relished the knowledge of the intimate details of lives and doings of others especially his neighbours. The most obvious and conflicting value is the public interest in news and information which must of necessity run counter to the individual interest of privacy. Even if the nature of the interest involved in privacy is understood it will not resolve this conflict of values except perhaps to make it clear that one of the values to be weighed is that interest.

One may desire to live a life of seclusion, another a life of publicity. Still another a life of publicity concerning certain matters and privacy as respects other matters of life. Neither an individual nor the public has a right arbitrarily to take away from him that liberty. It is difficult to find words adequate to express the mental conditions resulting from the pain on the violation of the right of privacy. We speak without sufficient discrimination of it as distress, anguish, anxiety, mental illness, indignity, mental suffering.

The common interest involved in all these conditions resulting from violation of privacy is spiritual in character rather than any interest in reputation or property. Although the American Federal Constitution does not mention the right to privacy explicitly, the Supreme Court has declared it as a fundamental right emanating from the totality of the constitutional provisions, having its roots in particular in the First, Third, Fourth, Fifth and Ninth Amendments; and intended to secure "inviolate personality" and thus promote the pursuit of happiness (*Roe* vs. *Wade* and *Grisswold* vs. *Connecticut*).

What distinguishes the invasion of privacy as a tort from other torts which involve insult to human dignity and individuality is merely the means used to perpetuate the wrong. The woman who is petted indecently suffers the same indignity as the woman whose birth pangs are overseen. The woman whose photograph is exhibited for advertisement is degraded and demeaned as surely as the woman who is kept aboard in a pleasure yacht against her will. Intrusion upon personal intimacy and using techniques of publicity is to make a public spectacle of an otherwise private life.

*

VI

KINDS

> "Each new claim to constitutional protection must be considered against a background of constitutional purposes, as they have been rationally perceived and historically developed. Though we exercise limited and sharply restrained judgement, yet there is no "mechanical yardstick", to "mechanical answer". The decision of an apparently novel claim must depend on grounds which follow closely on well-accepted principles and criteria. The new decision must take "its place in relation to what went before and further (cut) a channel for what is to come."
>
> –*Irvine* Vs. *California* (1953) 347 U.S. 128, 147.
> 98 Led. 561, 578; 74 S.ct. 381
> (dissenting opinion).

(1) *The Privacy Act*

The Privacy Act created a right of access for individuals to their own files, a right to correct mistakes contained in those files, and a responsibility on the part of the Government to protect personal information from misuse and disclosure which constituted an invasion of the privacy of the subject of that information. The *Freedom of Information Act* amendments speeded access by the public to Government records, strengthened the rights of the public to obtain disclosure of public information and limited the scope of the Government's authority to withhold certain kind of information. *The Freedom of Information Act* had always recognised the Government's authority to withhold information whose disclosure would constitute a clearly unwarranted invasion of personal privacy.

The forces seeking greater disclosure of government operations and information often are found in opposition to forces seeking protection of individual privacy. Some of the leading cases interpreting the *Freedom of Information Act* deal with the kinds of information about individual citizens which can be released without invading their privacy.

"Public policy about the management of information must embrace three policy objectives": *freedom of expression*; *personal privacy;* and the *public's right to know.* In a free society, these three objectives are always in contention, and the challenge to public policy is to strike a proper balance among them. No public policy on the management of recorded information about people can be formulated that will accommodate all three of these objectives, if the right of *personal privacy* is understood as the *right to be let alone. Freedom of expression* and the *public's right to know* require traficking in information in ways that impact on people. The issues that arise in achieving these objectives relate to how people will be affected not whether they will be affected. Records about people are made to mediate and reflect actions affecting them."

In other words, if information about an individual would be released under an FOI Act request, it could be released under b (2) of the Privacy Act. The standard for release under the FOI Act is in section b(6) which permits the withholding of information the release of which would constitute a "*clearly unwarranted invasion of personal privacy*".

A concern that government and business accumulates too much data on private citizens is making the protection of the individual privacy an issue high on the priority list of scores of government policy makers. While part of the rush to action is in response to abuses of government power documented in the watergate scandals, it also is an inevitable result of the rapid growth of government record keeping made possible by the increasing sophisticated use of computers.

This review of the government's impact on privacy may bear results similar in scope to those generated a few years ago by the concern for protecting the environment. And, as with the ecology boom, privacy may be an issue that is easy to support in general terms but raises complex policy and cost questions. Action also has been frustrated by bureaucratic inertia in many federal agencies in U.S.A.

The problem of insuring personal privacy in a computerized society which threatens to open the most personal affairs of each of us to anyone with access to computer-stored information is one of the "most serious" and "least realised" problems facing the nation. A review of privacy developments during the first nine months of 1974 demonstrates the involvement of a substantial number of executive and congressional officials in the struggle to develop regulations to deal with the real and potential threats to individual liberties posed by the growth of computer technology.

The ancient concept that "a man's home is his castle" into which "not even the king may enter" has lost none of its vitality. At the same time, that a broad philosophy of "freedom of information" is enacted into law, it is necessary to protect certain equally important rights of privacy with respect to certain information in Government files, such as medical and personal records. It is also necessary for the very operation of our Government to allow it to keep confidential certain material, such as the investigatory files of the Federal Bureau of Investigation.

(2) *The Freedom of Information Act*

The Freedom of Information Act states generally that each federal agency shall make available to the public certain specified information. Section 552 (b) of Title 5 represents a recognition by Congress that "certain information in Government files" should be exempt from disclosure. While the case involving exemption (6), are numerous, every effort was made to include only those cases which construe by definite analysis the provisions of the exemption. Exemption (6) protects from disclosure "personal and medical files" and similar files the disclosure of which would constitute a clearly unwarranted invasion of personal privacy.

Congressional awareness of possible conflicts between the right of the public to know and the intrusion into individual privacy would appear to be the reason for the creation of exemption (6) as the privacy balancing machinery. A general exemption for the category of information is much more practical than separate statutes protecting each type of personal record. The limitation of a clearly unwarranted invasion of personal privacy provides a proper balance between the protection of an individual's right of privacy and the preservation of the public's right to government information by excluding those kinds of files the disclosure of which might harm the individual. The exemption is also intended to cover detailed Government records on an individual which can be identified as applying to that individual and not the facts concerning the award of a pension or benefit or the compilation of unidentified statistical information from personal records.

It is not an easy task to balance the opposing interests, but it is not an impossible one either. It is not necessary to conclude that to protect one of the interests, the other must, of necessity, either be abrogated or substantially subordinated. Success lies in providing a workable formula which encompasses balances, and protects all interests yet places emphasis on the fullest responsible disclosure. Professor Davis takes the position that balancing was not intended under the Act. The requests of all information seekers are equal since the provision of former section 3 providing for disclosure was changed from "to persons properly and directly concerned" to "any person".

(3) *Clearly Unwarranted Invasion of Personal Privacy*

In one of the earlier cases decided under the Act the Court of Appeals for the district of Columbia in *Ackerley* vs. *Ley 420 F. 2d. 1336, (1969)* stated in dictum that medical files received under a pledge of confidentiality cannot, in and of itself justify non-disclosure under Exemption 6, even though the records are explicitly mentioned in it and are the kind which the exemption intended to protect from disclosure. In another case *Robles* vs. *Environmental Protection Agency 484 F. 2d. 843,* the court applying a general public interest standard as against weighing the interest of the particular individual obtaining the information held that plaintiff's interest in surveys dealing with the existence of trailings found in foundations of individual homes may provide a beneficial colouring effect on the reasonable apprehensions of citizens and would override any interest of privacy that the right to disclosure under the Act is not to be resolved by a balancing of equation or a weighing of need or benefit; the only ground for denial of disclosure here is that the disclosure would represent a "*clearly unwarranted invasion of personal privacy*".

In *Getman* vs. *NLRB (1971)* and *Wine Hobby, U.S.A. Inc.* vs. *United States Bureau of Alcohol, Tobacco and Firearms (1973)*, the courts interpreted Exemption 6 as requring "a court reviewing the matter *de novo* to balance the right of privacy of affected individuals against the right of the public to be informed". In *Getman* lists of containing names and addresses of employees eligible to vote in certain representation elections were requested by two labour law professors. The requesters had planned to communicate with the employees appearing on the list in order to evaluate the voting regulations of the NLRB. The court ruled in favour of disclosure after concluding that the invasion of privacy was "*very minimal*" and that the study could benefit the public significantly. However in *Wine Hobby* where the requester stipulated that it sought the information for "*private commercial exploitation*" the court denied the release of the information in light of the requester's failure to assert a public interest purpose for disclosure. The court concluded that the "invasion of privacy caused by disclosure would be clearly unwarranted" even though the invasion of privacy in this case (was) not as serious as that considered by the court on other cases.

In *Tuckinsky* Vs. *Selective Service System* (1969) the court held that a draft counsellor was entitled to the names of the local Selective Service Board officials, but was not entitled to personal information in regard to such matters as their home addresses, occupations, races, dates of appointment, military affiliations and citizenship under the *Freedom of Information Act*, in view of a Selective Service Regulation permitting the release of personal information only "if the person involved, determines in writing that disclosures would not harm that person and would not be a clearly unwarranted invasion of that person's personal privacy."

The 1967 Attorney General's Memorandum does not set forth any guidelines for determining what constitutes an invasion of personal privacy; however, it referred to the House Report which "noted that the Civil Service Commission....ruled that the names, position, titles, grades, salaries and duty stations of Federal employees are public information". (U.S. Department of Justice Attorney General's Memorandum on the Public Information Section of the Administrative Procedure Act). The Memorandum concludes by stating that "whether such addresses are protected by this exemption would depend upon the context in which they are sought.

In balancing interests, the courts have considered in their determination of whether there may be an invasion of privacy the extent of the invasion of privacy, the public interest that would be served by disclosure, whether the interest could be satisfied without that requested materials. [*Getman vs. NLRB (1971), Rural Housing Alliance* Vs. *Department of Agriculture (1974)*], (*Ditlow* Vs. *Shultz*) promises of confidentiality [*Robles* vs. *EPA* (1973)] and whether the affected individual is willing to give permission to release the information [*Rural Housing Alliance* vs. *Department of Agriculture* (1974)].

Similar to *Robles* vs. EPA the court in *Rose* vs. *Department of the*

Air Force (1974), appeared to have considered the seriousness of the intrusion on the individual privacy rather than balancing that intrusion on the individual with the public interest which would be served as a result of the disclosure. In Rose, the United States Court of Appeals for the second circuit held that the Air Force Academy Cadet Honour and Ethics code case summarises were not exempt from disclosure under Exemption (6). In addition the court refused to deny disclosure of the case summaries by utilising a broad power of equitable discretion to prevent harm to the public interest.

Expressing its primary concern for privacy, the Rose Court set forth a basis upon which each potential privacy intrusion will be evaluated.

"Each case involves an essentially unique investigation into the nature of the privacy interest invaded and the extent of the proposed invasion viewed in the light of contemporary mores and sensibilities as applied to the particular facts." Although the court concluded that the case summaries all or in part were not protected from disclosure by Exemption (6) the conclusion did not affect the court's primary concern for privacy. On remand the District Court was instructed to delete all personal reference and all other identifying information and "if in the opinion of the District Judge, this (was) not sufficient to safeguard privacy then the summaries should not be disclosed.

By accepting *Rose* vs. *Department of Air Force* for review, the Supreme Court will have before it the following questions under Exemption 6:

> Whether Exemption 6 covers all personal files rather than only those whose disclosure "would constitute a clearly unwarranted invasion of personal privacy?"
>
> Whether the exemption bars diclosure of summaries of proceedings against cadets at *Air Force Academy* accused of violation of Honour and Ethics codes because such disclosure "would constitute a clearly unwarranted invasion of personal privacy?"

Both House and Senate Reports can only be read as disclosing a congressional purpose to eschew a blanket exemption for "personnel" ....and "similar files" and to require a balancing of interests in either case. Thus the House Report states, "The limitation of a 'clearly unwarranted invasion of personal privacy' provides a proper balance between the potential of an individual's right of privacy and the preservation of the public's right to Government information by excluding those kinds of files the disclosure of which might harm the individual."

The phrase "clearly unwarranted invasion of personal privacy" enunciates a policy that will involve a balancing of interests between the protection of an individual's private affairs from unnecessary public scrutiny and the preservation of the public's right to government information. Plainly Congress did not itself strike the balance as to "personal files" and confine the courts to striking the balance only as to "similar files". To the contrary Congress enunciated a single policy to be enforced in both cases by the courts "that will involve a balancing of the private and public interests". This was the conclusion of the Court of Appeals of the District of Columbia Circuit as to medical files and this conclusion is equally applicable to personnel files.

"Exemption 6 of the Act covers....medical files...the disclosure of which would constitute a clearly unwarranted invasion of personal privacy." Where a purely medical file is withheld under authority of Exemption 6 it will be for the District Court ultimately to determine any dispute as to whether that exemption was properly invoked.

Deletion of names and identifying characteristics of individuals would in some cases serve the underlying purpose of Exemption 6, which exempts "personnel and medical files and similar files" the disclosure of which would constitute a clearly unwarranted invasion of personal privacy. At the same time that a broad philosophy of "freedom of information" is enacted into law, it is necessary to protect certain equally important rights of privacy with respect to certain information in Government files such as medical and personal records.

It is not an easy task to balance the opposing interests but it is not an impossible one either. It is not necessary to conclude that to protect one of the interests, the other must of necessity either be abrogated or substantially subordinated. Success lies in providing a workable formula which encompasses balances and protects all interests yet places emphasis on the fullest responsible disclosure. The limited statutory exemptions do not obscure the basic policy that disclosure, not secrecy, is the dominant legislative objective of the FOIA.

(2) Exemption 2 does not generally apply to matters such as the summaries here involved in which there is a genuine and important public interest.

(a) The phrasing of that exemption reflected congressional dissatisfaction with the "internal management" exemption of former section 3 of the Administrative Procedure Act and was generally designed, as the Senate Report made clear to delineate between, on the one hand trivial matters, and, on the other, more substantial matters, in which the public might have a legitimate interest.

(b) The public has a substantial concern with the Academy's administration of discipline and procedures that affect the training of Air Force officers and their military careers.

(3) Exemption 6 does not create a blanket exemption for personal files with respect to such files and "similar files" Congress enunciated a policy to be judicially enforced involving a balancing of public and private interests. Regardless of whether the documents whose disclosure is sought are in "personnel" or "similar" files, non-disclosure is not sanctioned unless there is a showing of a clearly unwarranted invasion of personal privacy and reduction of documents to permit disclosure of non-exempt portions is appropriate under Exemption 6.

(4) Even if "personnel files" were to be considered as wholly exempt from disclosure under Exemption 6 without regard to whether disclosure would constitute a clearly unwarranted invasion of personal privacy, the case summaries here were not in that category although they constituted "similar files" relating as they do to the discipline of Cadets and their disclosure implicating similar privacy values.

(5) The Court of Appeals did not err in ordering the Agency to produce the case summaries for the District Court's *in camera* examination a procedure that represents a workable compromise between individual rights and the preservation of public rights to Government information which is the statutory goal of Exemption 6.

(a) The limitation in Exemption 6 to cases of "clearly unwarranted" invasion of privacy indicates that Congress did not intend a matter to be exempted from disclosure merely because it could not be generated that disclosure would not trigger recollection of identity in any person whatever, and Congress vested the courts with the responsibility of determining *de novo* whether the exemption was properly invoked.

(b) Respondents' request for access to summaries "with personal references or other identifying information deleted" respected the confidentiality interests embodied in Exemption 6 and comported with the Academy's tradition of confidentiality.

A society numbered, punched and filed by government cannot be free. In solving a problem giant invasions of privacy are authorised as a consequence. Privacy is valued in our society as a hallmark of freedom. There are those in our country who believe that to enforce the laws government should investigate everything and there are those who believe that to preserve liberty, government should investigate nothing. There are those who believe that government must have ample power to investigate and to gather information in order to govern but who also believe that there are certain things which are none of the business of the government. There are those who believe that a free society must take some risks in order to remain free, but who also believe that, similarly, the individual under a government of law must assume the risks and the legal consequence for his actions.

There must be a proper balance between the needs of the government and the freedom of the individual guaranteed by the constitution. Another force is computer technology and the use of scientific methods of systems analysis which it encourages. In a study by the Constitutional Rights Sub-committee, we found that the increased use of government and private computer-based systems is making it vastly more economical to acquire and store information about people for reasons which should give Americans serious pause. It is creating not only an army of specialists in the information processing field but battalions of investigators and analysts specialising in seeking out and reporting derogatory information on individuals. The individual's privacy and right to *due process* of law are threatened by the very existence of the files the agencies collected. While the requirements of privacy and of access are in many ways consistent, there is a point of clear conflict where privacy taken alone would require that personal material held by a government agency must always be disclosed and access would require that any material held by a government agency must always be disclosed obviously neither privacy nor access can ever be considered alone, both must be considered in relation to other needs and in relation to each other.

VII

DEFINITION

> "Without doubt, it denotes not merely freedom from bodily restraint but also the right of an individual to contract, to engage in any of the common occupations of life, to acquire useful knowledge to marry, establish a home and bring up children, to worship God according to the dictate of his own conscience, and generally to enjoy those privileges long recognised at common law as essential to the orderly pursuit of happiness by free man.... The established doctrine is that this liberty may not be interfered with under the guise of protecting the public interest by legislative action which is arbitrary or without reasonable relation to some purpose within the competency of the state to effect."
>
> —*Justice Mc Reynolds* in *Meyer* Vs. *Nebraska (1923)* 67 *L Ed.* 1042

The concept of right to privacy does not lead itself to easy logical definition. This is so partly because as Tom Gaiety said in his Article "*Redefining Privacy*" (12 *Harv. Civ. Rights. Civil Lib.Rev. p. 233*), the concept was thrown up in great haste from a miscellany of legal rock and stone and partly because of inherent difficulties in defining such an elusive concept. The difficulty arises out of the fact that this concept is not unitary concept but is multidimensional susceptible more for enumeration than definition. But it can be confidently asserted that any plausible definition of right to privacy is bound to take human body as its first and most basic reference for control over personal identity. Such a definition is bound to include body's inviolability and integrity and intimacy of personal identity including marital privacy. A few representative samples would bear this out. Gaiety defined privacy as "an autonomy or control over the intimacies of personal identity". Richard B. Parker in his "A definition of Privacy" quoted in "Philosophy and Public Affairs" (1975), Vol. 4, No. 4, pp. 295-314, wrote:

".....Privacy is control over when and by whom the various parts of us can be sensed by others. By 'sensed' is meant simply seen, heard, touched, smelled or tasted."

Gary L. Bostwick writing in California Law Review, Vol. 64, p. 1447 suggests that "privacy" is divisible into three components:

(a) repose,

(b) sanctuary, and

(c) intimate decisions.

Of these three components he holds that the last one is an eminently more dynamic privacy concept as compared to repose and sanctuary (p. 1466). Prof. Tribe in his American Constitutional Law, p. 921 stressed another fundamental facet of the right to privacy problem. He wrote *inter alia*:

> "Of all decisions a person makes about his or her body the most profound and intimate relates to two sets of questions: first, whether, when and how one's body is to become the vehicle for another human being's creation."

(1) *Starting Point*

The usual starting point in any discussion of the growth of legal concept of privacy though not necessarily the correct one, is the famous article "*The Right to Privacy*" by *Charles Warren* and *Louis D. Brandeis, 4 Harward Law Review 193*. What was truly creative in that article was their insistence that privacy – the right to be let alone – was an interest that man should be able to assert directly and not derivately from his efforts to protect other interests. To protect man's "inviolate personality" against the intrusive behaviour so increasingly evident in their times, Warren and Brandeis thought that the law should provide both a criminal and a private law remedy:

> "Once a civilisation has made a distinction between the "outer" and the "inner" man between the life of the soul and the life of the body, between the spiritual and the material, between the sacred and the profane, between the realm of God and realm of Caesar, between church and State, between rights inherent and inalienable and rights that are in the power of government to give and take away, between public and private, between society and solitude, it becomes impossible to avoid the idea of

> privacy by whatever name it may be called – the idea of a private sphere in which man may become and remain 'himself'."

There can be no doubt that makers of our Constitution wanted to ensure conditions favourable to the pursuit of happiness. They certainly realised as Brandeis J. said in his dissent in *Olmstead* vs. *United States, 277 U.S. 438*, the significance of man's spiritual nature, of his feelings and of his intellect and that only a part of the pain, pleasure, satisfaction of life can be found in material things and therefore they must be deemed to have conferred upon the individual as against the government a sphere where he should be let alone.

The liberal individualist tradition has stressed in particular three personal ideals to each of which corresponds a range of private affairs. The first is the ideal of personal relations; the second the Lockean ideal of the politically free man in a minimally regulated society; the third, the Kantian ideal of the morally autonomous man, acting on principles that he accepts as rational.

There can be no doubt that privacy-dignity claims deserve to be examined with care and to be defined only when an important countervailing interest is shown to be superior. If the court does find that a claimed right is entitled to protection as a fundamental privacy right, a law infringing it must satisfy the compelling state interest test. Then the question would be whether a state interest is of such paramount importance as would justify an infringement of the right. Obviously, if the enforcement of morality were held to be compelling as well as a permissible state interest, the characterization of a claimed right as a fundamental privacy right would be of far less significance.

Individual autonomy perhaps the central concern of any system of limited government is protected in part under our Constitution by explicit constitutional guarantees. "In the application of the Constitution our contemplation cannot only be of what has been but what may be." Time works changes and brings into existence new conditions. Too broad a definition of privacy raises serious questions about the propriety of judicial reliance on a right that is not explicit in the Constitution. Of course privacy primarily concerns the individual. It therefore relates to and overlaps with the concept of liberty. The most serious advocate of privacy must confess that there are serious problems of defining the essence and scope of the right. Privacy interest in autonomy must also be placed in the context of other rights and values.

Any right to privacy must encompass and protect the personal intimacies of the home, the family, the marriage, motherhood, procreation and child rearing. This catalogue approach to the question is not as instructive as it does not give any analytical picture of that distinctive characteristics of the right of privacy. Perhaps the only suggestion that can be offered as unifying principle underlying the concept has been the assertion that a claimed right must be a fundamental right implicit in the concept of ordered liberty. Rights and freedoms of citizens are set forth in the Constitution in order to guarantee that the individual, his personality and those things stamped with his personality shall be free from official interference except where a reasonable basis for intrusion exists. "Liberty against Government" a phrase coined by Professor Corwin expresses this idea forcefully. In this sense, many of the fundamental rights of citizens can be described as contributing to the right to privacy. As Ely says: "There is nothing to prevent one from using the word "*Privacy*" to mean the freedom to live one's life without governmental interference. But the court ordinarily does not so use the term. Nor could it for such a right is at stake in every case."

There are two possible theories for protecting privacy of home. The first is that activities in the home harm others only to the extent that they cause offence resulting from the mere thought that the individuals might be engaging in such activities and that such harm is not constitutionally protectible by the state. The second is that individuals need a place of sanctuary where they can be free from societal control. The importance of such a sanctuary is that individuals can drop the mask, desist for a while from projecting on the world the image they want to be accepted as themselves, an image that may reflect the values of their peers rather than the realities of their natures.

The right to privacy in any event will necessarily have to go through a process of case-by-case development. Therefore even assuming that the right to personal liberty, the right to move freely throughout the territory of India and the freedom of speech create an independent right of privacy as an emanation from them which one can characterise as a fundamental right, it cannot be said that the right is absolute.

The European Convention on Human Rights which came into force on 3-9-1953 represents a valiant attempt to tackle the new problem. Art. 8 of the Convention is worth citing ("Privacy and Human Rights" Ed. A.H. Robertson, p. 176):

"1. Everyone has the right to respect for his private and family life, his home and his correspondence.

"2. There shall be no interference by a public authority with the exercise of that right except such as is in accordance with the law and is necessary in a democratic society in the interests of national security, public safety or the economic well-being of the country for the prevention of disorder or crime for the protection of health or morals or for the protection of the rights and freedoms of others."

Some of the Justices of the Supreme Court of America who have spoken about it have attempted to define privacy as an aspect of the pursuit of happiness [*Poe* Vs. *Willman 367 U.S. 497*, *Public Utility Commission* Vs. *Pollock 343 U.S. 451*, *Goldman* Vs. *United States, 316 U.S. 129*]. Pursuit of happiness requires certain amount of liberty to do as one likes. Privacy requires a private enclave as it were, where an individual is at liberty to do what he wants. An intrusion on privacy threatens that liberty just as assault, battery or imprisonment. It is really an offence "to the reasonable sense of personal dignity". There can perhaps be no objection in regarding intrusion upon our privacy as a dignity tort. The harm caused by this intrusion is incapable of being repaired and the loss suffered in dignity is not susceptible of being made good in damages. The injury is to the spiritual element in our otherwise mundane composition.

The American Federal Constitution does not mention the right to privacy explicitly, the Supreme Court has declared it as a fundamental right emanating from the totality of the constitutional provisions having its roots in particular in the First, Third, Fourth, Fifth and Ninth Amendments; all intended to secure "*inviolate personality*" and thus promotes the pursuit of happiness *Roe* Vs. *Wade* and *Griswold* Vs. *Connecticut*).

The idea of privacy is a vague one and difficult to get into a right perspective. Numerous meanings crowd in on the mind that tries to analyse privacy: the privacy of private property; privacy as proprietary interest in name and image; privacy as the keeping of one's affairs to one's self; the privacy of the internal affairs of a voluntary association or of a business corporation; privacy as the physical absence of others who are unqualified by kinship, affection, or other tributes to be present; respect for privacy as respect for the desire of another person not to disclose or to have disclosed information about what he is doing or has done, the privacy of sexual and familial affairs; the desire for privacy as a desire not to be observed by another person or persons, the privacy of the private citizen in contrast with the public official, and there are only a few. But not only are there many usages of the concept of privacy; there are also the numerous related and contrasting terms; freedom, autonomy, publicity, secrecy, confidentiality, intimacy and so forth.

(2) *Privacy: A zero-relationship*

Privacy is a "zero-relationship" between two persons or two groups or between a group and a person. It is a "zero-relationship" in the sense that it is constituted by the absence of interaction or communication or perception within contexts in which such interaction, communication or perception is practicable – *i.e.*, within a common ecological situation such as that arising from spatial contiguity or membership in a single embracing collectivity such as that a family, a working group, and ultimately a whole society. Privacy may be the privacy of a single individual, it may be the privacy of the individuals, or it may be the privacy of three or more numerous individuals. But it is always the privacy of those persons, single or plural, *vis-a-vis* other persons.

The phenomenon of privacy exists only in contexts in which interaction, communication or perception is physically practicable and within the range of what can be expected of human beings. The situation must, therefore be one in which the abrogation of privacy by intrusion from the outside or by renunciation from the inside is practically possible. Privacy presupposes the prior existence of a system of interaction among persons in a common space, it might be face-to-face interaction within a household, a neighbourhood, or village or within a unit in a corporate body such as a firm, an army or a congregation; the presupposed system of interaction might be one in which there is ordinarily no face-to-face interaction between authority and subject within a corporate body like a large church, a large firm, a large army, or the state, and in which the interaction or perception is initiated by an agent of authority with the intention of intruding on the privacy of the subject.

It is a matter of the possession and flow of information. We say that privacy exists where the persons whose actions engender or become the objects of information retain possession of that information, and any flow outward of that information from the persons to whom it refers (and who share it where more than one person is involved) occurs on its inititives of its possessers. This means that other persons do not come into possession of the information, they do not observe the actions that are the objects from which such information is generated; nor do they receive it from records or from other persons who have observed the actions in question.

Privacy in one of its aspects may therefore be defined as the existence of a boundary through which information does not flow from the persons who possess it to others. The actions of the former are not reported to or observed or recorded or otherwise perceived by the latter. It is the acquisition or transmission of information without the voluntary consent or initiative of those whose actions and words generate the information. Where the latter disclose the information entirely voluntarily and on their own initiative, we speak of sharing of privacy. Where the information is acquired by manipulation, deception, coercion or through a market mechanism, we speak of a disruption of or intrusion into privacy. Voluntariness on the part of the person or persons whose privacy is in question is an essential component.

Private property, the private life and private information refer to relationships in which the individual or group of individuals retain "possession of something that might otherwise be shared and that if shared is shared on the initiative of the possessor. The nature of the "something" is less important than the retention of "possession". Possession means here the control over the movement of these properties across a boundary from person to person or from person to group or from group to group or from group to individual. Whatever the "something" is, it belongs to the individual or group of individuals. Individuals and groups of individuals have a substantive existence which is recognised by the consciousness that inheres in individual and in collective existence and that is acknowledged by those who deal with it. Secrecy too, involves information and boundaries affecting its flow. In secrecy, disclosure or acquisition beyond the boundary is prohibited, and the prohibition is attended by sanctions in event of a breach. In privacy disclosure is at the discretion of the possessor and such sanctions as laws provide are directed only against coercive acquisition by persons outside the boundary. Possession of them entails right to their possession. Related with intrusions on personal and primordial privacy and intrusions into corporate privacy, the following questions are matters of concern:

(1) How much privacy can a human being or group of human beings enjoy, given the fact of being born into and living in any society whatsoever?

(2) How much privacy can be enjoyed by an individual or group of individuals, given the facts of existence in contemporary large scale industralised urban societies?

(3) To what extent do individuals or groups of individuals desire privacy?

Kinship constricts the privacy of the individual because it presents claims on him to be responsible for and to know about other members of the group and for them to know about him. Common residence makes him more observable, and absences raise questions that seek answers. Kinship establishes claims that intrude into the individual's private sphere, that demand information about actions and resources.

No society can obliterate all privacy. The separateness of places, the impenetrability of their physical boundaries, the limited curiousity of equals, and the limited powers of rulers, and indifference, have been the main bulwarks of that privacy which human beings have possessed or desired to possess through most of history. Changes in any of these affect the magnitude of the privacy that a society enjoys. Certain sections of the legal profession, the judiciary and legislative bodies have repeatedly attempted, since the end of the 2nd World War, to restrict and diminish the amount of intrusion into personal privacy. In the past few years, the enormities of intrusion have activated a quite new concern to protect personal privacy. But the resistance thus far is largely an elite resistance. Governments, Journalists, Employers and social scientists have been the main intruders into personal privacy. They want to share in privacy. This paradoxical combination of control over what belongs to the self and its transcedence in a relationship of sharing runs throughout the whole complex of the phenomena which are subsumed under the term "*privacy*". That which is solitarily private is often impelled outward into a community of two persons, that which is personally private between two persons is often impelled outward into a society between one of the two and a third person, and so it goes – but nearly always with the intention that it should not pass beyond the third or nth sharer. Voluntary self-disclosure is not usually intended to be boundless. The disclosure does not entirely annihilate the boundedness characteristic of privacy.

The desire for privacy is nearly always partial. There is a desire to be simultaneously in production in "public" relations with particular other persons. Thus not everything is shared with those with whom certain things are shared. Certain private matters might be shared with some persons; other private things might be shared with other persons. A great deal of the intrusion into personal privacy is not only on immoral affront to human dignity, it is also quite useless and unnecessary from any serious standpoint. Much of it is unnecessary to effective government, efficient administration, national security, the progress of knowledge, or individual productivity. Much of it is the frivolous self-indulgence of the professionals of intrusion.

Intrusions on privacy are baneful because they interfere with an individual in his disposition of what belongs to him. He does not acquire them through purchase or inheritance. He possesses them and is entitled to possess them by virtue of the charisma which is inherent in his existence as an individual soul – in his indiviudality – and which is inherent in his membership in the civil community. They belong to him by virtue of his humanity and civility. A society that claims to be both humane and civil is committed to their respect. When its practice departs from that respect, it also departs to that degree from humanity and civility.

Privacy is an outcome of a person's wish to withhold from others certain knowledge as to his past and present experience and action and his intentions for the future. The wish for privacy expresses a desire to be an enigma to others, or more generally, a desire to control others' perceptions and beliefs *vis-a-vis* the self-concealing person. Privacy is essential for that disclosure which illumines a man's being-for-himself, changes his being for others, and potentiates desirable growth of his personality. Privacy is experienced as "room to grow in" as freedom from interference, and as freedom to explore, to pursue experimental projects in science, art, work, play and living. In the name of the *status quo* and others, even more attractive goals, privacy may be eroded. But without privacy and its concomitant freedom, the cost for to be paid for the ends achieved in terms of lost health, weak commitment to the society, and social stagnation may be too great.

There is no historical consensus, in philosophy, politics or law, that privacy is a right. Few philosophers would argue that privacy is a natural right or that the intrinsic nature of privacy establishes it as a legal right. The circumstances of existence in modern society are in many ways more restrictive of privacy than conditions in the past. Some degree of privacy is necessary in order to ensure to the individual the possibility of moral choice and action. The claim that privacy is a right to be protected by law is a question of value discrimination, and the justification of privacy in this context is a problem of moral definition and analysis.

After centuries of failure to recognise privacy as a factor pertinent to moral and political speculation, we suddenly find ourselves concerned with the right of privacy as one of the most critical problems of contemporary political and legal analysis. The right of privacy seems to be an integral and essential ingredient protected by law. Such an analysis is casual, a thoroughly inadequate description of the development of the concept of privacy in our thought, but the persistence of the ill-defined assumption in the face of the facts of the contemporary social organisation is indicative of the confusion and ambiguity that characterize the idea of privacy.

Perhaps the last philosopher who gave any significant attention to the privacy of the individual was Jeremy Bentham, his strongly expressed view that law was an invasion of privacy that must be justified on the ground of necessary utility was somewhat but not profoundly modified by John Stuart Mill.

The analytic requirements imposed by the problems of privacy are two-fold: the definition of values and the specification of procedure. The first is the task of moral philosophy, reflected in the political function of legislation. The second depends upon legal process, especially as it operates to control the various administrative functions to which the individual is subject. Failure in or neglect of either of these tasks leaves only the alternative of an increasing latitude of arbitrary administrative discretion that can actively circumvent any achievement of values by the individual. Legal control of administrative processes is mandatory but if it is to be other than a sheer exhibition of force its procedures must be justified. That justification can be provided only by a value judgement as to what the moral and political rights of the individual ought to be. If privacy is defined as an essential requirement for the achievement of morality, then privacy is a right that the law must protect and provide. Modern man is born in chains, only the law can set him free.

Art. 21 of Indian Constitution

Art. 21 prevents the state from treating the human life as that of any other animal. It is now well-established by the decisions of the Supreme Court that the word "life" occurring in the above Art. 21 has spiritual significance as the word "life" occurring in the famous 5th and 14th Amendments to the American Constitution does. In those constitutional provisions of the American Constitution, the "life" is interpreted by Mr. Justice Field in his dissenting judgement in ***Munn*** Vs. ***Illinois (1877) 24 L Ed., p. 17*** to mean and signify "more than a person's right to lead animal or vegetative existence." Field J. said in the above Munn's case: "By the term life as here used something more is meant than the mere animal existence." The contrast drawn by Field J. emphasising the difference between existence of a free willing human and that of an unfree animal was accepted by our Supreme Court first in ***Kharak Singh*** vs. ***State of U.P. (1964), 1 S.C.R. 332*** and next in ***Govind*** vs. ***State of M.P. (1975) 3 S.C.R. 946*** transforming Art. 21 of our Constitution into a charter for civilisation. In ***Kharak Singh's*** case Rajagopala Ayyangar J. for the majority and Suba Rao J. for the concurring minority accepted the above meaning and significance given to the word "life" by Field J. in Munn's case. Both held that Art. 21 of our Constitution to be the source for the protection of our personal liberty and life in the elevated senses. Suba Rao J perceptively observed that right to privacy forms a part of the guaranteed right of personal liberty in Art. 21 of the Constitution. In a scientific age, psychological fears and restraints generated by the use of scientific methods, he feared may constitute even greater denial of personal liberty than mere crude physical restraints of a bygone age.

In a later decision of the Supreme Court in ***Govind*** Vs. ***State of M.P. (AIR 1975 SC 1378)***, Mathew J. taking the lead given by the minority judgement of Suba Rao J in the above-mentioned ***Kharak Singh's*** case (AIR 1963 SC 1295) and adverting to the American legal and philosophical literature on right to privacy and to the American cases reported in ***Griswold*** Vs. ***Connecticut (1965) 14 L Ed. 2d. 510*** and ***Jane Roe*** Vs. ***Henry Wade (1973) 35 L Ed 2d., p. 147*** ruled that Art. 21 of our Constitution embraces the right to privacy and human dignity. The centrepiece of the judgement in Govind's case is to hold that right to privacy is part of Art. 21 of our Constitution and to stress its constitutional importance and to call for its protection. The learned judge then examined the content of the right to privacy and observed that "any right to privacy must encompass and protect the personal intimacies of the home, the family, marriage, motherhood, procreation and child rearing". The learned judge stressed the primordial importance of the right to privacy for human happiness and directed the courts not to reject the privacy-dignity claims brought before them except where the countervailing state interests are shown to have overweighing importance. He observed that "there can be no doubt that the makers of our Constitution wanted to enforce conditions favourable to the pursuit of happiness. They certainly realised as Brandeis J. said in his dissent in *Olmstead* vs. *United States of America (1927) 277* U.S.*438*, "the US significance of man's spiritual nature, of his feelings and of his intellect and that only a part of the pain, pleasure, satisfaction of life can be found in material things and therefore, they must be deemed to have conferred upon the individual as against the Government a sphere where he should be let alone". The learned judge also stated "there can be no doubt that privacy-dignity claims deserved to be examined with care and to be denied only when an important countervailing interest is shown to be superior". *Govind's case* thus firmly laid it down that Art. 21 protects the right to privacy and promotes the individual dignity mentioned in the preamble to our Constitution. *Govind's case* also lays it down that the courts should protect and uphold those important constitutional rights except where the claims of those rights for protection are required to be subordinated to superior state interests.

In *Griswold* Vs. *Connecticut (1965) 14 L. Ed. 2d. 510*, Mr. Justice while invalidating a Connecticut statute which made the use of contraceptives a criminal offence, wrote for the court that "this law, however, operates directly on an intimate relation of husband and wife and their physician's role in one aspect of that relation....", implying that the right to privacy encompasses within their intimate relationships such as those between husband and wife about the use of contraceptives. Of course, the question from where this right to privacy should be derived gave rise to different answers in that case. Mr. Justice Douglas in *Griswold* Vs. *Connecticut (1965 14 L Ed. 2d. 510)* has found penumberal areas of specific guarantees in the

Bill of Rights as providing the basis for the right of privacy. But Mr. Justice Goldberg, wrote in that case highlighting in the process the theoretical confusions in the situation that the right of marital privacy falls within the category right to privacy. *Griswold's case* is an authority for the proposition that the reproductive choice to beget and bear a child does not belong to the state and that belongs to an individual. In *Jane Roe* Vs. *Henry Wade (1973) 35 L Ed. 2d. 147*, Mr. Justice Blackman for the court observed that the decisions of the American Supreme Court held that "only personal rights that can be deemed fundamental" or implicit in the concept of ordered liberty "....are included in the guarantee of personal privacy. They also make it clear that the right has some extension to activities relating to marriage ..., procreation, contraception, family relationships and child rearing and education...."

> "Yet the marital couple is not an independent entity with a mind and heart of its own, but an association of two individuals each with a separate intellectual and emotional make up. If the right of privacy means anything, it is the right of the INDIVIDUAL married or single, to be free from unwanted governmental intrusions into matters so fundamentally affecting a person as the decision whether to bear or beget a child."

This is a clear recognition of the legal position that right to privacy belongs to a person as an individual and is not lost by marital association. In *Planned Parenthood of Missouri* Vs. *Danforth (1976–49 L Ed 2d.788)*, the court reiterated the position taken by the American Supreme Court in *Eisenstadt* Vs. *Baird (1972) 405 U.S. 438* that the right to privacy belongs to each one of the married couple separately and is not lost by reason of their marriage. The court observed, invalidating a statutory condition, that the husband's consent is necessary for termination of pregnancy. "We cannot hold that the state has constitutional authority to give a spouse unilaterally the ability to prohibit a wife from terminating her pregnancy." The court further observed that "inasmuch as it is the woman who physically bears the child and who is the more directly and immediately affected by the pregnancy, as between the two, the balance weighs in her favour. Earlier in *Skinner* Vs. *Oklahoma (1941–86 L Ed 1655*), the American Supreme Court characterised the right to reproduce as one of the basic civil liberties of man. In the same case, Justice Jackson spoke of the state interference with reproductive decisions as involving dignity and personality. The decisions in *Loving* Vs. *Virginia* (1967) 168 L Ed. 2d. 1010 and *Zeblocki* Vs. *Redhall (1978) 54 L Ed. 2d. 618* are also relevant on this point. The above cases of the American Supreme Court clearly establish the proposition that the reproductive choice is fundamental to an individual's right to privacy. They uphold the individual's reproductive autonomy against the state intrusion and forbid the state from usurping that right without overwhelming social justification. That this right belongs even to a married woman is clear from Justice Brennan's opinion quoted above.

It cannot be denied that among the few points that distinguish human existence from that of animals, sexual autonomy an individual enjoys to choose his or her partner to a sexual act, is of primary importance. Sexual expression is so integral to one's personality that it is impossible to conceive of sexuality on any basis except on the basis of consensual participation of the opposite sexes. No relationship between man and woman is more rested on mutual consent and personality forged than sexual relationship. The coercive act of the state compelling sexual co-habitation must be regarded as a great restraint and torture imposed on the mind of the unwilling party. The life of a man or woman which the soveriegn can commandeer through the coercive power of the state for performing an unwilling act of sexual co-habitation cannot but be regarded as that of a human beast denied of all spirituality. In *Rusell* Vs. *Rusell (1897) A.C. 395* Lord Hershell long-ago noted the barbarity of this judicial remedy.

In the process of making such a fateful choices as to when, where and how if at all she should beget, bear, deliver and rear a child, the wife consistent with her human dignity, should never be excluded. Conception and delivery of a child involves the most intimate use of her body. The marvel of creation takes place inside her body and the child that would be born is of her own flesh and blood.

(3) *Restitution of Conjugal Rights and Privacy*

The British Law Commission presided over by Mr. Justice Scarmen (as he then was) recommended recently on 9-7-1969 the abolition of this uncivilised remedy of restitution of conjugal rights. Accepting the recommendation of the British Law Commission, the British Parliament through Section 20 of the Matrimonial Proceedings and Property Act, 1970 abolished the right to claim restitution of conjugal rights in the

English courts. But our ancient Hindu system of matrimonial law never recognised this institution of conjugal rights although it fully upheld the duty of the wife to surrender to her husband. This could have been only because of its realisation that in a matter so intimately concerned the wife or the husband, the parties are better left alone without state interference. The plain question that arises is whether our Parliament now functioning under the constitutional constraints of the fundamental rights conceived and enacted for the preservation of human dignity and promotion of personal liberty can legally impose sexual cohabitation between unwilling opposite sexual partners even if it be during the matrimony of the parties?

Sexual cohabitation is an indispensable ingradient of a decree for restitution of conjugal rights. It follows, therefore, that a decree for restitution of conjugal rights passed by a civil court extends not only to the company of the other spouse, but also embraces the right to have marital intercourse with the other party. The consequences of the enforcement of such a decree are firstly to transfer the choice to have or not to have marital intercourse to the state from the concerned individual and secondly, to surrender the choice of the individual to allow or not to allow one's body to be used as a vehicle for another human being's creation to the state. Belief of restitution of conjugal rights fraught with such serious consequences to the concerned inividual where granted under section 9 enables the decree-holder through application of financial sanctions provided by Order 21, Rules 32 and 33 of C.P.C. to have sexual cohabitation with an unwilling party. There can be no doubt that a decree of restitution of conjugal rights thus enforced offends the inviolability of the body and the mind subjected to the decree and offends the integrity of such a person and invades the marital privacy and domestic intimacies of such a person.

(4) *American Position*

Given the reluctance of the courts to enforce the Fourth Amendment in areas it plainly encompasses, there seems little likelihood it will be invoked to govern great intrusions in privacy never envisaged by its authors. There is no area of constitutional law today where the citizen can expect so little help from the courts as if he has a claim that his right to privacy under the Fourth Amendment has been breached.

The case *Griswold* Vs. *Connecticut* overturned a law against the use of contraceptive devices because it interfered with the privacy of the marital relationship. Citing the narrow protections for privacy derived from other amendments to the Constitution (including the Third Amendment's prohibition against compulsory quartering of soldiers in private homes in times of peace), the justices said that together the Constitution forms a "penumbra" guaranteeing privacy. The Ninth Amendment guaranteed in broader terms rights such as privacy emanating "from the totality of the constitutional scheme under which we live," as Justice Brandeis stated it a generation earlier.

Despite the sweeping protection for privacy suggested by Griswold, its principles have rarely been followed. *Griswold* was the high water mark of the Warren Court's expansive reading of the *Bill of Rights*. In the intervening decade, the courts have backed away from the Ninth Amendment and its potential as a protection for privacy.

The word privacy never appears in the Constitution. It is only in the last century that this word has been used as a legal concept to describe the state's duty to let people alone. "The right to be let alone", said Brandeis in *Olmstead* Vs. *United States* in 1928, is "the most comprehensive of rights and the right most valued by civilised men. When the Founding Fathers assembled to draft the Constitutions of the United States, they did not anticipate the need to establish privacy as an inalienable right. However, because of the need to reinterpret democratic values in changing social contexts, the State of California amended its Constitution in 1972 in order to list privacy as a fundamental right.

Privacy is not an abstract concept. It has meaning only in relation to a national culture, a particular political system and a specific period of time. It has become an issue in modern democratic societies which are characterised by large-scale, sophisticated bureaucratic structures and advanced technology in communications and information systems. Technological development has been permitted to evolve without regard for its impact on our democratic political system.

A major factor of the privacy problem is the absence of legislation and organisational rules ensuring privacy, confidentiality and due process to the subjects of computerised information. Data banks have been established at all levels of government, business and the military services without any real knowledge or concern for their potential impact over individual rights.

Privacy is the guarantor of individual moral autonomy, a basic value in a democratic system of government. Privacy can be defined as the right to control one's information system and one's physical being. The latter right has been traditionally conceived in American society as the right to be secured against unauthorised entries and seizures. Both rights are closely related to the principle of respect for persons. Both must be reinterpreted in the light of changing technological and social contexts. Privacy is violated whenever a person's moral autonomy or self-image are impinged upon even without affecting his conduct. Altering an individual's self perception against his will offends human dignity. If we are able to regulate a person's conduct or keep it under surveillance (as in the system of dispensing welfare) we are, in fact, curtailing his responsibility as a moral agent making free choice. This limits the options open to persons regarding their relationship with others, their physical mobility and their own self-perception.

Privacy, the control of one's own person and of the extension of one's person in the form of information, is at the basis of man's claim for human dignity. Information about a person is an extension of self-hood, for him to communicate or withhold as he sees fit. A person's control over personal information and access to and dissemmination of that information are at the heart of individual autonomy. The relationship of individual autonomy to the functioning of an open society requires renewed attention and emphasis at all levels of civic education.

The privacy issue involves other concerns often emotionally associated with, but not actually included in the concept of privacy. People may feel threatened by the very existence of massive and efficient information systems even though their privacy has not actually been invaded. Concomitantly with increasing legal recognition of privacy, there has developed a technological ability to invade it by a number of means heretofore not known.

This right is not defined nor specified in our Constitution. Yet, the principle of privacy permeates this document. Though privacy is not specifically mentioned, it is certainly a factor in the First Amendment (religion, speech, press, assembly); Third Amendment (quartering troops); Fourth Amendment (unreasonable search and seizure); Fifth Amendment (self-incrimination); and Ninth Amendment (rights enumerated in the Constitution not to be construed to deny or disparage others retained by the people). Therefore, privacy is what freedom is all about.

The security of one's privacy against arbitrary intrusion by the police, which is at the core of the IVth Amendment – is basic to a free society....The knock at the door, whether by day or by night, as a prelude to a search without authority of law but solely on the authority of the police, did not need the commentary of recent history to be condemned as inconsistent with the conception of human rights enshrined in the history and the basic constitutional documents of English-speaking peoples.

In a famous dissenting opinion in *Olmstead* Vs. *United States* (1938), Mr. Justice Brandeis characterised the "*right to be let alone*" by the Government as "the most comprehensive of rights and the rights most valued by civilised men". In his book "*The Assault on Privacy*" Prof. Arthur Miller observed that while the Fourth Amendment was probably conceived to protect tangible objects, it has since been extended in *Kats* Vs. *United States, 389 U.S. 34*, *(1967)* to restrict the Government's right to seek personal information. The right of individual privacy is vital to any free society. The right is a basic concept which permeates the very fabric of our Constitution even though it is not an explicit constitutional guarantee. By privacy is meant what the U.S. Supreme Court has referred to as the embodiment of "our respect for the inviolability of the human personality" and as right which is so rooted in the traditions and conscience of our people as to be ranked as fundamental. In order for the individual to truly exist, some reserve of privacy must be guaranteed to him. Privacy is vital for the flourishing of the individual personality and to the imaginativeness and creativity of the society as a whole. By privacy is meant the great common law tradition that a person has a right not to be defamed whether it is by a machine or a person meaning the right "*to be let alone*" – from intrusions by Big Brother in all his guises. It also means the right to be protected against disclosure of information given by an individual in circumstances of confidence and against disclosure of irrelevant embarrassing facts relating to one's own private life, both rights having been included in the authoritative definition of privacy agreed upon by the *International Commission of Jurists* at its world Conference of May, 1967.

*

VIII

CONSTITUTION AND PRIVACY

> "The Court....cannot accept the view that in a State where Constitution guarantees personal rights, it is enough to look to statute only as the warrant for one's actions."
>
> – *The State (Quinn)* Vs. *Ryan*
>
> (1965) I.R. 70
>
> *(A Decision of the Irish Supreme Court)*

Rights and freedoms of citizens are set forth in the Constitution in order to guarantee that the individual, his personality and those things stamped with his personality shall be free from official interference except where a reasonable basis for intrusion exists. "Liberty against Government" a phrase coined by Professor Corwin expresses this idea forcefully. In this sense, many of the fundamental rights of citizens can be described as contributing to the right to privacy. The struggle for constitutional government for the extension of the franchise and particularly for the freedom of the press... was directed against privacy in Government. Almost as much as the extention of the franchise and constitutional restraint on monarchial absolutism, publicity regarding political and administrative affairs was a fundamental aim of the modern liberal democratic movement. The demand for the publicity of governmental affairs was attended by a demand for the protection and reinforcement of privacy in other spheres – a demand which was itself the child of the aspiration for individual liberty. The result Shils says was a balancing of rights. The traditions of liberal and individualistic democracy maintained an equilibrium of publicity, privacy and secrecy. The equilibrium was enabled to exist as long as the beneficiaries and protagonists of each spector.... respected the legitimacy of the two and were confident that they would not use their power and opportunities to disrupt the equilibrium. The principles of privacy, secrecy and publicity are not harmonious among themselves. The existence of each rests on a self-restrictive tendency in each of the others. Nothing can be more sacred to our democratic society than the security of the citizen in his home, and the privacy of the individual in the conduct of his personal affairs.

The issue of the right to privacy is at a crossroads. The policy choices to be made in the next few years will determine whether our nation will leash technology to prevent its stampede over the right to privacy or whether enormous interconnected data systems carrying information above all of us will grow unchecked. Until recently, the available technology made difficult the automatic transfer of information gathered by one agency for one purpose to another agency for another purpose without the knowledge of the individual. By living in a diffuse society, certain rights to privacy are automatically surrendered by everyone. There are other rights to privacy that some citizens choose to give up voluntarily. When a person wants a privilege that others do not have whether it is a government job, a credit card, or an educational scholarship – there is an implicit understanding that the goal is important enough to warrant giving out some relevant personal information. In that case, since it is a conscious decision made with the knowledge of how it will be used, the individual retains his or her free choice.

Suddenly, people have become intensely aware that the situation has changed. Now they are faced with an erosion of their privacy, for which they will receive no benefit or right in exchange. In fact, the entire process of collection and transfer of information can and does occur without the individual's knowledge, yet alone his or her consent what is lost, as much as the right to privacy, is the right to control one's life.

(1) *American Position*

The Privacy Act specifically excludes gathering of information about the political or religious beliefs of any person, unless authorised by law, and requires the written consent of the individual before any information is used in other than a routine way. The civil liberties of all Americans is at stake. History has shown, the Watergate scandals have shown, that the executive branch alone cannot impose the controls required to protect each citizen's constitutional rights. Yet with inadequate controls, and with no checks, it is possible that we could all be victims of surveillance technology. With a balanced approach, we can continue to fight crime and the loss of its privacy. We must move ahead on both fronts without substituting one right for another.

Warrantless taps pose a grave danger to fundamental constitutional liberties. Generally they are not supported by concrete evidence to justify the invasion of an individual privacy. And always they escape the scrutiny of the courts and the public at large because the government is not required to disclose their existence unless it prosecutes the individual involved – a rare occurrence in the history of national security wiretaps. The danger of warrntless wiretaps is not confined to the truly criminal and subversive element within our society. Warrantless wiretaps are a serious threat to everyone, regardless of his or her station in life.

These cases demonstrate that often these taps are employed to ensure the political scrutiny of the nation. They also demonstrate the wisdom of the Fourth Amendment's protection. The Fourth Amendment was intended to protect each citizen from unreasonable invasion of privacy. It guarantees that privacy can be invaded only when there is a judicial warrant based on probable cause. The Founding Fathers did not contemplate the advent of telecommunications. The individual's right to privacy is nonetheless equally violated when the government breaks into someone's telephone conversation as when, it breaks into someone's home.

In the 1967 decisions of *Berger* Vs. *New York* & *Katz* Vs. *United States*, the Supreme Court held that the Fourth Amendement generally requires the government to obtain a judicial warrant before it can wiretap. The Court later reaffirmed this decision in *Alderman* Vs. *United States* [394 U.S. 165 (1969)] and *United States* Vs. *United States District Court [407* U.S. *297 (1972)]* commonly referred to as the *Keith Case*. The court stated in the *Keith Case* that the government cannot use warrantless wiretaps even when the citizens' activities threatened the domestic security of the nation.

The court has not yet ruled on whether the Fourth Amendment also applies to cases involving foreign powers and their agents.

In *Keith*, the Court specifically stated it did not consider cases where citizens "have significant connection" with foreign power and their agents. Because the court has not ruled on these national security matters, the government has maintained that it can still install warrantless wiretaps in certain situations. In a September, 1973 letter to Senator William Fullbright, then the Chairman of the Senate Foreign Relations Committee, then Attorney General Elliot Richardson stated that the Administration would continue to install warrantless wiretaps against private individuals and domestic Organisations, if the Administration believed their activities affected national security.

Johnson nevertheless ordered that wiretaps be permitted in national security cases where there was specific authorisation from the Attorney General. Johnson apparently believed in good faith that this authorisation would safeguard the individual's constitutional right to privacy. Sadly but not unexpectedly, this belief proved illusory. Examples of abuse abound.

Regardless of how beneficient the government's intentions, warrantless wiretaps pose serious danger to constitutional rights and liberties. Whatever the rationale for past inaction, it is clear that Congress must act now to misuse the preservation of precious constitutional rights – especially the right to privacy. Innocation of "national security" cases should not enable the government to wiretap without regard to traditional constitutional limitations.

Before the government could wiretap American citizens in national security cases it would have to obtain a judicial warrant based on probable cause that a crime had been, or was about to be, committed. This change would merely be a reaffirmation of the individual's rights under the Fourth Amendment, which requires all government searches – including wiretaps to have the prior approval of a judicial warrant based on probable cause. The courts could guard the right to privacy in one of two ways, either they could refuse to issue a warrant authorising a government search or they could respond to an individual's complaint that the government had conducted an unconstitutional search. In the present situation there is usually no way for the individuals to know that their calls are being intercepted.

For decades the government has used warrantless wiretaps to serve its view of the national security. These wiretaps have always posed a fundamental danger to the freedom guaranteed by the Constitution. The Watergate scandals have dramatically demonstrated the danger in our midst. The right to privacy, as well as the other constitutional liberties, are the cornerstone of our democratic system. If these rights and liberties, are eroded the very fabric of our constitutional system is imperilled. Congress should therefore, act now to protect our cherished rights and liberties from abusive national security wiretaps.

Privacy in a free society has suddenly come alive – an issue that must be reckoned with if we are to preserve one of the fundamental rights of our democracy. Thus privacy in our free society – the conflict during the last decade and a half over the rights of the citizens and the rights of the government and business–becomes a vocal issue. Watergate in demonstrating how the invasion of citizens' privacy became a threat to our democratic free society gives Samson-like strength to the vocal action. Both technology with its surging seemingly uncontrollable momentum, and the arrogance of ambitious politicians threaten the vitality of individual rights. But the fault does not lie entirely with men on technology or self-serving politicians. It lies with the people.

(2) *The Constitution of the United States*

> "The enumeration in the Constitution of certain rights, shall not be construed to deny or disparage others retained by the people."

The current doctrine of a "right to privacy" finds its origins in an even broader concept – that specifically guaranteed constitutional rights cast protective penumbras, a notion that infuriated strict constructionists like Justice Hugo Black. Justice Black objected to William O. Douglas notions of penumbras. Despite repeated and emphatic insistence on a literal reading of the Constitution, Black could quote with approval from an earlier case in some subsequent case, the following:

> "Constitutional provisions for the security of the persons should be liberally construed. A close and literal construction deprives them of half their efficacy and leads to gradual depreciation of the right, as if it consisted more in s: und than in substance. It is the duty of the courts to be watchful for the constitutional rights of citizens, and against any stealthy encroachment."

[Quoted from *Boyd* vs. *United States 116* U.S. *616 (1886)* in *Reid* Vs. *Covert 354* U.S. *1 (1957).]*

The U.S. Supreme Court's general approach to constitutional interpretation contrasts sharply with that of the Judicial Committee of the Privy Council which until 1949 functioned as Canada's super Supreme Court. Those British judges tended to look on Canadian

Fundamental law as a contract between private citizens, to be rigidly and narrowly interpreted. In so doing, the Privacy Council showed that judges could make just as much policy by speaking narrowly as by speaking broadly. American judges' rejection of strict construction also distinguishes their work, although less sharply from that of Australian and Canadian judges, who in the tradition of the Privy Council view law as separate from politics and tend to see themselves a legal technicians rather than as national leaders. Recent German and Irish judges also fit the American model more closely than that of the Privy Council, although the Irish understandably often name British verbal style. The Japanese Supreme Court has been cautiously grooping its way in constitutional interpretation a field doubly alien because of a cultural bias against litigation and the novelty of judicial review.

AMENDMENT IV (1791):

The right of the people to be secure in their persons, houses, papers and effects, against unreasonable searches and seizures, shall not be violated, and no warrants shall issue but upon probable cause, supported by oath or affirmation, and particularly describing the place to be searched, and the persons or things to be seized.

AMENDMENT V (1791):

No person shall be held to answer for a capital, or otherwise infamous crime, unless on a presentment or indictment of a Grand Jury, except in cases arising in the land or naval forces, or in the militia, when in actual service in time of war or public danger; nor shall any person be subject for the same offence to be twice put in jeopardy of life or limb; nor shall be compelled in any criminal case to be a witness against himself, nor shall be deprived of life, liberty or property, without due process of law, nor shall private property be taken for public use, without just compensation.

AMENDMENT IX (1791):

The enumeration in the Constitution, of certain rights, shall not be construed to deny or disparage others retained by the people.

AMENDMENT XIV (1868):

Section 1: All persons born or naturalised in the United States, and subject to the jurisdiction thereof, are citizens of the United States and of the State wherein they reside. No state shall make or enforce any law which shall abridge the privileges or immunities of citizens of the United States, nor shall any state deprive any person of life, liberty or property, without due process of law, nor deny to any person within its jurisdiction the equal protection of the laws.

The broad principles involved in what is conventiently called "the individual right of privacy" are deeply rooted in our history and derived from the Bill of Rights of the United States Constitution. The Fourth Amendment to the Constitution was written as the result of the American colonial experience with warrants and writs issued under King George III of England which often gave his officers an excuse to search anyone, anywhere, any time. In their famous 1890 Harward Law Review Article "***the right to privacy***", Samuel Warren and Louis D. Brandeis concluded:

It would doubtless be desirable that the privacy of the individual should receive the added protection of the criminal law, but for this, legislation would be required.... The common law has always recognised a man's house as his castle; impregnable, often, even to its own officers engaged in the execution of its commands. Shall the courts thus close the front entrance to continued authority, and open wide the back door to idle or prurient curiosity?

Almost 40 years later, Justice Brandeis, in his famous dissent in the case of *Olmstead* Vs. *United States* set forth the basic constitutional principles of individual privacy.

The makers of our Constitution undertook to secure conditions favourable to the pursuit of happiness. They recognised the significance of man's spiritual nature of his feeling and of his intellect.... They conferred as against the Government, the right to be let alone – the most comprehensive of rights and the right most valued by civilised man. To protect that right, every unjustifiable intrusion by the Government upon the privacy of the individual, whatever the means employed must be deemed a violation of the Fourth Amendment.

He went on to say further in his dissent even more relevant in these days of wholesale abuses of governmental power in our modern democratic society. Experience should teach us to be most on our guard to protect liberty when the government's purposes are beneficient. Men born to freedom are naturally alert to repel invasions to their liberty by evil minded rulers. The greatest dangers to liberty work in insidious encroachment by men of zeal, well-meaning, but without understanding.

While there can be no right of absolute privacy in our complex civilisation, there is an urgent need today to assert the fundamental right of privacy for all of us to the maximum extent consistent with the overall welfare of our Nation. The Federal Government can and must take the lead to achieve this important objective. On August 12, 1974 in his famous address to the Congress as Chief Executive, President Ford pledges his personal and official dedication to the individual right of privacy. "There will be but pursuit of tough laws to prevent illegal invasion of privacy in both government and private activities."

In 1890 Louis Brandeis wrote an historic essay for the Harward Law Review. In that essay he noted that an advancing communications technology imperilled the individual's right of privacy. Brandeis pointed to the development of telephone and the snapshot camera as mechanical devices that would seriously and irrevocably alter a person's fundamental right to be let alone. He warned legislators and legal scholars of his time that a "next step" was needed to protect that right. That "next step" is long overdue.

Today, now that we have very sophisticated electronic bugging devices, we have computers, the types of devices Brandeis profitably never even conceived of. People are now prepared to take that next step by passing legislation to safeguard privacy. Communications technology has now achieved a speed and facility that far outstrips anything. Brandeis may have dreamed possible. It is increasingly apparent that in the long series of technological break-throughs that have made the gathering, use and trading of personal data both efficient and economical, privacy safeguards have simply not kept pace. This has resulted in a tremendously increased potential for damaging misuse of personal information, and burgeoning abuses of our privacy.

Today, almost every fact about us is on file somewhere in the United States. Federal Census surveys record our household, family, and personal lives. The Internal Revenue Service gathers our Income-tax data. Motor Vehicle Registries keep track of our driving records and automobile ownership. Credit Card Files reveal how we spend our money and credit reporting companies monitor how we pay our bills. Hospital and physician files register intimate facts about our physical and mental well being. Police agencies account for our dealings with the law and law enforcement agencies. Schools retain teachers' comments and records of our academic achievement and social adjustment. The list may be virtually endless because new systems of files are constantly being created.

In and of itself, any one of these personal files is not particularly ominous. Most people readily accept the fact that data gathering systems are necessary to our institutions if they are to keep pace with the complex needs of a modern society, without records there would be chaos. The real problem comes, however, when these information systems are linked with one another and are used to exchange information without the knowledge or consent of the individuals concerned. When personal data is collected by one organisation for a completely unrelated purpose, individual rights could be seriously threatened.

Many of our Federal agencies have become omniverous fact collectors – gathering, combining, using and trading information about persons without regard for his or her rights of privacy. Simultaneously, numerous private institutions have also amassed huge files and information retrieval systems containing millions of files of unprotected information on millions of people. Our ability as individuals to control access to personal information about us has all but completely faded.

Where personal rights, benefits, privileges, and opportunities are determined by the contents of an individual's file, he should be given the rights necessary to assure these determinations are based upon accurate up-to-date and relevant information. He should be kept fully aware of the uses to which personal data he is asked to be disclosed will be used. And this includes knowing what organisations will have access to his file and knowing the purposes for which they will use his data.

Federal agencies are given a mandate to hold open public hearings to establish rules to protect the confidentiality of personal information they maintain. These open proceedings are an essential means of obtaining the input of trained privacy experts and private citizens, to assure that agency rules are responsible and equitable. Once these rules are determined, all Federal employees involved in the design and operation of systems of records on individuals must be trained to understand and to obey these rules.

When substantial changes or entire new computer systems are proposed by an agency, careful attention must at least be paid to their potential impact on personal privacy. These proposals must be evaluated by the Administration and by private experts before they are so far along that they cannot be stopped even if they pose a serious and unwarranted threat to our personal privacy. If a proposal does not comply with the private standards in this act or with the privacy regulation of the agency involved, it will be set aside for 60 days. This will afford Parliament and responsible executives branch officials an opportunity to decide what additional safeguards are needed or whether the project should be halted completely.

The Federal Agencies have expanded their information gathering and surveillance activities to such an extent that they pose serious threats to our basic privacy rights. Until the agencies develop and adopt adequate rules and procedures, effective oversight can and must be performed by experts who understand the technology and yet who are sensitive to the basic question of how to safeguard privacy. This is a central reason for establishing the commission. Equally important is the need to develop effective solutions to privacy problems outside the realm of the Federal Government.

While the concern for the rights of American citizens to be secure from government invasion has run from the adoption of the Bill of Rights to present day times, it has not found widespread recognition in the courts outside the area of criminal law. In applying the provisions of the IVth Amendment to the Constitution to this issue Mr. Justice Frankfurter observed in *Wolf* Vs. *Colorado*:

> The security of one's privacy against arbitrary intrusion by the police, which is at the core of the IVth Amendment – is basic to a free society.... The knock at the door, whether by day or by night, as a prelude to a search without authority of law but solely on the authority of the police, did not need the commentary of recent history to be condemned as inconsistent with the conception of human rights enshrined in the history and the basic constitutional documents of English-speaking peoples.

In a famous dissenting opinion in *Olmstead* Vs. *United States* (1938), Mr. Justice Brandeis characterised the "***right to be let alone***" by the Government as the most comprehensive of rights and the rights most valued by civilised men. In his book, "***The Assault on Privacy***", Prof. Arthur Miller observed that while the Fourth Amendment was probably conceived to protect tangible objects, it has since been extended in *Katz* Vs. *United States (389* U.S. *347, 1967)* to restrict the Government's right to seize personal information.

While the courts have begun to recognise the capacity of Government to invade individual privacy by the gathering or misuse of information, it is the responsibility of the Parliament to develop specific legislative guidelines in this area. The Federal Privacy Act draws upon the constitutional and judicial recognition accorded to the right of privacy and translates it into a system of procedural and substantive safeguards against obstrusive Government information gathering practices. Uptil now we have allowed technological advances in Federal record keeping to outpace our efforts to control and safeguard the use of the information we have collected. This Act would balance these advances with specific safeguards and add a new dimension of rights to the citizen. In effect, it would bring the law in line with a concept that "Government is not the owner of the information on individuals, but only the trustee."

If an agency, asks a citizen for information he would have the right to know if he is required to divulge it and to know what use the agency will make of it. He would be entitled to know what information systems or files a Federal agency operates and whether those systems or files contain information about him. He would be entitled to see what is in those files and if necessary to challenge the accuracy, the completeness, the timeliness, and the relevancy to the needs of the agency of their contents. He would be entitled to know who has seen information about him, and if the agency makes changes at his request, to inform past recipients of that data about those changes. Finally each citizen would be entitled to enforce the right of access and challenge in a Federal District Court and to seek an award of damages for injuries resulting from the misuse of personal information.

These are fundamental rights to be included in any privacy legislation, and they should help begin to restore public faith in our Government's information practices. Supreme Court Justice Felix Frankfurter described the evolution of tyrannical power in the executive branch:

> The accretion of dangerous power does not come in a day. It does come however slowly, from the genenative force of unchecked disregard of the restrictions that fence in even the most disinterested assertion of authority.

Unfortunately, Justice Frankfurter's observation does much to explain why individual liberty has been eroded by an expanding web of snooping conducted at all levels of Government. For many years now, the Government has used both simple and sophisticated techniques to exercise almost unlimited power over the individual. The Government instals wiretaps, plants electronic bugs, uses computerized information to assemble dossiers on individuals and engages in other surveillance activities which make a mockery of the individual freedoms guaranteed by our Constitution.

The numbers, and dangers, of this official spying, have surely increased since 1967. But even those 1967 figures (as well as the examples) should be more than sufficient to demonstrate what should be clear to everyone; uncontrolled Government snooping is a dangerous assault on our constitutional liberties. These liberties are the cornerstone of our democratic system and any aassault on them cannot be treated lightly. A society cannot remain free and tolerate a Government which can invade an individual's privacy at will.

Government snooping is particularly dangerous because often it is executed without the knowledge or approach of those officials who are accountable to the public. This in turn, increases the probability that Government invasions of individual privacy, as well as other fundamental constitutional liberties, will be accomplished by illicit means and for illegitimate purposes. As Supreme Court Justice Brandeis once observed:

> Experience should teach us to be most on our guard to protect liberty when the Government's purposes are beneficient. Men born to freedom are naturally alert to repel invasions of their liberty by evil-minded rulers. The greatest dangers to liberty lurk to insidious encro-achment by means of zeal, well-meaning but without understanding.

Individual privacy and freedom which are at the heart of our system of democratic self-government, are under severe pressure today. Modern technology has vastly increased the ease with which intrusions on individual privacy may be conducted. The American people are deeply disturbed about evidence that has accumulated in recent years of widespread Government insensitivity and disregard for the rights of individual citizens. Watergate and related scandals have brought to light a callous disregard for the law and for the sanctity of individual rights within the highest circles of government.

Such activities as the formation of the "plumbers" for the purpose of carrying on internal securing operations, which included wiretapping and burglary smacks of a secret police operation that has no place in American life.

In order for the individual to truly exist, some reserve of privacy must be guaranteed to him. Privacy is vital for the flourishing of the individual personality and to the imaginativeness and creativity of the society as a whole. By privacy is meant the great common law tradition that a person has a right not to be defamed whether it is by a machine or a person, meaning thereby the right "to be let alone" – from intrusions by Big Brother in all his guises. It also means the right to be protected against disclosure of information given by an individual in circumstances of confidence and against disclosure of irrelevant embarrassing facts relating to one's own private life, both rights having been included in the authoritative definition of privacy agreed upon by the International Commission of Jurists at its world conference of May, 1967.

By privacy is also meant what the U.S. Supreme Court has referred to as the embodiment of "our respect for the inviolability of the human personality", and as a right which is so rooted in the traditions and conscience of our people as to be ranked as fundamental. The spread of the data bank concept, the increasing computerization of sensitive subject areas relating to people's personal lives and activities, and the tendency of the Government to put information technology to uses detrimental to individual privacy was Professor Arthur Miller. He stated:

> "Americans today are scrutinised, measured, watched, counted and integrated by more governmental agencies, law enforcement officials, social scientists and poll takers than at any other time in our history. Probably in no Nation on earth is as much industralised information collected, recorded and disseminated as in the United States.

The information gathering and surveillance activities of the Federal Government have expanded to such an extent that they are becoming a threat to several of every American's basic rights, the rights of privacy, speech, assembly, association and petition of the government.

In dealing with troublesome privacy problems, let us not scapegoat the computer itself as a Frankenstein's monster. But let us be aware of the implications posed to freedom and privacy emerging from the ways we use computers to collect and disseminate personal information. A concerned inadvertent by all who use computers is the only way to produce standards and policies that will do the job. It is upto us to assume that information is not fed into the computer unless it is relevant.

Even if it is relevant, there is still a need for discretion. A determination must be made if the social harm done from some data outweighs its usefulness. The decision-making process is activated by demands of the people on the Government and business for instant credit and instant services. Computer technology has made privacy an issue of urgent national significance. It is not the technology that concerns me but its abuse. I am also confident that technology capable of designing such intricate systems can also design measures to assure security.

The right of individual privacy is vital to any free society. That right is a basic concept which permeates the very fibre of our Constitution even though it is not an explicit constitutional guarantee. The freedoms guaranteed by the first amendment – free speech, a free speech and freedom of assembly and religion – at the very least imply the right to be "let alone" by the Government. The principle is further demonstrated by the constitutional prohibition against the Government invading the privacy of the homes or business by conducting unreasonable search and seizure and the right against self-incrimination is another section that deals with privacy.

The individual's right to privacy has long been recognised by the courts which have consistently protected it from both governmental and non-governmental intervention. As technological advances, cameras, wiretaps, sound recordings and so forth provided new opportunities for infrigement upon these rights, the courts responded in an affirmative manner. Unfortunately due to the nature of the courts, this response has often been slow and incomplete case law is built gradually over a period of years and is often incomplete because it is usually decided on narrow issues of law. Thus, what is needed now is a coordinated and comprehensive approach to the problems that can be provided only by the Parliament.

Technology is again advancing, this time in the form of computers. This new technology brings with it, as advancements often do, the possibility of negligent use or deliberate misuse. This is what we must guard against. With the development of the computer, it has become possible to collect, instantly retrieve and analyse vast amounts of personal information. Access to this personal data has been expanded by the computer's ability to retrieve data access, agency, institutional, governmental and geographic boundaries.

Our recent experience with Watergate and related matters points up the need for enacting safeguards to protect the collection and use of such information. The compilation of an enemies list, for example, must be viewed, as only the first step in an abuse of power, for the next logical step would be the compilation of useful information about these on the list. Justice Brandeis' wisdom in his dissenting opinion in the first wiretap case to reach the Supreme Court, *Olmstead* Vs. *United States* (1927), in crediting the framers of the Constitution with having "conferred", as against the Government, the right to be let alone – the most comprehensive of rights and, the right most valued by civilised men must be protected by nothing less than the prevention of "every unjustifiable intrusion by the Government upon the privacy of the individual, whatever the means employed".

(3) *The Basic Law of the Federal Republic of Germany*

The listing of rights is much wider than those explicitly protected by any other Constitution discussed below. Most of the protections are not written in absolute terms. For example, the right to free development of personality extends only in so far as a person does not violate the rights of others or offered against the constitutional order, or the moral code. Freedom of expression is expressly, is specifically limited "by the provisions of the general law, the provisions of law for the protection of youth, and by the right to inviolability of personal honour". Although as the *Mephisto* and *Privacy of Communications* decisions of the Federal Constitutional court explain, the restriction of "the general laws" carries a narrower meaning in Germany than it would in the United States, these qualifications give German executive and legislative officials considerable discretion and frequently bring interesting cases to the constitutional court.

Basic Rights

Art. I (PROTECTION of HUMAN DIGNITY):

(1) The dignity of man shall be inviolable; to respect and protect it shall be the duty of all state authority.

(2) The German people therefore acknowledge inviolable and inalienable human rights as the basis of every community, of peace and of justice in the world.

(3) The following basic rights shall bind the legislature, the executive and the judiciary as directly enforceable law.

Art. 2 (RIGHTS of LIBERTY):

(1) Everyone shall have the right to the free development of his personality in so far as he does not violate the rights of others or offend against the constitutional order or the moral code.

(2) Everyone shall have the right to life and to inviolability of his person. The liberty of the individual shall be inviolable; These rights may only be encroached upon pursuant to a law.

Art. 10 (PRIVACY of POSTS AND TELECOMMUNICATIONS):

(1) Privacy of posts and telecommunications shall be inviolable.

(2) The right may be restricted only pursuant to a law. Such law may lay down that the person affected shall not be informed of any such restriction if it serves to protect the free democratic basic order or the existence or security of the Federation or a land, and that recourse to the courts shall be replaced by a review of the case by bodies and auxiliary bodies appointed by Parliament.

Art. 13 (INVIOLABILITY OF THE HOME):

(1) The home shall be inviolable.

(2) Searches may be ordered only by a judge or, in the event of danger in delay, by other organs as provided by law and may be carried out in the form prescribed by law.

(3) In all other respects, the inviolability may not be encroached upon or restricted except to avert a common danger or a mortal danger to individuals, or, pursuant to a law, to prevent imminent danager to public safety and order, especially to alleviate the housing shortage, to combat the danger of epidemics or to protect endangered juveniles.

Art. 18 (FORFEITURE of BASIC RIGHTS):

Whoever abuses freedom of expression of opinion, in particular freedom of the press [paragraph (1) of Art. 5], freedom of teaching, [paragraph (3) of Art. 5], freedom of assembly (Article 8), freedom of association (Art. 9), privacy of posts and telecommunications (Art. 10), property (Art. 14), or the right of asylum [paragraph (2) of Art. 16] in order to combat the free democratic basic order, shall forfeit these basic rights. Such forfeiture and the extent thereof shall be pronounced by the Federal Constitutional Court.

Art. 19: (RESTRICTION of BASIC RIGHTS):

(1) In so far as a basic right may, under this Basic Law, be restricted by or pursued to a law, such law must apply generally and not solely to an individual case. Furthermore, such law must name the basic right, including the Article concerned.

(2) In no case may the essential content of a basic right be encroached upon.

(3) The basic rights shall apply also to domestic juristic persons to the extent that the nature of such rights permits.

(4) Should any person's right be violated by public authority, recourse to the courts shall be open to him. If jurisdiction is not specified, recourse shall be to the ordinary courts. The second sentence of paragraph (2) of Article 10 shall not be affected by the provisions of this paragraph.

(4) *The Constitution of Japan*

(Chapter III) – RIGHTS AND DUTIES OF THE PEOPLE

Art. 11: The people shall not be prevented from enjoying any of the fundamental human rights. These fundamental human rights guaranteed to the people by this Constitution shall be conferred upon the people of this and future generation as eternal and inviolate rights.

Art. 12: The freedoms and rights guaranteed to the people by this Constitution shall be maintained by the constant endeavour of the people, who shall refrain from any abuse of these freedoms and rights and shall always be responsible for utilising them for the public welfare.

Art. 13: All of the people shall be respected as individuals. Their right to life, liberty, and the pursuit of happiness shall to the extent that it does not interfere with the public welfare, be the supreme consideration in legislation and in other governmental affairs.

Art. 21 (2): No censorship shall be maintained nor shall the secrecy of any means of communication be violated...

Art. 24 (2): With regard to choice of spouse, property rights, inheritance, choice of domicile, divorce and other matters pertaining to marriage, and the family laws shall be enacted from the standpoint of individual dignity and the essential equality of the sexes.

Art. 31: No person shall be deprived of life or liberty nor shall any other criminal penalty be imposed, except according to the procedure established by law.

Art. 32: No person shall be denied the right of access to the courts.

Art. 33: No person shall be apprehended except upon warrant issued by a competent judicial officer which specifies the offence being committed.

Art. 34: No person shall be arrested or detained without being at once informed of the charges against him or without the immediate privilege of counsel, nor shall he be detained without adequate cause; and upon demand of any person such cause must be immediately shown in open court in his presence and the presence of his counsel.

Art. 35: (1) The right of all persons to be secure in their homes, papers and effects against entries, searches and seizures shall not be impaired except upon warrant issued for adequate cause and particularly describing the place to be searched and things to be seized or except as provided by Art. 33.

(2) Each search or seizure shall be made upon separate warrant issued by a competent judicial officer.

Art. 36: The infliction of torture by any public officer and cruel punishments are absolutely forbidden.

(5) *Constitutional Position in Canada*

The founding fathers seem not to have concerned themselves about civil liberties. The BNA Act contains no explicit guarantees of such fundamental rights as freedom of speech and press, habeas corpus or due process of law.

Some Canadian judges have maintained that the Preamble's reference to "a Constitution similar in principle to that of the United

Kingdom" and more particularly a popularly elected House of Commons preclude invasion of fundamental rights by provincial legislatures and; perhaps even by the Canadian Parliament. But neither the Privy Council nor an unambiguous majority of the Supreme Court has ever endorsed such libertarian implications of the Preamble.

In 1960, however, the Parliament of Canada enacted a statutory Bill of Rights that recognise the existence "without discrimination by reason of race, national origin, colour, religion or sex," of such rights as those to "life, liberty and security of person and enjoyment of property, and the right not to be deprived thereof without due process of law," equality before the law, and freedom of speech, press, assembly, association and religion. Furthermore, the Bill directs judges to construe every federal statute, unless it explicitly states otherwise, not to abridge these rights.

Until the *Queen* Vs. *Drybones* in 1970, judges offered little comfort to those who had hoped that this Bill of Rights would have more than symbolic value. Then in a startling track, a solid majority in *Drybones* gave the *Bill of Rights* a status that chief Justice Laskin has called "*quasi-constitutional*".

Mr. Justice Roland Ritchie in an opinion endorsed by other members of the Court, said:

"Section 2 is intended to mean and does mean that if a law of Canada cannot be sensibly construed and applied" so that it does not abrogate, abridge or infringe one of the rights and freedoms recognised and declared by the Bill, then such law is inoperative "unless it is expressly declared by an Act of the Parliament of Canada that it shall operate notwithstanding the Canadian Bill of Rights."

As of 1976, however, *Drybones* marked the outer limits of judicial enforcement of the *Bill of Rights*, not the norm. Perhaps somewhat startled by their own boldness and worried about lower Court judges' treading a path of judicial activism, the justices have hesitated to extend – or even to apply, some critics argue – the rationale of *Drybones* to later cases.

THE CANADIAN BILL OF RIGHTS

Part I: Bill of Rights

1. It is hereby recognised and declared that in Canada there have existed and shall continue to exist without discrimination by reason

of race, national origin, colour, religion or sex, the following human rights and fundamental freedoms, namely:

(a) the right of the individual to life, liberty, security of the person and enjoyment of property, and the right not to be deprived thereof except by due process of law;

(b) freedom of the press.

2. Every law of Canada shall, unless it is expressly declared by an Act of the Parliament of Canada that it should operate notwithstanding the Canadian Bill of Rights be so construed and applied as not to abrogate, abridge or infringe or to authorise the abrogation, abridgement or infringement of any of the rights or freedoms herein recognised and declared, and in particular, no law of Canada shall be construed or applied so as to:

(a) authorise or effect the arbitrary detention, imprisonment or exile of any person;

(b) impose or authorise the imposition of cruel and unusual treatment or punishment,

(c) deprive a person who has been arrested or detained –

  (i) of the right to be informed promptly of the reason for his arrest or detention,

  (ii) of the right to retain and instruct counsel without delay, or

  (iii) of the remedy by way of *habeas corpus* for the determination of the validity of his detention, and for his release if the detention is not lawful;

(d) authorise a court, tribunal, commission, board or other authority to compel a person to give evidence if he is denied counsel, protection against self-crimination or other constitutional safeguards;

(e) deprive a person of the right to a fair hearing in accordance with the principles of fundamental justice for the determination of his rights and obligations;

(f) deprive a person charged with a criminal offence of the right to be presumed innocent until proved guilty according to law in a fair and public hearing by an independent and impartial tribunal, or of the right to reasonable bail without just cause; or

(g) deprive a person of the right to the assistance of an interpreter in any proceedings in which he is involved or in which he is a party or a witness before a court, commission, board or other tribunal, if he does not understand or speak the language in which such proceedings are conducted.

Part II:

Art. 5 (1): Nothing in Part I shall be construed to abrogate or abridge any human right or fundamental freedom not enumerated therein that may have existed in Canada at the commencement of this Act.

(6) *Constitutional Position in Australia*

(The Commonwealth of Australian Constitution Act)

The founding fathers' enthusiasm for American constitutional arrangements did not extend to a Bill of Rights. To them the responsible government and the common law seemed sufficiently stalwart guarantors of civil liberties. And so, like the B.N.A. Act, the Australian Constitution entrenched few fundamental rights. It makes no reference to protection against self-incrimination, bills of attainder, cruel and unusual punishment, or unreasonable searches and seizures, or rights to freedom of speech, press, assembly, counsel or due process of law generally.

Extended attention, during 1956-1959, failed to pursuade the Parliamentary Joint Committee on constitutional revision of the need to entrench additional liberties. The Committee believes that as long as governments are democratically elected and there is full Parliamentary responsibility to the electors, the protection of personal rights will, in practice, be secure in Australia. The Committee has not chosen, therefore, to recommend the writing into the Constitution of a charter of individual liberties.

Developments at the 1973 Constitutional Convention did not deter Prime Minister Whitlam's Labour Government, elected in 1972 on a Platform that promised increased protection for civil rights, from proceeding with plans for statutory action. In November, 1973, the Government introduced two measures, a bill against racial discrimination and a human rights bill to protect a wide range of civil and political liberties. The Labour Government maintained that ratification of the

International Convention for Elimination of Racial Discrimination and the International Covenant on Civil and Political Rights obliged Australia to take positive action.

Speaking for a unanimous Court in the early case of *D'Emden* Vs. *Pedder*, Chief Justice Griffith stated:

> We are entitled to assume – what, after all, is a fact of public notoriety – that some, if not all, of the framers of [our] Constitution were familiar....with the Constitution of the United States....when ....we find embodied in the Constitution provisions undistinguishable in substance, though varied in form, from provisions of the Constitution of the United States which had long been judicially interpreted by the Supreme Court of that Republic, it is not an unreasonable inference that its framers intended that like provisions should receive like interpretation [1904] 1 C.L.R. 91.

Decisions of the U.S. Supreme Court provided "most welcome aid and assistance" though not "infallible guidance". The High Court used the implications doctrine, or the doctrine of political necessity, as the approach to constitutional construction reflected in *D'Emden* Vs. *Pedder* was variously known, to read into the Constitution unwritten limitations on powers assigned to the States and, above all, to the commonwealth.

In *Amalgamated Society of Engineers* Vs. *Adelaide Steamship Co. Ltd.*, the *Engineers'* case, the new majority staged a constitutional revolution. The Court, in a majority opinion by Justice Issacs, held that the Australian Constitution is a British statute and, as such, must be construed in accordance with the principles of statutory interpretation observed by British Courts. *Engineers* quoted the Privy Council with approval:

> In the interpretation of a completely self-governing Constitution founded upon a written organic instrument.... if the text is explicit the text is conclusive, alike in what it directs and what it forbids. When the text is ambiguous....recourse must be had to the context and scheme of the Act.

Fundamental differences between the American and Australian Political systems, moreover Issacs said, rendered decisions of the

U.S. Supreme Court unsuitable as "standards" for interpreting the Commonwealth Constitution. With this deft double thrust the High Court freed itself from the implications doctrine. Not until a generation later did the Court return, and then cautiously, to the use of implications to limit federal power.

(7) *The Constitutional Position of Ireland*

The Irish Constitution itself implies a rejection of positivism, for it speaks of guaranteeing rather than conferring certain "inviolable" and "inalienable" rights. Justice Walsh's judgement invalidated a statutory prohibition against importation of contraceptives:

> Articles 40, 41 and 43 [of the Constitution] emphatically reject the theory that there are no rights without laws, no rights contrary to the law and no rights anterior to the law. They indicate that justice is placed above the law and acknowledge that natural rights or human rights are not created by the law but that the Constitution confirms their existence and gives them protection. The individual has natural and human rights over which the State has no authority.

FUNDAMENTAL RIGHTS (PERSONAL RIGHTS)

Art. 40: (1) All citizens shall, as human persons, be held equal before the law.

This shall not be held to mean that the State shall not in its enactments have due regard to differences of capacity, physical and moral, and of social function.

(3) (1°) The State guarantees in its laws to respect, and as far as practicable, by its laws to defend and vindicate the personal rights of the citizen.

(3) (2°) The State shall, in particular, by its laws protect as best it may from unjust attack and in the case of injustice done, vindicate the life, person, good name and property rights of every citizen.

(4) (1°) No citizen shall be deprived of his personal liberty save in accordance with law.

(4) (2°) Upon complaint being made by or on behalf of any person to the High Court or any judge thereof

alleging that such person is unlawfully detained, the High Court .... shall forthwith enquire into the said complaint and may order the person in whose custody such person is detained to produce the body of such person before the High Court on a named day and to certify in writing the grounds of his detention, and the High Court shall .... order the release of such person from such detention unless satisfied that he is being detained in accordance with the law.

4(3°): Where the body of a person alleged to be unlawfully detained is produced before the High Court in pursuance of an order in that behalf made under this section and that court is satisfied that such person is being detained in accordance with a law but that such law is invalid having regard to the provisions of the Constitution, the High Court shall refer the question of the validity of such law to the Supreme Court by way of case stated and may, at the time of such reference or at any time thereafter, allow the said person to be at liberty on such bail and subject to such conditions as the High Court shall fix until the Supreme Court has determined the question so referred to it...

(5) The dwelling of every citizen is inviolable and shall not be forcibly entered save in accordance with law.

(8) *The Constitutional Position of India*

In *Kharak Singh* Vs. *The State of U.P. and others (1964)SCR332*, the Supreme Court had occasion to consider the validity of Regulation 236 of the U.P. Police Regulation which is in *pari materia* with Regulation 856 of the *Madhya Pradesh Regulation*. There it was held by a majority that Regulation 236 (b) providing for domiciliary visits was unconstitutional for the reason that it abridged the fundamental right of a person under Art. 21 and since Regulation 236 (b) did not have the force of law, the regulation was declared bad. The other provisions of the Regulation were held to be constitutional. In *Kharak Singh* Vs. *The State of U.P. and others*, the majority said that 'personal liberty' in Art. 21 is comprehensive to include all varieties of rights which go to make up the personal liberty of a man other than those dealt with in Art. 19 (1) (d). According to the Court while Art. 19 (1) (d) deals with the particular types of personal freedom, Art. 21 takes in and deals with the residue. The Court said:

> We have already extracted a passage from the judgement of Field J. In *Munn* Vs. *Illinois (1877) 94 U.S. 113, 142*, where the learned judge pointed out that life in the 5th and 14th Amendments of the U.S. Constitution corresponding to Art. 21 means not merely the right to the continuance of a person's animal existence, but a right to the possession of each of his agent – his arms and legs etc. We do not entertain any doubt that the word 'life' in Art. 21 bears the same signification. Is then the word 'personal liberty' to be construed as excluding from its purview an invasion on the part of the police of the sanctity of a man's home and an intrusion into his personal security and his right to sleep which is the moral comfort and a dire necessity for human existence even as an animal? It might not be inappropriate to refer here to the words of the preamble to the Constitution that it is designed to "assure the dignity of the individual" and therefore of those cherished human value as the means of ensuring his full development and evolution. We are referring to these objectives of the framers merely to draw attention to the concepts underlying the Constitution which would point to such vital words as 'personal liberty' having to be construed in a reasonable manner and to be attributed that sense which would promote and achieve those objectives and by no means to stretch the meaning of the phrase to square with any preconceived notions or doctrinaire constitutional theories."

The Court then quoted a passage from the judgement of Frankfurter J. in *Wolf* Vs. *Colorado (1949) 338 U.S. 25* to the effect that the security of one's privacy against arbitrary intrusion by the police is basic to a free society and that the knock at the door, whether by day or by night, as a prelude to a search, without authority of law but solely on the authority of the police, did not need the commentary of recent history to be condemned as inconsistent with the conception of human rights enshrined in the history and the basic constitutional documents of English-speaking peoples. The court then said that at common law every man's house is his castle and that embodies an abiding principle transcending mere protection of property rights and expounds a concept of "personal liberty" which does not rest upon any element of feudalism or any theory of freedom which has ceased to exist. The Court ultimately came to the conclusion that Regulation 236 (b) which authorised domiciliary visits was violative of Art. 21 and 'as there is no law' on the basis of which the same could be justified, it must be struck down as unconstitutional. The court was of the view that the other provisions in Regulation 236 was not bad as no right of privacy has been guaranteed by the Constitution.

Suba Rao J. writing for the minority was of the opinion that the word 'liberty' in Art. 21 was comprehensive enough to include privacy also. He said that although it is true our Constitution does not expressly declare a ***right to privacy*** as a fundamental right, but the right is an essential ingredient of personal liberty, that in the last resort, a person's house where he lives with his family is his "castle", that, nothing is more deleterious to a man's physical happiness and health than a calculated interference with his privacy and that all the acts of surveillance under Regulation 236 infringe the fundamental right of the petitioner under Art. 21 of the Constitution....

The question whether right to privacy is itself a fundamental right flowing from the other fundamental rights guaranteed to a citizen under Part III is not easy of solution.

There are two possible theories for protecting privacy of home. The first is that activities in the home harm others only to the extent that they cause offence resulting from the mere thought that the individuals might be engaging in such activities and that such harm is not constitutionally protectible by the State. The second is that individuals need a place of sanctuary where they can be free from societal control. The importance of such a sanctuary is that individuals can drop the mask, desist for a while from projecting on the world the image they want to be accepted as themselves, an image that may reflect the values of their peers rather than the realities of their natures.

The right to privacy in any event will necessarily have to go through a process of case-by-case development. Therefore, even assuming that the right to personal liberty, the right to move freely throughout the territory of India and the freedom of speech create an independent right of privacy as an emanation from them which one can characterize as a fundamental right, we do not think that the right is absolute.

The contrast drawn by Field J. in *Munn* Vs. *Illinois* between existence of a free willing human and that of an unfree animal was accepted by our Supreme Court first in *Kharak Singh* Vs. State of U.P. *(1964) I.S.C.R. 332* and next in *Govind* Vs. *State of U.P. (1975) 3 S.C.R. 946*, transforming Art. 21 of our Constitution into a charter for civilisation. In *Kharak Singh Case*, Rajagopala Ayyangar J. for the majority and Suba Rao J. for the concurring minority accepted the above meaning and significance given to the word "life" by Field J. in *Munn's Case*. Both held that Art. 21 of our Constitution to be the source for the protection of our personal liberty and life in the elevated sense. Suba Rao J. perceptively observed that right to privacy forms a part of the guaranteed right of personal liberty in Art. 21 of the Constitution. In a scientific age, psychological fears and restraints generated by the use of scientific methods, he feared may constitute even greater denial of personal liberty than mere crude physical restraints of a bygone age.

In a later decision of the Supreme Court in *Govind* Vs. *State of M.P.* (*AIR 1975* SC *1378*) Mathew J. taking the lead given by the minority judgement of Suba Rao J. in the above-mentioned *Kharak Singh's Case* (AIR 1963 SC 1295) and adverting to the American legal and philosophical literature on right to privacy and to the American cases reported in *Griswold* Vs. *Connecticut (1965) 14 L Ed. 2d. 510* and *Jane Roe* Vs. *Henry Wade (1973) 35 L Ed. 2d. 147* ruled that Art. 21 of Indian Constitution embraces the right to privacy and human dignity. The centrepiece of the judgement in *Govind's Case* is to hold that right to privacy is part of Art. 21 of Indian Constitution and to stress its constitutional importance and to call for its protection. The learned judge then examined the content of the right to privacy and observed that "any right to privacy must encompass and protect the personal intimacies of the home, the family, marriage, motherhood, procreation and child rearing." The learned judge stressed the primordial importance of the right to privacy for human happiness and directed the courts not to reject the privacy-dignity claims brought before them except where the countervailing State interests are shown to have overweighing importance. He observed that "there can be no doubt that the makers of our Constitution wanted to ensure conditions favourable to the pursuit of happiness. They certainly realised as Brandeis J. said in his dissent in *"Olmstead* Vs. *United States of America (1927) 277 U.S. 438*, "the significance of man's spiritual nature, of his feelings, and of his intellect and that only a part of the pair, pleasure, satisfaction of life can be found in material things and therefore, they must be deemed to have conferred upon the individual as against the Government a sphere where he should be let alone". The learned judge also stated "there can be no doubt that privacy-dignity claims deserves to be examined with care and to be denied only when an important countervailing interest is shown to be superior". *Govind's Case* firmly laid it down that Art. 21 protects the right to privacy and promotes the individual dignity mentioned in the preamble to Indian Constitution. *Govind's Case* also lays it down that the courts should protect and uphold those important constitutional rights except where the claims of those rights for protection are required to be subordinated to superior State interests. *Art. 21 of Indian Constitution reads*:

> "No person shall be deprived of his "*life*" or "*personal liberty*" except "*according to the procedure established by law.*"

*

IX

INVESTIGATIVE JOURNALISM AND PRIVACY

"Let me add that one of the more dangerous pretensions of the media is that there is some right to invade privacy if it seems what is called "*public interest*" to do so and the further pretension that the only person to judge what is a "*public interest*" is the person who wants to make the invasion. I should like to see more lawyers giving attention to maintaining the reasonable boundaries between what is a person's own business and what is a matter of legitimate public concern."

–Governor-General of Australia, Sir Pali Hasluck

"It has been generally if not universally considered that it is the chief purpose of the guaranty to prevent previous restraints upon publication."

–Near vs. *Minnesota 283 U.S. 697 (1931)*

The right to communicate ideas creates a peculiar set of problems for constitutional democracies. First of all, this right is substantially valuable in itself. True freedom would be impossible where citizens not able to speak their minds, write their thoughts, or associate with others who might have their interests and opinions. The right of free expression is usually considered essential to the development of personality. As Justice Cardozo said: "[I]t is the matrix, the indispensable condition of nearly every other form of freedom."

Cardozo's evaluation of this right as touching "the very essence of the scheme of ordered liberty" leads to a second dimension. Not only is freedom of expression an end in itself, it also serves an indispensable function in a democratic system.

Speech, writing and association can also threaten other values. Every liberal democracy has had to confront problems of reconciling the potential – and frequently actual conflict of values inherent here.

This formal answer, as embodied in constitutional documents, vary the First Amendment to the U.S. Constitution is worded, if not applied in absolute terms: "Congress shall make no law abridging the freedom of speech, or of the press; or the right of the people peaceably to assemble, and to petition the government for a redress of grievances." In contrast, the Australian and Canadian Constitution are silent on matters of speech, press and assembly. On middle ground, the German, Irish and Japanese Constitutions talk of freedom of expression in glowing terms. None of these provisions, however, neither the absolutist First Amendment, the Australian and Canadian silences, nor the German, Irish and Japanese qualifications, settles many of the truly difficult issues.

The liberty of the press, and of speech is within the liberty safeguarded by the due process clause of the Fourteenth Amendment from invasion by state action. Liberty of speech and of the press is also not an absolute right, and the state may punish its abuse. Liberty of the press, historically considered and taken up by the Federal Constitution, has meant principally although not exclusively immunity from previous restraint or censorship. The conception of the liberty of the press in the U.S. had broadened with the exigencies of the Colonial period and with the efforts to secure freedom from oppressive administration. That liberty was expressly cherished for the immunity it afforded from previous restraint of the publication of censure of public officers and charges of official misconduct.

Publicity is short-hand expession for the freedom of information held vital for the democratic political process. Publicity simply means the freedom of the press in its broadest interpretation. Privacy, of course, is the right of the individual to be let alone, to enjoy solitude, intimacy, reasonable anonymity and to reserve personal information. And secrecy really means official secrecy — the right of the government to withhold information. When can publicity expose secrecy? When can secrecy invade privacy?

Few can doubt that these elements are getting out of balance, with the passion for official secrecy overriding both the right of the individual to privacy and the right of the citizen to free access to essential information about the actions of his government. Out of the Watergate era, similarly may come legislation and executive rulings in the name of privacy which in fact advance secrecy and penalise legitimate publicity. The clear measure of the shifting balance over these decades is that secrecy already has advanced too far. The real issue is not between privacy and publicity allied in the fight to regain their balance against secrecy.

Many critics of journalism think differently. They maintain that the most invaders of privacy are newspapers, magazines, and broadcasters. One reason for this impression is the relative visibility and noiseness of journalism. The Governmental war against privacy, on the contrary is carried on quietly, in the name of 'national interest' or 'national security'. These tendencies can be found under all forms of government. But they reach their ultimate expression in totalitarian societies, where governmental secrecy and the lack of privacy accorded to individuals approach the absolute – the literal negative of the libertation aims of our own Constitution.

When compared to invasions of privacy practised by governments in the name of secrecy, the cause of irresponsible intrusions by journalists into the privacy of individuals, however, inexcusable shrink to a regretable but relatively small proportion. These cases are publicly litigated, and most privacy law is written around them. These battles are carried on in the open and we witness them. We tend therefore to think of them as being the whole war. They are not. A journalistic invasion of privacy may afront dignity and might damage someone financially, but such journalistic abuses seldom tend to destroy liberty itself. Alexander Solzhzmitsyn (it is suspected), for example, preferred to endure occasional invasions of his privacy by journalists rather than forever surrender all his privacy to government.

"For achieving a balance, in both the public and private sectors between the individual's right to privacy and society's 'need to know'. The intensified assault on press freedom threatens us all. Journalistic freedom and independence must be strengthened. That is not to say that the press is above criticism. In fact, vigorous criticism of American journalism is healthy for both the press and the nation, and the criticism is, often richly deserved. But many of today's attacks threatened the bounds of mere critical comment. There is no doubt that the society with a free, unregulated press, despite its defects, will be the freest, most desirable society in which to live. Perhaps James Madison most eloquently expressed the view that "if a society is going to strive to be democratic, its press must be free".

Nothing could be more irrational than to give the people power, and to withhold from them information without which power is abused. A people who means to be their own governors must arm themselves with power which knowledge gives. A popular government without popular knowledge or the means of acquiring it is but a prologue to a farce or a tragedy or perhaps both.

If a reporter violates a trust – or is even perceived as violating a trust – the journalist source relationship is destroyed. Before a person will talk openly to a reporter, he must believe that the reporter will respect what is told in confidence. All of us are injured, when confidential information between reporter and source is disclosed; our right to know is impaired. And this injury is greater than the benefit to be gained by the court in receiving the confidential information.

(1) *Freedom of the Media*

Freedom of expression is the basic prerequisite of democratic set up to which we have pledged ourselves in our Constitution. One of the important features of democracy which distinguishes it from dictatorship and other forms of government is the freedom to express a view different from that of the ruling party or the individual. Freedom of expression is the well-spring of our Constitution. For social development of the human race wherein there is bound to be experimentation involving trial and error, the fullest possible opportunity for the free play of the human mind is an indispensable prerequisite. Liberty of man to search for truth ought not, be fettered, no matter what orthodoxies he may challenge.

Freedom of the press and freedom of expression are the most cherished values, values which are a part of the common heritage of the mankind in a democratic world, values without which life would lose all meaning and bereft of all decencies. The freedom of expression and freedom to dissent are two facets of one of the most cherished rights, a right which indeed is a true index of the prevalance of democratic values in a country. The enlightened sections of the community have to safeguard against erosion or abridgement of that right – a right so essential for the moral health of the community. In respect of freedom of speech, Cardozo observed that it is the matrix, the indispensable condition, of nearly every other form of freedom. The essential function of a free press in a democracy is to serve the governed and not the governors. No one can underrate the importance of freedom of the press for the health and growth of the society.

There are one or two matters to which printed reference in the context of the freedom of the press is required to be made. One of them relates to the danger of trial by the press. Certain aspects of a case are so much highlighted by the press that the publicity gives rise to strong public emotions. The inevitable effect of that is to prejudice the case of one party or the other for a fair trial. We must consider the question as to what extent are restraints necessary and have to be exercised by the press with a view to preserving the purity of the judicial process. At the same time, we have to guard against another danger. A person cannot by starting some kind of judicial proceedings in respect of matter of vital public importance stifle all public discussions of that matter on pain of contempt of court. A line to balance the whole thing has to be drawn at some point. It also seems necessary in exercising the power of contempt of court or legislature *vis-a-vis* the press that no hyper sensitivity is shown and due account is taken of the proper functioning of a free press in a democratic society. This is vital for ensuring the health of democracy. At the same time the press must also keep in view its responsibility and see that nothing is done as may bring the courts or the legislatures into disrepute and make the people loose faith in these institutions. One another matter which must not be lost sight of is that while comment is free, facts are sacred.

The demand of the security of the state and the country's relations with foreign powers also on occasions raises questions of importance in the context of restraints on the freedom of the press. Linked with the above is the question whether diplomacy shall proceed frankly and in public or in secrecy. The function of democracy it has been said, might well require some rough but rational balance between secrecy and disclosure, between official control of information and public need for it. We have also to consider the question as to whether a code of conduct for the journalists recognises that there can be and are legitimate national secrets.

In the above context, it is necessary to state that secrecy can be preserved only when credibility is also maintained and there is no seeming clash or confrontation between the two. Danger arises when in the words of a writer legitimate secrecy balloons into illegitimate secrecy and the administration runs the system in the interest not of the nation but of itself. Every bureaucracy it is said, seeks to increase the superiority of the professionally informed by keeping their knowledge and their intentions secret. The concept of the official secrecy is the specific invention of bureaucracy. If secrecy in some cases remains a necessity it also can easily become the means by which the government dissenables its purposes, buries its mistakes, safeguards its reputation, manipulates its citizens, maximises its power and corrupts itself. At the same time, we must recognise that there are some matters in the affairs of the state wherein it would be most dangerous and nothing short of quixotic madness to do away with secrecy. Likewise in the negotiation of treaties of whatever nature perfect secrecy and immediate despatch are often requisite. Although some idealists like ***Woodrow Wilson*** have advocated that diplomacy should proceed always frankly and in the public view and called for open covenants of peace, openly arrived at, many others have questioned the correctness of that approach in the world of real politic. According to a distinguished diplomat, the day secrecy is abolished, negotiation of any kind will become impossible. It is because of that documents came to be classified as secret, confidential and private after the war of 1812. Since then various categories of documents have been specified as those of which the disclosure would not be in public interest.

Another question in the above context is of the imposition of prior restraint by the government on a newspaper from publishing material the disclosure of which in the opinion of the government would not be in national interest. The U.S. Supreme Court in 1971 in one case held that any system of prior restraint of expression bears a heavy presumption against constitutional validity and the government carried a heavy burden of showing justification for the enforcement of such restraint.

Questions have also been posed as to whether there are any limitations on a journalist's right to obtain information in respect of matters of public interest. The question is whether in his quest for facts or what is called ***investigative journalism*** is a reporter, hot on the trail of some official wrong-doing, subject to some restraints? Is he entitled to pry into secret documents and use all kinds of means for this purpose? Shall he not be liable for infraction of some law and should he not be hauled up before a court on that account. Another connected question is as to whether a journalist who obtains such information can be compelled to disclose the source of his information. There have been occasions when some journalists have preferred to go to jail rather than disclose their source when asked to do so in judicial proceedings. There are matters which must engage the attention of law-makers for there is need for evolving some broad guidelines on these issues. A journalist can sometimes be faced with a dilemma in a situation wherein he comes into possession of material of great public interest but the disclosure of which would be detrimental to the national interests.

Indian Constitution, unlike many other Constitutions, contains no express provision relating to the freedom of the press. The First Amendment to U.S. Constitution provides *inter alia*, that Congress shall make no law abridging the freedom of speech or of the press. According to *Clause (1) of Art. 5 of the Constitution of the German Federal Republic*, everyone shall have the right freely to express and disseminate his opinion by speech, writing and pictures and freely to inform himself from generally accessible sources. Freedom of the press and freedom of reporting by radio and motion pictures are guaranteed. There shall be no censorship. *Art. 18 of the Constitution of Belgium* states that the press is free. No form of censorship may ever be instituted. No cautionary deposit may be demanded from writers, publishers, or printers. *Clause (6) of Art. 40 of the Constitution of Ireland* provides that the State guarantees liberty for the exercise of the right of citizens, subject to public order and morality to express freely their convictions and opinions. The article further states that the education of public education being, however a matter of such grave import to the common good, the state shall endeavour to ensure that organs of public opinion, such as the radio, the press, the cinema, while preserving their rightful liberty of expression, including criticism of government policy, shall not be used to undermine public order or morality or the authority of the State. According to *Art. 21 of the Japanese Constitution*, freedom of assembly and association as well as speech, press and other forms of expression are guaranteed. The article further states that no censorship shall be maintained, nor shall the secrecy of any other means of communication be violated.

There is no provision relating to freedom of the press in Indian Constitution. It was, however, settled by a judicial decision in 1950 in *Ramesh Thapar's Case* that freedom of the speech and expression guaranteed to all citizens by *Art. 19 (1) (a)* includes freedom of the press and circulation. It was held in that case that the liberty of the press stands on no higher footing than the freedom of speech and expression of a citizen and that no privilege attaches to the press as such or as distinct from the freedom of the citizens. It is, therefore, plain that the freedom of the press is to operate within the limit of *Art. 19(1) (a)* and *Clause (2) of Art. 19* of the Indian Constitution. In the United States where the First amendment to the Constitution contains provisions in absolute terms relating to the freedom of the press reasonable restrictions on the exercise of that freedom were evolved by the courts.

The freedom of the press and the independence of the judiciary are two of the most important indices of democracy in a country. It is essentially to pressure both. Pliable press and subservient judiciary are the first step in the process of extinguishment of democratic lights. There is some element of similarity between the functions of the press which acts as a sentinel against deviations from norms of decent public life and the courts which act as sentinels against deprivations from norms set down by the Constitution and the laws. It is essential that points of conflict between the two as far as possible be avoided. This is particularly vital because on occasions both of them are the targets of criticism at the hands of those who make no secret of their chagrin against the want of subservience on the part of these institutions.

Toleration of criticism is an essential attribute of democracy. It is indeed the strength of democracy that it alone can tolerate criticism of the ruler and that criticism when tolerated instead of being a weapon of destruction is an instrument of better government. Equally wrong is the attitude to find nothing but dark and ignoble in our national life. Such an attitude can corrode the people's faith and belief in nation's destiny. It would also result in an attitude of cynicism and scepticism towards not only many of those controlling different institutions, but also institutions themselves. It has to be ensured that in the political game of denunciation of individuals, we do not destroy the institutions. It is, therefore, essential to keep the balance and strive for an integrated approach so as not to allow the things to tilt one way or the other.

The allegiance of the press in the final analysis can only be to the country and the nation and not to those who may for the moment be in the seats of power. Its commitment can only be to democratic values and decencies of public life. At a time when the official media is concerned and preoccupied with giving publicity mainly to the views and activities of the ministers, it is only in the columns of the newspapers that one can read about the views of others who have not set up an equation with those in power. It is therefore, necessary to ensure that the freedom of the press may be maintained and no inroads are made into it.

What are the limitations of this right to privacy, and what remedies may be granted for the enforcement of that right? To determine in advance of experience the exact line at which the dignity and convenience of the individual must yield to the demands of the public welfare or of private justice would be a difficult task; but the more general rules are furnished by the legal analogies already developed in the law of *slander* and *libel*, and in the law of literary and artistic property.

(1) The right to privacy does not prohibit any publication of matter which is of public or general interest. It is the unwarranted invasion of individual privacy which is reprehended, and to be, so far as possible, prevented. The general object in view is to protect the privacy of private life, and to whatever degree and in whatever connection a man's life has ceased to be private, before the publication under consideration has been made, to that extent, the protection is to be withdrawn.

In general, then, the matters of which the publication should be repressed may be described as those which concern the private life, habits, acts and relations of an individuals and have no legitimate connection with his fitness for a public office which he seeks or for which he is suggested, or for any public or quasi-public position which he seeks or for which he is suggested, and have no legitimate relation to or bearing upon any act done by him in a public or quasi-public capacity. Some things all alike are entitled to keep from particular curiosity, whether in public life or not, while others are only private because the persons concerned have not assumed a position which makes their doings legitimate matters of public investigation.

(2) The right to privacy does not prohibit the communication of any matter, though in its nature private, when the publication is made under circumstances which would

render it a privileged communication according to law of *slander* and *libel*.

Under this rule, the right to privacy is not invaded by any publication made in a court of justice, in legislative bodies, or the committees of those bodies; in municipal assemblies, or the committees of such assemblies or practically by any communication made in any other public body, municipal or parochial, or in any body quasi-public, like the large voluntary associations formed for almost every purpose of benevolence, business or other general interest; and reports of any such proceedings would in some measure be accorded a like privilege. Nor would the rule prohibit any publication made by one in the discharge of some public or private duty, whether legal or moral, or in conduct of one's own affairs, in matters where his own conduct is concerned.

(3) The law would probably not grant any redress for the invasion of privacy by oral publication in the absence of special damage. The injury resulting from such oral communications would ordinarily be so trifling that the law might well, in the interest of free speech, disregard it altogether.

(4) The right to privacy ceases upon the publication of the facts by the individual, or with his consent. A private communication of circulation for a restricted purpose is not a publication within the meaning of the law.

(5) The truth of the matter published does not afford a defence. It is not for injury to the individual's character that redress or prevention is sought, but for the injury to the right of privacy.

(6) The absence of "*malice*" in the publication does not afford a defence.

The invasion of the privacy that is to be protected is equally complete and equally injurious, whether the motives by which the speaker or writer was actuated are, taken by themselves, culpable or not. The remedies for an invasion of the right of privacy are also suggested by those administered in the law of defamation, and in the law of literary and artistic property, namely:

(i) An action of tort for damages in all cases.

(ii) An injunction, in perhaps a very limited class of cases.

It would doubtless be desirable that the privacy of the individual should receive the added protection of the criminal law, but for this legislation would be required. Perhaps it would be deemed proper to bring the criminal liability for such publication within narrower limits; but that community has an interest in preventing such invasions of privacy, sufficiently strong to justify the introduction of such a remedy, cannot be doubted. The common law has always recognised a man's house as his castle, impregnable, often even to its own officers engaged in the execution of its commands.

The claim to speak and to publish without inhibition or constraint has been a persistent theme of philosophical and public debate. The importance of free expression is accepted without question in the liberal society; there are, however, important and difficult questions about the limits which may properly be imposed upon such expression. The claim to a free press has been stated in very sweeping terms. Thomas Jefferson said that our liberty depends upon the freedom of the press and that cannot be limited without being lost, while *Alexis de Tocquaville* wrote that there is no medium between servitude and extreme licence, in order to enjoy the inestimable benefits which the liberty of the press ensures, it is necessary to submit to the inevitable evils which it endangers.

(2) *Privacy* versus *the Press*

The right to privacy – perhaps the most cherished right of all – is guaranteed, but more and more lately it is coming into conflict in the courts with the press's First Amendment right to report freely news... How much privacy does a person who is not a public figure have when his privacy collides with the rights of the press?

The person's right to disseminate information was explicitly guaranteed in the Constitution, and an individual's right to privacy has been obtained through a series of judicial rulings, each one put atop the other like so many bricks in a wall, since the begining of the century.

It was the first time that the court had been asked to rule that an individual's right to privacy could outweigh the First Amendment when the news report was true. The court ruled that "once true information is disclosed in public court documents open to public inspection the press cannot be sanctioned for publishing it".

The court then dampened the ruling somewhat by saying that it was confining the ruling to "the narrower interface between press and privacy" involved in printing the name of a rape victim rather than "the broadest question whether truthful publications may ever be subjected to civil or criminal liability".

Still, the reality of the law is such that lawyers who defend newspapers in privacy cases will now bring appeals based on the broader words of the ruling, hoping finally to inch the court toward absolutely guaranteeing the press the right to print whatever information it wants. It probably will take many more cases, involving crimes other than rape, to determine how far the court is willing to go.

Do private people who are connected to events of a public interest have a buffer of privacy against reporting and, if so, how wide a buffer?

Most legal experts think it will be a slow process to define the distinction between private facts and public news, and to determine precisely when the printing of a private fact is offensive.

Every Candidate automatically gives up most rights to privacy, and the political system already invades privacy to a great degree. A candidate must disclose campaign financing details, there are investigations into his private income, and there are even, questions about an offspring's love life.

The presentation of privacy seems to be one of the main legitimate passions of the moment – a passion in part created out of congressional reaction to public indignation over the Watergate disclosures. Obviously, this concern for privacy is welcome – as long as it is not used as an excuse to strengthen the opportunities for secrecy in the government. It should come as no surprise in the present climate, that legislation has been and probably will again be considered by Congress that in the name of privacy would forbid access by the press to such traditionally public records or public blotters and criminal records. The framers of legislation on privacy in U.S. have been aware that there are problems in this approach, and have tried to solve them.

The struggle for constitutional government for the extension of the franchise, and particularly for the freedom of the press... was directed against privacy in government. Almost as much as the extension of the franchise and constitutional restraint on the monarchal absolutism, publicity regarding political and administrative affairs was a fundamental aim of the modern liberal democratic movement. The demand for the publicity of governmental affairs was attended by a demand for the protection and reinforcement of privacy in other spheres – a demand which was itself the child of the aspiration for individual liberty.

The tradition of liberal individualistic democracy maintained an equilibrium of publicity, privacy and secrecy. The equilibrium was enabled to exist as long as beneficiaries and protagonists of each spector....respected the legitimacy of the other two and were confident that they would not use their power and opportunities to disrupt the equilibrium. The principles of privacy, secrecy and publicity are not harmonious among themselves. The existence of each rests on self-restrictive tendency in each of the others.

Publicity is a short-hand expression for the free flow of information held vital to the democratic political process. Publicity simply means the freedom of the press in its broadest interpretation. Privacy is the right of the individual to be let alone, to enjoy solitude, intimacy, reasonable anonymity and to reserve personal information. And secrecy really means official secrecy – the right of the government to withhold information.

When can publicity expose secrecy? When can secrecy invade privacy?

These elements are getting out of balance, with the passion for official secrecy overriding both the right of the individual to privacy and the right of the citizen to free access to essential information about the actions of his government. Out of the Watergate era, similarly may come legislation and executive rulings in the name of privacy which in fact advance secrecy and penalise legitimate publicity. The clear measure of the shifting balance over these decades is that secrecy already has advanced too far. The real issue is not between privacy and publicity, but between both privacy and publicity allied in the fight to regain their balance against secrecy.

Many critics of journalism think differently. They maintain that the worst invaders of privacy are newspapers, magazines, and broadcaster. One reason for this impression is relative visibility and noiseness of journalism. The governmental war against privacy, on the contrary, is carried on quietly, in the name of "national interest" or "national security". These remedies can be found under all forms of government. But they reach their ultimate expression in totalitarian societies, where governmental secrecy and the lack of privacy accorded to individuals approach the absolute – the literal negative of the libertarian aims of U.S. Constitution.

When compared to invasions of privacy practised by governments in the name of secrecy, the cases of irresponsible intrusions by journalists into the privacy of the individuals, however inexcusable shrink to a regretable but relatively small proportion. These cases are publicly litigated, and most privacy law is written around them. These battles are carried on in the open, and we witness them. We tend therefore to think of them as being the whole war. They are not. A journalistic invasion of privacy may afront dignity and might damage someone financially, but such journalistic abuses seldom tend to destroy liberty itself. It is suspected that Alexander Solzhznitsyn, for example, preferred to endure occasional invasions of his privacy by journalists rather than forever surrender all his privacy to government.

For achieving a balance, in both the public and private sector between the individual's right to privacy and society's "need to know". For decades the government has used warrantless wiretaps to serve its view of the national security. These wiretaps have always posed a fundamental dangers to the freedoms guaranteed by the Constitution. The *Watergate scandals* have dramatically demonstrated the danger in our midst. The right to privacy, as well as the other constitutional liberties are the cornerstone of our democratic system. If these rights and liberties are eroded the very fabric of our constitutional system is imperilled. Privacy in a free society has come alive – an issue that must be reckoned with if we are to preserve one of the fundamental rights of our democracy. Privacy in our free society – the conflict during the last decade and a half over the rights of the citizens and the rights of the government and business – becomes a vocal issue. Watergate in demonstrating how the invasion of citizen's privacy became a threat to our democratic free society gives *Samson-like* strength to the vocal action.

(3) *Art. 19 (1) (a) of the Indian Constitution*

Art. 19 deals with those great and basic rights which are recognised and guaranteed as the natural rights inherent in the status of a citizen of a free country. The Constitution has treated civil liberties as distinct Fundamental Rights and made separate provisions in Articles

19, 21 and 22 as to the limitations and conditions subject to which alone they could be taken away or abridged. Art. 19 only protects some of the important attributes of personal liberties even of a free citizen. A freeman has far more and wider rights than those enumerated in clause (1) of Article 19.

Article 19 protects some of the important attributes of personal liberty as independent rights and the expression *'personal liberty'* means in Article 21 all the varieties of rights which make up the personal liberty of men. The attributes of personal freedom which are not enumerated in Article 19 but which, may be taken as constitutionally guaranteed by Art. 21, are not immune from legislative interference.

Where a Fundamental Right, which is beyond the competence of a legislature to affect, is involved, the proceedings of a statutory body can be questioned in a court of law, even though such body may be acting within the limits of its sttutory powers.

None of the fundamental rights under Art 19 is an absolute right. Each of the sub clauses (a) to (g) in clause (1) is saddled with a restrictive provision enacted in clause (2) to (6) of Art. 19. Hence, in determining the extent of a right guaranteed under any of the sub-clause must be taken along with the corresponding provision in clauses (2) to (6) of Art. 19. Art. 19, while guaranteeing some of the most valued phases or elements of liberty to every citizen as civil rights provides for their regulation for the common good by the state imposing certain restrictions on their exercise.

In considering the validity of restrictions imposed under the law by the state on Fundamental Rights, it is the right which is fundamental and not the limitation. Art. 19 only applies where the Fundamental Rights conferred by it are hit directly and not indirectly as a consequence of the invasion of some other Fundamental Rights which may be covered by some other provision of the Constitution. The rights guaranteed by the several sub-clauses of clause (1) are all distinct and independent of each other. The validity of an enactment is liable to be questioned under each of the sub-clauses (a) to (g) and unless the impugned enactment is found to be valid under each of the sub-clauses read with the corresponding clause of the Article, the enactment will have to be declared valid. In order to determine whether any enactment falls under any of the sub-clauses of clause (1), it must be seen whether the enactment falls directly under that sub-clause.

In order to determine whether an enactment is violative of more than one sub-clause of clause (1), it must be seen whether the impugned enactment directly falls under both the sub-clauses by applying the rule of pith and substance. If the enactment directly falls only under one of the sub-clauses of clause (1) and is found justified by the application of the corresponding clause among clauses (1) to (6) of the Article, its validity cannot be impeached merely because it indirectly falls under another sub-clause of clause (1) also.

Where the impugned enactment directly falls under a particular sub-clause of clause (1) and is not justified by the application of the corresponding clause in clauses (2) to (6) of Article 19, such enactment cannot be held to be valid merely because it falls indirectly under some other sub-clause of clause (1) and the infirmity with reference to such sub-clause is cured by the application of the corresponding clause in clauses (2) to (6) of Art. 19.

Infringement of the freedom guaranteed under Article 19 can be excused only on grounds mentioned in clauses (1) to (6) and not on the ground that the infringment is not the main object of the law but only an incidental effect of enforcement of its provision. The provisions of Art. 19 must be interpreted in a broad manner and not in a narrow and pedantic sense. The court must interpret them in a manner which would enable citizens to enjoy the rights guaranteed by the Constitution in the fullest measure subject to permissible restrictions. Each of the guaranteed rights must be interpreted as involving or including concomitant rights necessary to achieve the object which must be supposed to underlie the grant of each of those rights.

Art. 19 does not include as a fundamental right any guarantee against the impairment of subsisting rights and obligations under contracts, unlike under the American Constitution Article, Section 10(1). A law which affects or varies rights and obligations under contracts is not *per se* unconstitutional under Article 19.

The rights guaranteed under Art. 19 are subject to exercise of similar or other rights by other citizens. The rights guaranteed by Article 19 are exercisable throughout the territory of India. The contents of the freedom guaranteed under clauses (a) to (c) of Article 19 (1) do not include the right to exercise them in the properties belonging to others. The right wil come to an end as soon as the right of some one else to avoid the property intervenes. Such limitation is inherent in it. Fundamental rights guaranteed under Art. 19 is not violated by the Constitution (Thirtieth Amendment) Act (1972). A combined reading of all the sub-articles of Art. 19 would reveal that it does not contemplate violation of or challenge to a fundamental right by anyone except the State. Any violation of or challenge to fundamental right as defined in Art. 19 by an individual would be outside the scope of the said Article.

Article 19 refers to the rights of citizens in their free State and is not concerned with the question of taking away that basic freedom itself and putting a citizen in confinement. This latter question is the subject matter of Articles 20, 21 and 22. Article 19 is not applicable to the question of detention of a person, preventive, punitive or otherwise. Where a person is totally deprived of his personal liberty and detained in confinement, Article 21 and not Article 19 will apply. The articles mentioned in Article 19 will only apply where a legislation hits a citizen's liberties as enumerated in Article 19 already and not where the restitution on or the deprivation of those liberties results from the application of some other law. Where a person's personal liberty is not actually taken away by his being kept in confinement, and only certain restrictions are placed upon the freedom of his movement and as the instance by means of an externment order, Article 19 will apply and not Article 21. Art. 19 does not contain the entire substantive law or the question of personal liberty and Article 21 does not deal merely with procedure and not merely complementary to Art. 19. Article 21 itself is a substantive provision with a distinct and individual scope.

While Article 19 enacts that a citizen shall have the various rights enumerated and proceeds to lay down the extent to which these rights may be curtailed by the State by means of laws, Articles 21 and 22 are couched in a negative form and purport to enact restrictions on the power of the State. Where personal liberty is restricted by a particular law and the law does not relate to topics mentioned in Article 19, the examination of its reasonableness is an exclusive legislative function. Our Constitution does not contain a provision corresponding to the due process clause of the American Constitution. There are five distinct lines of thought in the matter of reconciling Article 21 with Article 19 namely:

(1) If one loses his freedom by detention, he loses all the other attributes of freedom enshrined in Article 19.

(2) Personal liberty in Article 21 is the residue of personal liberty after excluding the attributes of that liberty embodied in Article 19.

(3) The personal liberty included in Article 21 is wide enough to include some or all of the freedoms mentioned in Art. 19 but they are two distinct fundamental rights – a law to be valid shall not infringe both the rights.

(4) The expression 'law' in Article 21 means a valid law and therefore, even if a person's liberty is deprived by law of detention, the said law shall not infringe Art. 19.

(5) Article 21 applies to procedural law, whereas Article 19 to substantive law relating to personal liberty.

It is not the object of the Constitution of India to enable the citizens of India to break obligations arising under formal contracts entered into by them under the guise of that obligation being something that is repugnant to the recognition of a Fundamental Right. Such an idea is foreign to the Constitution of India. The rule of estoppel does not apply in case of fundamental rights. Hence a person who has taken the benefit of a provision of law to start a business can challenge its constitutionality under Art. 19. Art. 19 does not contain any guarantee against infringement of rights by private individuals. The Article was intended to protect the fundamental freedoms assured to the citizen by clause (1) against state action other than the legitimate exercise of its powers to regulate private rights in the public interest.

Article 19 is not directed against the infringement by private individuals for which remedies should be sought under the ordinary law. Laws restricting fundamental rights should be strictly construed. In order to determine whether any enactment amounts to an interference with any of the rights conferred by Art. 19, it is the direct effect of an enactment and not its indirect or incidental effect that should be considered.

Where a statute is impugned on the ground that it adversely affects rights guaranteed by Article 19 the courts would first have to ascertain whether the right claimed is one of the rights guaranteed by the Constitution and secondly whether the right is affected in a manner not warranted by the Constitution. The presumption is always in favour of the constitutionality of the enactment and this principle also applies when an Act is impugned on the ground of its infringement of any of the fundamental rights under Article 19. Where on fair construction of an enactment it is found to violate one of the fundamental rights guaranteed by clause (1) of Art. 19, it must be held to be invalid unless those who support the enactment can bring it within the clause of the Article which relates to the particular fundamental right involved. In order to describe whether a particular legislative measure contravenes any of the fundamental rights it is necessary to examine with some strictness the substance and the true nature of the legislation.

In the case of pre-Constitution laws which conflict with fundamental rights such laws become *void* on the coming into force of the Constitution. But their unconstitutionality will automatically be removed if and when, subsequent to the coming into force of the Constitution, the relevant provisions relating to fundamental rights are amended, and the pre-Constitution law does not conflict with the constitutional provision as amended. Where a post-Constitution Act conflicts with a fundamental right the subsequent amendment of the relevant provision relating to fundamental right will not validate the unconstitutional law.

Under Article 19, the freedom of speech and expression including the freedom of the press has only been conferred on citizens. This however does not mean that in India, a foreigner or non-citizen has no freedom of speech or expression at all. It only means that such right cannot be claimed as a fundamental right. Where the executive places restrictions on the liberty of speech and expression or on the liberty of press of a non-citizen without the authority of a law, the action of the executive can be called in question in a court of law. All citizens including Government servants are entitled to the fundamental rights under Article 19. Although citizenship is the foundation of the fundamental rights under Art. 19, it is not itself a fundamental right beyond the reach.

A post-Constitution law which takes away or abridges the rights conferred by Article 19 will be operative in regard to non-citizens as it is *void* only to the extent of the contravention of the rights conferred on citizens, namely, those under Article 19 if a law is otherwise good and does not contravene any of their fundamental rights non-citizens cannot take advantage of the *voidness* of the law for the reason that it contravenes the fundamental right of the citizens and claim that there is no law at all. In the absence or a law expressly taking away the right referred to in Article 2 of *International Bill of Human Rights*, it would be wholly fallacious to argue that the mere absence of a declaratory law as regards the foreigner should be construed as negativing the rights of a foreigner which he ordinarily possessed.

Unlike Article 21, which deals with the right to personal liberty of any person, Art. 19 deals with and confers fundamental rights mentioned therein upon every citizen of this country and a foreigner or a non-citizen like a joint-stock company incorporated under the Companies Act or a society registered under Societies Registration Act and such other entities, are outside the conferral of the rights mentioned in Art. 19 and it is clear that even the unqualified Presidential order dated Jan. 8, 1976 which suspends the right to move any court for enforcement of any of the rights conferred by Art. 19 cannot take within its sweep such foreigner or a non-citizen.

When it is shown that *prima facie* one of the Fundamental Rights under Art. 19 is violated by a law, it is for the State to show how the provisions of the law are reasonable and otherwise satisfy the conditions which would make it valid under clauses (2) to (6). None of the fundamental rights guaranteed by Art. 19 is absolute. Each of them is liable to be restricted by legal provisions under clauses (2) to (6) of Art. 19. The object of the several clauses (2) to (6) is to reconcile the fundamental rights granted by the Article with the power of the State to enact suitable legislation for ensuring the welfare of the members of the State. The restrictions permitted by clauses (2) to (6) follow a pattern *viz.*, they are imposed by the legislature for reasons of public policy. When an enactment is found to infringe any of the fundamental rights guaranteed under Art. 19(1), it must be held to be invalid unless those who support it can bring it under the protective provisions of clauses (2) to (6) of that Article. To do so the burden is on those who seek that protection and not on the citizen to show that the restrictive enactment is invalid. Articles 19 (2) to (6) also save the validity of all existing laws to the extent to which they may impose reasonable restrictions upon the restrictive fundamental freedoms for the purposes mentioned in the several clauses.

The general principles as to the tests of reasonableness are fairly well established. Legislation which arbitrarily or excessively invades the right cannot be said to contain the quality of reasonableness and unless it strikes a proper balance between the freedom guaranteed in

Article 19(1) and the social control permitted by clauses (2) to (6) of Article 19, it must be held to be wanting in that quality.

The purpose of the guarantee under Art. 19 (1) (a) is to prevent public authorities from assuming the guardianship of the public mind. Article 19 (1) (a) has to be read with clause (2) and if an Act directly falls under clauses (1) (a) but only incidentally under clause (1) (g), the enactment cannot be justified by recourse to clause (6), where it is not possible to justify it under clause (2).

The law of contempt of court is an existing law for purposes of Art. 19 (2). Any law including that which has been in force since before the passing of the Constitution either customary or based on statute must be subject to the test of Article 19 (2). The purpose of the guarantee under Art. 19 (1) (a) is to prevent public authorities from assuming the guardianship of the public mind. Art. 19 (1) (a) has to be read with clause (2) and if an Act directly falls under clause (1) (a) but only incidentally under clause (1) (g), the enactment cannot be justified by recourse to clause (6), where it is not possible to justify it under clause (2). It is only where an enactment is aimed directly at the right of freedom of speech that it would come under clause (1) (a) and the question of the validity under clause (2) would arise for decision. *Newspaper Price and Page Act (1956)* directly infringed clause (1) (a).

Where the object of an enactment was not to affect the freedom of speech and expression or the freedom of the press, but its object was the amelioration of the conditions of service of persons employed in the newspaper industry, the enactment would not fall under clause (1) (a) [Working Journalists (Conditions of Services) Act, 1955]. Where an enactment is directed merely of a certain kind of commercial advertisements which are considered to be objectionable from the point of view of the interests of the general public, the enactment will not come under clause (1) (a). Art. 19 (1) (a) is not intended to cover the question of official languages which is separately dealt with under Part XVII of the Constitution. Section 3 of M.P. Official Languages Act (24 of 1950) does not offend Art. 19 (1) (a). The fundamental right of freedom of speech and expression under clause (a) should not be confused with constitutional right under Art. 194 (1) regarding freedom of speech in Legislative Assembly.

The right of speech and expression is but one right and not two separate rights. They are two aspects of one and the same right, one being complementary to the other. The essence of the right does not consist merely making use of the human voice but, it lies in the ability to convey one's views to others. Right to freedom of speech and expression carries with it the right to propagate and circulate one's views and opinions subject to reasonable restrictions.

Freedom of speech goes to the heart of the natural right of an organised freedom-loving society to impart and acquire information: If any limitation is placed which results in the society being deprived of such right, it would fall within the guaranteed freedom under clause (1) (a). But if all it does is that that it deprives a trader from commending his wares, it would not fall within that term. It was held in the cases decided before the amendment of 1951 that a law restricting the freedom of speech and not relating to defamation or Contempt of Court and not also concerned with any offence against decency or morality, would be *ultra vires* unless it related to any matter which undermined the security of or tended to overthrow the State. These decisions must be regarded as no longer good law after the amendment of 1951 to the extent the decisions related to public order and incitement to an offence. Even before the amendment of 1951, it was held by the Supreme Court that even under the unamended clause (2) restrictions against incitement to crimes of violence were constitutional. It was pointed out that speeches or expressions of an individual which incite or encourage the commission of violent crimes, such as murder, cannot but be matters which would undermine the security of the State and come within the ambit of Art. 19 (2) as it stood prior to the amendment.

The importance of freedom of speech and expression guaranteed by Art. 19 (1) (a) cannot be overestimated because it lies at the foundation of all democratic governments. The provisions of clause (1) (a) are based on the provisions contained in Amendment 1 of the Constitution of the United States of America and it would therefore be legitimate and proper to refer to decisions of the Supreme Court of America, in order to appreciate the true nature, scope and extent of the right under our Constitution.

The contents of the freedoms guaranteed under clause (a), (b) and (c) do not include the right to exercise them in the properties belonging to others. Therefore, the directions issued by the General Manager of Northern Railway prohibiting the railway employees from holding meeting within the railway premises including open grounds forming part of those premises does not deprive the workers of any of the freedoms guaranteed to them under Art. 19 (1). There are no geographical limitations to freedom of speech and expression guaranteed Art. 19 (1) (a) and this freedom is exercisable not only in India but also outside and if State action sets up barriers to its citizens freedom of expression in any country in the world it would violate Art. 19 (1) (a). This will equally apply in relation to fundamental right to practise any profession or to carry on any occupation, trade or business guaranteed under Art. 19 (1) (g).

A petition under Art. 226 of the Constitution must fail if the challenge made therein to the impugned orders is founded upon a violation or infringement of the petitioner's right under Art. 19 (1) but not if the ground of challenge is *debors* the infrigement or violation of any such right; the right to freedom of speech and expression mentioned in Art. 19 (1) (a) is not a right created or conferred for the first time in the laws of India by Art. 19 (1) (a). It is a right under the Common Law of England which has been recognised and enforced by the courts in India prior to the coming into force of the Constitution and it has been continued in force by the Constitution.

Though sub-clause (a) of clause (1) of Art. 19 only refers expressly to freedom of speech and expression, it guarantees also the freedom of the press. The non-reference to the liberty of the press in the Article was merely due to the fact that express mention of the liberty of the press was considered unnecessary. Being only a right flowing from the freedom of speech and expression, the liberty of the press in India in relation to the Law of Contempt of Court or Defamation stands as on no higher footing than the freedom of speech and expression of a citizen and no privilege attaches to the Press as such that is to say, as distinct from the freedom of the citizen.

Freedom of speech and expression under Art. 19 (1) (a) of the Constitution is the same for the Press and the citizen. It is not absolute, however, and is subject to limitations in clauses (2) to (6) of Art. 19. Freedom of speech and expression prevails except where the contempt is manifest and mischievous. Courts like other institutions are not immune from criticism. Justice is not a closed virtue. The freedom of press includes also the freedom of circulation. Putting of a ban on the entry of a newspaper or magazine into a State would be an infringement of the right under Art. 19 (1) (a). Any enactment which directly affects the circulationof a newspaper will therefore be a violation of clause (1) (a). A law which fixes the maximum number of pages that might be published by a newspaper for a certain price and also prescribes the number of supplements that can be published virtually fixes a minimum price below which a newspaper cannot be sold and thus puts a limitation on the circulation of the paper as the minimum price fixed may make the paper unattractive to a number of persons. (*Price and Page*) *Act, 1956* and *Daily Newspaper* (*Price and Page*) *Order 1960* were held invalid.

A limitation on the amount of matter or information or news that a newspaper can publish is a direct infringement of the freedom of speech and expression guaranteed by Art. 19 (1) (a). If the area for advertisements in newspapers is curtailed by law, the price of the newspaper will be forced up and this will directly affect their circulation. Freedom of press includes freedom in the matter of employment of the editorial staff. Newspapers can be subjected to all ordinary taxes. Licence and privilege taxes are however exception.

A restriction in order to fall under clause (1) (a) must be directly aimed at the freedom of the press and expression and the freedom of the press and not only indirectly or incidentally. *Working Journalists and Conditions of Service and Miscellaneous Provisions Act, 1955* does not directly infringe the freedom of the press under clause (1) (a).

Where a direct restriction by law on the freedom of the press is not covered by clause (2), the mere fact that incidentally or indirectly it is also covered by clause (1) (g) as a restriction on the right of carrying on business and that the restriction viewed in that light would be valid under clause (6) will be no ground for holding that it is valid. A non-citizen (*e.g.*) a foreigner who runs a newspaper cannot claim the freedom of press as a fundamental right. The liberty of the press means complete freedom to write and publish without censorship or restriction save such as is absolutely necessary for the preservation of Society.

The newsprint policy is not a reasonable restriction within the ambit of Article 19(2). In the garb of distribution of newsprint, the Government has tended to control the growth and circulation of newspapers. Freedom of the press is both qualitative and quantitative. Freedom lies both in circulation and in content. The newsprint policy which permits newspapers to increase circulation by reducing the number pages, page area and periodicity, prohibits them to increase the number of pages, page area and periodicity by reducing circulation. These restrictions constrict the newspapers in adjusting their page number and circulation. The restrictions imposed by Section 12 M.P. Public Security Act on freedom of the press are reasonable and constitutional. An order under Section 12 M.P. Public Security Act totally prohibiting sale, distribution or circulation of paper is violative of Art. 19 (1) (a) and (g) of the Constitution of India.

If number of pages is restricted and made to depend upon the price to be charged, the right of the newspapers to freedom of speech and expression is infringed. However, if the only object of the Government for setting up the fact finding committee is in the fair price of the newspapers, there is no question of interference with the fundamental rights of the newspaper. Fair price is a price which is fair to all, that is, to the newspapers as also to the readers. If however, the price is not considered to be fair, it may affect both the newspapers, as also the readers. Whether the price which has to be fixed is fair or not is a matter to be considered after it is fixed. ***Provisions of the Press (Objectionable Matter) Act, 1951*** being in interest of decency and morality are reasonable restrictions in interests of general public. Exercise of the power under Section 11 of the Act is not arbitrary and the restriction upon freedom of speech and expression is not an unreasonable restriction.

The imposition of pre-censorship on a journal or newspaper is clearly an infringement of the freedom of the press which is an essential part of the right to the freedom of speech and expression declared by sub-clause (a) of clause (1). Every free man has an undoubted right to lay what sentiments he pleases before the public to forbid this is to destroy the freedom of the press. There is a clear distinction between the imposition of pre-censorship and the requirement of licence. In the case of pre-censorship the citizen is required to submit his views to the authorities concerned as a condition precedent to its publication, while in the case of license all that he is required to do as to take out a licence before exercising the right of free speech.

Demanding security from the press is a form of restriction on the freedom of the press which will be ***prima facie*** unconstitutional as violating the freedom of speech and expression under Art. 19 (1) (a) of the Constitution. Section 3 (1) of the ***Indian Press (Emergency Powers) Act*** is invalid. A speech advocating a change in the system of

Government cannot be said to involve a threat to the security is not unconstitutional. Incitement to crimes of violence like murder would undermine the security of the State, and a law against such incitement would have been constitutional even under clause (2) as it stood prior to its amendment by the Constitution (First Amendment) Act (V of 1951) when it included "Security of the State" but did not expressly, include "incitement to an offence" as one of the matters in respect of which freedom of speech and expression could be lawfully restrained.

Right to punish contempt under Art. 129 cannot be said to have been conferred on the Supreme Court in order to curb the right of freedom of speech. The law relating to contempt as it stands in United States of America cannot be followed in India as the American Constitution does not contain any provision parallel to Art. 19 (2) of the Constitution of India. Freedom of speech and expression can be said to be prejudicial to public safety, when there is immediate or imminent threat to the State or community. Before the amendment of clause (2) of Art. 19 by the Constitution (First Amendment) Act, 1951, it was held by the Supreme Court of India that criticism of Government, exciting disaffection or bad feelings towards it is not to be regarded as a justifying ground for restricting the freedom of expression and of the press unless it is such as to undermine the security of or tends to overthrow the State.

The constituent elements of the offence under Section 505 of the Penal Code refer to the Security of State and public order and hence the restriction on the freedom of speech and expression enacted by the Section, is covered by clause (2) and valid. A law punishing people for commending an intoxicant will be *void as* an uncalled for restriction on the freedom of expression which is not justified by any demands of morality or decency. The right to freedom of speech and expression does not embrace the freedom to commit contempt of court. Contempt jurisdiction is a special and to some extent an unusual type of jurisdiction wherein the prosecutor and the judge are combined in one. To some extent, it trenches upon the fundamental right of free speech and expression and stifles criticism of a public officer concerned with administration of public justice in discharge of his public duty. The contempt jurisdiction has to be sparingly exercised with utmost restraint and considerable circumspection. Clause (2) expressly permits restrictions on the freedom of speech and expression when such restrictions are imposed by a law relating to contempt of Court. The fundamental rights guaranteed under Articles 19 (1) (a) and (b) and 25 of the Constitution are not unfettered and absolute. The right freely to propagate religion is subject to the condition that it does not violate similar fundamental rights of the followers of other religions.

Even if a right is not specifically named in Art. 19 (1) it may still be a fundamental right covered by some clause of that Article, if it is an integral part of a named fundamental right or partakes of the same basic nature and character as that fundamental right. It is not enough that a right claimed flows or emanates from a fundamental right. Right to go abroad cannot in all circumstances be regarded as included in freedom of speech and expression.

*

X

PRIVACY AND SURVEILLANCE

> "It's not the number that's the evil, and it's not the information that's the evil, it's the decision to collect and use the information".
>
> —*Hope Eastman, a lawyer for the American Civil Liberties Union*

Privacy has become an issue in modern democratric societies which are characterised by large-scale, sophisticated bureaucratic structures and advanced technology in communications and information systems. Technological development has been permitted to evolve without regard for its impact on our modern democratic political system. A major factor of the privacy problem is the absence of legislation and organised rules ensuring privacy, confidentiality and due process to the subjects of computerized information. Data banks have been established at all levels of Government, business and the military services without any real knowledge or concern for their potential impact over individual rights. The privacy issue is all the more urgent because of the widespread use of information systems to administer services which many people may consider essential to their well being. Along with the values of a democratic system people have constantly rising expectations in terms of medical services, health, insurance, credit, family assistance and education. Those in search of jobs, credit, housing, welfare and other services must disclose extensive information of a particular nature, in order to obtain these benefits. This information further accumulates into the files maintained by various private and public institutions. If the facts about a person are freely disclosed with the knowledge and consent that they may be shared with others, there has been no violation of privacy.

The privacy issue involves other concerns often emotionally associated with, but not actually included in the concept of privacy. People may feel threatened by the very existence of massive and efficient information systems even though the privacy has not actually been invaded. They are often concerned about the endless search for personal data by social scientists, market researchers, opinion pollsters and the institutions that use the data. When the institutions that use the data when the institution seeking information also control funds, the threat appears much greater. Although people may change institutions that operate information systems with invasion of privacy, their real complaint is often about institutional power and its linkage to possession of information. An issue frequently aassociated with privacy is the relationship of the individual to any large institution operating a data bank. These concerns focus on the place of the individual in a technological society and reveal not that too much power is held by too few, but that so little is held by so many. In the relationship between individuals and organisations, the scales are balanced in favour of the latter. The information process is one way in which institutions learn more about individuals, but individuals learn no more about institutions or even what institutions learn about them.

Concern for privacy is caught up in the more general debate regarding the effect of technology on society. Some contemporary thinkers share a pessimistic view of this relationship and conclude that what is technically feasible is allowed to occur without regard for the consequences. ***Hannab Arendt, Herbert Marcuse*** and ***Lewis Mumford*** share this attitude. At the other end of the spectrum are those who argue with ***Alvin Toffler*** that technology has allowed the individual a greater range of choice than he has ever enjoyed before, one that may further even be bewildering broad. They argue that problems resulting from modern technology can be solved by the use of more technology. The privacy issue, however, will suffer from being embroiled in this debate. Since technology is here to stay, the privacy discussion should not focus on its desirability, but rather on finding ways to protect humanistic values and goals. Given the ease and speed with which information passes from one organisation to another, it could become the basis for unjust discrimination. But concomitantly with increasing legal recognition of privacy, there has developed a technological ability to invade it by a number of means heretofore not known. Data on individuals is easily collected and as easily stored. What is technologically possible will be done.

Professor Miller is right in believing that technological advances tend inexorably to narrow the defensible area. It is not only the

Justice Department that has a compendium of data on private citizens. There is a Medical Information Bureau that dispenses data to insurance companies on the medical history of applicants for insurance. A television camera on a utility pole, using infra-red light, can look into darkened rooms and provide entertainment for policemen monitoring the picture without the knowledge of the room's inhabitants. It is discouraging true that the invention has usually done substantial damage before the litigation can be started, let alone concluded.

In 1890, Louis Brandeis wrote an historic essay for the Harward Law Review. In that essay he noted that an advancing communications technology imperilled the individual's right of privacy. Brandeis pointed to the development of telephone and the snap-shot camera as mechanical devices that would seriously and irrevocably alter a person's fundamental right to be let alone. He warned legislators and legal scholars of his time that a "next step" was needed to protect that right. That "next step" is long overdue. Today, now that we have very sophisticated electronic bugging devices, we have computers, the type of devices Brandeis profitably never even conceived of.

Communications technology has now achieved a speed and facility that far outstrips anything. Brandeis may have dreamed possible. It is increasingly apparent that in the long series of technological break-throughs that have made the gathering, use and trading of personal data both efficient and economical, privacy safeguards have simply not kept pace. This has resulted in a tremendously increased potential for damaging misuse of personal information, and burgeoning abuses of our privacy.

The individual's right to privacy has long been recognised by the courts which have consistently protected it from both governmental and non-governmental intervention. As technological advances — cameras, wiretaps, sound recordings and so forth — provided new opportunities for infringement upon these rights, the courts responded in an affirmative manner. Unfortunately due to the nature of the courts, this response has often been slow and incomplete. Technology is again advancing, this time in the form of computers. This new technology brings with it, as advancements often do, the possibility for negligent use or deliberate misuse. This is what we must guard against. With the development of the computer it has become possible to collect, instantly retrieve and analyse vast amounts of personal information. Access to this personal data has been expanded by the computer's ability to retrieve data access agency, institutional, governmental and geographic boundaries.

Our recent experience with *Watergate* and related matters points up the need for enacting safeguards to protect the collection and use of such information. The compilation of an enemies list, for example, must be viewed as only the first step in an abuse of power, for the next logical step would be the compilation of useful information about those on the list. Certainly the demands of a complex technological society call for some concessions, but we have before us today an opportunity to help balance the recent trend of legislative activity by enacting legislation to help restore individual rights and individual privacy. Symbolic of this balance is the controversy over the use of social security numbers for identification purposes. While such a proposal may make a sound technological sense, to many citizens it implies removal of an important element of their privacy and individuality. Some of the principles are – the right of the individual to maintain his privacy and personal identity.

The right to privacy goes far beyond a claim to be protected from the unjustifiable intrusion of the press and the other media. A rapidly developing technology which makes it easily possible to exercise surveillance over the activities and conduct of individual by the use and exploration of a variety of devices has become, a matter of increasing and anxious concern. Almost forty years after the publication of the Warren and Brandeis article, Brandeis, by this time a distinguished judge of the Supreme Court of the United States, wrote in *Olmstead* vs. *United States (1928) 277* U.S. 438, a case which raised the issue of the admissibility of evidence obtained by eavesdropping (specifically by Telephone tapping) against a man charged with crime. Brandeis at the time in dissent declared that it was not admissible. In a famous and prophetic passage, he wrote:

> "Discovery and invention have made it possible for the Government by means far more effective than stretching upon the rack to obtain disclosure in court of what is whispered in the closet....The progress of science in furnishing the Government with means of espionage is not likely to stop wire-tapping. Ways may some day be developed by which the Government without removing papers from secret drawers, can reproduce them in Court, and by which time it will be enabled to expose to

> a jury the most intimate occurrences of the home. Advances in the psychic and related sciences may bring means of exploring unexposed beliefs, thoughts and emotions. The makers of the Constitution....sought to protect Americans in their beliefs, their thoughts, their emotions and their sensations. They conferred as against the Government, the right to be let alone – the most comprehensive of rights and the right most valued by civilised man."

In the course of time, Brandeis' view expressed in *Olmstead* in dissent, became the law. Brandeis spoke of surveillance by Government which has special dangers. Such devices of course are not only available to, and have not been used exclusively by governmental instrumentalities. They are part of the armoury of an army of snoopers. As one contemporary writer [*Miller, Computers and Privacy (1969) 67 Michigan L.R. 1091 at 1176*-7] in this field has put it:

> "The accelerating development of technology and the almost exponential expansion of the ability to manipulate personal information in variegated ways may be altering the balance between the individual citizen and those institutions in society that seek to exercise control over him. The individual has little ability to protect himself against governmental and private snoopers who can employ sophisticated electronic surveillance to monitor his activities and to obtain information about him. More substantial legal sufeguards than those currently available are required merely to maintain the *status quo* in the privacy field."

Computer technology makes a special and formidable contribution to the problem. The capacity of the computers to assimilate and store and print out a mass of information provides the possibility of comprehensive surveillance by dossier over individuals, with an ease and to an extent hence before-comprehended. Whatever the present dimension of the threat, the possibilities of far-reaching surveillance are very real.

Advancing technology has enabled the media to make even more searching intrusions into individual privacy and the reach of the Television, with the assist of the satellite, is formidable. The Younger

Committee spoke of a growing tendency on the part of the media to engage in "*investigative journalism*" and devoted a substantial part of its report to the problems associated with the media. The Younger Committee noted that from a wider point of view, concern for the protection of privacy has been stimulated by the growing pressures exerted by modern industrial society upon the home and daily life including such factors as the consequent difficulty of escaping from the observation of neighbours.

It is also likely that the threats to privacy represented by assembly of massive computerized data banks are potential rather than actual. The Younger Committee noted that the computer problem as it affects privacy in Great Britain is one of apprehensions and fears and not so far, one of facts and figures. Computer organisations displayed the greater sensitivity to the possible effects on privacy of what they were doing and the utmost anxiety to see that privacy was fully protected. There, are, however, seriously and deeply-felt fears concerning the use to which such computer data banks may be put, especially in such fields as credit, medical and police records. There is certainly deep concern at the use of the battery of sophisticated devices available and constantly becoming available for surveillance and information gathering. Spectacular and widely publicised events add to the unease, the revelation of wire-tapping, bugging and break-ins associated with Watergate have brought to many a new or renewed awareness of the scale and character of intrusions into individual privacy.

Most would agree that the need for secrecy in matters relating to national defence probably outweighs the benefits which might accrue to individual as a consequence of their having access to such information. But there is a great deal of information which is secret though it has nothing to do with security matters, indeed, the fact of its being kept at all is sometimes 'secret' at least to the extent that we are not necessarily always informed as to who is in possesion of certain information, and to what ends, such information may even concern us personally. In such a situation, the public interest, which is claimed to justify secrecy must be weighed against the private interests of the individual concerned. Even information which does not concern a private individual directly but is of a "public" nature does not necessarily preclude the possibility of a 'right of access'.

(1) *Computerized Data*

The scope for abuse in relation to computerised data has been highlighted in recent years by a number of highly elaborate computer frauds some of which have proved well-nigh impossible to detect. Our concern here is not the use of computers for criminal purposes as such, but the threat posed by computerization to the individual's privacy. Not that this problem is confined to the misuse of automatic systems of data storage, the general trend has been for those countries which have legislation creating a public right of access to official records to make provision for the protection of privacy. Thus Sweden, which has had a Freedom of the Press Act since 1768, passed its Data Act, in 1973, following the model of the *Hesse Data Protection Act, 1970*. The USA whose Freedom of Information Act was passed in 1966, enacted a Privacy Act in 1974. Other countries have passed privacy laws which bear on the use of data, sometimes (as with the Canadian Human Rights Act) as part of a broader legislative enactment. Indeed in Europe, at any rate, the U.K. is virtually alone in not having passed any such laws, most European States having some sort of data protection legislation, if not privacy laws generally.

Attempts have been made to establish some form of regulation or control in respect of the use of data in the U.K. In 1961, Lord Mancroft introduced a Bill in the House of Lords "to protect a person from any unjustifiable publication relating to his private affairs and to give him right at law in the event of such a publication.

Bills concerned primarily with computerized information were introduced in 1969 and in 1972. In 1975, the Home Secretary Mr. Roy Jenkins, presented a white paper entitled Computers and Privacy in which the Government announced its intention to appoint a non-statutory body to be known as the Data Protection Committee. Owing to the death of the chairman-designate, Sir Kenneth Younger, the committee was eventually chaired by Sir Norman Lindop. It reported in 1978. Unlike the Younger Committee which has preceded it the Lindop Committee was not concerned with those aspects of privacy which are not connected with the handling of personal data in information systems, such as intrusions into private premises, 'snooping' and so on. Also the committee was aware that there were certain aspects of data protection which have no immediate connection with privacy – the use of inaccurate information as the basis of taking decisions affecting individuals, for instance.

The problem confronting the committee was, as ususal, the need for a balance to be struck between the interests of the individual and those of society. This is, perhaps, rather more difficult in the realm of data protection than in relation to certain other areas where the permissible bounds of freedom can be fairly readily drawn. Thus, the interests of law and order can be quite readily weighed against the individual's interest in freely demonstrating his views orally or by, say, marching with other, like-minded individuals, and a point of balance drawn. In connection with data protection, however, things are a little more complicated. It is not only the public interest in, say, security which must here be weighed against the individual interest in having access to information, or his interest in privacy. Data which is stored in computer banks, in particular, tends to be used by a variety of individuals and organisations for a variety of reasons. As Lindop pointed out, "a balance must be found between the interests of the rest of the society which include the efficient conduct of industry, commerce and administration." Clearly, than such legislation as to the use of data, and computerized data collection in particular, must apply to the private as well as the public sector, a fact which finds expression in Lindop's recommendations.

Whilst Lindop is concerned with data protection generally, it is the implications for individual privacy which comprise the central theme in a survey of the potential abuse of data and most of the objectives to the growing use of automatic (computerized) systems of data processing inevitably relate to its implications for privacy. It is true that certain safeguards do exist in the U.K. in relation to certain areas at least. An individual has the right to request that a credit reference agency supply him with copies of their files on him, for instance, and he is entitled to seek to have incorrect information amended. Such safeguards are both piecemeal and inadequate, however, certainly Lindop's proposals go a great deal further, and would, if implemented, bring us into line with the countries mentioned earlier.

The committee proposed a Data Protection Act which should apply to the "automatic" handling in the U.K. of personal data by any use ('personal data' was taken to mean any data which could be related to an identifiable person). A Data Protection Authority should be established, whose duties would be to ensure that the handling of such data would be carried out with adequate safeguards for the interests of the 'data subjects', and in particular their privacy. To that end, compliance with certain principles would be sought. The principles involved are:

(1) Data subjects should know what personal data relating to them are handled, why those data are needed, how they will be used, who will use them for what purpose and how long ?

(2) Personal data should be handled only to the extent and for the purposes made known, when they are obtained, or subsequently authorised.

(3) Personal data handled should be accurate and complete, and relevant and timely for the purpose for which they are used.

(4) No more personal data should be handled than are necessary for the purposes made known or authorised.

(5) Data subjects should be able to verify compliance with these principles.

The above are in the interests of "data subjects", the interests of data users, and of the community at large, should also be served of course, and to that end Lindop proposed that users should not, in their legitimate handling of personal data, be subjected to excessive cost.

(2) *Snooping, Bugging and Tapping*

Devices for eavesdropping on conversation for 'bugging' a person's home or office, long-distance telephoto, even infra-red, camera lenses, all have facilitated prying by a person or agency, into the affairs of another. We must also consider more traditional means whereby a man's privacy may be invaded. Such as publicity or even harassment by the press and good old-fashioned trespass with regard to the former, perhaps, the means of making intrusions upon a persons' privacy has advanced far more quickly than the law protecting him, and it is certainly true that these techniques, in particular, highlight the relative inadequacy of the law in the U.K., which once again seems to fall short by comparison with some other countries.

A number of cases, Warren and Brandeis argued lead to the conclusion that the protection afforded to thought, sentiments and emotions, expressed through the medium of writing or of the arts, so far as it consists in preventing publication is merely an instance of the enforcement of the more general right of the individual to be let alone. This development, they said was a sort of extension of the law-protecting the individual from physical interference or from interference to his property – indeed the right to be let alone and the right not to be assaulted, or to freely enjoy one's property, were actually similar, in that in each of these rights'......there inheres the quality of being owned or possessed – and ....there may be some property in speaking of such rights as property. In other words, such things as a man's thoughts, sentiments and emotions like his physical person and his land or chattels, "could be conceived of as his property", the law should (and according to Warren and Brandeis actually did) protect his rights in relation to such property.

Whilst the law on trespass has afforded the individual in the U.K. some protection, our courts – unlike those in the U.S.A. – have not conceived of such protection as amounting to a right of privacy. In the U.S.A. whilst there is no constitutional right to privacy as such the courts have tended to assume that the individual is entitled to a 'reasonable expectation of privacy' arising in particular, from the Fourth Amendment. Apart from the obvious fact of its embodiment in a written Constitution, this does not differ to any substantial degree from the legal position in the U.K. The U.S. courts have clearly been willing to contemplate a general right of privacy, where ours have not. The idea of a "***reasonable expectation of privacy***" arising from the Fourth Amendment has been held in one American case to extend to telephone conversations. In *Katz* Vs. *U.S.* [*389 U.S. 347 (1967)*], a man was convicted of illegal gambling on the basis of evidence obtained by the FBI by means of a tap which they had placed on a public telephone booth used by him. The U.S. Supreme Court held that this was an unreasonable search, the fact that it did not involve physical entry but an electronic device was irrelevant. One Judge at least, Mr. Justice Stewart, stated specifically – the Government's activities in electronically listening to and recording the petitioners words violated the privacy upon whch he justifiably relied while using the telephone booth and thus constituted a "***search and seizure***" within the meaning of the Fourth Amendment.

In 1973 case in ***Malone*** vs. ***Commissioner of Police of the Metropolis***, the matter of telephone tapping as a means of surveillance by the British authorities was considered by Sir Robert Megarry, the Vice-Chancellor. Sir Robert felt that tapping was lawful, so long as certain requirements were satisfied. These were. first, that there should be grounds for suspecting that the tapping was lawful, so long as certain requirements were satisfied. These were: first, that there should be grounds for suspecting that the tapping of the particular phone will be of material assistance in detecting or preventing crime or discovering the criminals, or otherwise assisting in the discharge of the functions of the police in relation to crime. Second, that no use should be made of material obtained except for these purposes. Third, that any knowledge of information which is not relevant to these purposes should be confined to the minimum number of persons reasonably required to carry out the process of tapping.

In his book "The Protection of Privacy" Raymond Wacks suggests four main categories of privacy – invasion, intrusion (including interception of communications, snooping, and physical intrusions such as searches, the activities of private detectives and the press); publicity (and the disclosure of private information about individuals in particular); the use of computers and the use of an indiviudal's identity (either by way of appropriating it, or by presenting it in a false light), with regard to many of the activities referred to by Wacks, English Law is virtually devoid of remedies. Intrusions on the part of the press confined to the publication of personal information obtained by "*investigative journalism*" or some such method.

The demand that individual privacy be respected is becoming more common and more insistent in our age. This probably reflects a rapidly increasing need for privacy arising from converging ecological, cultural, technical and social changes. The population explosion together with modern urbanisation have made it much more difficult for the individual to get away physically and psychologically, from the crowd of strangers around him. The growing allegiance to political individualism and moral autonomy have caused the individual to resent and resist legal regulation and social interference more intensely. At a time when bugging and other techniques of *surveillance* have been perfected to an alarming degree the development of computers enables us to store and retrieve vastly increased amounts of information about any specified individual in even very large populations. Finally as organisations have grown larger in size and more bureaucratic in structure, their tendency to invade the life of the individual has grown apace.

(3) *American Position*

The Ninth Amendment's reservation that "the enumeration in the Constitution of certain rights shall not be construed to deny or disparage others retained by the people" clearly shows that the

Founding Fathers contemplated that certain basic individual rights not specifically mentioned in the Constitution – such as privacy –should nevertheless be safe from governmental interference. The Supreme Court has held many aspects of individual privacy to be constitutionally protected. In recognising that "specific guarantees in the Bill of Rights have penumbras formed by emanations from these guarantees that help give them life and substance" (*Griswold* Vs. *Connecticut – 381 U.S. 479*), the Court has found that those penumbras protect the right to give and receive information, the right to family life and child rearing according to one's conscience, the right to marry, the right to procreation, the right to contraception, and the right to abortion.

All Americans can testify to the power of those protections of the individual's rights. The Constitution assures these rights to all citizens whether their exercise is pleasing to Government or not. And by the same token, it assures the individual, the reverse of these rights, the right not to speak what he believes, whether his silence is pleasing to Government or not, and his right not to act, not to associate, not to assemble, whether his inaction is pleasing to Government or not. It seems that now as never before, the appetite of Government and private organisations for information about individuals threatens to usurp the right to privacy which is among the most basic of civil liberties as a free people.

If we have learned anything in the last year of Watergate, it is that there must be limits upon what the Government can know about each of its citizens. Each time we give up a bit of information about ourselves to the Government, we give up some of our freedom. For the more the Government or any institution knows about us, the more power it has over us, when the Government knows all of our secrets, we stand naked before official power. Stripped of our privacy we lose our rights and privileges. The Bill of Rights then becomes just so many words. The importance of being a free individual with certain inalienable rights, an individual seems in the knowledge that his thoughts and judgements are beyond the reach to the State or any man.

Privacy like many of the other attributes of freedom, can be easiest appreciated when it no longer exists. A complacent citizenry only becomes outraged about its loss of integrity and individuality when the aggrandizement of power in the Government becomes excessive. By then, it may be too late. Protesting against the loss of a little liberty is the best means of safeguarding against the loss of our freedom.

The protection of personal privacy is no easy task. It will require foresight and the ability to forecast the possible trends in information technology and the information policies of the Government and private organisationss before they actually take their toll in wide-spread invasions of the personal privacy of large number of individual citizens.

The Founding Fathers had that foresight when they wrote the *Bill of Rights*. The First, Fourth and Fifth amendments are among the most effective bulwarks to personal freedom conceived by the mind of man. Justice Brandeis in his classic dissent in the *wiretapping case, Olmstead* Vs. *United States* [*(277 U.S. 438 (1927)*] described with unsurpassed eloquence the importance of the right to privacy set out in the Constitution. These words do not go stale from repetition.

Government and private Data collection on individuals is not a brand new phenomenon. The Federal Government has been collecting immense amounts of very sensitive information on individuals for decades. Income Tax, social security and census come to mind immediately. Nevertheless, the effect on the right to privacy of massive information gathering and dissemination through the use of sophisticated computer technology is just beginning to be realised. Rich or poor, male or female, whatever one's cultural styles or religions or political views, each of us is subject to cumulative records being stored by a variety of Government agencies and private organisations. One of the most obvious threats the computer poses to privacy comes in its ability to collect, store and disseminate information without any subjective concern for human emotion and fallibility. Yet the increasing growth of information gathering by Government and private organisations proceeds without any standards or procedures to regulate these organisations. It is because of this vaccum of authority....safeguards must be created against the present and potential abuse of information about people.

Under the provisions of the Bill, information may be gathered by Federal agencies, State and local Governments, or any private organisations only to accomplish the proper purpose of those agencies and organisations. In gathering information the individual must be the source of that information to the greatest extent possible; however, no individual may be forced to disclose any information not required by law; and he is to be informed of his right not to disclose. The individual is to be notified of the existence of any information being maintained on him and the uses to which that information is being put. No public or private organisations may collect information on any individual, political or religious beliefs or affiliations unless specified by law. Restrictions on the maintenance of information systems used by Federal agencies, State and local Governments, and other organisations include requirements that all information in these systems be accurate, complete, timely and pertinent. Any individual has the right to inspect the information maintained in a system relating to him with the exception of medical records. He has the right to know the nature of the source and the recipients of that information.

The individual also has the right to challenge any information on the basis of its accuracy, completeness, timeliness, pertinence or necessity. Upon receipt of any challenge to its information by an individual, an organisation must : first investigate and record the current status of such information; second, purge any information that is found to be incomplete, not pertinent, not timely, not necessary to be maintained, or that can no longer be verified. The Bill places strict restrictions on the dissemination of information in personal information systems, both private and public. All information systems must request permission from the individual before disseminating any information to any person or organisation not having regular authorised access to the information system.

Organizations maintaining information systems are required to keep an accurate list of all persons having access to the information including but not limited to those having access on a regular basis. The Bill also provides for the removal of any name and address from a mailing list upon the written request of the individual. Certain types of information are exempted from coverage of this Act. Those information systems exempted include : any information maintained by a Federal agency and determined to be vital to national defence; criminal investigatory files of Federal, State or local law enforcement agencies; and any information maintained by the press or news media – except that information related to the employees of such organisations.

The term "personal information" means all information that describes, locates or indexes, anything about an individual including his education, financial transactions, medical history, criminal or employment record, or that affords a basis for interfering personal characteristics, such as finger and voice prints, photographs or things done by or to such individual; and the record of his presence, registration or membership in an organisation or activity or admission to an institution.

The term "disseminate" means to release, transfer or otherwise communicate information orally, in writing or by electronic means. There are benefits to the computer age. Apparently, it is like blowing into a gale. The benefits are so obvious and so easily stated that we are willing to give up our privacy in order to get them.

"Nothing in this Act shall be construed to permit the withholding of any personal information other than that required to be disclosed by law or any regulation thereunder."

Americans today are scrutinized, measured, watched, counted, and interrogated by more governmental agencies, law enforcement officials, social scientists and poll takers than at any other time in our history. Probably in no nation on earth is as much industrialised information collected, recorded and disseminated as in the United States.... The information gathering and surveillance activities of the Federal Government have expanded to such an extent that they are becoming a threat to several of every American's basic rights, the rights of privacy, speech, assembly, association, and petition of the Government.

The *HEW* (Health, Education and Welfare) Report found that "concern about computer-based record keeping usually centres on its implications for personal privacy, and understandably so if privacy is considered to entail control by an individual over the uses made of information about him. In many circumstances in modern life, an individual must either surrender some of that control or forego the services, that an organisation provides. Although there is nothing inherently unfair in trading some measures of privacy for a benefit, both parties to the exchange should participate in settling the terms.

A computer storage device now exists which make it entirely practicable to record thousands of millions of characters of information, and to have the whole of this always available for instant retrieval. Distance is no obstacle, communications, circuits, telephone lines, radio waves, even laser beams, can be used to carry information in bulk at speeds which can match the computer's own. Time sharing is normal.

Details of our health, our education, our employment, our taxes, our telephone calls, our insurance, our banking and financial transactions, pension contributions, our books borrowed, our airline and hotel reservations, our professional societies, our family relationships, all are being handled by computers right now. Unless these computers, both governmental and private, are specifically programmed to erase unwanted history, these details from our past can at any time be reassembled to confront us.... we must programme the programmers while there is still some personal liberty left.

The committee has found that the concern for privacy is a bipartisan issue and knows no political boundaries. President Ford once stated:

In dealing with troublesome privacy problems, let us not however, scapegoat the computer itself as a Frankenstein's monster. But let us be aware of the implications posed to freedom and privacy emerging from the ways we use computers to collect and discriminate personal information. A concerned involvement by all who use computers is the only way to produce standards and policies that will do this job. It is upto us to assure that information is not fed into the computer unless it is relevant.

Even if it is relevant, there is still a need for discretion. A determination must be made if the social harm done from some data outweighs its usefulness. The decision-making process is activated by demands of people on the Government and business – for instant credit and instant services. Computer technology has made privacy an issue of urgent national significance. It is not the technology alone but its abuse which is a matter of concern. Technology capable of designing such intricate systems can also design measures to assure security.

> Watergate has thus been the symbolic catalyst of a tremendous upsurge of interest in securing the right of privacy wiretapping and bugging political opponents, breaking and entering enemies lists, the Hustoon Plan, national security, justifications for wiretapping, and burglary, misuse of information compiled by government agencies for political purposes, access to hotel telephone and bank records; all of these show what government can do if its actions are shrouded in secrecy and its vast information resources are applied and manipulated in a punitive, selective or political fashion.

The premise underlying the Privacy Act of 1974 is that good Government and efficient management require that basic principles of privacy, confidentiality, and due process must apply to all personal information programs and practices of the Federal Governments and should apply to those of State and local Governments as well as to those of the organisations, agencies and instruments of the private sector.

Privacy is independent of technological safeguards it involves the social policy issues of what information should be collected at all and how much information should be assembled in any one information system. For purposes of the principles implemented by the Privacy Act for the Federal Executive branch, the Committee means this to include constitutional and statutory prohibitions or restraints.

Confidentiality is the central issue for which technological safeguards are relevant, where an organisation has promised those from whom it collects information that unauthorised uses will not be made by persons inside or outside that agency making good that promise of confidentiality requires record scrutiny controls in both manual and computerized files.

Privacy, then is a shorthand term for the restraint on the power of the Government to investigate individuals, to collect information about their personal lives and activities in society or in ways which are banned by the Constitution, or for reasons which have little or nothing to do with the purpose of the Government or of the agency involved as their powers are defined by the Constitution and specific statutes.

First, an important cause of fear and distrust of computerized data systems has been the feelings of powerlessness they provoke in many citizens. The computer has come to symbolise the unresponsiveness and insensitivity of modern life. Whatever may be thought of these reactions, it is at least clear that genuine rights of access and challenge would do much to discern this hostility.

Second, such rights promise to be the most viable of all the possible methods to guarantee the accuracy of data systems. Unlike more complex internal mechanisms, they are triggered by the most powerful and consistent of motives, individual self-interest.

Finally, it should now be plain that if any future system is to win public acceptance, it must offer persuasive evidence that it is quite seriously concerned with the rights and interests of those whose lives it will record. The committee can imagine no more effective evidence than authentic rights of access and challenge

The Committee recognises however, that there are two general classes of files maintained by agencies with law enforcement functions, criminal history or record files on the one hand and intelligence and investigative files on the other. The second class of information generally maintained by law enforcement agencies are intelligence or investigative files. These files contain highly sensitive and usually confidential information collected by law enforcement officers in anticipation of criminal activity, such as by organised crime figures, or in the course of investigating criminal activity which has already occurred. It was the committee's judgement, shared by most criminal justice privacy experts and reflected in the pending criminal justice privacy legislation that all of the provisions of Title II of Sec. 3418 could not be applied to such sensitive information. In particular, it would not be appropriate to allow individuals to see their own intelligence or investigative files.

A major avenue by which personal privacy and confidentiality may be invaded is the practice of the Federal Government of selling and renting names, addresses and personal data in their files for use in commercial and other mailing lists. Such practices may cause a violation of the tacit or formal agreement by which the agency collected or acquired the information for its own authorised purposes. Laws promoting open records in government have resulted or may result in administrative contracts on agreements to sell the data in bulk, either as convenience to commercial or other users, or to promote and publicize the purposes of the agency.

The threat to individual privacy from the selling and renting of names and personal information from Government files and the use of the mailing lists by the mailing list industry was found to be an appropriate subject for privacy legislation by the *National Academy of Sciences Project Report*. The committee agrees with the report that the standard of *Direct Mail Marketing Association*, mere removal of one's name, is not enough for Government agencies. As the Academy report states: "For many people, this does not resolve the basic privacy issue; when individuals give information about themselves to governmental agencies for one purpose, usually under legal compulsion to report, should their names, addresses and data about their occupations, ownership, military service or other activities be made available to organisations that would use the information for purposes that these individuals consider intrusive."

In time of major problems of housing, education, crime, race relations, pollution, and peace, it may seem a disturbingly trivial matter to worry about government records leading to the receipt of mail advertisements that some individuals do not want. But the issue symbolizes something we cannot afford to ignore how do we make the individual's informed consent a more respected and controlling feature in organisational society? Our approach to this problem should not be to make matters confidential which have long been considered open for public access; rather it should be to find a way to accommodate those who feel their privacy is intruded upon by such direct mail practices.

Privacy is "the primary civil liberties issue, since both confidentiality and due process questions disappear if the data are not gathered in the first place, or once they are destroyed." The individual also has the right to know the source of the personal information. If such source is required to be kept confidential by statute, then the individual may be informed only of the nature of the sources. The privacy of an individual is directly affected by the collection, maintenance, use and dissemination of personal information by Federal agencies. The increasing use of Computers and sophisticated information technology has greatly magnified the harm that can occur from any collection, maintenance, use and dissemination of personal information. The opportunities for an individual to secure employment, insurance and credit, and his right to due process and other legal protections are endangered by the misuse of certain information systems, the right to privacy is a personal and fundamental right protected by the Constitution of the United States. In order to protect the privacy of individuals identified in information systems maintained by Federal Agencies, it is necessary and proper, for the Congress to regulate the collection, maintenance, use and dissemination of information by such agencies.

To permit an individual to determine what records pertaining to him are collected, maintained, used or disseminated by such agencies. To permit an individual to prevent records pertaining to him obtained by such agencies for a particular purpose from being used or made available for another purpose without his consent, to permit an individual to gain access to information pertaining to him in Federal

Agency records to have a copy made of all or any portion thereof, and to correct or amend such records; to collect, maintain, use or disseminate any record of identifiable personal information in a manner that assures that such action is for a necessary and lawful purpose that the information is current and accurate for its intended use, and that adequate safeguards are provided to prevent misuse of such information. To permit exemptions from the requirements with respect to records provided in the Privacy Act only in those cases where there is an important public policy need for such exemption as has been determined by specific statutory authority; and subject to civil suit for any damages which occurs as a result of wilful, arbitrary or capricious action which violates any individual's rights under the Privacy Act.

No agency shall disclose any record which is contained in a system of records by any means of communications to any person, or to another agency, except pursuant to a written request by or with the prior written consent of, the individual to whom the record pertains, unless disclosure of the record would be:

(1) to those officers and employees of the agency which maintain the record who have a need for the record in the performance of their duties;

(2) for a routine use;

(3) to the Bureau of the census for purposes of planning or carrying out a census or survey or related activity;

(4) to a recipient who has provided the agency with advance adequate written assurance that the record will be used solely as a statistical research or reporting record, and the record is to be transferred in a form that is not individually identifiable;

(5) to the National Archives of the United States as a record which has sufficient historical or other value to warrant its continued preservation by the U.S. Government or for evaluation by the Administrator of General Services or his designee to determine whether the record has such value;

(6) to another agency or, to an instrumentality of any governmental jurisdiction within or under the control of the U.S. for a law enforcement activity if the activity is

authorised by law and if the need of the agency or instrumentality has made a written request to the agency which maintains the record specifying the particular portion desired and the law enforcement activity for which the record is sought;

(7) pursuant to a showing of compelling circumstances affecting the health or safety of an individual, if upon the disclosure notification is transmitted to the last known address of the individual;

(8) to either House of Congress or to the extent of matter within its jurisdiction, any Committee or Sub-committee thereof or any Joint Committee of Congress or Sub-committee of any such Joint Committee.

The purpose of the Privacy Act is to provide certain safeguards for an individual against an invasion of personal privacy by requiring Federal agencies, except as otherwise provided by law to,

(1) permit an individual to determine what records pertaining to him are collected, maintained, used or disseminated by such agencies;

(2) permit an individual to permit records pertaining to him obtained by such agencies for a particular purpose from being used or made available for another purpose without his consent.

(3) permit an individual to gain access to information pertaining to him in Federal agency records to have a copy made of all or any portion thereof and to correct or amend such records;

(4) collect, maintain, use or disseminate any record of identifiable personal information in a manner that assures that such action is for a necessary and lawful purpose that the information is correct and accurate for its intended use, and that adequate safeguards are provided to prevent misuse of such information;

(5) permit exemptions from the requirements with respect to records provided in the Privacy Act only in those cases where there is an important public policy need for such exemptions, as has been determined by specific statutory authority; and

(6) be subject to civil suit for any damages which occur as a result of wilful or intentional action which violates any individual's rights under the Privacy Act.

The purpose of the Privacy Act is to insure safeguards for personal privacy from Federal agencies by adherence to the following principles of information practice :

(1) There should be no personal information system whose existence is secret.

(2) Information should not be collected, unless the need for it has been clearly established in advance.

(3) Information should be appropriate and relevant to the purpose for which it has been collected.

(4) Information should not be obtained by fraudulent or unfair means.

(5) Information should not be used unless it is accurate and current.

(6) There should be a prescribed procedure for an individual to learn the information stored about him. the purpose for which it has been recorded, and particulars about its use and dissemination.

(7) There should be a clearly prescribed procedure for an individual to correct, erase or amend inaccurate obsolete, or irrelevant information.

(8) Any Federal Agency holding personal information should assure its reliability and take precautions to prevent its misuse.

(9) There should be a clearly prescribed procedure for an individual to prevent personal information collected for one purpose from being used for another purpose without his consent.

(10) The Federal Government should not collect personal information except as authorised by law.

The Congress finds –

(1) that an individual's privacy is directly affected by the extensive collection, maintenance, use, and dissemination of personal information;

(2) that the increasing use of computers and sophisticated

information technology has greatly magnified the harm that can occur from these practices;

(3) that an individual's opportunities to secure employment, insurance, credit, and his right to due process and other legal protections are endangered by these personal information systems;

(4) that in order to preserve the rights guaranteed by the first, third, fourth, fifth, ninth and fourteenth amendments of the United States Constitution, uniform Federal legislation is necessary to establish procedures to govern information systems containing records on individuals.

H.R. 16373 of the Bill prescribes legislative guidelines within the framework of the *Freedom of Information Act* to protect the privacy of individuals by regulating the Federal Government's collection, maintenance, use, or dissemination of personal identifiable information. H.R. 16373 provides a series of basic safeguards for the individual to help remedy the misuse of personal information by the Federal Government and reassert the fundamental rights of personal privacy of all Americans that are derived from the Constitution of the United States. At the same time, it recognises the legitimate need of the Federal Government to collect, use, store and share among various agencies certain types of personal data. This information includes Income Tax returns, social security records, civil service records, census data, economic statistics, governmental payroll records, law enforcement records and other similar types of personally identifiable information about many millions of individuals. H.R. 16373 attempts to strike that delicate balance between two fundamental and conflicting needs – on the one hand, that of the individual American for a maximum degree of privacy over personal information he furnishes his government, and on the other, that of the government for information about the individual which it finds necessary to carry out its legitimate functions.

*

XI

PRIVACY AND SEARCH & SEIZURE

> "Belief however well founded, that an article sought is concealed in a dwelling house furnishes no justification for a search of that place without a warrant. And such searches are.....unlawful notwithstanding, facts unquestionably showing probable cause."
>
> –*Agnella* vs. *United States (1925) 269 U.S. 20*
> *(The United States Supreme Court)*

Society, of course, has a legitimate interest in suppressing crime and detecting criminals. It is established by an abundance of authority that the officers of the State cannot degrade the individual in their search for proof of crime and the identity of criminals.

The court in *Breithaupt* vs. *Abram* (1957) *352 U.S. 432* observed:

> "As against the right of an individual that his person be held inviolable, even against so light an intrusion as is involved in applying a blood test of the kind to which millions of Americans submit as a matter of course nearly every day, must be set the interests of the society in the scientific determination of intoxication, one of the great causes of the mortal hazards of the road."

The Supreme Court in *Schmerber* vs. *California (1966) 384 U.S. 757* noted: "The overriding function of the Fourth Amendment is to protect personal privacy and dignity, against unwarranted intrusion by the state." It added:

"History and precedent have required that we today reject the claim that self-incrimination clause of the Fifth Amendment require the human body in all circumstances to be held inviolate against State expeditions seeking evidence of crime. But, if compulsory administration of a blood test does not indicate the fifth amendment, it plainly involves the broadly conceived reach of a search and seizure under the Fourth Amendment. That Amendment expressly provides that 'the right of the people to be secure in their persons.... against unreasonable search and seizures, shall not be violated'....Such testing procedures plainly constitute searches of 'persons'.....the Fourth Amendment's proper function is to constrain, not against all intrusions as such, but against intrusions which are not justified in the circumstances or whch are made in an improper manner. In other words, the questions we must decide in this case are whether the police were justified in requiring petitioner to submit to the blood test, and whether the means and procedures employed in taking his blood respected relevant Fourth Amendment standards of reasonableness."

The court concluded that the search was necessary and performed in a reasonable manner. It thought wise to add this dictum, however:

"The integrity of an individual's person is a cherished value of our society. That we today hold that the Constitution does not forbid the States' minor intrusions into an individual's body under stringently limited conditions in no way indicates that it permits more substantial intrusions, or intrusions under other conditions" said Justice Fortas in dissent. "As prosecutor, the state has no right to commit any kind of violence upon the person, or to utilise the results of such a tort, and the extraction of blood, over protest is an act of violence."

Society has a worthy interest in attempting to prevent anti-social conduct, and it is sometimes thought that physically punishing those convicted of crime deters them and others from wayward behaviour. The Eighth Amendment in the case of the Federal Government and the Fourteenth in the case of the states, prevent the imposition of cruel and unusual punishment even upon those convicted of the most heinous offences. Another way of protecting society's interest in the dignity of the individual, notwithstanding his anti-social behaviour, is the free exercise of religion guarantee of the First Amendment.

(1) *Ban upon unreasonable searches and seizures*

Society has a strong interest in the privacy of the individual, and this interest is represented by the constitutional ban upon unreasonable searches and seizures. The U.S. Supreme Court in *Silverman* vs. *United States (1961) 365 U.S. 505* has said:

> "The decisions of this court have time and again underscored the essential purpose of the Fourth Amendment to shield the citizen from unwarranted

> intrusions into his privacy." On another instance the court added: "The Fourth Amendment, and the personal rights which it secures, have a long history. At the very core stands the right of a man to retreat into his own home and there be free from unreasonable governmental intrusion."

The ban upon unreasonable searches and seizures is made applicable to the Federal Government directly by the Fourth Amendment, and to the states and their political subdivisions indirectly by the Fourteenth Amendment. The standard of reasonableness has been said by the Supreme Court to be "the same under the Fourth and Fourteenth Amendments".

By the general rule a person or his property cannot be searched unless the authorities have a search warrant. Illustrative of the general rule, a man's house may not be searched without a search warrant, even though the police have probable cause to suspect that there is within the house some article the possession of which is forbidden by law.

The court said in 1958 in *Jones* Vs. *United States (1958) 357 U.S. 493*: "It is settled doctrine that probable cause for belief that certain articles subject to seizure are in a dwelling cannot of itself justify a search without a warrant."

The Supreme Court in *Johnson* Vs. *United States (1948) 333 U.S.10*, has invalidated a search of hotel room made by officers when they detected a strong odor of burning opium coming from the room. The court observed:

> "No reason is offered for not obtaining a search warrant except the inconvenience to the officers and some slight delay necessary to delay papers and present the evidence to a magistrate. These are never very convincing reasons and in these circumstances, certainly are not enough to by-pass the constitutional requirement."

The Supreme Court held in 1961 that the Fourth Amendment extends to the recording of oral statements, overheard without any technical tresppass under local property law [*Silverman* vs. *United States (1961) 365 U.S. 505)*]. Six years later the court held that the earlier *Olmstead* [*(Olmstead* vs. *United States (1928) 277 U.S. 438*] and *Goldman* [*Goldman* vs. *United States (1942) 316 U.S. 129*] decisions allowing the use of detectaphones placed on the outer wall of a hostel room and the use of microphones to pick up conversations "can no longer be regarded as controlling". [*Katz* Vs. *United States (1967) 389 U.S. 347*]. In the Katz decision, the court re-emphasized that the reach of the Fourth Amendment does not turn upon the presence or absence of a physical intrusion into any given enclosure. The court there ruled that the Amendment protects a person making a telephone call from a public booth from governmental use of an electronic listenting and recording device affixes to the outside of the booth. Henceforth, the Fourth Amendment will protect the individual from intrusion into the areas of his life he desires to keep private from all forms of mechanical and electronic intrusion.

The *Katz* case has added interest because the court said by way of dictum that a magistrate could have authorised such a search as occurred "with appropriate safeguards". The court emphasized that before such a search can be made, it is necessary to present the estimate of probable cause to a neutral magistrate, there must be precise limits established in advance of the search of specific court order and the officers must be directed after the search is completed, to notify the authorising magistrate the detail of all that was seized.

The Federal Communications Act provides "No person not being authorised by the sender shall intercept any communication and divulge or publish the existence, contents, substance, purport, effect, or meaning of such intercepted communication to any person. The Act bars the use in Federal prosecutions of illegal wire-taps by Federal or State officers. However, the court has allowed State courts to use such evidence. And this evidence can be used in Federal Court if one person to the conversation has consented to the wire-tap. In concluding, the court noted that it had condoned the use of eaves-dropping devices "under specific conditions and circumstances".

(2) *The U.S. Constitutional Right of Disclosural Privacy*

In interpreting certain provisions of the Bill of Rights to protect the individual from governmental intrusions, the Supreme Court has spoken broadly of a right of privacy. Although there is no explicit constitutional recognition of such a right, the court "has recognised that a right of personal privacy, or a guarantee of certain areas or zones of privacy does exist under the Constitution". A right of privacy has been found in the Fourth Amendment, the First Amendment, the

Ninth Amendment and the concept of ordered liberty guaranteed by the due process clauses of the Fifth and the Fourteenth Amendments (significantly, in discussing the right of privacy, the court has not distinguished between disclosural privacy – the right to control the flow of information concernting the details of one's individuality – and that aspect of privacy concerning the individual's ability to decide whether to perform certain acts or to undergo certain experiences, an aspect accurately characterized as privacy relating to personal autonomy). Many of these cases, especially the privacy cases have focused on the privacy of autonomy. It is the purpose of the *Bill of Rights* to analyse the degree of protection, to determine whether these separate protections are capable of being generalised into a unitary right of disclosural privacy, and to ascertain when government interests in information acquisition, retention and dissemination will override individual privacy interests.

The Fifth Amendment privilege against self-incrimination does not deal with an individual's interest in disclosural privacy. *Boyd* Vs. *United States 116 U.S. 616 (1886); Mapp* Vs. *Ohio 367 U.S. 643 (1961)*, but the privacy protection afforded by that amendment is minimal because incriminating testimony can be compelled, if either use or traditional immunity from prosecution is conferred on the witness. (*Kastigar* Vs. *United States, 406 U.S. 441 (1972). Zicaselli* Vs. *State Commissioner of Investigations, 406 U.S.472 (1972),* the Fifth Amendment privilege against self-incrimination also does not apply to the compelled production of privately held but legally required records. *Wilson* Vs. *United States 221 U.S. 361 (1911)*. Nor does the privilege apply to records required by law to be kept in order that there may be suitable information of transactions which are the appropriate subjects of governmental rights. [*Wilson* Vs. *United States 221 U.S. 361 (1911)* and *Davis* Vs. *United States 328 U.S. 582 (1946)*].

Except for the Third Amendment's ban on the quartering of soldiers in any house without the owner's consent in terms of peace – a very narrow prohibition – the Fourth Amendment comes closer to mentioning a right of privacy than any other provision of the Constitution. An examination of some of the principal search and seizure cases suggests a broad concern for privacy underlying the Fourth Amendment. For example in *Boyd* Vs. *United States*, the court struck down a statute empowering a court to require a defendant to produce personal papers, it reasoned that the essence of an unreasonable search and seizure is "not the breaking of his doors and the rummaging of his drawers....but....the invasion of his indefeasible right of personal security, personal liberty and private property...." In holding that the Fourth Amendment limits the compulsory production of evidence in addition to prohibiting unlawful searches, the court provided protection for a privacy concept broad enough to include both disclosure and autonomy. [The Fourth Amendment to the Constitution provides: "The right of the people to be secure in their papers, persons, houses, and effects, against unreasonable search and seizures, shall not be violated, and no warrants, shall issue but upon probable cause, supported by oath or affirmation, and particularly describing the place to be searched and the persons or things to be seized."]

Boyd demonstrates that the Fourth Amendment served two purposes. The protection of individual privacy and the protection of the individual against the compulsory production of evidence to be used against him, as well as against unlawful searches [*Davis* Vs. *United States 328 U.S. 582 (1946)*].

Based on this dual purpose analysis, one could argue that the "right to be let alone" attaches only in a criminal context, since as the court noted in *Boyd*, the Fourth and Fifth Amendments "run almost into each other" 116 U.S. at 630. However, the inference that privacy is fully protected by the Fourth Amendment only when the individual is suspected of criminal activity was rejected by the court *in camera* Vs. *Municipal Court 387 U.S. 523 (1967)* .

In *Olmstead* vs. *United States 277 U.S. 438 (1928)*, the Supreme Court retreated from the broad "formulation of *Boyd* to a mechanistic interpretative of the Fourth Amendment by sanctioning a home telephone tap that did not constitute a technical trespass. Chief Justice Taft, writing for the court, interpreted the Fourth Amendment, as forbidding only "an actual physical invasion of [one's] house". By emphasizing the manner rather than the effect of invasion, the holding narrowed the concept of privacy, underlying the Fourth Amendment. In an often, quoted dissent, Justice Brandeis adhered to the broader view.

The makers of the Constitution conferred, as against the Government, the right to be let alone – the most comprehensive of right, and the right most valued by civilised men. To protect that right, every unjustifiable intrusion by the Government, upon the privacy of the individual, whatever the means employed, must be deemed a violation of the Fourth Amendment.

One author (Beaney) interpreted Justice Brandeis' construction of the Fourth Amendment to require that "all government intrusions on a person's privacy at home, in his papers and effects, and on his free movement would have ....to be justified with the government forced to bear the burden of showing why a particular form of interference was reasonable. Privacy though not absolute, would have a high place in the hierarchy of protected values.

In *Katz* vs. *United States, 389 U.S. 347* (1967), the court returned to a more expansive view of the Fourth Amendment by excluding evidence obtained by the use of an electronic listening and recording device attached to the outside of a public telephone booth. Abadoning the ***Olmstead trespass doctrine***, the court based its decision on the sweeping proposition that the "Fourth Amendment protects people, not places. What a person knowingly exposes to the public even in his own home or office, is not a subject of Fourth Amendment protection.... But what he seeks to preserve as private, even in an area accessible to the public, may be constitutionally protected. The Fourth Amendment applied in this instance, the court stated, because the defendants had "justifiably relied" upon the privacy afforded by the public phone booth. In his concurrence, Justice Harlan understood the court's holding to require.

First, that a person have exhibited an actual (subjective) expectation of privacy, and second, that the expectation be one that society is prepared to recognise as "***reasonable***". Thus, a man's home is, for most purposes, a place where he expects privacy, but objects activities or statements that he exposes to the "***plain view***" of the outsiders are not "***protected***" because no intention to keep them to himself has been exhibited. On the other hand, conversations in the open would not be protected against being overheard, for the expectation of privacy under the circumstances would be unreasonable.

While the *Katz* view of the privacy concept underlying the Fourth Amendment goes only to disclosure and not to autonomy, and is therefore not as broad as the implications of *Boyd*, the decision suggests that the Fourth Amendment – equally applicable in the non-criminal context – gives rise to a zone of privacy adhering to the individual at times even in situations outside the home. Because, the test turns on what society deems a reasonable expectation of privacy, the individual of course, receives more protection within his house than without, in accordance with the common law prior to the Constitution. But, while applicable in broad range of contexts, the Fourth Amendment rights of disclosural privacy affords minimum protectioin because it must yield in the face of reasonable Government intrusion. While the Fourth Amendment has been interpreted to require probable cause or a warrant for searches in the criminal context, and in administrative searches involving physical intrusion by Government agents into the home, it is satisfied in the case of questionnaires, if the information sought is "reasonable related to governmental purposes and functions". Under this test, census questionaire have been sustained, despite the wide scope of census questions. In sum, Fourth Amendment privacy poses at most a minor barrier to government collection of information from the population at large.

[The notion of a "Zone of Privacy" outside his home was apparently rejected in *Paris Adult Theatre I* vs. *Slation, 413 U.S. 49 (1973)*. However, unlike *Katz* which was a disclosure case, *Paris* involved the privacy of autonomy. Petitioner, in *Paris* had been enjoined by the Georgia Supreme Court from exhibiting two allegedly obscene films. They argued that the constitutional doctrine of privacy laid down in *Stanley* Vs. *Georgia, 394 U.S. 557 (1969)*, where the court held that the possession of obscene materials in the home was beyond the reach of the State's criminal law because the Constitution protected the right to receive information and ideas and to be generally free from government intrusion, applied outside the home as well. The court rejected this extension of *Stanley*, holding that the privacy of the home could not be equated with a general zone of privacy that follows a consumer of obscene materials, wherever he goes, *413 U.S. at 66*. These cases indicate that certain aspects of privacy of autonomy, while protected inside the home, are not necessarily protected outside the home. The privacy of disclosure however, is oriented to the person not to the place, and thus should follow "*the individual*", wherever he may be. Thus, *Paris* should not be interpreted as rejecting the zone of privacy notion with respect to disclosure.]

A list of cases beginning in the 1950's suggests that the First Amendment is a source of a right of disclosural privacy. The court concluded that "privacy of association" was a necessary concomitant to First Amendment freedoms, that forced disclosure would abridge those freedoms, and that to justify such an abridgement a State must convincingly show a substantial relation between the information sought and a subject of overriding and compelling State interest. Other related cases have similarly made clear that a State's power to make inquiries about a person's beliefs or associatons is limited by the First Amendment. Although these cases have focused on the "chilling effect" that disclosure would have on the exercise of First Amendment freedoms, that clearly hold that the First Amendment protects disclosural privacy interests and lend at least some support for the construction of a right of a disclosural privacy.

There are, however, two limitations on the general rule that Governments cannot violate constitutional rights when acquiring information that may restrict an individual's ability to assert a First Amendment privacy right as a defence to a governmental demand for information. First, recipients of information requests generally are unable to assert by way of defense violations of the constitutional rights of third parties, at least where no inquiry in fact is demonstrated by the recipient. In *NAACP* Vs. *Alabama, 357 U.S. 449 (1958), the NAACP* was allowed to assert the First Amendment rights of its members in response to a State request for its membership list. Similarly in *Griswold* Vs. *Connecticut*, a doctor and a birth control official were permitted to assert the privacy rights of the recipients of contraceptives as a defence to criminal charges of aiding and abetting the use of birth control devices. Second, as pointed out in *Eastland* Vs. *United States Serviceman's Fund*, the speech and debate clause limits the ability to raise constitutional defences in response to requests for information from members of Congress or their aides. While significant, the restriction on the assertion of constitutional rights resulting from the speech and debate clause is of limited force; it arises only at the federal governmental level when information is requested of third parties by members of Congress or by congressional aids carrying out legislative tasks.

The final three possible constitutional bases for a right to privacy – the penumbras emanating from the first Eight Amendments, the Ninth Amendment and the concept of ordered liberty guaranteed by the due process clauses of the Fifth and Fourteenth Amendments – have been explored collectively in a series of cases dealing with the privacy of autonomy. In *Griswold* vs. *Connecticut* the court struck down statutes prohibiting the prescription or use of contraceptives in so far as the statutes related to married couples. Six Justices, in their opinions, found an independent right of privacy, although they could not agree on its source. Justice Douglas, writing for the court, advanced the penumbra theory. He attempted to demonstrate that the Bill of Rights applies to the States through the due process clause of the Fourteenth Amendment and protects the right of marital privacy by arguing that the specific guarantees of the first eight Amendments give rise to "peripheral rights" without which the specific rights would be less secure. Thus, he asserted that the First Amendment whose penumbra includes associational privacy, the Third Amendment, which prohibits quartering soldiers in any house in time of peace without the owner's consent, the Fourth Amendment, which protects against unreasonable search and seizure, and the Fifth Amendment, which protects the citizen against self-incrimination when taken together gave rise to "*Zones of Privacy*".

Rejecting the penumbra approach, Justice Harlan considered the right of privacy so fundamental that it was "implicit in the concept of ordered liberty" and hence protected by *"due process"*. Justice Harlan had previously advanced the fundamental rights approach to privacy in *Poe* vs. *Ullman* where he stated that "it is not the particular enumeration of rights in the first eight Amendments which spell out the reach of the Fourteenth Amendment due process, but rather....those concepts which are considered to embrace those rights which are....fundamental, which belong ...to the citizens of all free governments. This approach was also adopted by Justice Goldberg, even though he joined in the court's opinion and stated that he was adding his own opinion merely to "emphasize the relevance of the Ninth Amendment." Justice Goldberg argued that the Ninth Amendment shows a belief of the Constitution's authors that fundamental rights exist that are not expressly enumerated in the first eight Amendments and an intent that the list of rights included there not be deemed exhaustive. One must look, he stated, to the traditions and collective conscience of our people to determine whether a principle is so rooted there....as to be ranked as fundamental. The right of privacy in Justice Goldberg's view was just such a fundamental personal right, which emanated "from the totality of the constitutional scheme under which we live."

One other Supreme Court case, *Stanley* vs. *Georgia, 394 U.S. 557*

(1969), expanded the privacy concept to include the right to possess obscene materials in one's home. While the court based ostensibly its holding on the first amendment, the decision drew in part upon a "fundamental right to be free, except in very limited circumstances from unwanted governmental intrusions into one's privacy. The privacy underpinning in *Stanley* was clearly significant because the case is difficult to reconcile with other cases holding that the first Amendment does not apply to obscenity and because the right recognised in *Stanley* is limited to the house, unlike most First Amendment rights. Moreover, the court cited *Griswold* in addition to First Amendment cases to support the proposition that "the right to receive information and ideas" is "fundamental to our free society". In short, the court apparently relied on First Amendment considerations to justify expanding the incipient privacy right.

[As early as *Meyer* vs. *Nebraska, 262 U.S. 390 (1923)*, the court recognised certain "fundamental rights" that would be protected despite their lack of explicit recognition in the Constitution. In subsequent cases, the court recognised as fundamental rights included in the liberty clause of the Fifth and Fourteenth Amendments, the personal intimacies of the home, the family, procreation, motherhood, marriage and child rearing. *Eisenstadt* vs. *Baird, 405 U.S. 438 (1972), Stanley* vs. *Georgia, 394 U.S. 567 (1969), Loving* Vs. *Virginia, 388 U.S. 1 (1967), Griswold* vs. *Connecticut, 381 U.S. 479 (1965), Skinner* vs. *Oklahoma, 316 U.S. 535 (1942), Pierce* vs. *Society of Sisters, 268 U.S. 510 (1925)*. In *Village of Belle Terra* Vs. *Boraas, 416 U.S.I (1974)* (Marshall J. Dissenting) Justice Marshall stated that the right of privacy should extend to the selection of living companions. "The choice of household companions -- of whether a person's intellectual and emotional needs are best met by living with family, friends, professional associate or others – involves deeply personal considerations as to the kind and quality of intimate relationship within the home. That decision surely falls within the ambit of the right to privacy protected by the Constitution". *416 U.S. at 16*. If these rights apply to the states through the due process clause of the Fourteenth Amendment, one may also find a right of privacy either in that same clause or in the liberty clause of the Fifth Amendment applying to the Federal Government.]

The contours of the privacy rights developed by these cases seem extraordinarily difficult to determine for the activities it has been invoked to protect lack a clear interrelationship. The court often speaks of privacy as if it were a single right, but it seems more accurate to conceive of privacy as that characteristic common to those individual actions that the court has been willing to recognise as fundamental rights. Thus, the court has stated that "only personal rights that can be deemed fundamental or 'implicit in the concept of ordered liberty',... are included in this guarantee of personal privacy". It is clear that not all fundamental rights fall within the ambit of the privacy right, but an underpinning of strong privacy interests seems to enhance the possibility that a particular right will be deemed fundamental. The actions protected thus far in the name of privacy relate to the home, the family, and individual sexuality. The court seems to be guided by its perception of activities that society views as private and that are thus not fit subjects for Government regulations. But it is not at all clear what other actions popularly considered private will receive constitutional protection.

The above discussed privacy cases involve autonomy, not disclosure. A right of disclosural privacy, however, can be derived from the fundamental privacy rights by analogy to the First Amendment Right of disclosural privacy. Disclosure of information relating to an individual's participation in particular activities may deter an individual from engaging in those activities. Where the activities have the status of fundamental rights, any such deterrent effect would be an impermissible "chill". But the disclosural privacy right derived from the privacy cases arguably should go beyond those situations in which a chilling effect can be shown. For example, requiring disclosure of the reasons why a woman decides to have an abortion may not deter the exercise of this fundamental right because the consequences of having an unwanted child are so enormous. Nevertheless, this information seems so private that the Government should not in most instances be able to require its disclosure. The same high regard for privacy that led the court to conclude that government regulation of abortion is improper, at least in the first trimester, should mandate disclosural privacy with regard to information concerning abortions in the first trimester. In situations where the State's regulatory purposes are outweighed by a concern for individual privacy, the State should be unable to investigate, even for a tangentially related purpose such as public health, without showing a very strong interest. Thus, with regard to information relating to contraception, the bearing and rearing of children, private obscenity and any other activities recognised as fundamental private rights, it can be argued that there is a corresponding fundamental right of disclosural privacy, although no case to date has so held. While the right of disclosural privacy derived in this manner from fundamental rights would not be as broad as the disclosural privacy right inferred from the Fourth Amendment, its exceptions would be more restricted. A State infringement of fundamental rights can only be justified by a compelling State interest and the infringing legislation "must be narrowly drawn" to express only the legitimate State interests at stake. Thus it seems possible to develop a right of disclosural privacy offering more protection than the broad but low walls of the Fourth Amendment.

(3) *Indian Position*

Art. 20 (3) of the Constitution of India embodies a fundamental principle of British Jurisprudence, and has also its counterpart in the Federal Constitution of the United States of America. The basic principle of clause (3) is the presumption of innocence of the accused casting the burden of proof on the prosecution to prove the guilt. The principle of this clause finds expression in the provisions of the Code of Criminal Procedure, the Evidence Act etc. Clause (3) does not create a new right but only gives a new status to an old right by making it a fundamental right under the Constitution. Clause (3) must be construed strictly and unless the condition of this clause are fully satisfied, a person cannot claim the immunity conferred by it. The effect of clause (3) is to make any evidence which is prohibited by the clause inadmissible against an accused person.

In order that clause (3) of Art. 20 may apply the person compelled to be a witness against himself must have filled the character of an accused person at the time of the compulsion. The "person compelled" must have been an accused person in a criminal prosecution. Where a person who is not accused of any criminal offence, is compelled to give evidence and such evidence ultimately leads to a criminal prosecution being launched against him, there is no violation of clause (3). "*Compulsion*" during police investigation is covered by clause (3) provided the compelled person is an "accused" at that stage. He need not be figuring as an accused person before a court of law at that time. The protection conferred by clause (3) is not limited to testimonial compulsion in court.

"*To be a witness*" is not equivalent to "furnishing evidence" in its widest significance, that is to say, as including not merely making of oral or written statement but also production of documents or giving materials which may be relevant at a trial to determine the guilt or innocence of the accused. Giving thumb impressions or impressions of foot or palm or fingers or specimen writings or showing parts of the body by way of identification are not included in the expression "*to be a witness*". "*To be a witness* " means imparting knowledge in respect of relevant facts by an oral statement or a statement in writing made or given in court or otherwise.

Section 73 of the Evidence Act which provides that the court may direct any person including an accused person present in court to write any words or figures or to give his thumb impressions does not conflict with clause (3) of Art. 20. Even the compelled production of documents or other incriminating material by the accused will not make him "*a witness*" for the purpose of clause (3) of Art. 20. Where the document which is compelled to be produced contains a statement by the accused himself of a self-incriminatory nature, he would be acting as a witness against himself within the meaning of clause (3) of Art. 20.

The search and seizure of documents or other incriminating material, whether under the orders of the court, or by the police during investigation will not be a proceeding by which the accused is compelled to be a witness against himself. An order for production of documents under section 94 of the Criminal P.C. cannot be passed against an accused person. Accused cannot be compelled to produce articles likely to implicate him or may be proved as incriminatory circumstances against him at trial.

The words "*the person*" in section 91 Criminal Procedure Code 1974, do not include an accused. Article 20 (3) has been construed to mean that an accused person cannot be compelled to disclose documents, which are incriminatory and based on his knowledge. Therefore, the accused who is tried for offence under section 468 of Penal Code cannot be directed to produce alleged forged document. In an American case the scope of the Fourth Amendment of the Constitution of the United States was invoked with reference to the word "*houses*". Protection afforded by the Fourth Amendment extends to commercial premises. A search was conducted without warrant in Union office. Document searched admitted in evidence for conviction on charge of conspiracy and coercion. Conviction was held illegal.

Privilege against self-incrimination by production of corporate records applies only against the record themselves and all oral testimony by individuals can properly be compelled only by exchange of immunity for waiver of the privilege (Fifth Amendment of the Constitution of the United States). In privilege against self-incrimination, rule permitting compelled production of corporate records by their custodian may be invoked only against a party who is in fact the custodian of the records in question.

Where the property has passed into the custody of the court, the production by the person entrusted with its temporary custody even if he happens to be an accused in obedience to the order of the court would not amount to his making any statement, written or oral, or imparting any knowledge in regard thereto within Article 20 (3), he can be compelled to produce the seized document made over to him.

In proceedings under Section 67 of the Factories Act, it is not competent for the Magistrate to issue a summons under section 94 Cr. P.C. to the accused to produce certain documents which were in his custody. The documents are likely to be self-incriminatory. An Income-Tax practitioner was called upon to produce documents in his possession during course of investigation pertaining to the firms. In such a case Art. 20 (3) is not applicable. An order by a Magistrate directing the accused charged for publishing inflammatory articles in newspapers, to produce the original of newspapers so as to enable the prosecution to adduce secondary evidence of the contents of newspapers on record, does not amount to testimonial compulsion forbidden by Art. 20. An attempt by prosecution to comply with the provisions of the Evidence Act, so as to enable it to adduce secondary evidence in a case cannot possibly amount to compelling the accused to give evidence against himself.

Section 27 of Evidence Act enabling disclosure statement of an accused admissible in evidence is an exception to the general rule under Art. 20 (3) barring self-incrimination. Persistent questioning of the accused in custody of the Police negatives the impression that the confessional statements are voluntary. If the information by the accused leading to the discovery of facts referred to in Section 27 of Evidence Act has been obtained by compulsion, it will be inadmissible under clause (3). If the information from the accused leading to discovery of facts has not been obtained by compulsion, it will be inadmissible under clause (3) of Art. 20 of the Indian Constitution.

Previous to the Constitution, the information under Section 27 of the Evidence Act, would have been admissible in evidence although it had been obtained under compulsion.

A mere voluntary confession of guilt by an accused person or any statement obtained from the accused without the use of any compulsion is not inadmissible in evidence against him at the inquiry or trial against him. Article 20 (3) strikes at confessions and self-incriminations but leaves untouched other relevant facts. Merely because the accused fancied that by such answer he would incriminate himself, he could not claim the privilege of silence. It must appear to the court that the implications of the question in which it is asked, make it evident that a responsive answer on an explanation of why it cannot be answered might be dangerous because injurious disclosure could result. The apprehension of incrimination from the answer sought must be substantial and real as distinguished from danger of remote possibilities or fanciful flow of inference.

Section 5 (1) (e), Prevention of Corruption Act does not contravene Art. 20 (3) of the Constitution. If a person accused of an offence makes a voluntary statement which is incriminating or is forced by circumstances to make a statement which may be incriminatory, it cannot be said that he is being "compelled" to be a witness against himself. It is open to the accused to waive the privilege of immunity from self-incrimination granted by clause (3) of Art. 20.

"*Compulsion*" in clause (3) of Art. 20 means duress and unless duress was exercised against the accused he cannot be held to have been compelled to be a witness against himself. Compulsion may take many forms. A person accused of an offence may be subject to physical or mental injury. He may be starved or beaten and a confession may be extorted from him. By deceitful means he may be induced to believe that his son is being tortured in an adjoining room and by such inducement he may be compelled to make an incriminating statement. Police officer is certainly a person in authority. Insistence on answering is a form of pressure especially in the atmosphere of the police station under certain safeguards erasing duress are adhered to. Frequent threats of prosecution if there is failure to answer may by itself not amount to duress but the manner of mentioning it to the victim of interrogation may introduce an element of tension and tone of command perilously hovering near compulsion.

Whether "*compulsion*" was exercised depends on the circumstances of each case. The mere fact that the police asked the accused to do a certain thing, will not amount to "*compulsion*". The mere fact that the accused made the statement while in police custody does not prove that the accused was compelled to make the statement. The use of third degree methods for obtaining information no doubt amounts to "*compulsion*". The mere questioning of an accused person by police officer resulting in a voluntary statement is not "*compulsion*". Being bound to answer questions or furnish informatin on threat of being sentenced to imprisonment or other punishment is legal compulsion within clause (3) of Art. 20.

Search of premises occupied by the accused without the accused being compelled to be a party to such search would not be violative of the constitutional guarantees enshrined in Art. 20 (3). Where any document or other incriminating material is secured by a Government Officer as a result of search and seizure the accused is not being "*compelled*" to be witness against himself. In an American case, a person was arrested in his home. The whole house was searched without warrant. 4th and 15th Amendments of the American Constitution were contravened. As the scope of the search being unreasonable, the conviction on that basis was illegal. The provisions relating to search contained in *Section 93 (1) Cr. P.C. (1974)* are not hit by Art. 20 (3). A doctrinaire insistence that no such search warrant should be issued to find out articles in the possession or control of the accused which may have undesirable results. Where an accused, even on being warned that he is not bound to make any statement, makes a statement, there cannot be said to be any compulsion. Whereupon an order to produce certain documents, the accused made a statement under protest, it was held that there was "*compulsion*". Where the talk between the accused and another person was tape-recorded, without the knowledge of the accused it cannot be said there was any compulsion on the accused in as much as the statements made by him were not extracted by force or in an appropriate manner.

In a case from U.S.A., a tax-payer has no privilege under the constitutional right against self-incrimination to file a false return when faced with the choice of prescription for failure to file a return or for incriminating statements in a truthful return the resulting pressure is not "*testimonial compulsion*". The Fifth Amendment privilege grants a right to a witness to refuse to answer self-incriminating questions and to remain silent. But the Fifth Amendment privilege does not endow the witness with a licence to commit perjury. Even the predicament of being forced to choose between incriminatory truth and falsehood as opposed to refusing to answer does not justify perjury. If the citizen answers the question, the answer must be truthful.

*

XII

DIGNITY AND PRIVACY

> " ... Privacy is control over when and by whom the various parts of us can be sensed by others. By 'sensed' is meant simply seen, heard, touched, smelled or tasted."
>
> – *Richard B. Parker in his "A Definition of Privacy" quoted in "Philosophy and Public Affairs" (1975) Vol. 4, No. 4, p. 295-314.*

Privacy is the guarantor of individual moral autonomy, a basic value in a democratic system of government, Privacy can be defined as the right to control one's information system and one's physical being. The latter right has been traditionally conceived in American society as the right to be secured against unauthorised entries and seizures. Both rights are closely related to the principle of respect for persons. Both must be reinterpreted in the light of changing technological and social contexts. Privacy is violated whenever a person's moral autonomy or self-image are impinged upon, even without affecting his conduct. Altering an individual's self-perception against his will offends human dignity. If we are able to regulate a person's conduct or keep it under surveillance (as in the system of dispensing welfare), we are, in fact, curtailing his responsibility as a moral agent making free choice. This limits the option open to persons regarding relationship with others, their physical mobility and their own self-perception. Privacy, the control of one's own person and of the extension of one's person in the form of information, is at the basis of man's claim for human dignity.

Clinton Rossiter has said that privacy is a special kind of independence which can be understood as an attempt to secure autonomy in at least a few personal and spiritual concerns, if necessary in defiance of all pressures of modern society. Privacy according to him, seeks to erect an unbreakable wall of dignity and reserve against the entire world. The free man is the private man, who keeps some of his thoughts and judgements entirely to himself, who feels no overriding compulsion to share everything of value with others, not even with those he loves and trusts. Some of the Justices of the Supreme Court of America who have spoken about it have attempted to define privacy as an aspect of the pursuit of happiness [*Poe* Vs. *Ullman, 367 U.S. 497; Goldman* Vs. *United States, 316 U.S. 129; Public Utility Commission* vs. *Pollock, 343 U.S. 451*]. Pursuit of happiness required certain amount of liberty to do as one likes. Privacy requires a private enclave as it were where an individual is at liberty to do what he wants. An intrusion on privacy threatens that liberty just as assault battery or imprisonment. It is really an offence "*to the reasonable sense of personal dignity*". There can perhaps be no objection in regarding intrusion upon our privacy as a dignity tort. The harm caused by this intrusion is incapable of being repaired and the loss suffered in dignity is not susceptible of being made good in damages. The injury is to the spiritual element in our otherwise mundane composition.

One may desire to live a life of seclusion, another a life of publicity. Still another a life of publicity concerning certain matters and privacy as respects other matters of life. Neither an individual nor the public has a right arbitrarily to take away from him that liberty. It is difficult to find words adequate to express the mental conditions resulting from the pain on the violation of the right of privacy. We speak without sufficient discrimination of it as distress, anguish, anxiety, mental illness, indignity and mental suffering.

The common interest involved in all these conditions resulting from violation of privacy is spiritual in character rather than any interest in reputation or property. Although the American Federal Constitution does not mention the right to privacy explicitly, the Supreme Court has declared it as a fundamental right emanating from the totality of the constitutional provisions; having its roots in particular in the First, Third, Fourth, Fifth and Ninth Amendments all intended to serve "inviolate personality" and thus promote the pursuit of happiness [*Roe* vs. *Wade* and *Griswold* vs. *Connecticut*].

(1) *Distinction between invasion of Privacy as a tort from other Torts*

What distinguishes the invasion of privacy as a tort from other torts which involve insult to human dignity and individuality is merely the means used to perpetuate the wrong. The woman who is petted indecently suffers the same indignity as the woman whose birth pangs are overseen. The woman whose photograph is exhibited for advertisement is degraded and demeaned as surely as the woman who is kept aboard in a pleasure yacht against her will. This is an example of intrusion upon personal intimacy and using techniques of publicity to make a public spectacle of an otherwise private life.

Generally speaking a civilised man has a different concept of life and consequently of his home. The danger of not having a private zone for every individual was indicated by Douglas J. He said, "that a time may come when no one can be recorded for use at some future time. When every one will be in fear that his most sacred thoughts are no longer his own but belong to the Government. When the most confidential conversations are open to eager, prying ears; when that time comes privacy and with it liberty is gone. If a man's privacy is invaded at will, who can say that he is free? If his every word is taken down and evaluated or if he is afraid of every word he says, who can say he enjoys freedom of speech? If every association of man is known and recorded, if his conversation with his associates are purloined, who can say that he enjoys the freedom of association?"

The right of privacy attempts to preserve individuality by placing sanction upon outrageous or unreasonable violations of conditions for its sustenance. This then is the social value to be served by the law of privacy. It is served not only in the law of tort but in other areas. Protection of privacy is the central purpose of the privilege against self-incrimination in Article 20 (3). The privilege reflects the respect which we accord to the inviolability of human personality and the right of each individual to a private zone where he may have his private life. It reflects the private inner sanctions of the individual feeling and thought and prescribes state intrusion to extract self-condemnation.

We are all of necessity subject to some minimum amount of scrutiny by our neighbours as a condition of civilized life in a society. Man has always relished the knowledge of the intimate details of lives and doings of others especially his neighbours. The most obvious and conflicting value is the public interest in news and information which must of necessity run counter to the individual interest of privacy. Even if the nature of the interest involved in privacy is understood it will not resolve this conflict of values, except perhaps to make it clear that one of the values to be weighed is that interest. All tort privacy cases involve the same interest in preserving human dignity and individuality will have important consequences for this development of tort.

(2) *Sanctity of the individual as limited by various other interests of society*

Society has a strong interest in protecting the sanctity, the dignity and the integrity of the human person. John Stuart Mill once wrote:

> "There is a circle around every individual human being, which no Government, be it that of one of a few, or of the many, ought to be permitted to overstep; there is a part of the life of every person who has come to years of discretion, within which the individuality of that person ought to reign uncontrolled either by any other individual or by the public collectively. That there is, or ought to be, some space in human existence thus entrenched around and sacred from authoritative intrusion, no one who professes the smallest regard to human freedom or dignity will call in question."

[*Principles of Political Economy* (1848) *Vol II, pp. 560, 561*]

The American Judiciary has generally acknowledged that there is such a societal interest – an "*inherent right of bodily integrity*". Furthermore the privacy of the individual from assault upon his person by officers of the state is a right so basic and fundamental that it is binding upon the states under the due process clause of the Fourteenth Amendment. [*Rochin* Vs. *California (1952) 342 U.S. 165*].

One of the most important societal interests is that of safeguarding and protecting the public health and it can be expected that this interest will prevail over most other interests. Perhaps a majority of our people feel that society has a legitimate interest in preventing the propagation of congenital mental defectives. Such interest, according to the U.S. Supreme Court justifies a state in exposing such defectives to compulsory sterilisation [*Buck* Vs. *Bell (1927) 274 U.S. 200*]. In *Skinner* Vs. *Oklahoma* (1942) 316 U.S. 535, the U.S. Supreme Court has referred to the right to enter into the marriage relation and procreate children as "fundamental" among "*the basic civil rights of man*" and truly a basic liberty. In area involving interests less precious than the sanctity of the person, the court has demanded that the state explore reasonable alternatives that will as adequately protect the interests of society without infringing upon the person. Here reasonable alternatives seem to be available to a state concerned with the perpetuation of congenital mental defectives – these unfortunate individuals can be institutionalised and segregated from members of the other sex without prohibitive costs to society. Justice Wiest of the Michigan Supreme Court once wrote:

> "The bodies of citizens may not, under legislative mandate, be cut and power of procreation destroyed by litigation or mutilation or carrying out of organs."

The United States Supreme Court has invalidated a State Sterilization Act which authorised the sterilisation of those convicted for the third time of larceny but made no similar assault upon the bodies of those for the third time convicted of such crimes as embezzlement. The Supreme Court stated:

> "When the law lays an unequal hand on those who have committed intrinsically the same quality of offence and sterilizes one and not the other, it has made as invidious a discrimination as if it had selected a particular race or nationality for oppressive treatment." [*Skinner* vs. *Oklahoma (1942) 316 U.S. 525*].

Under equal protection of the laws any semblance of unreasonable differentiation in sterilisation statutes or their practice will invalidate the same. Sterilisation cannot be imposed upon persons as punishment for crime; courts rather generally agreeing that such is cruel and unusual punishment. [*Davis* vs. *Berry (1914) D.C. Iowa, 216 F 413, Mickle* vs. *Henrichs (1918) DC Nev. 262 F. 687*].

(3) *Detecting Crime*

Society has a legitimate interest in suppressing crime and detecting criminals. However, it is established by an abundance of authority that the officers of the State cannot degrade the individual in their search for proof of crime and the identity of criminals. The court in *Breithaupt* vs. *Abram (1957) 352 U.S. 432*, observed:

"As against the right of an individual that his person be held inviolable, even against so light an intrusion as is involved in applying a blood test of the kind to which millions of Americans submit as a matter of course nearly every day must be set the interests of the society in the scientific determination of intoxican, one of the great causes of the mortal hazards of the road."

The Supreme Court in *Schemerber* vs. *California (1966) 384 U.S. 757* noted: "The overriding function of the Fourth Amendment is to protect personal privacy and dignity against unwarranted intrusion by the Sate." It added:

> "The integrity of an individual's person is a cherished value of our society. That we today hold that the Constitution does not forbid the states' minor intrusions into an individual's body under stringently limited conditions in no way indicates that it permits more substantial intrusions, or intrusions under other conditions."

Said Justice Fortan in dissent:

> "As prosecutor, the State has no right to commit any kind of violence upon the person, or to utilise the results of such a tort, and the extraction of blood, over protest is an act of violence."

Society has a worthy interest in attempting to prevent anti-social conduct, and it is sometimes thought that physically punishing those convicted of crime deters them and others from wayward behaviour. The Eighth Amendment in the case of the Federal Government, and the Fourteenth in the case of the States, prevent the imposition of cruel and unusual punishment even upon those convicted of the most heinous offences. Another way of protecting society's interest in the dignity of the individual notwithstanding his anti-social behaviour is the free exercise of religion guarantee of the First Amendment.

(4) *Autonomy and State Interference: Indian Viewpoint*

In the process of making such a fateful choice as to when, where and how if at all she should beget, bear, deliver and rear a child, the wife consistent with her human dignity should never be excluded. Conception and delivery of a child involves the most intimate use of her body. The marvel of creation takes place inside her body and the child that would be born is of her own flesh and blood. In a matter which is so intimately concerns her body and which is so vital for her life, a decree of restitution of conjugal rights by a court of law completely excludes her.

Our ancient Hindu system of matrimonial law fully upheld the duty of the wife to surrender to her husband. This could have been only because of its realisation that in a matter so intimately concerned the wife or the husband, the parties are better left alone without State interference. Can our Parliament now functioning under the constitutional constraints of the Fundamental Rights conceived and enacted for the preservation of human dignity and promotion of personal liberty, can legally impose sexual cohabitation between unwilling opposite sexual partner even if it be during the matrimony of the parties?

Art. 21 of the Indian Constitution prevents the State from treating the human life as that of any other animal. It is now well-established by the decisions of the Supreme Court that the word "life" occurring in Art. 21 has spiritual significance as the word "life" occurring in the famous 5th and 14th Amendments to the American Constitution does. In those constitutional provisions of the American Constitution, the "life" is interpreted by Mr. Justice Field in his dissenting judgement in ***Munn*** vs. ***Illinois (1877) 24 L Ed. p. 17*** to mean and signify more than a person's right to lead animal or vegetative existence. Field J. said in the above ***Munn's*** case, "By the term life as here used something more is meant than mere animal existence." The contrast drawn by Field J. emphasizing the difference between existence of a free willing human and that of an unfree animal was accepted by Indian Supreme Court first in ***Kharak Singh*** Vs. *State of U.P. (1964) I.S.C.R.* 332 and next in ***Gobind*** Vs. *State of M.P. (1975) 3 SCR 946* transforming Art. 21 of Indian Constitution into a charter for civilisation.

In a later decision of the Supreme Court in ***Govind*** vs. ***State of M.P.*** *(AIR 1975 SC 1378)* Mathew J. taking the lead given by the minority judgement of Suba Rao J. in the above-mentioned ***Kharak Singh's Case*** *(AIR 1963* SC *1295)* and adverting to the American legal and philosophical literature on right to privacy and to the American cases reported in ***Griswold*** Vs. ***Connecticut*** *(1965) 14 L Ed. 2d. 510* ***and Jane Roe*** Vs. ***Henry Wade*** *(1973) 35 L Ed. 2d, p. 147* ruled that Art. 21 of Indian Constitution embraces the right to privacy and human dignity. The centrepiece of the judgement in ***Govind's Case*** is to hold that right to privacy is part of our Constitution and to stress its constitutional importance and to call for its protection. The learned judge then examined the content of the right to privacy and observed that "any right to privacy must encompass and protect that personal intimacies of the home, the family, marriage, motherhood, procreation and child rearing." The learned judge stressed the primordial importance of the right to privacy for human happiness and directed the courts not to reject the privacy-dignity claims brought before them except where the countervailing State interests are shown to have over- weighing importance. Meaning thereby that privacy-dignity claims deserve to be examined with care and to be denied only when an important countervailing interest is shown to be superior. Govind's case thus firmly laid it down that Art. 21 protects the right to privacy and promotes the individual dignity mentioned in the preamble to our Constitution."

*

XIII

PRIVACY AND OTHER CIVIL LIBERTIES

> "The phrase "procedure established by law" seems to be borrowed from Art. 31 of the Japanese Constitution. It is not shown that the word "law" means "jus" in the Japanese Constitution... The omission of the word "due" the limitation imposed by the word "procedure" and the insertion of the word "established" thus brings out more clearly the idea or legislative prescription in the expression used in Art. 21. By adopting the phrase "procedure established by law" the Constitution gave the legislature the final word to determine the law."
>
> – *A.K. Gopalan's Case*
> *(AIR 1950 SC 21)*

Under the American Constitution, safeguards for individual liberty are provided by the "due process clause" and other provisions of the Bill of Rights. Under the Indian Constitution, its founders without being dógmatic about any particular formula or phraseology, have achieved the same objective in a different way. The due process means both procedural as well as substantive limitation, though the former is more important and has been often relied on by the U.S. Supreme Court, as a limitation on the exercise of governmental power, Federal as well as State. Further due process requirement is a limitation on both executive and legislative power of the governments.

Art. 21 as adopted by the Indian Constituent Assembly and as later interpreted by the Supreme Court, authorises the legislature to pass a law prescribing the procedure by which a person may be deprived of his life or personal liberty, and in so far as the Article shields such a law passed by an Indian legislature from being challenged in a Court of Law on the ground of being an 'unjust' law, it does not lay down a constitutional system comparable to one adopted by the American Constitution, with the due process concept lying at the base of it. The Indian Constitution, on the whole lays down a system of fair procedure for deprivation of life and personal liberty and at some points the procedural guarantees provided by it even exceed those provided by the American *due process clause* as interpreted by the U.S. Supreme Court.

(1) ***Liberty–Its Restraint and Limitation***

Liberty stands behind the very exercise of power. Whatever kind of power one has, there is usually a liberty to exercise it or not. The giving of equal liberties could reach the point of anarchy and the disintegration of society; so once again the question is whether liberties to destroy society should be allowed at all or else how their exercise is to be restricted. Even where the law restricts liberty by replacing it with a duty not to do some act so that the individual no longer has any liberty at law he still has an inner moral liberty to obey the law or to disobey.

It is superficial attractive to contend that there should be equal liberty all round, or at least that it should be curtailed equally. The matter is not so simple, whether minorities or individuals are allowed certain liberties at all depends, not on equality but on the priority of values. The competing values are those of individual liberty of action and the social interest. If everyone insisted one complete liberty of action in using the highway, traffic would seize up; so certain limitations on liberty are imposed on various other kinds of liberties in order to hold society together.

Social existence depends upon co-ordination, which in turn requires restraint in individual action. Such restraint may spring from laws imposing duties to limit liberties or it may spring spontaneously from moral sense. Freedom and duty are jurally opposite each beginning where the other ends. Accordingly, legal restrictions may only be relaxed safely when there is a sufficient degree of self-control bred from moral discipline. To relax legal restraints at a time when there is less and less assurance of self-discipline is the path to social destruction; which is why the reinforcement of moral discipline by law must continue.

Professor Hart says that "some shared morality is essential to the existence of any society." "*Essential*" has two aspects, on the one hand, it means that some shared morality is an ingredient of any and every community *i.e.*, a part of every community is its morality. On the other hand, it may also connote certain additional moral ideas which have become part of the fabric of a particular society. This distinction provides the respective basis for what might be termed the "Institutional" and the "Utilitarian" interpretations of "moral position".

(A) *The "Institutional" Basis*: In order to preserve itself society is entitled to use its laws when the limit of tolerance is reached. The following are the limits within which legislators should act:

(a) There should be the maximum of freedom consistent with the integrity of society.

(b) The limit of tolerance is reached when the ordinary man would feel indignation and distrust.

(c) Law-makers should be slow to change.

(d) Privacy should be respected as far as possible.

(e) Laws should be concerned with minimum, not maximum standards.

(B) *The "Utilitarian"* Basis: Professor Hart proceeds from John Stuart Mill's utilitarianism. He admits that "some shared morality is essential to the existence of any society," but the significance of this is that it connotes morality which is the *sine qua non* of the existence of any and every kind of society, not just of a particular society.

Mill's plea for liberation was that laws should not uphold morality as such, but should only seek to prevent harm to others as this is disruptive of any kind of society. It may be observed in passing that Mill's position concedes a moral premise, namely that it is morally wrong, to uphold morality as such.

Harm to others includes many things. According to Mill, "The principle of freedom cannot require that he should be free not to be free. It is not freedom to be allowed to alienate his freedom." So, laws should indeed uphold some moral positions, though they advance different reasons, the dispute touches on the limits which should be set on their use. According to Utilitarians they should only uphold that aspect of morality which is a *sine qua non* of any type of society, whereas according to Lord Devlin they should be concerned with all the morality that constitutes the *sine qua non* of the particular society. Apart from this, the Utilitarians only mask, but fail to expel morality from considerations, while Lord Devlin fails to provide a workable test as to where legal reinforcement should stop. Perhaps, the answer is not be found in a single formula.

Granting that laws should uphold morality at least to some extent, something has now to be said about the word *"uphold"*. The two concepts that may be invoked are disability and duty. Abolishing the duty not to indulge, *e.g.*, in homosexuality does not affect its immoral quality, just as adultery remains immoral though it is no longer forbidden in this country. The moral attitude might still be "upheld" by rules attaching disabilities with regard to immoral conduct. Direct prohibition of immoral conduct by means of duty is more troublesome. Its functioning should be taken into account alongwith other considerations. The following factors would seem to be relevant:

(1) the danger of the activity to others;
(2) the danger to the actor himself;
(3) economy of forces needed for detention and pursuit;
(4) equality of treatment;
(5) the nature of the sanction;
(6) possible hardship caused by the sanction;
(7) possible side effects.

Even where the law abolishes liberty by imposing a duty, the individual still has the moral liberty to obey, or not to obey. The ultimate check, therefore, on such liberty, and *a fortiori* on the liberty to exercise power, is one of self-restraint born of a sense of responsibility, when the point of moral liberty is reached any restraining influence on it must spring from inner motivations, whether through fear of punishment or through a sense of responsibility, which in turn is bound up with the extent to which people are prepared to accept standards and have a sense of purpose and faith in a way of life.

Resort to legal prohibition of undesirable behaviour may safely be kept to a minimum as long as there is acceptance of moral standards which discourage it for the self-restraint which these inspire will check any abuse of the liberty allowed at dare. The law can however, only help in the acceptance of standards by discouraging their abandonment. For instance, where there are laws, especially those embodying the standards of that shared morality, which according to Professor Hart is essential to any society, the upholding of such laws not only points to the existence of the standards, but also helps to preserve them by acting as a brake on their abandonment. It is precisely at a time when standards are being questioned that it becomes socially suicidal to relax laws simply because they are being questioned or are difficult to apply.

Upholding laws helps by preserving a "moral atmosphere", which is essential to preserving that shared morality, which in turn is essential to encouraging obedience and social existence. A commonly advanced reason for abolishing laws especially those concerning moral standards is that these may have become difficult to enforce (*i.e.*, detect and visit with sanctions). This is a dangerous argument. Unenforceability is a matter of degree, and difficulty of enforcement, however great, should never be a ground *per se* for abolishing any law. The argument rests on the premise that only enforceable laws should be preserved. But enforceability is less significant in ensuring obedience than the psychological pressure towards conformity exerted by the fact of other people's conformity. The more numerous the cases of disobedience, the weaker becomes the pressure. The danger of abolishing a law because it is unenforceable and is being disobeyed is that it weakens at one stroke the pressure to conform even to other enforceable laws, which is how laws once enforceable become unenforceable in time. In short, to talk of maintaining only enforceable laws is to take the first step towards undermining their enforceability.

(2) *Bodenheimer's view*

The element of generality is an important ingredient of the concept of law. First the approach produces a semantic uniformity in the use of the term "*law*". Second, by applying a uniform standard of adjudication to an indefinite number of equal or closely similar situations, we introduce an element of stability and coherence into the social order which guarantees internal peace and lays the groundwork for a fair and impartial administration of Justice without this necessarily imperfect striving for stability, law cannot exist.

The liberty of each is to be limited only by the equal liberties of all. This conception of justice was cast by Spencer into the mold of a celebrated formula. "Every man is free to do that which he wills, provided he infringes not the equal freedom of any other man." A position very similar to Spencer's was taken by the German philosopher Kant. He also used the concept of liberty for the purpose of defining the meaning of law and justice. Proceeding from the premise that liberty was the only original, natural right belonging to each man in his capacity as a human being, he described law (in the sense of just, adequate law) as "the totality of the conditions under which the arbitrary will of one can coexist with the arbitrary will of another under a general law of freedom".

In the opinion of Ward, justice consists in the "enforcement by society of an artificial equality in social conditions which are naturally unequal". While Ware concurs with Aristotle in making equality, the central idea in describing the goals of justice, his notion of equality is different from Aristotle's. Aristotle was ready to accept many natural inequalities, such as those created by sex and superior intelligence, and to make these natural inequalities the basis and justification for the unequal treatment of persons by the law. Ward, on the other hand, was convinced that natural inequality had nothing to do with justice. The "artificial equality" by which he sought to cut down the incidence and consequences of natural inequality was to be the deliberate objective of a social policy designed to achieve an unlimited equalization of opportunity for all members of a community or State. Each individual regardless of sex, race, nationality, class and social origin, was to be given a full chance to make good in life and lead a worthwhile existence.

The first and foremost condition for creating the widest possible equality of opportunity, in Ward's view, is the necessity for equalising intelligence among the members of the upper and lower classes of society. He admitted that not all men are equals intellectually but insisted that intellectual inequality was common to all classes. The general level of intelligence prevailing in the various strata of society could be equalized, in his view, and under a condition of universal enlightenment it would appear that the lower class was not inferior in intellectual ability to the upper class.

Most of the theories made either equality or freedom the focal point for approaching the problem of justice. A Scotish philosopher, W. R. Sorley claimed that no satisfactory doctrine of justice could be developed without finding a place for both equality and freedom in the scheme of societal organisation and without attempting to reconcile the potentially anti-thetical character of these two human values. He pointed out that liberty and equality may easily come into opposition in the social order, since the extension of liberty does not necessarily promote human equality. Each step taken for the purpose of preventing gross inequalities from arising in the social and economic sphere involves some interference with the abstract right to freedom.

The social idea which Sorley proposed as an alternative to either abstract liberty or abstract equality was the idea of positive freedom. Its realisation requires the following conditions:

(1) The development and direction of human mental and physical powers by education;

(2) Such access to the materials and instruments of production as would give suitable employment to people; and

(3) The establishment of physical and social surroundings which will and not hamper, individual development.

An order fashioned upon such principles, Sorley maintained, would faster the growth of genuine freedom while it would at the same time bring the ideal of freedom into closer harmony with equality. Reception of justice in human social affairs must be looked upon as the superior to all rival conceptions that a latter are ***a priori*** condemned to failure and bankruptcy.

Justice, according to this point of view demands an objective, unbiased and considerate attitude towards others, a willingness to be fair, and a readiness to give or leave to others that which they are entitled to have or retain. The just man, either in private or public life is a person who is able to see the legitimate interests of others and to respect them. Thus, understood, justice is a principle of rectitude which requires integrity of character as a basic precondition.

A rational individual may insist on scrupulous respect for his own feelings and due recognition of his personal rights but at the same time, he accords an equal respect to the personality of other human beings. A rational being tends to act in moral and socially responsible manner, while anti-social and immoral action is normally irrational in character.

(3) *Scope and Application of Art. 21*

Art. 21 clarifies and crystalises the general principle that no person shall be deprived of his life or personal liberty except according to procedure established by law. Articles 19, 20, 21 and 22 form one group entitled "***Right to Freedom***". Art. 21 guarantees the most essential of all rights the right to life and personal liberty. Article 21 does not abrogate to any extent ***parens patriae*** jurisdiction of court and High Court can in the best interest of child entrust it to one of its parents who is residing outside India and permit the child to be removed out of India. Article 21 unlike Art. 19 applies to all persons and not only to citizens. Art. 21 has no application to a corporate body *e.g.*, co-operative society (The liquidation of a co-operative society, *i.e.*, a corporate body cannot be equated to "*deprivation of life or personal liberty*"). Even though an offence of murder is proved and the accused is sent to jail, the court is to ensure that the deprivation of liberty is accompanied by curative strategy and human dignity. Art. 21 of the Constitution is the jurisdictional root for this legal liberalism. The Supreme Court can intervence with prison administration when constitutional rights or statutory prescriptions are transgressed to the injury of the prisoner.

Articles 21 and 22 apply to all persons including members of Legislatures and they can be deprived of their personal liberty "*according to procedure established by law*". The right to life or personal liberty is not an absolute one but is one which is not subject to the provisions of any "law". Art. 21 is not a limitation on the powers of the Legislature but only on those of the executive. Art. 21 only applies to the deprivation of life or personal liberty by the State and not by a private individual.

The right to life though the most fundamental of all, is also one of the most difficult to define and its protection generally takes the form of a declaration that no person shall be deprived of it save by the process of law or by authority of law. Words "except according to procedure established by law" control and qualify both life and "personal liberty". By the term "life" something more is meant than mere animal existence. The inhibition against its deprivation extends to all those limits and faculties by which life is enjoyed. The word "life" does not take in its scope matters like individual status enjoyed by a person. Cessation of office of Sarpanch does not come within the scope of the word "life" as occurring in Art. 21.

(4) *Deprivation of Personal Liberty*

The word "deprivation" conveys the idea of total loss of personal liberty as contrasted with mere restriction on personal liberty. Art. 21 applies not only to the initial deprivation of personal liberty but also to the continuation of such deprivation. And hence the continuation of deprivation of personal liberty also must be according to procedure established by law. A person who has been deprived of his personal liberty in the sense that he has been detained in prison cannot be subjected to any restrictions otherwise than in accordance with law.

The secret picketing of the house of a suspect or keeping watch over his movements under Police surveillance does not amount to deprivation of the personal liberty of such suspect as such "deprivation" should be something tangible and direct. The shadowing of a suspect by police and keeping a watch over his activities by the police does not amount to a deprivation of his personal liberty. Police Regulations, which has the force of law does not violate fundamental right of the citizen guaranteed under Art. 21. Domiciliary visits to the house of a police suspect at night involving the intrusion into the privacy of his home, disturbance of his sleep etc. will amount to deprivation of his personal liberty. The administrative circulars directing police officers and district officers to obtain Labour Minister's direction before discharging their statutory duties where managerial staff is confined by *Gherao* in industrial establishment have been held not to violate Article 21. Deprivation of freedom by refusal of bail is not for punitive purpose but for bi-focal interests of justice to the individual involved and society affected and does not violate Art. 21. Detention in jail for period longeer than what they would have been sentenced if convicted is illegal as being in violation of Art. 21. Where the prisoner seeks to file an appeal or revision, every facility for exercise of that right shall be made available by the Jail Administration. Any Jailor who, by indifference or vendetta, withholds the copy of the judgement thwarts the court process and violates Art. 21.

(5) *Article 21 and Art. 19 – Effect of Gopalan's Case*

Article 19 and Article 21 are two entirely distinct provisions dealing with distinct topics. The question of total deprivation of personal liberty is as between the two Articles exclusively within the purview of Article 21 and not that of Article 19. Article 19 deals with certain important individual rights of personal liberty in the case of citizens of India and the restrictions that could be validly placed upon such rights. The rights enumerated in Article 19 do not form the subject-matter of Article 21. The Constitution protects the freedom of citizen by Article 19 (1) (a) to (e) and (g) but empowers the State even while those freedoms last to impose reasonable restrictions on them in the interest of the State or of public order or morality or of the general public as mentioned in clauses (2) to (6). Further the moment even this regulated freedom of the individual becomes incompatible with and threatens the freedom of the community the State is given power by Art. 21 to deprive the individual of his life and personal liberty in accordance with procedure established by law subject of course to the provisions of Article 22.

"Personal Liberty" under Art. 21 is not identical with the right of freedom of movement throughout the territory of India under Article 19 (1) (d). Personal liberty includes all aspects of personal liberty. Art., 19 does not apply to a case where a person is incarcerated and is totally deprived of his personal liberty in such a case; Article 21 alone applies and the validity of the law under which the person is deprived of his personal liberty cannot be tested in the light of the provisions of Article 19. Both Articles 19 and Article 21 are substantive provisions dealing with Fundamental Rights and each of the articles has a distinct scope and subject-matter. Articles 21 and 22 confer a Fundamental Right and give fundamental guarantee. It is the duty of the court to ensure that the right and the guarantee are not rendered illusory and meaningless. While certain important individual attributes of freedom are dealt with separately in Article 19, Article 21 deals with the total deprivation of personal liberty. Art. 19 deals with rights of a citizen as long as he is free and does not apply to a person who has ceased to be free and has been incarcerated either under preventive or punitive legislation. Article 19 only applies where a legislation directly hits the rights enumerated in the article and not where the loss of the rights mentioned in the Article is the result of the operation of a legislation relating to punitive or preventive detention.

(6) *"Personal Liberty", Meaning of*

The words "personal liberty" taken by themselves do not mean only liberty of the person and mean liberty or the rights attached to the person (*jus personam*). Thus, the words are capable of including the rights mentioned in Art. 19. But the Constitution treats the two rights as distinct and provides for them separately in two different Articles. Hence Art. 19 does not apply to a law authorising the total deprivation of personal liberty although the rights under Article 19 are lost in the process of such deprivation. "Personal Liberty" means freedom of information. "Personal Liberty" means liberty of the person or body *i.e.* freedom from imprisonment and physical coercion.

The expression "life and personal liberty" includes a variety of rights though they are not enumerated in Part III of the Constitution, provided that they are necessary for the full development of the personality of the individual and can be included in the various aspects of the liberty of the individual. "Personal Liberty" in Article 21 means not merely freedom from physical restraint but includes all aspects of personal liberty except those which are specifically enumerated in Art. 19. The right of a student to educate himself by participating in the activities of the students union including election of its office-bearers is included in Article 21. Right to receive higher education or professional education is a fundamental right. Where a person is sought to be deprived of the opportunity to pursue medical education by an improper order, that will constitute an infraction of his fundamental right. The right of an Indian citizen to go abroad and travel outside India is part of his "*personal liberty*" under Art. 21. Hence he cannot be refused a passport for leaving the country except when such refusal is warranted by a valid law. Section 18-B of the *Foreign Exchange Regulation Act (1947)* which deprives persons of their personal liberty in so far as they cannot go out of India without booking their passages through an airline shipping company or travel agent is the "*procedure established by law*" within the meaning of Art. 21. Unauthorised interference with a citizen's right to carry his personal effects by searching them amounts to an intrusion into his privacy and an invasion of his personal right to travel about. Procedure established by the Passports Act, 1967 for impounding a passport is in conformity with the requirement of Article 21 and does not fall foul of that Article.

The procedure evolved by The Government of India with the agreement of foreign Governments that invitations of Indian citizens extended by Foreign Diplomatic Missions on behalf of their Governments should be okayed by the Government of India is not unreasonable. The compulsory medical examination of a person against his will is unconstitutional unless it is warranted by law. The compulsory extraction of blood for testing is an interference with personal liberty and will be unconstitutional unless it is warranted by any law. The term "Personal Liberty" does not extend to intellectual or educational freedom and the Article is not infringed in making reservation in educational institution for backward classes. Order requiring accused to give specimen of hair for the purpose of identification is not violative of fundamental rights granted by Article 20 (3).

(7) *Article 21 and Article 22*

Article 22 applies to preventive detention. Article 22 (1) and (3), prescribe limitations on the right given by Article 21. If the procedure mentioned in those Articles is followed the arrest and detention contemplated by Article 22 (1) and (2) although they infringe the personal liberty of the individual, will be legal because that becomes the established legal procedure in respect of arrest and detention. There is a significant difference in the wording of Articles 19, 20, 21 and 22. Under Article 19 certain freedoms are declared and certain restrictions on those freedoms are permitted. But under Articles 20, 21 and 22 the restriction is not on the freedom or the liberty of the person but on the power of the State to take away the liberty.

(8) *"Procedure Established By Law*

This phrase means positive State-made law. Art. 21 is an example of the fusion of substantive and procedural law. It contains a negative as well as a positive aspect. The provision that no one can be deprived of these rights except according to procedure established by law itself clearly amounts to a substantive provision of law and the mere fact that it states that a certain procedure must be followed if the right of life or personal liberty is to be affected does not render the Article a merely procedural enactment. The expression "*procedure established by law*" connotes an enacted law and not law in the abstract or the principles of natural justice. The expression "*procedure established by law*" in this Article is not to be given the wide and rather fluid meaning if the expression "*due process of law*" under the Federal Constitution of the United States of America but means only State-made law of statutory origin.

Law in Article 21 means not *jus* i.e., law in the abstract in the sense of the principles of natural justice as mentioned in the standard works of jurisprudence, but *lex,* i.e., enacted law. But mere executive orders or administrative orders are not "*law*". U.P. Police Regulations regarding police surveillance over suspects are not "*law*". Section 4 of the *Prevention of Corruption Act* (1947) is not unconstitutional as Section 4 lays down "*procedure established by law*" within Art. 21. Reasonableness or otherwise of law is not open for examination by court. The mere fact that the word "*law*" occurs both in the expression "*due process of law*" under the American Constitution and in the expression '*procedure established by law*' in Art. 21 does not make the same meaning applicable to both the expressions and does not require that the meaning of the word '*law*' under the decisions on the American Constitution must be imported into the interpretation of Art. 21.

Though the expression '*procedure established* by *law*' is not to be taken in the fluid sense of the words "due process of law" as referring to the fundamental principles of natural justice, any and every piece of legislation cannot be covered by the expression "*procedure established by law*". The procedure under Article 21 must be one established by a general law of procedure and must not be a mere change in the law made *ad hoc* for any special purpose or occasion. The expression "*procedure established by law*" refers to the procedure prescribed by any law of the Legislature which is duly made. It is open to the Parliament or other Legislative body or after the prescribed procedure and such altered procedure also will be procedure established by law within the meaning of Art. 21. "Law" within the meaning of Art. 21 is a valid law. The meaning of "law" under Art. 21 is narrower than under Article 13 (1) (a) under which "*law*" includes even custom or usage having the force of law. Mere executive or administrative orders or instructions are not "*law*" within the meaning of Art. 21. "Law" in the expression "*procedure established by law*" will include the provisions of the Constitution. Thus the procedure under Article 22 clauses (1) and (2) is covered by the expression "*procedure established by law*". The provisions of Art. 22 relating to preventive detention will constitute "*procedure established by law*" within the meaning of Article 21 and will have to be complied with in the case of any person who is detained under any law relating to preventive detention.

Where a person is tried and convicted of a criminal offence and sentenced to imprisonment under the relevant law, his detention will be one in accordance with procedure established by law. Detention under the preventive sections of the Criminal P.C., Chapter VIII is one in accordance with procedure established by law. The inherent power of the High Court or the Supreme Court to punish for contempt of court is covered by the expression "*procedure established by law*". High Court has jurisdiction to initiate contempt proceedings *suo motu* even in a civil contempt. No particular form of procedure is necessary so long as the proceedings are initiated giving an opportunity to the contemner to defend himself. Art. 21 is not in any way violated thereby. The rules of procedure for enforcement of a power privileges and immunities of a State Legislature under Art. 208 constitute "*procedure established by law*" and the deprivation of the personal liberty of a citizen under such rules is valid.

Section 30 of the *Insecticides Act* (*1969*) does not infringe the Fundamental Rights guaranteed to a citizen under Art. 21 of the Constitution. Prescription of entrance test by State Government in accordance with law for admission to Medical College does in no way affect personal liberty of candidates secured under Art. 21. An accused who obdurately refuses to be defended by a Counsel may thereby injure himself but such injury cannot be said to be the result of any non-observance of the procedure established by law and therefore there is no violation of Art. 21. Maintenance of Internal Security Act does not violate Article 21. In the case of an arrest under Preventive Detention Law, it is not obligatory for the detaining authority to communicate grounds of detention within twentyfour hours of detention. Section 8(1) of M.I.S. Act (1971) setting out maximum time limit of five days or 15 days in exceptional circumstances for communication of grounds to the detenu is not inconsistent with Art. 21 or Art. 22. Having paramount regard to the security of the State rights under natural law or the common law and the rules of natural justice are explicitly excluded by the statute itself under Sections 16-A and 18 of the MISA.

In the following cases the deprivation of personal liberty was held to be not in accordance with procedure established by law:

(1) Arrest and imprisonment of income-tax assessee under order beyond authority of law.

(2) Absence of statutory provision compelling medical examination of party.

(3) Arrest and detention by Head Constable under Section 151, Criminal Procedure Code.

(4) Warrant of arrest illegally issued.

(5) Illegal arrest of petitioner not authorised by Co-operative Societies Act, 1912 or any other law.

(6) Bail given on Saturday – Release of prisoner on Monday – Detention continued on Sunday is illegal.

(7) Detention under Preventive Detention Act – Procedure not strictly followed – Article 21 held violated.

(8) Preventive Detention – Detention after expiration of time for giving grounds and opportunity – Detention held illegal.

(9) Detention under Preventive Detention Act – Delay in

submission of report under Act not satisfactorily explained – Detention held not in accordance with procedure established by law.

(10) To recover debts by putting a defaulter in prison is too flagrantly violative of Art. 21 unless there is some proof of the minimal fairness of his wilful failure to pay in spite of his sufficient means.

The provisions of Section 167 Cr. P.C. which authorises detention of an accused person to the maximum time limit of 60 days are mandatory. Detention of accused beyond period of 60 days prescribed under Section 167 Cr. P.C. is illegal and violative of individual liberty guaranteed under Art. 21. Not a single day's delay can be condoned even if 60th day happens to be holiday or Sunday, in a non-cognizable offence investigated by police without taking previous order of Magistrate. Non-conformance to mandatory provisions in Section 155 (2), Cr. P.C. is a non-conformance to the procedure established by law vitiating the ultimate proceeding. In the case of issue of writ of proclamation, non-conformance of Section 87(1) and (2) Cr. P.C. is but a non-conformance to the procedure established by law. Such a performance is all the more necessary after the passing of the Constitution. Article 21 lends assurance to the same.

Any order of detention of a person who is discovered under a warrant issued under Section 100 Cr. P.C. would inevitably offend against fundamental right of personal liberty when no accusation is made that the person has committed or is likely to commit any offence. In matters where the liberty of the subject concerned and a highly cherished right is involved the representations made by the detenu should be construed liberally and not technically so as to frustrate or defeat the concept of liberty which is engrained in Article 21. Where the representation has not been considered at all by the Government which it was duty bound to consider that itself vitiates the order of detention.

(9) *"Due Process of Law" – Meaning of, under American Constitution*

Four marked points of distinction between the '*due process*' clause in the American Constitution and Art. 21 are:

(1) The first is that in the U.S.A. Constitution, the word 'liberty' is used simpliciter while in India it is restricted to personal liberty.

(2) In the U.S.A. Constitution the same protection is given to property while in India the Fundamental Right in respect of property is contained in Art. 31.

(3) The word "due" is omitted altogether and the expression "due process of law" is not used deliberately.

(4) The word "established" is used and is limited to "procedure" in Article 21.

The fundamental constitutional right of access to the courts requires prison authorities to assist inmates in the preparation and filing of meaningful papers by providing prisoners with adequate law libraries or adequate assistance from persons trained in the law. Under Fifth and Fourteenth Amendments of the Constitution of U.S.A., imposition of death sentence on basis of confidential information not disclosed to accused or his counsel was held to violate *due process clause*. In all criminal prosecutions, the accused shall enjoy the right to a speedy and public trial, by impartial jury of the State and district wherein the crime shall have been previously ascertained by law, and to be informed of the nature and cause of the accusation; to be confronted with the witnesses against him; to have compulsory processes for obtaining witnesses in his favour and to have the assistance of counsel for his defence. In a trial for murder prosecution eliminating nearly half the venire of prospective jurors by challenging under the authority of an *Illinois Statute* any venireman expressing qualms about capital punishment. Jury found accused guilty fixing the penalty of death. Reversing the penalty U.S. Supreme Court by a majority held that the sentence of death could not be carried out if the jury that imposed or recommended it was chosen by excluding veniremen simply because they voiced general objections to the death penalty or expressed conscientious or religious scruples against its infliction. No accused could constitutionally be put to death at the hands of a tribunal so selected.

(10) *Can the Right under Article 21 be called a Fundamental Right*

The effect of holding that the word "law" in this Article means only enacted law and that Art. 19 does not apply to the subject of deprivation of life or personal liberty is that the reasonableness or otherwise of statutory provisions under which the lives and liberties of persons can be taken away are not subject to judicial review as in the case of legal provisions imposing restrictions on the exercise of the Fundamental Rights under Art. 19. The final word to determine the law on the subject of the right to life and personal liberty is given to the legislature. Art. 21 is not a limitation on the power of the Legislature but on that of the Executive. Although no doubt, the power of the Legislature overrides and controls the right conferred by this Article and to that extent cannot but be felt as an infirmity in the provision, yet it must also be remembered that the position in point of law in England is not different and there in spite of the supremacy of Parliament, the Parliament has not been known to legislate against well-recognised principles of natural justice accepted as such in all civilised countries.

Independently of any Fundamental Rights provided by any written Constitution, it is an established principle of law that the Executive cannot take away the life and the liberty of a person on its own responsibility unless it has the support of some legal provision for doing so and is acting within the bounds of the law. The State must act within the limits of the law in any proceeding affecting the life or liberty of a person.

(11) *Has Art. 21 marked an advance?*

In effect, this Article has only guaranteed a principle which was already well established and does not include any advance over the previous position so far as the right of a person to his life or liberty is concerned. The Article has crystallised and given a permanent place as a fundamental principle of the Constitution, to a principle which was only part of the common law.

*

XIV

INTERNATIONALIZING PRIVACY

> Whereas recognition of the inherent dignity and of the equal and inalienable rights of all members of the human family is the foundation of freedom, justice and peace in the world.
>
> Whereas disregard and contempt for human rights have resulted in barbarous acts which have outraged the conscience of mankind, and the advent of a world in which human beings shall enjoy freedom of speech and belief and freedom from fear and want has been proclaimed as the highest aspiration of the common people.
>
> Whereas it is essential, if a man is not to be compelled to have rècource, as a last resort, to rebellion against tyranny and oppression, that human rights should be protected by the rule of law.
>
> Whereas it is essential to promote the development of friendly relations between nations.
>
> Whereas the peoples of the United Nations have in the charter reaffirmed their faith in fundamental human rights in the dignity and worth of the human person and in the equal rights of man and women and have determined to promote social progress and better standards of life in larger freedom.
>
> Whereas Member States have pledged themselves to achieve, in co-operation with the United Nations, the promotion of universal respect for and observance of human rights and fundamental freedoms.
>
> Whereas a common understanding of these rights and freedoms is of the greatest importance for the full realization of this pledge.
>
> *– Preamble to the Universal Declaration of Human Rights 1948*

The General Assembly proclaimed this *Universal Declaration of Human Rights* as a command standard of achievement for all peoples and all nations, to the end that every individual and every organ of society, keeping the Declaration constantly in mind, shall strive by teaching and education to promote respect for these rights and freedoms and by progressive measures, national and international, to secure their universal and effective recognition and observance both among the peoples of Member States themselves and among the people of territories under their jurisdiction.

The relevant Articles of the *Universal Declaration of Human Rights* are as follows:

Article 1: All human beings are born free and equal in dignity and rights. They are endowed with conscience and should act towards one another in a spirit of brotherhood.

Article 3: Everyone has the right to life, liberty and security of person.

Article 5: No one shall be subjected to torture or to cruel, inhuman or degrading treatment or punishment.

Article 6: Everyone has the right to recognition everywhere as a person before the law.

Article 7: All are equal before the law and are entitled without any discrimination to equal protection of the law. All are entitled to equal protection against any discrimination in violation of this Declaration and against any incitement to such discrimination.

Article 8: Everyone has the right to an effective remedy by the competent national tribunals for acts violating the fundamental rights granted to him by the Constitution or by law.

Article 9: No one shall be subjected to arbitrary arrest, detention or exile.

Article 10: Everyone is entitled in full equality to a fair and public hearing by an independent and impartial tribunal, in the determination of his rights and obligations and of any criminal charge against him.

Article 11: (i) Everyone charged with a penal offence has the right to be presumed innocent until proved guilty according to law in a public trial at which he has had all the guarantees necessary for his defence.

(ii) No one shall be held guilty of any penal offence on account of any act or omission which did not constitute a penal offence under national or international law, at the time when it was committed. Nor shall a heavier penalty be imposed than the one that was applicable at the time the penal offence was committed.

Article 12: No one shall be subjected to arbitrary interference with his privacy, family, home or correspondence nor to attacks upon his honour and reputation. Everyone has the right to the protection of the law against such interference or attacks.

Article 16: (1) Men and women of full age, without any limitation due to race, nationality or religion, have the right to marry and to found a family. They are entitled to equal rights as to marriage, during marriage and at its dissolution.

(2) Marriage shall be entered into only with the free and full consent of the intending spouses.

(3) The family is the natural and fundamental group unit society and is entitled to protection by society and the state.

Article 22: Everyone, as a member of society has the right to social security and is entitled to realization through national effort and international co-operation and in accordance with the organisation and resources of each state of the economic, social and cultural rights indispensable for his dignity and the free development of his personality.

Article 24: Everyone has the right to rest and leisure, including reasonable limitation of working hours and periodic holiday with pay.

Article 25: (1) Everyone has the right to a standard of living adequate for the health, and well-being of himself and of his family including food, clothing housing and medical care and necessary social services, and the right to security in the event of unemployment, sickness, disability, widowhood, old age, or other lack of livelihood in circumstances beyond his control.

(2) Motherhood and children are entitled to special care and assistance. All children whether born in or out of wedlock shall enjoy the same social protection.

Article 26 (2): Education shall be directed to the full development of the human personality and to the strengthening of respect for human rights and fundamental freedoms. It shall promote understanding tolerance and friendship among all nations, racial or religious groups and shall further the activities of the United Nations for the maintenance of peace.

Article 27: (1) Everyone has the right freely to participate in the cultural life of the community, to enjoy the arts and to share in scientific advancement and its benefits.

(2) Everyone has the right to the protection of the moral and

material interests resulting from any scientific literary or artistic production of which he is the author.

Article 28: Everyone is entitled to a social and international order in which the rights and freedoms set forth in this Declaration can be fully realised.

Article 29: (1) Everyone has duties to the Community in which alone the free and full development of his personality is possible.

(2) In the exercise of his rights and freedoms, everyone shall be subject only to such limitations as are determined by law solely for the purpose of securing due recognition and respect for the rights and freedoms of others and of meeting the just requirements of morality, public order and the general welfare in a democratic society.

(3) These rights and freedoms may in no case be exercised contrary to the purposes and principles of the United Nations.

(1) *Text of Resolution III adopted by the Second Committee at its 9th Meeting on 6th May 1968*

The international conference on Human Rights considering that scientific discoveries and their technological applications open up vast prospects for economic, social and cultural progress and for raising the level of living, and that they can by that token constitute a decisive factor in the effective application of Human Rights for all individuals and all peoples. Considering, however, that these discoveries and technological development may entail certain dangers for the right of the individual or of the group and for human dignity and that, in any event, their utilisation raises complex ethical and legal problems with respect to human rights:

(i) Is of the opinion that these problems require thoughts and continuous inter-disciplinary studies at both the national and the international level, so that they may serve as a basis for drawing up appropriate standards should the need arise.

(ii) Recommends that the organisations of the United Nations family should undertake a study of the problems with respect to human rights arising from developments in science and technology particularly with regard to –

(a) respect for privacy in view of recording techniques;

(b) protection of the human personality and its physical

and intellectual integrity in view of the progress in biology, medicine and bio-chemistry;

(c) the use of electronics which may affect the rights of the person and the limits which should be placed on its uses in a democratic society;

(d) and, more generally, the balance which should be established between scientific and technological progress and the intellectual, spiritual, cultural and moral advancement of humanity.

(2) *Montreal Statement of the Assembly for Human Rights, March 22–27, 1968*

(IX) NEW DANGERS CAUSED BY SCIENTIFIC DEVELOPMENTS

The Assembly recognised the debt which the peoples of the world owe to the efforts of scientists and technologicians. Nevertheless, the Assembly points out that many aspects of technological advance represent positive threats to human rights and to human dignity and that the world community must be alerted to the nature of these threats.

The Assembly also recognised that protection against such threats must be embodied in convention or other instruments until their nature can be identified, and until there is a general awareness of their implications. The dangers were considered under four heads:

(i) Electronic and other forms of intrusion on the right of privacy.

(ii) Implications of computer-based technology for domestic governments.

(iii) Protection of traditional cultures against the homogenizing influence of technological civilization.

(iv) New developments in medicine and biology and their impact on human rights.

(3) *International Covenant on Civil and Political Rights, 1966*

Preamble: The State Parties to the present Covenant considering that, in accordance with the principles proclaimed in the Charter of the United Nations, recognition of the inherent dignity and of the equal and inalienable rights of all members of the human family is the foundation of freedom, justice and peace in the world;

Recognising that these rights derive from the inherent dignity of the human person;

Recognising that, in accordance with the Universal Declaration of Human Rights, the ideal of free human beings enjoying civil and political freedom and freedom from fear and want can only be achieved if conditions are created whereby everyone may enjoy his civil and political rights, as well as his economic, social and cultural rights;

Considering the obligation of State under the Charter of the United Nations to promote universal respect for and observance of human rights and freedoms;

Realising that the individual having duties to other individuals and to the community to which he belongs, is under a responsibility to strive for the promotion and observance of the rights recognised in the present Covenant.

Part III

Article 6 (i). Every human being has the inherent right to life. This right shall be protected by law. No one shall be arbitrarily deprived of his life.

Article 7: No one shall be subjected to torture or to cruel, inhuman or degrading treatment or punishment. In particular no one shall be subjected without his free consent to medical or scientific experimentation.

Article 8: (1) No one shall be held in slavery. Slavery and the slave-trade in all their forms shall be prohibited.

(2) No one shall be held in servitude.

Article 9 (1): Everyone has the right to liberty and security of person. No one shall be subjected to arbitrary arrest or detention. No one shall be deprived of his liberty except on such grounds and in accordance with such procedure as are established by law.

(4) Anyone who is deprived of his liberty by arrest or detention shall be entitled to take proceedings before a court, in order that that court may decide without delay on the lawfulness of his detention and order his release if the detention is not lawful.

Article 10 (1): All persons deprived of their liberty shall be treated with humanity and with respect for the inherent dignity of the human person.

Article 17 (1): No one shall be subjected to arbitrary or unlawful interference with his privacy, family, home or correspondence nor to unlawful attacks on his honour and reputation.

(2) Everyone has the right to the protection of the law against such interference or attacks.

Article 23: (1) The family is the natural and fundamental group unit of society and is entitled to protection by society and the State.

(2) The right of men and women of marriageable age to marry and to found a family shall be recognised.

(3) No marriage shall be entered into without the free and full consent of the intending spouses.

(4) States parties to the present Covenant shall take appropriate steps to ensure equality of rights and responsibilities of spouses as to marriage, during marriage and at its dissolution. In the case of dissolution provision shall be made for the necessary protection of any children.

(4) *Convention for the Protection of Human Rights and Fundamental Freedoms signed at Rome on 4.11.50*

Article 5(1): Everyone has the right to liberty and security of person. No one shall be deprived of his liberty save in the following cases and in accordance with a procedure prescribed by law.

Article 8: (1) Everyone has the right for his private and family life, his home and his correspondence.

(2) There shall be no interference by a public authority with the exercise of this right except such as is in accordance with the law and is necessary in a democratic society in the interest of national security, public safety or the economic well-being of the country, for the prevention of disorder of crime, for the protection of health or morals, or for the protection of the rights and freedoms of others.

5. *Resolutions adopted by the General Assembly on International Covenants on Human Rights*

The General Assembly

Considering that one of the purposes of the United Nations, as stated in Articles 1 and 55 of the Charter is to promote universal respect for, and observance of human rights and fundamental freedoms for all without distinction as to race, sex, language or religion;

Considering that in Article 56 of the Charter all members of the United Nations have pledged themselves to take joint and separate action in co-operation with the organisation for the achievement of that purpose;

Recalling the proclamation by the General Assembly on 10 December, 1948 of the Universal Declaration of Human Rights as a common standard of achievement for all peoples and all nations;

Having considered since its Ninth Session the draft International Covenants on Human Rights prepared by the Commission on Human Rights and transmitted to it by Economic and Social Council Resolution 545 B (XVIII) of 29 July, 1954 and having completed the elaboration of the Convenants at its Twenty-first Session.

*

XV

APPLICATIONS OF PRIVACY

> "... There is no statutory authority for an evergrowing use of numbers as an identifier.... The average citizen has no legal remedy for such use of the number.... The universal use of a numeric identifier permits the linking of files and the tracing of a person from cradle to grave.
>
> – *Report of the Secretary of HEW entitled "Records, Computer and Rights of Citizens."*

The great contribution of Brandeis in his famous Olmstead dissent was his drawing of the distinction between the interest to be protected and particular forms of invasion of this interest. In his view, the devising and ingenuity of man in substituting new scientific technique for the older, heavy-handed secret observation of the thoughts, acts and words of others should not be allowed to succeed in outflawing the law. One of the most interesting of constitutional developments has been the search for a suitable rationale for protecting the privacy of groups against State efforts to identify members and through various other stratagems to make hazardous the enjoyment of a right to association. Clearly, there cannot be an unlimited right to the privacy of association that seek undesirable social objectives on whose methods of operation runs afoul of reasonably applied conspiracy doctrines. In undertaking this very ticklish process of separating permissible from prohibitable associational activity the Supreme Court has taken a long step toward bringing constitutional guarantees into closer alignment with social realities. For better and for worse, individuals today frequently find meaningful avenues for asserting personal and social claims only through associational activity. But some form of associational activity may threaten the freedom, including the right to privacy of other individuals and groups. A weighing of ends and means is clearly required, and, as in so many other situations where we seek to use law to shape conduct, resolutions of issues in individual cases is difficult and any rule of law than a rule of reason is virtually unthinkable, whether or not one agrees with the court's performance in balancing interests to protect the *NAACP* while allowing harassment of the Ku Klux Klan and the Communist Party of U.S.A; there are sufficient differences between both means and ends to make plausible a different treatment in law of these associations. With respect to privacy values, which have often been viewed as a primary concern only of higher status individuals, the efforts through law to enhance the privacy and dignity of disadvantaged individuals and groups, whether criminal suspects, religious or racial minorities or welfare clients tends to strengthen the claims to privacy and dignity of all citizens.

(1) *The weighing of privacy and conflicting claims*

The cases in *Public Utilities Commission* Vs. *Pollock* (1952) and *Griswold* Vs. *Connecticut* have focused heavily on this point in the past. Acceptance of the use by law enforcement officials of electronic devices to obtain evidence where no trespass has been committed points up the reluctance of the court to extend the concept of a right to privacy. In *Silverman* Vs. *United States* (1961), the Court agreed that the use of a spike microphone constituted a trespass and thus the resulting eavesdropping was a violation of the Fourth Amendment. The earlier cases had relied on the much criticised Olmstead rationale that in the absence of a trespass there is no illegal search when electronic eavesdropping takes place. [The decision in *Lopez* Vs. *United States* (1963)].

With the growing public concern over public and private use of electronic devices, the public interest in security of homes and offices will tend to outweigh the official need to use these devices for law enforcement and security purposes, when the courts are confronted with ordinary cases. The spirit that infused the court's decision in *Boyd* Vs. *United States* and *Brandeis* dissent in *Olmstead* is likely to pervade application of the Fourth Amendment in the future, with the stress on protection of the interest in privacy rather on the specific warner in which that interest is adversely affected.

What we see emerging is a substantial acceptance by the court of the importance of individual privacy-dignity and the need to protect that sort of interest against unreasonable government action. The replacement of the human eye, ear and nose by more sophisticated technical devices is increasingly seen not merely as a refinement in the older techniques of surveillance but as a revolutionary step in stripping individuals of their privacy.

The Supreme Court of United States has upheld administrative searches by health officials acting under laws that authorised searches of homes and other premises without warrant. One would assume that routine inspections might be preceded by at least a general notice of intention to inspect in certain areas, but in the *Ohio* case, no notice was given. If a similar case were to arise today the court might well invalidate an inspection system that lacked both warrant and notice provisions at least when there was a lack of evidence tending to show a need for inspection without delay. Public opinion may serve as a significant limiting facts but the most likely targets of overzealous inspectors will be the homes and establishments of those of lower socio-economic status and not those of the opinion-leaders of the community.

In the foregoing cases and others the Supreme Court has toiled valiantly though with difficulty to fashion a legal concept protective of privacy from constitutional provisions and principles. There is every reason to believe that a right to privacy with constitutional underpinnings will find increasing recognition and application in the future. As an essential facet of human freedom and dignity, a right to privacy has found a stout champion in a court devoted to the protection of the freedom and equality of individuals and groups at a time when they are increasingly threatened by public and private action. To say that the court has not yet succeeded in discovering a formula that can be applied readily to any situation that may arise is only to recognise a condition of constitutional jurisprudence that is characteristic whenever important claims or interests clash. What the court has been doing in a somewhat tentative way is to insist that privacy-dignity claims deserve to be examined with care and to be denied only when an important countervailing interest is shown to be superior.

(2) *Privacy in Welfare Public Assistance and Juvenile Justice*

Government intervention into the lives of public assistance recipients is inevitable so long as dispensation of income maintenance proceeds on a determination of individual needs. The inherently offensive aspect of need determination and redetermination lies not in investing need *per se* but in the application of investigatory techniques and eligibility standards that are alien to the conduct of other governmental affairs, and that reach, far beyond the point that honesty and efficiency in programme administration reasonably require. The basic issues revolve around the attitudes we take toward less fortunate persons, the degree of double-checking assumed to be necessary to assure that legislative objectives are carried out and the adequacy of the payments to be provided.

Recognition that current programmes degrade individual recipients by exposing them to a kind of scrutiny and control from which the rest of us are ordinarily exempt may hasten further adoption of statutes, administrative procedures and professional practice that are consonant with individual freedom and dignity. The new welfare programs expand the areas of official concern into additional aspects of private life and personality. If the character of a recipient is to be changed in order to better equip him for life, then techniques must be used to explore social and psychological defects. The programs legitimize governmental concern in those matters that affect the process of rehabilitation. The price of rehabilitation is the increased vulnerability of welfare recipients to the humanitarian regulator of personal life. The more increasing and difficult issues of privacy arise in the humanitarian progressive programs. This is ironic but changing. Conceptions of "need" have expanded the legitimate activity of government into the lives of its clientale. Techniques of changing behaviour whether monetary incentives, education blandishments, or force, conflict with deeply held values of freedom, individualism and dignity.

(3) *The Privacy of Government Employees*

Notwithstanding the people's long-standing interest in privacy, it is disturbingly common in our society for employers both private and governmental – to make searching inquiries into the actions, habits, associations and thoughts of their employees. Important technological and scientific advances have greatly facilitated the invasion of individual privacy. Almost all of the various privacy-invading techniques that are decried by journalists and other observers of society have been used from time to time by employers in dealing with their employees. Common practice has long established the privilege of an employee – private or governmental – to inquire into certain areas of a person's personal and professional background when he applies for employment. The employer's interest in the applicant's past is presumptively legitimate, although the relevance of particular inquiries may occasionably be in doubt. Moreover the job applicant in seeking a particular position can fairly be said to have consented to an investigation of his qualifications for that employment. This consent is freely enough given to authorise investigation of matters that are obviously relevant, but there is some doubt that implied consent supports a full background investigation involving contacts with persons other than previous employers and those expressly listed as reference on an employment application. Obviously, implied consent ought to be relied upon where the applicant is ignorant of the type of investigation that will be conducted or if he is misled by the interview or the application form.

Unfortunately improper invasions of employee privacy by federal agencies are not restricted to unwarranted prying into personal life of prospective employees but includes many kinds of surveillance and probing of employees activities after they have been hired. In situations where implied consent does not operate submission to an invasion of privacy has often been made voluntary, but even here employees have often felt varying degrees of coercion to allow their privacy to be usurped. The case with which administrators can thus encroach upon the privacy of their subordinate makes vigilance especially desirable. Until investigations are firmly linked to the overriding issue of the employee's right to personal privacy abuses will be difficult to detect and correct.

Perhaps the leading type of privacy invasion by private industry is the widespread use of covert surveillance and eavesdropping techniques. These techniques include closed-circuit television, one-way mirrors, hidden microphones tapped telephones, and so forth. The purpose may be to detect pilferage or to check up on employee diligence or morale or on the quality of service being rendered to the public. Similar motivations may also prompt public employers to adopt such expedients.

(4) *The Constitutional Status of Government Employees*

Although the scope of the court's mandate in *Griswold* is not clearly defined and the criteria for its application are as yet undrawn, it is possible that the area of employee privacy will be one of the fields of application. The combination of *Griswold* case's recognition of privacy as a constitutionally protected interest with the Supreme

Court's new willingness to accord constitutional protections to public employees suggests a possible judicial role in protecting employee privacy. It is too early to tell what may develop, but a few random possibilities may be listed:

(1) Certain kinds of private employee conduct may prove to be beyond the range of legitimate government inquiry and may therefore be unacceptable as grounds for dismissal or other adverse treatment,

(2) Lie detectors may be held to infringe personal liberties of the results are made the basis for adverse personal action;

(3) Psychological testing may be subjected to judicial scrutiny concerning its validity and the relevance of the results in screening for particular jobs.

(4) Refusals to submit to particular inquiries may be held an inadequate basis for dismissing of refusing employment; and

(5) Concern with privacy values may prompt imposition of strict procedural standards and influence construction of relevant legislation and administrative directives.

The contemporary people's lethargy in reacting to invasions of privacy by employers both governmental and private is a sad commentary on our national heritage and traditions. The type in many respects preferable to those of the actions, habits and innermost thoughts of our citizens. The insidiousness of the latter researches – made in many instances without the employer's knowledge–makes them all the more frightening. That the public has submitted to these incursions on their liberties has undoubtedly accounted in large measure for the increasing and widespread assault of their privacy.

If the spirit of the Constitution is to be upheld, the employee must fully exercise his rights as a citizen to protect his own privacy as well as that of every fellow employee. Furthermore administrators must realize that adherence to that high moral principle demands that his decisions affecting the public and his own personnel reflect a respect for the dignity of the individual and for his basic rights under our system of government. His observance of these moral principles, his devotion to the values protected by our Constitution impose on him the duty to raise his voice against orders to utilise privacy invading practices and devices.

(5) *The Freedom of Information Act and Privacy*

Perhaps the most difficult task in drafting federal privacy legislation was that of determining the proper balance between the public right to know about the conduct of their government, and their equally important right to have information which is personal to them maintained with the greatest degree of confidence by Federal agencies. The House Bill made no specific provision for Freedom of Information Act requests of material which might contain information protected by the Privacy Act. Instead, in the Committee report on the Bill, it recognised that:

> "The legislation would have an effect on sub-section (b) (6) of the Freedom of Information Act which states that the provisions regarding discharge of information to the public shall not apply to the material the disclosure of which constitute a clearly unwarranted invasion of personal privacy. H.R. 16373 would make all individual identifiable information in government files exempt from public disclosure. Such disclosures could be made available to the public only pursuant to rules published by agencies in the Federal Register permitting the transfer of particular data to persons other than the individuals to whom they pertain."

The Committee Report went on to express a desire that agencies continue to make certain individually identifiable records open to the public because such disclosure would be in the public interest. The Senate Bill reflected the position of an earlier draft of the House measure in section 205 (b) where it provided that nothing in this Act shall be construed to permit the withholding of any personal information which is otherwise required to be disclosed by law or any regulation thereunder. This Section was intended as specific recognition of the need to permit disclosure under the Freedom of Information Act.

The compromise amendment would add an additional condition of disclosure in the House Bill which prohibits disclosure without written request of an individual when disclosure of the record would be pursuant to Section 552 of the Freedom of Information Act. The compromise is designed to preserve the *status quo* as interpreted by the courts regarding the disclosure of personal information under that Section, A related amendment taken from the Senate Bill would prohibit any agency from relying upon any exemption contained in Section 552 to withhold from an individual any record which is otherwise accessible to such individual under the provisions of this Section.

Privacy is not a privilege, it is a basic right, a fundamental freedom which is deeply rooted in the heritage. It is the ability to be secure in our homes, persons and papers. We simply must take firm and specific action to protect the people from the erosion of their personal liberties.

This Bill, which addresses itself to the use and abuse of Federal Data Banks, establishes several basic standards. First, only relevant personal information can be collected, and the individual must be informed as to which data is required, which is voluntary, why it is needed and under which authority. Second, only timeless data may be maintained and disseminated, and access to and security of the data must be regulated. Additionally, the nature of all data banks must be announced. Individuals must be told the source of the data and how it is used. Finally, information challenged by an individual must be reinvestigated and where proper, modified or corrected.

This legislation requires that Federal agencies in making determinations on individuals, utilise records which are accurate, relevant, timely and complete. This assures fairness to the individual, is going to result in much better decisions by Government officials. There are three basic weaknesses in the Bills the numerous and unjustified exemption provisions the failure to provide either liquidated or punitive damages, and the lack of any administrative mechanism to oversee the implementation of the Bill.

First, exemptions from the provisions of this Bill, or of any Bill designed to protect individual rights of privacy can be justified only in the face of overwhelming societal interests. There are, at most, only three areas where societal interests can be paramount to the individual rights provided in this Bill. First, where granting an individual access to his or her records would seriously damage national defense or foreign policy. Second, where such access would interfere with an active criminal prosecutions, and third, where records are required by law to be maintained for statistical research or reporting purposes and are not, in fact, used to make determinations about identifiable individuals.

Not only in the past has this been done for any nefarious

purpose, but the system of records may be instituted and maintained and the public just not know about it. So that is the first thing that will be done; identify the system of records and make public the fact that such records are being maintained. Second, again a public record would be made of the purpose for which the system is being maintained. Then we would limit in the Bill access to these records for those purposes so that information contained in those systems would be used only for those routine purposes, and unless the individual about whom the information related agreed to its use for other than routine purposes, it could not be so used.

It could be used then only for the routine purposes. This limits the purpose and the use of these information systems to the public purpose which has been made known the purposes identified in the Federal Register.

Third, we provide for access by individuals to information in these record systems pertaining to himself or herself. So that a person about whom information has been collected will have an opportunity to get a copy of that information and to see if it is accurate and will have the procedure where he can request the amendment of the information to make it accurate and will have an opportunity if the information is misused under the terms of the Act for recourse in a civil action through the courts.

*

XVI

CASE LAW

> "The right to privacy in any event will necessarily have to go through a process of case-by-case development. Therefore, even assuming that the right to personal liberty, the right to move freely throughout the territory of India and the freedom of speech create an independent right of privacy as an emanation from them which one can characterise as a fundamental right, we do not think that the right is absolute."
>
> – *Govind* Vs. *State of M.P. 1975 (3) SCR 946*

(1) *U.S. Supreme Court: ....We must weigh the importance of the general privilege of confidentiality of presidential communications ....against the inroads of such a privilege on the fair administration of criminal Justice.*

UNITED STATES Vs. NIXON 418 U.S. 683

Following the indictment of seven high-ranking White House officials – including former special presidential assistants H.R. Halderman and John Ehrlichman and former Attorney General John Mitchell – for conspiracy to defraud the U.S. Government and obstruction of Justice, the special prosecutor obtained a subpoena directing President Richard M. Nixon to deliver to the trial judge certain tape recordings and memoranda of conversation held in the White House. The trial judge would then examine those tapes and documents and give to the prosecution and defense those portions relevant to the issues at trial. The remainder would be returned to the President. Nixon produced some of the subpoenaed material but withheld other portions, invoking executive privilege, which, he claimed, placed confidential presidential documents beyond judicial control. The trial judge denied the President's claim and he appealed to the Court of Appeals. The special prosecutor asked the Supreme Court to review the case before the Court of Appeals had passed judgement and the Justices agreed

Neither the doctrine of separation of powers, nor the need for confidentiality of high level communications, without more, can sustain an absolute, unqualified presidential form of immunity from judicial process under all circumstances. The President's need for complete candor and objectivity from advisers calls for great deference from the courts. However, when the privilege depends solely on the broad, undifferentiated claim of public interest in the confidentiality of such conversations, a confronation with other values arises. Absent a claim of need to protect military, diplomatic or sensitive national security secrets, we find it difficult to accept the argument that even the very important interest in confidentiality of presidential communications is significantly diminished by production such material *in camera* inspection with all the protection that a district court will be obliged to provide.

The expectation of a President to the confidentiality of his conversations and correspondence, like the claim of confidentiality of judicial deliberations, for example, has all the values to which we accord deference for the privacy of all citizens and added to those values, the necessity for protection of the public interest in candid, objective, and even blunt or harsh opinions in presidential decision-making....These are the considerations justifying a presumptive privilege for presidential communications. The privilege is fundamental to the operation of government and inextricably rooted in the separation of powers under the Constitution. In *Nixon* vs. *Sirica* ...(1973) the Court of Appeals held that such presidential communications are "presumptively privileged, ...and the position is accepted by both parties in the present litigation. We agree with Mr. Chief Justice Marshall's observation, therefore, that in no case of this kind would a court be required to proceed against the President as against on ordinary individual". *United States* vs.*Bun*....

But this presumptive privilege must be considered in the light of our historic commitment to the rule of law. This is nowhere more profoundly manifest than in our view that "the two-fold aim [of criminal Justice] is that guilt shall not escape or innocence suffer". *Berger* vs. *United States*....we have elected to adopt an adversary system of criminal justice in which the parties contest all issues before a court of law. The need to develop all relevant facts in the adversary system is both fundamental and comprehensive...The very integrity of the judicial system and public confidence in the system depend on full disclosure of all the facts, within the framework of the rules of evidence. To ensure that justice is done, it is imperative to the function of courts that compulsory process be available for the production of evidence needed either by the prosecution or by the defense.

No case of the court....has extended this high degree of deference to a President's generalised interest in confidentiality. Nowhere in the Constitution.... is there any explicit reference to a privilege of confidentiality, yet to the extent this interest relates to the effective discharge of a President's power, it is constitutionally based.

The right to the production of all evidence at a criminal trial similarly has constitutional dimensions. The Sixth Amendment explicitly confers upon every defendant in a criminal trial the right "to be confronted with the witnesses against him" and "to have compulsory process for obtaining witnesses in his favour". Moreover, the Fifth Amendment also guarantees that no person shall be deprived of liberty without due process of law. It is the manifest duty of the courts to vindicate those guarantees and to accomplish that it is essential that all relevant and admissible evidence be produced.

The allowance of the privilege to withhold evidence that is demonstrably relevant in a criminal trial would cut deeply into the guarantee of due process of law and gravely impair the basic function of the courts. A President's acknowleged need for confindentiality in the communications of his office is general in nature, whereas the constitutional need for production of relevant evidence in a criminal proceeding is specific and central to the fair adjudication of a particular criminal case in the administration of justice. Without access to specific facts a criminal prosecution may be totally frustrated....

We conclude that when the ground for asserting privilege as to subpoenaed materials sought for use in a criminal trial is based only on the generalised interest in confidentiality, it cannot prevail over the fundamental demands of due process of law in the fair administration of criminal justice. The generalised assertion of privilege must yield to the demonstrated, specific need for evidence in a pending criminal trial.....

(2) ***Irish Supreme Court: "The Court ....cannot accept the view that in a state where constitution guarantees personal rights, it is enough to look to statute only as the Warrant for one's actions."***

THE STATE (QUINN) *Vs.* RYAN (1965) I.R. 70

Walsh J.: Among the personal rights guaranteed by the Constitution is the right not to be deprived, of personal liberty save in accordance with law. (Art. 40, Section 4, sub-section 1). At sub-section 2 it is provided that upon complaint being made by any person to the High Court (and, therefore, on appeal to this court), that he is being unlawfully detained, his release must be ordered unless the court is satisfied that he is being detained in accordance with law. At Section 3 the State guarantees in its laws to defend and vindicate the personal rights of the citizens and in particular by its laws to protect as best – it may from unjust attack, and in the case of injustice done, vindicate the right, person, good name and property rights of every citizen. At Section 4, sub-section 3 of Art. 40, the Constitution recognises the possibility of a person's detention being in accordance with a law but such law being invaded having regard to the provisions of the Constitution.

(3) *In re o' Laighleis [1960] I.R. 93*

MAGNIRE C.J.: CONVENTION FOR THE PROTECTION OF HUMAN RIGHTS AND FUNDAMENTAL FREEDOMS

Art. 1: "The High Contracting Parties shall secure to everyone within their jurisdiction the rights and freedoms defined in Section 1 of this convention. Section 1 inciudes the following Articles:

"*Article 5* "(1) Everyone has the right to liberty and security of person.

"No one shall be deprived of his liberty save in the following cases and in accordance with a procedure established by law:

> "(c) the lawful arrest or detention of a person effected for the purpose of bringing him before the competent legal authority on reasonable suspicion of having committed an offence or when it is reasonably considered necessary to prevent his committing an offence or fleeing after having done so;

"(2) Everyone who is arrested or detained in accordance with the provisions of paragraph 1(c) of this Article shall be brought promptly before a Judge or other officer authorised by law to exercise judicial power and shall be entitled to trial within less reasonable time or to release pending trial. Release may be conditioned by guarantees to appear for trial.

(4) Everyone who is deprived of his liberty by arrest or detention shall be entitled to take proceeding by which the lawfulness of his detention shall be decided speedily by a court and his release ordered if the detention is not lawful...."

HUMAN DIGNITY AND PUBLIC HEALTH, MORALS AND SAFETY

For a liberal, democratic society, after all, has a real and fundamental interest in protecting individual liberty as well as public health, morals and safety. Indeed, the very notions of a written Constitution and judicial review indicate that governmental or even majoritarian concepts of what the public weal demands should not automatically take precedence over individual liberty. Moreover, the dignity of man forms one of the fundamental principles on which constitutional democracy is grounded. Police practices which uncover crime at the expense of human dignity are thus to some extent dysfunctional. One might also argue that it is similarly dysfunctional to allow a person to die slowly, with pain but without dignity.

Constitutionally typically speak glowingly of both the general welfare and the sanctity of individual rights. Where a Constitution includes no Bill of Rights, as in Canada and Australia general phrases such as "peace, order and good government" appear to supply ample justification for exercise of police power, Constitutions that include Bills of Rights often take refuse in vague phrases, such as prohibition in the Fifth and Fourteenth Amendments to the U.S. Constitution against governments' depriving "any person of life, liberty or property without due process of law". Combining oriental mysticism with American jurisprudence, Art. 13 of the Japanese Constitution stipulates.

All of the people shall be respected as individuals. Their right to life, liberty and the pursuit of happiness shall, to the extent that it does not interfere with the public welfare, be the supreme consideration in legislation and in other governmental affairs. Similarly, other Constitutions use language that extols individual rights while permitting governmental interference. Art. 1, Sec. 2 of the West Germany's Basic Law states:

> Everyone shall have the right to life and physical inviolability. The freedom of the individual shall be inviolable. These rights must be interfered with only on the basis of a law.

Even the meaning of the first clause of Art. I of the Basic Law is hardly self-evident as applied to specific cases, although one cannot help but admire its tersely eloquent statement of much of the political philosophy that underpins constitutional democracy:

> The dignity of man shall be inviolable to respect and protect it shall be the duty of all state authority.

Statutes against abortion may protect the lives of some fetuses, especially those carried by mothers who are too poor to travel to other jurisdictions where abortions are legal or too frightened to trust their lives to back-alley practitioners. But woman with many can easily travel in a country or State that has legalised abortion. Other women may be able to pursuade – by emotion, logic or money – competent physicians to perform the operation at home. Still other women may risk the tender skills of the back-alley abortionist and pay a fearful price. On the other hand, close governmental restrictions on abortion may encourage respect for human life and dignity and both help pursuade a woman not to kill her potential child and lead her and others to cherish humanity. The net balance in lives is hard to calculate, but certainly the less affluent or persuasive the woman, the narrower her range of choices.

Current dangers of overpopulation, for instance make earlier bans on dissemination of information about birth control appear passing strange. At a later time and under different circumstances, current arguments for sterlizing people who have produced more than three or four children may seem absurd.

(4) *Griswold Vs. Connecticut 381 U.S. 479*

> U.S. Supreme Court: ".....specific guarantees in the Bill of Rights have penumbras..."

The executive director of the Planned Parenthood League of Connecticut and a physician teaching at the Yale Medical School were convicted in a state court for giving information about birth control to a married couple. Connecticut Law made the use of contraceptives, as well as counselling aiding or abetting such use; a criminal offence. State appellate courts sustained the convinction, and Defendants appealed to the U.S. Supreme Court.

Justice Douglas: This law, however, operates directly on an intimate relation of husband and wife and their physician's role in one aspect of that relation.

The association of people is not mentioned in the Constitution nor in the Bill of Rights. The right to educate a child in the school of the parent's choice–whether public or private or parochial–is also not mentioned. Nor is the right to study any particular subject or any foreign language. Yet the First Amendment has been construed to include certain of these rights.

By *Pierce* Vs. *Society of Sisters*.....the right to educate one's children as one chooses is made applicable to the states by the force of the First and Fourteenth Amendments. By *Meyer* Vs. *Nebraska*....the same dignity is given the right to study the German language in a private school. In other words, the state may not, consistently with the spirit of the first Amendment, contract the spectrum of available knowledge. The right of freedom of speech and press includes not only the right to utter or to print but the right to distribute, the right to receive, the right to read (*Martin* Vs. *Struthers*) and freedom of inquiry, freedom of thought, and freedom to teach (*Wieman* Vs. Updegraff) – indeed the freedom of the entire University community, *Sweezy* vs. *New Hampshire*....without those peripheral rights the specific rights would be less secure. And so we reaffirm the principle of the *Pierce* and the *Meyer* cases.

In *NAACP* vs. *Alabama* ....we protected the "freedom to associate and privacy in one's associations," noting that freedom of association was a peripheral First Amendment right...In other words, the First Amendment has a penumbra where privacy is protected from governmental intrusion.

The foregoing cases suggest that specific gurantees in the Bill of Rights have penumbras formed by emanations from those guarantees that help them give life and substance....various guarantees create zones of privacy. The right of association contained in the penumbra of the First Amendment is one.... The Third Amendment in its prohibition against the quartering of soldiers "in any house" in time of peace without the consent of the owner is another facet of that privacy. The Fourth Amendment explicitly affirms the "right of the people to be secure in their persons, houses, papers and effects, against unreasonable searches and seizures. The Fifth Amendment in its Self-Incrimination clause enables the citizen to create a zone of privacy which government may not force him to surrender to his detriment. The Ninth Amendment provides: "certain rights shall not be construed to deny or disparage others retained by the people."

The Fourth and Fifth Amendments were described in *Boyd* vs. *United States*.....as protection against all governmental invasions "of the sanctity of a man's home and the privacies of life". We recently referred in *Mapp* vs. *Ohio*....to the Fourth Amendment as creating a "right to privacy, no less important than any other right carefully and particularly reserved to the people".

The present case, then, concerns a relationship lying within the zone of privacy created by several fundamental constitutional guarantees. And it concerns a law which, in forbidding the use of contraceptives rather than regulating their manufacture or sale, seeks to achieve its goals by means having a maximum distinctive impact upon that relationship. Such a law cannot stand in the light of familiar principle, so often applied by this court that a "governmental purpose to control or prevent activities constitutionally subject to state regulation may not be achieved by means which sweep unnecessarily broadly and thereby invade the area of protected freedoms.". *NAACP* vs. *Alabama*....would we allow the police to search the sacred precincts of marital bedrooms for tell-tale signs of the use of contraceptives? The very idea is repulsive to the notions of privacy surrounding the marriage relationship.

Marriage is a coming together for better or for worse, hopefully enduring, and intimate to the degree of being sacred. It is an association that promotes a way of life, not causes, a harmony in living not political faiths, a bilateral loyalty, not commercial or social projects. Yet it is an association for as noble a purpose as any involved in our prior decisions.

Mr. Justice Goldberg whom the Chief Justice [Warren] and Mr. Justice Brennan join concurring:

I agree with the court that Connecticut's birth control law unconstitutionally intrudes upon the right of marital privacy. I do agree that the concept of liberty protects those personal rights that are fundamental, and is not confined to the specific term of the Bill of Rights. My conclusion that the concept of liberty is not so restricted and that it embraces the right of marital privacy though that right is not mentioned explicitly in the Constitution is supported both by numerous decisions of this court.

To hold that a right so basic and fundamental and so deep-rooted in our society as the right of privacy in marriage may be infringed because that right is not guaranteed in so many words by the first eight amendments to the Constitution is to ignore the Ninth Amendment and to give it no effect whatsoever....While it may shock some of my brethren that the court today holds that the Constitution protects the right of marital privacy, in my view it is far more shocking to believe that the personal liberty guaranteed by the Constitution does not include protection against such totalitarian limitation of family size; which is at complete variance with our constitutional concepts; yet, if upon a showing of a slender basis of rationality a law outlawing voluntary birth control by married persons is valid, then, by the same reasoning, a law requiring compulsory birth control also would seem to be valid. In my view, however, both types of law would unjustifiably intrude upon rights of marital privacy which are constitutionally protected....

(5) *Mcgree* Vs. *Attorney General and Revenue Commissioners (1974) I.R. 284*

Arts. 40, 41, 42 and 44 of the Constitution all fall within that Section of the Constitution which is titled "Fundamental Rights". Arts. 41, 42 and 43 emphatically reject the theory that there are no rights without laws, no rights contrary to the laws and no rights anterior to the law. They indicate that justice is placed above the law and acknowledge that natural rights or human rights are not created by law but the Constitution confirms their existence and gives them protection. The individual has natural and human rights over which the state has no authority and the family as the natural, primary and fundamental unit group of society has rights as such which the State cannot control. At the same time however, it is true, as the Constitution acknowledges that the State is the guardian of the common good and that the individual, as a member of society and the family as a unit of society, have duties and obligations to consider and respect the common good of that society. I agree with the view expressed by Mr. Justice Byrne in *Backley and others* Vs. *The Attorney General* that the power of the State to act for the protection of the common good or to decide what are the exigencies of the common good is not one which is peculiarly reserved for the legislative organ of government.

Section 17 of the Act of 1935 in so far as it unreasonably restricts the availability of contraceptives for use within marriage is, in my opinion, inconsistent with the provisions of Art. 41 of the Constitution for being an unjustified invasion of the privacy of husband and wife in their sexual relations with one another.

The Development of the constitutional law of the United States of America is ample proof of this. There is a Constitution, which while not professing to be governed by the precepts of Christianity, also in the Ninth Amendment recognises the existence of rights other than those referred to expressly in the Constitution and its Amendments. The views of the United States Supreme Court as reflected in the decisions interpreting the constitutional law also appear firmly to reject legal positivism as a jurisprudential guide.

Budd J.: Whilst "personal rights" are not set out specifically, it is scarcely to be doubted that in our society, the right to privacy is universally recognised and accepted with possibly the rarest of exceptions and the matter of marital relationship must rank as one of the most important of matters in the realm of privacy. When the preamble to the Constitution speaks of seeking to promote the common good by the observance of Prudence Justice and charity so that the dignity and freedom of the individual may be assured it must surely inform those charged with its Constitution as to the mode of application of its Articles.

(6) *West German Constitutional Court.*

Enemies of the Constitution must not be allowed to endanger, impair or destroy the existence of the state.

PRIVACY OF COMMUNICATIONS CASE 30 B VENF GE1 (1970)

Initially Art. 10 of the Basic Law read:

"Secrecy of the mail and secrecy of posts and telecommunications shall be inviolable. Restrictions may be ordered only pursuant to a law. But even when this provision was in effect, Great Britain, France, and the United States continued, as they had during the occupation, to supervise German mails and telephonic, telegraphic and radio communications to protect against espionage and sabotage. The Bonn Govt. was unhappy with foreign control but had to consent when it signed the treaty in 1952 providing for restoration of sovereignty. The Allies agreed to relinquish supervision when the German Govt. obtained authority to assume the task. In response to this opportunity and to copy with serious problems of espionage, thefts of documents, and defections of intelligence officials that were playing West Germany, the Govt. adding a lengthy sentence to Art. 10 so that Parliament could permit restrictions on communications without having to inform people put under surveillance. The new sentence also authorised substitution of review by administration bodies appointed by Parliament for more normal judicial supervision. Parliament then quickly approved a statute to carry out these provisions and the Land of Hesse and the Free Hamseatic City of Bremen, asked the second Senate of the constitutional court to declare both the statute and the amendment unconstitutional. A group of lawyers and judges filed a constitutional complaint making a similar request, and the court consolidated the two petitions. The question of an unconstitutional provision of the Constitution had arisen in the Southwest case 1B Verf GE 14 (1951) in a general way. It came up here because Art. 79 forbids an amendment to Art. I's protection of human dignity or to the terms of Art. 20, recognising the Federal Republic as a "social and democratic" federal polity dependent on popular sovereignty expressed through elections and executed by a Govt. characterised by separation of powers, with the legislature confined by the constitutional order and judges and administrators bound by law.

From the outset, the Basic Law did not unreservedly protect privacy of mails and telecommunications, rather, restrictions were always admissible, but in all cases had to be based on a law. In this respect newly added sentence 2 of Art. 10, para 2 does not introduce anything novel.

Wherever the Basic Law restricts basic rights, it is always to protect effectively another individual or supraindividual legal interest which has priority. The existence of the Federal Republic and its liberal constitutional order are a predominant legal interest for whose effective protection basic rights may, if absolutely necessary, be restricted.

(a) What is really new in the constitutional amendment is authorisation not to inform the person affected of those restrictions and to replace recourse to the courts by a review of the case by bodies appointed by Parliament. The connection between these special measures and the restrictions is clear. Efforts, plans, and measures directed against the constitutional order and against the security and existence of the state are mostly initiated by groups who disguise their work and manoeuvre in secret, who are well-organised and rely to a great extent on undisturbed functioning of their communications system. An office to protect the Constitution can effectively counter such an apparatus only if the measures of surveillance remain secret.

Even subsequent disclosure can furnish forces hostile to the Constitution with clues as to methods of operation and specific areas of observation by the office for the protection of the Constitution.

(b) Constitutional provisions must not be interpreted in isolation but rather so that they are consistent with the Basic Law's fundamental principles and its system of values.

The constitutional directive to limit measures or surveillance to what is absolutely necessary requires that only persons who are under coercive suspicion may be kept under surveillaance. Surveillance of other persons does not, however, become unlawful, if, during an investigation, communications are intercepted linking them to the suspect.

A regulation or instruction that restricts a citizen's freedom or imposes duties on him does not violate human dignity. Neither does a measure which subjects a citizen, even without his knowledge or consent, to governmental surveillance. Under the circumstances at hand, absence of notification is not an expression of disrespect for a human being and his dignity, but a burden imposed upon a citizen to protect his existence of his state and of the free democratic order. Possibility of illegal and unconstitutional abuse, does not make the rule unconstitutional, in interpreting and assessing a regulation one must rather proceed from the assumption that in a free democracy based on the rule of law it will be applied in a correct and just manner.

Neither does substitution of recourse to the courts by some other legal control violate the dignity of man. It is true that respect for the individual quality of man normally requires that he be not only holder of subjective rights, but that he also be capable of taking legal action to defend and assert his rights. But there have always been exceptions to this rule which do not offend the dignity of man. In any case, the dignity of man is not violated if the exclusion of judicial protection is not motivated by contempt or disrespect for the human being, but by the necessity to keep measures secret in order to protect the democratic order and the existence of the state. The dignity of man would, however, be affected if the person affected were left at the mercy of public authorities.

(7) *Other Communication Cases*

Privacy of communication encourages comparison with decision on similar problems by other countries. The U.S. Supreme Court avoided the whole issues of surveillance in *Laird* vs. *Tatum 408 U.S. 1(1972)*, subsequent revelations from the Watergate scandals of illegal surveillances of Govt. officials, newsmen and private citizens that President Nixon had authorised; and later documentation that, while Nixon's use against political foes of the Army CIA, FBI, Internal Revenue Service, National Security Agency and his personal thing "the plumbers" was more extensive and systematic than related activities of his predecessors at least since Franklin Roosevelt the Federal Govt. had been illegally spying on political dissidents and sometimes harassing them. The jealous wary the Irish Supreme Court has reviewed executive power in *Quinn* vs. *Ryan* and *Buckley* vs. *Attorney General*, Irish judges also sternly rebuffed efforts by the Oireachtes to permit a bar association to exercise quasi-judicial powers, in disciplining lawyers. *In re solicitors Act* and the efforts by the executive to change, for reasons of health, sentences of convicted prisoners, *State (Coughlan)* vs. *Minister for Justice (1967) I.R. 106* and *State (O'Hara)* vs. *Governor of the Central Mental Hospital (1971)*.

Doctrine of proportionateness employed by the majority in privacy of communications clear and present danger test in *Dennison* Vs. *United States* and the balancing approach followed in *Homosexuality case*.

The constitutionality of wiretapping has a long judicial history in the United States. *Olmstead* vs. *United States 277 U.S. 438 (1928)* held that federal and by implication State-wiretapping without a warrant did not violate the Fourth Amendment. But later decision especially *Nardone* vs. *United States 302 U.S. 379 (1937)* held that in the Federal Communication Act of 1934, Congress had outlawed wiretapping. Thus evidence so obtained was not admissible in a federal court. The Attorney General, however, authorised the FBI to wiretap in cases involving national security or serious crimes such as kidnapping, extortion or murder. In 1967, the Supreme Court reversed *Olmstead* in *Katz* vs. *United States 389 U.S. 347*, and also held that the exclusionary rule applied to State courts.

BERGER Vs. NEW YORK 388 U.S. 31 (1967)

In the Omnibus Crime Control Act of 1968, Congress set out detailed rules regulating wiretapping. Under most circumstances, it is a crime for a private citizen to wiretap, and State or Federal officials can do so only after detaining a warrant. In an emergency the

Attorney General can authorize a tap for 48 hours provided he immediately seeks a court order. As in Germany, the person put under surveillance is not notified when the court issues the warrant.

Congress left open the question of any inherent presidential authority to wiretap pursuant to the Constitution's mandate that he "take care that the laws be faithfully executed". In *United States* Vs. *U.S. District Court 407 U.S. 297 (1972)*, the Supreme Court held that, whenever the President's inherent power to wiretap where foreign agents were concerned, he could authorise such surveillance in domestic security cases only after obtaining a warrant. For a unanimous court, Justice Powell wrote:

> Security surveillances are especially sensitive because of the inherent vagueness of the domestic security concept, the necessarily broad and continuing nature of intelligence gathering, and the temptation to utilise such surveillance to oversee political dissent. We recognise the constitutional basis of the President's domestic security role but we think it must be exercised in a manner compatible with the Fourth Amendment.

(8) *Freedom of Expression Case*

The right to communicate ideas creates a peculiar set of problems for constitutional democracies. First of all, this right is substantially valuable in itself. True freedom would be impossible were citizens not able to speak their minds, write their thoughts, or associate with others who might share their interests and opinions. Thus, the right of free expression is usually considered essential to the development of personality. As Justice Cardozo said: "[I]t is the matrix the indispensable condition of nearly every other form of freedom."

Cardozo's evaluation of this right as touching "the very essence of a scheme of ordered liberty" leads to a second dimension. Not only is freedom of expression an end in itself, it also serves an indispensable function in a democratic system.

Speech, writing and association can also threaten other values. Every liberal democracy has had to confront problems of reconciling the potential – and frequently actual conflict of values inherent here. Their formal answer, as embodied in constitutional documents vary. The First Amendment to the U.S. Constitution is worded, if not applied in absolute terms: "Congress shall make no law abridging the freedom of speech, or of the press; or of the right of the people peaceably to assemble, and to petition the government for a redress of grievances." In contrast, the Australian and Canadian Constitutions are silent on matters of speech, press and assembly. On middle ground, the German, Irish and Japanese Constitutions talk of freedom of expression in glowing terms. None of these provisions, however, neither the absolutist First Amendment, the Australian and Canadian silences, nor the German, Irish and Japanese qualifications, settles many of the truly difficult issues.

U.S. Supreme Court, "It has been generally, if not universally considered that it is the chief purpose of the guaranty to prevent previous restraints upon publication".

NEAR *Vs.* MINNESOTA 283 U.S. 697 (1931)

The liberty of the press, and of speech, is within the liberty guarded by the due process clause of the Fourteenth Amendment from invasion by State action. Liberty of speech, and of the press, is also not an absolute right, and the State may punish its abuse.

Liberty of the press, historically considered and taken up by the Federal Constitution, has meant, principally although not exclusively immunity from previous restraint or censorship. The conception of the liberty of the press in this country had broadened with the exigencies of the colonial period and with the efforts to secure freedom from oppressive administration. That liberty was especially cherished for the immunity it afforded from previous restraint of the publication of censure of public officers and charges of official misconduct.

(9) *Govind* Vs. *State of M.P. 1975 (3) SCR 946*

The petitioner in a petition under Art. 32, challenged the validity of Regulations 855 and 856 of the Madhya Pradesh Regulation made by the Government under the Police Act, 1961. Regulation 855 provides that where on information the District Superintendent believes that a particular individual is leading a life of crime, and his conduct shows a determination to lead a life of crime that individual's name may be ordered to be entered in the Surveillance Register, and he would be placed under regular surveillance. Regulation 856 provides that such surveillance *inter alia* may consist of domiciliary visits both by day and night at frequent but irregular intervals.

In *Kharak Singh* Vs. *The State of U.P. and others*[1964] 1 SCR 332, this court had occasion to consider the validity of Regulation 236 of the U.P. Police Regulations which is in *pari materia* with Regulation 856 here. There it was held by a majority that Regulation 236 (b) providing for domiciliary visits was unconstitutional for the reason that it abridged the fundamental right of a person under Art. 21 and since Regulation 236 (b) did not have the force of law, the regulation was declared bad. The other provisions of the Regulation were held to be constitutional.

In *Kharak Singh* vs. *The State of U.P. and others*, the majority said that personal liberty in Art. 21 is comprehensive to include all varieties of rights which go to make up the personal liberty of a man other than those dealt with in Art. 19(1) (d). According to the court while Art. 19(1)(d) deals with the particular types of personal freedom, Art.21 takes in and deals with the residue. The court said:

"We have already extracted a passage from the judgement of Field J. in *Munn* Vs. *Illinois (1877) 94 U.S. 113, 142,* where the learned judge pointed out that life in the 5th and 14th Amendments of the U.S. Constitution corresponding to Art. 21 means not merely the right to the continuance of a person's animal existence, but a right to the possession of each of his organs – his arms and legs etc. We do not entertain any doubt that the word "life" in Art.21 bears the same signification. Is then the word 'personal liberty' to be construed as excluding from its purview an invasion on the part of the police of the sanctity of a man's home and an intrusion into his personal security and his right to sleep which is the normal comfort and a dire necessity for human existence even as an animal? It might not be inappropriate to refer here to the words of the preamble to the Constitution that it is designed to "assure the dignity of the individual" and therefore of those cherished human value as the means of ensuring his full development and evolution. We are referring to these objectives of the framers merely to draw attention to the concepts underlying the Constitution which would point to such vital words as "personal liberty" having to be construed in a reasonable manner and to be attributed that sense which would promote and achieve those objectives and by no means to stretch the meaning of the phrase to square with any preconceived notions or doctrinaire constitutional theories".

The court then quoted a passage from the judgement of Frankfurter J. in *Wolf* vs. *Colorado (1949) 338 U.S. 25* to the effect that the security of one's privacy against arbitrary intrusion by the police is basic to a free society and that the knock at the door, whether by day or by night, as a prelude to a search, without authority of law but solely on the authority of the police, did not need the commentary of recent history to be condemned as inconsistent with the conception of human rights enshrined in the history and the basic constitutional documents of English-speaking peoples. The court then said that at common law every man's home is his castle and that embodies an abiding principle transcending mere protection of property rights and expounds a concept of 'personal liberty' which does not rest upon any element of feudalism or any thoery of freedom which has ceased to exist. The court ultimately came to the conclusion that regulation 236 (b) which authorised domiciliary visits was violative of Art. 21 and 'as there is no law' on the basis of which the same could be justified, it must be struck down as unconstitutional. The court was of the view that the other provisions in Regulation 236 were not bad as no right of privacy has been guaranteed by the Constitution.

Suba Rao J. writing for the minority was of the opinion that the word '*liberty*' in Art. 21 was comprehensive enough to include privacy also. He said that althought it is true our Constitution does not expressly declare a right to privacy as a fundamental right, but the right is an essential ingredient of personal liberty, that in the last resort, a person's house where he lives with his family is his "castle", that nothing is more deleterious to a man's physical happiness and health than a calculated interference with his privacy and that all the acts of surveillance under Regulation 236 infringe the fundamental right of the petitioner under Art. 21 of the Constitution...

The question whether right to privacy is itself a fundamental right flowing from the other fundamental rights guaranteed to a citizen under Part III is not easy of solution.

In *Griswold* Vs. *Connecticut 381 U.S. 479* a Connecticut statute made the use of contraceptives a criminal offence. The executive and medical directors of the planned Parenthood League of Connecticut were convicted in the Circuit Court on a charge of having violated the statute as accessories by giving information, instruction and advice to married persons as to the means of preventing conception. The Appellate Division of the circuit court affirmed and its judgement was affirmed by the Supreme Court of Errors of Connecticut. On appeal, the Supreme Court of the United States reversed. In an opinion by

Douglas, J. expressing view of five members of the court, it was held that the statute was invalid as an unconstitutional invasion of the right of privacy of married persons. He said that the right of freedom of speech, press includes not only the right to utter or to print but also the right to distribute, the right to receive, the right to read and that without those peripheral rights the specific right would be less secure and that likewise, the other specific guarantees in the Bill of Rights have penumbras, formed by emanations from those guarantees that help give them life and substance, that various guarantees create zones of privacy and that protection against all governmental invasion "of the sanctity of a man's home and the privacies of life" was fundamental. He further said that the inquiry is whether a right involved "is of such a character that it cannot be denied without violating those fundamental principles of liberty and justice which lie at the base of all our civil and political institutions" and that "privacy is a fundamental personal right, emanating from the totality of the constitutional scheme under which we (Americans) live."

In his dissenting opinion, Mr. Justice Black, berated the majority for discovering and applying a constitutional right to privacy. His reading of the Constitution failed to uncover any provision or provisions forbidding the passage of any law that might abridge the privacy of individuals.

In *Jane Roe* vs. *Henry Wade 410 U.S. 113*, an unmarried pregnant woman who wished to terminate her pregnancy by abortion initiated an action in United District Court for the Northern District of Texas, seeking a declaratory judgement that the Texas criminal abortion statutes, which prohibited abortion except with respect to those procured or attempted by medical advice for the purpose of saving the life of the mother, were unconstitutional. The Supreme Court said that although the Constitution of the United States does not explicitly mention any right of privacy, the United States Supreme Court recognises that a right of personal privacy, or a guarantee of certain areas or zones of privacy, does exist under the Constitution, and "that the roots of that right may be found in the First Amendment, in the Fourth and Fifth Amendments, in the penumbras of the Bill of Rights, in the Ninth Amendment, and in the concept of liberty guaranteed by the first section of the Fourteenth Amendment" and "that right to privacy is not absolute".

The usual starting point in any discussion of the growth of legal concept of privacy, though not necessarily the correct one, is the famous article "*The Right to Privacy*" by *Charles Warren* and *Louis D. Brandeis, 4 Harward Law Rev. 193*. What was truly creative in that article was their insistence that privacy – the right to be let alone – was an interest that man should be able to assert directly and not derivately from his efforts to protect other interests. To protect man's inviolate personality "against the intrusive behaviour so increasingly evident in their times, *Warren and Brandeis* thought that the law should provide both a criminal and a private law remedy." Once a civilisation has made a distinction between the "outer" and the "inner" man between the life of the soul and the life of the body, between the spiritual and the material, between the sacred and the profane, between the realm of God and the realm of Caesar, between Church and State, between rights inherent and inalienable and rights that are in the power of government to give and take away, between public and private, between society and solitude, it becomes impossible to avoid the idea of privacy by whatever name it may be called – the idea of a private sphere in which man may become and remain "himself".

There can be no doubt that makers of our Constitution wanted to ensure conditions favourable to the pursuit of happiness. They certainly realized as Brandeis J. said in his dissent in *Olmstead* vs. *United States, 277 U.S. 438*, the significance of man's spiritual nature, of his feelings and of his intellect and that only a part of the pain, pleasure, satisfaction of life can be found in material things and therefore, they must be deemed to have conferred upon the individual as against the government a sphere, where he should be let alone.

The liberal individualist tradition has stressed in particular, three personal ideals, to each of which corresponds a range of private affairs. The first is the *ideal of personal relations*; the second, the *Lockean ideal* of the politically free man in a minimally regulated society; the third the *Kantian ideal* of the morally autonomous man, acting on principles that he accepts as rational.

There can be no doubt that privacy-dignity claims deserve to be examined with care and to be defined only when an important countervailing interest is shown to be superior. If the court does find that a claimed right is entitled to protection as a fundamental privacy right, a law infringing it must satisfy the compelling state interest test. Then the question would be whether a state interest is of such paramount importance as would justify an infringement of the right. Obviously, if the enforcement of morality, were held to be compelling as well as permissible state interest, the characterization of a claimed right as a fundamental privacy right would be of far less significance. The question whether enforcement of morality is a state interest sufficient to justify the infringement of a fundamental privacy right need not be considered for the purpose of this case and therefore we refuse to enter the controversial thicket whether enforcement of morality is a function of State.

Individual autonomy, perhaps the central concern of any system of limited government, is protected in part under our Constitution by explicit constitutional guarantees. "In the application of the Constitution our contemplation cannot only be of what has been but what may be." Time works changes and brings into existence new conditions. Too broad a definition of privacy raises serious questions about the propriety of judicial reliance on a right that is not explicit in the Constitution. Of course, privacy primiarily concerns the individual. It therefore, relates to and overlaps with the concept of liberty. The most serious advocate of privacy must confess that there are serious problems of defining the essence and scope of the right. Privacy interest in autonomy must also be placed in the context of other rights and values.

Any right to privacy, must encompass and protect the personal intimacies of the home, the family, marriage, motherhood, procreation and child rearing. This catalogue approach to the question is not as instructive as it does not give any analytical picture of that distinctive characteristics of the right of privacy. Perhaps, the only suggestion that can be offered as unifying principle underlying the concept has been the assertion that a claimed right must be a fundamental right implicit in the concept of ordered liberty.

Rights and freedoms of citizens are set forth in the Constitution in order to guarantee that the individual, his personality and those things stamped with his personality shall be free from official interference except where a reasonable basis for intrusion exists. "*Liberty aginst government*", a phrase coined by Professor Corwin expresses this idea forcefully. In this sense, many of the fundamental rights of citizens can be described as contributing to the right to privacy.

As Ely says: "There is nothing to prevent one from using the word "privacy" to mean the freedom to live one's life without governmental interference. But the court obviously does not so use the term. Nor could it, for such a right, is at stake in every case.

There are two possible theories for protecting privacy of home. The first is that activities in the home harm others only to the extent that they cause offence resulting from the mere thought that the individual's might be engaging in such activities and that such harm is not constitutionally protectible by the State. The second is that individual need a place of sanctuary where they can be free from societal control. The importance of such a sanctuary is that individuals can drop the mask, desist for a while from projecting on the world the image that may reflect the values of their peers rather than the realities of their natures.

The right to privacy in any event will necessarily have to go through a process of case-by-case development. Therefore, even assuming that the right to personal liberty, the right to move freely throughout the territory of India and the freedom of speech create an independent right of privacy as an emanation from them which can characterize as a fundamental right, we do not think that the right is absolute.

The European Convention on Human Rights, which came into force on 3.9.1953, represents a valiant attempt to tackle the new problem. Art. 8 of the convention is worth citing (*"Privacy and Human Rights" Ed. A.H. Robertson, p. 176*):

"1. Everyone has the right to respect for his private and family life, his home and his correspondence.

"2. There shall be no interference by a public authority with the exercise of that right except such as is in accordance with the law and is necessary in a democratic society in the interests of national security, public safety or the economic well-being of the country for the prevention of disorder or crime, for the protection of health or morals or for the protection of the rights and freedoms of others."

(10) *T. Sareetha* Vs. *T. Venkata Subbiah AIR 1983 A.P. 356*

Sexual cohabitation is an indispensable ingredient of a decree for restitution of conjugal rights. It follows, therefore, that a decree for restitution of conjugal rights passed by a civil court extends not only to the grant of relief to the decree-holder to the co. of the other spouse, but also embraces the right to have marital intercourse with the other party. The consequence, of the enforcement of such a decree are firstly to transfer the choice to have or not to have marital intercourse to the state from the concerned individual and secondly, to surrender the choice of the individual to allow or not to allow one's body to be used as a vehicle for another human being's creation to the State. Belief of restitution of conjugal rights fraught with such serious consequences to the concerned individual where granted under section 9 enables the decree-holder through application of financial sanctions provided by O. 21, Rules 32 and 33 of C.P.C. to have sexual cohabitation with an unwilling party. There can be no doubt that a decree of restitution of conjugal rights thus enforced offends the inviolability of the body and the mind subjected to the decree and offends the integrity of such a person and invades the marital privacy and domestic intimacies of such a person.

It cannot be denied that among the few points that distinguish human existence from that of animals, sexual autonomy an individual enjoys to choose his or her partner to a sexual act, is of primary importance. Sexual expression is so integral to one's personality that it is impossible to conceive of sexuality on any basis except on the basis of consenual participation of the opposite sexes. No relationship between man and woman is more rested on mutual consent personality forged than sexual relationship.

The coercive act of the state compelling sexual cohabitation must be regarded as a great constraint and torture imposed on the mind of the unwilling party. The life of a man or woman which the sovereign can commander through the coercive power of the State for performing an unwilling act of sexual cohabitation cannot but be regarded as that of a human beast drained of all spirituality. In *Russel* vs. *Russel (1897) A.C. 395* Lord Hershell long ago noted the barbarity of this judicial remedy.

In the process of making such a fateful choice as to when, where and how if at all she should beget, bear, deliver and rear a child, the wife consistent with her human dignity, should never be excluded. Conception and delivery of a child involves the most intimate use of her body. The marvel of creation takes place inside her body and the child that would be born is of her own flesh and blood. In a matter which is so intimately concerns her body and which is so vital for her life, a decree of restitution of conjugal rights totally excludes her.

The British Law Commission presided over by Mr. Justice Scarmen (as he then was) recommended recently on 9.7.1969 the abolition of this uncivilised remedy of restitution of conjugal rights. Accepting the recommendation of the British Law Commission, the British Parliament through Section 20 of the *Matrimonial Proceedings and Property Act, 1970* abolished the right to claim restitution of conjugal rights in the English courts.

But our ancient Hindu system of matrimonial law never recognised this institution of conjugal right although it fully upheld the duty of the wife to surrender to her husband.

This could have been only because of its realisation that in a matter so intimately concerned the wife or the husband, the parties are better left alone without state interference.

The plain question that arises is whether our Parliament now functioning under the constitutional constraint of the fundamental rights conceived and enacted for the preservation of human dignity and promotion of personal liberty, can legally impose sexual cohabitation between unwilling, opposite sexual partners even if it be during the matrimony of the parties?

Art. 21 prevents the State from treating the human life as that of any other animal. It is now well-established by the decisions of the Supreme Court that the word "life" occurring in the above Article 21 has spiritual significance as the word "life" occurring in the famous 5th and 14th Amendments to the American Constitution does. In those constitutional provisions of the American Constitution, the "life" is interpreted by Mr. Justice Field in his dissenting judgement in *Munn* vs. *Illinois (1877) 24 L Ed. p. 17* to mean and signify "more than a person's right to lead animal or vegetative existence". Field J. said in the above Munn's case, "By the term life as here used something more is meant than mere animal existence". The contrast drawn by Field J. emphasizing the difference between existence of a free willing human and that of an unfree animal was accepted by our Supreme Court first in *Kharak Singh* Vs. *State of U.P. (1964) I.S.C.R. 332* and next in *Govind* Vs. *State of M.P. (1975) 3 S.C.R. 946* transforming Art. 21 of our Constitution, into a charter for civilisation. In *Kharak Singh's case* Rajagopala Ayyangar J. for the majority and Suba Rao J. for the concurring minority accepted the above meaning and significance given to the word "life" by Field J. in Munn's case. Both held that Art. 21 of our Constitution to be the source for the protection of our personal liberty and life in the elevated sense. Suba Rao J. perceptively observed that right to privacy forms a part of the guaranteed right of personal liberty in Art. 21 of the Constitution. In a scientific age, psychological fears and restraints generated by the use of scientific methods, he feared may constitute even greater denial of personal liberty than mere crude physical restraints of a bygone age.

In a later decision of the Supreme Court in *Govind* vs. *State of M.P.* (AIR 1975 SC 1378) Mathew J. taking the lead given by the minority judgement of Subarao J. in the above-mentioned *Kharak Singh's case (AIR 1963 SC 1295)* and adverting to the American legal and philosophical literature on right to privacy and to the American cases reported in *Griswold* Vs. *Connecticut (1965) 14 L Ed. 2d. 510* and *Jane Roe* Vs. *Henry Wade (1973) 35 L Ed. 2d. p. 147* noted that Art. 21 of our Constitution embraces the right to privacy and human dignity. The centrepiece of the judgement in *Govind's case* is to hold that right to privacy is part of Art. 21 of our Constitution and to stress its constitutional importance and to call for its protection. The learned judge then examined the content of the right to privacy and observed that "any right to privacy must encompass and protect the personal initimacies of the home, the family, marriage, motherhood, procreation and child rearing". The learned judge stressed the primordial importance of the right to privacy for human happiness and directed the courts not to reject the privacy-dignity claims brought before them except where the countervailing State interests are shown to have overwhelming importance. He observed that "there can be no doubt that the makers of our Constitution wanted to ensure conditions favourable to the pursuit of happiness. They certainly realised as Brandeis J. said in his dessent in *Olmstead* vs. *United States of America (1927–277 U.S. 438)* the significance of man's spiritual nature, of his feelings, and of his intellect and that only a part of the pain, pleasure, satisfaction of life can be found in material things and therefore, they must be deemed to have conferred upon the individual as against the Government a sphere where he should be let alone". The learned judge also stated "There can be no doubt that privacy-dignity claims deserve to be examined with care and to be denied only when an important countervailing interest is shown to be superior". *Govind's case* thus firmly laid it down that Art. 21 protects the right to privacy and promotes the individual dignity mentioned in the preamble to our Constitution. *Govind's case* also lays it down that the courts should protect and uphold those important constitutional rights except where the claims of those rights for protection are required to be subordinated to superior state interests.

However, it must be admitted that the concept of right to privacy does not lend itself to easy logical definition. This is so partly because as Tom Gaiety said in his Article "*Redefining Privacy*" *(12 Harv. Civ. Rights. Civil Lib. Rev. p. 233)* the concept was thrown up in great haste from a miscellancy of legal rock and stone and partly because of inherent difficulties in defining such an elusive concept. The difficulty arises out of the fact that this concept is not unitary concept but is multi-dimensional susceptible more for enumeration than definition. But it can be confidently asserted that any plausible definition of right to privacy is bound to take human body as its first and most basic reference for control over personal identity. Such a definition is bound to include body's inviolability and integrity and intimacy of personal identity, including marital privacy. A few representative samples would bear this out. Gaiety defined privacy as "an autonomy or control over the intimacies of personal identity". Richard B. Parker in his "A Definition of Privacy" quoted in "*Philosophy and Public Affairs*" *(1975) Vol.4, No.4, pp. 295-314* wrote:

> "....Privacy is control over when and by whom the various parts of us can be sensed by others. By 'sensed' is meant simply seen, heard, touched, smelled or tasted."

Gary L. Bostwick writing in California Law Review, Vol. 64, p. 1447 suggests that "privacy" is divisible into three components: (a) repose, (b) sanctuary, and (c) intimate decisions. Of these three components, he holds, that the last one is an eminently more dynamic privacy concept as compared to repose and sanctuary (p. 1466). Prof. Tribe in his American Constitutional Law, p. 921 stressed another fundamental facet of the right to privacy problem. He wrote, *inter alia*:

> "Of all decisions a person makes about his or her body, the most profound and intimate relates to two sets of questions. First, whether, when and how one's body is to become the vehicle for another human being's creation."

Applying the definitional aids to our discussion, it cannot but be admitted that a decree for restitution of conjugal rights constitutes the grossest form of violation of an individual's right to privacy. Applying Prof. Tribe's definition of right to privacy, it must be said, that the decree for restitution of conjugal rights constitutes the grossest form of violation of an individual's right to privacy. Applying Prof. Tribe's definition of right to privacy, it must be said, that the decree for restitution of conjugal rights denies the woman her free choice whether, when and how her body is to become the vehicle for the procreation of another human being. Applying Parker's definition, it must be said that a decree for restitution of conjugal rights deprives a woman of control over her choice as to when and by whom the various parts of her body should be allowed to be sensed. Applying the tests of Gaiety and Bostwick, it must be said, that the woman loses her control over her most intimate decisions clearly, therefore, the right to privacy guaranteed by Art. 21 of our Constitution is flagrantly violated by a decree of restitution of conjugal rights.

A few decided American cases have also taken the same view of the Constitutional right to privacy in that country.

The observations of Justice McReynolds in *Meyer* vs. *Nebraska* (1923) 67 L Ed. 1042 highlight certain facets of this right to privacy. There the learned judge observed:

> "Without doubt, it denotes not merely freedom from bodily restraint but also the right of any individual to contract to engage in any of the common occupations of life, to acquire useful knowledge to marry, establish a home and bring up children to worship God according to the dictates of his own evidence, and generally to enjoy those privileges long recognised at common law as essential to the orderly pursuit of happiness by free man ... The established doctrine is that this liberty may not be interfered with under the guise of protecting the public interest, without reasonable relation to some purpose within the competency of the state to effect."

In *Griswold* vs. *Connecticut* (1965) *14 L. Ed. 2d. 510* Mr. Justice Douglas while invalidating a Connecticut statute which made the use of contraceptives a criminal offence wrote for the court that "this law, however operates directly on an intimate relation of husband and wife and their physician's role in one aspect of that relation...", implying that the right to privacy encompasses within their intimate relationship such as those between husband and wife about the use of contraceptives. Of course, the question from where this right to privacy should be derived gave rise to different answers in that case.

Mr. Justice Douglas in *Griswold* Vs. *Connecticut (1965), 14 L. Ed. 2d. 510*, has found penumbral areas of specific guarantees in the *Bill of Rights* as providing the basis for the right of privacy. But Mr. Justice Goldberg wrote in that case highlighting in the process the theoretical confusions in the situation that the right of marital privacy falls within the category right to privacy. *Griswold's case* is an authority for the proposition that the reproductive choice to beget and bear a child does not belong to the State and that belongs to an individual. In *Jane Roe* Vs. *Henry Wade (1973) 35 L.Ed. 2d. 147*, Mr. Justice Blackman for the court observed that the decisions of the American Supreme Court held that "only personal rights that can be deemed fundamental" or implicit in the concept of ordered liberty "... are included in this guarantee of personal privacy. They also make it clear that the right has some extension to activities relating to marriage..., procreation, contraception, family relationships, and child rearing and education..."

> "Yet the marital couple is not an independent entity with a mind and heart of its own, but an association of two individuals each with a separate intellectual and emotional make up. If the right of privacy means anything, it is the right of the INDIVIDUAL married or single, to be free from unwanted governmental intrusions into matters so fundamentally affecting a person as the decision whether to bear or beget a child."

This is a clear recognition of the legal position that right to privacy belongs to a person as an individual and is not lost by marital association. In *Planned Parenthood of Missouri* Vs. *Danforth*, (1976) 49 L. Ed. 2d. 788, the court reiterated the position taken by the American Supreme Court in *Eisenstadt* Vs. *Baird (1972) 405 U.S. 438.* that the right to privacy belongs to each one of the married couple separately and is not lost by reason of their marriage. The court observed, invalidating a statutory condition, that the husband's consent is necessary for termination of pregnancy "we cannot hold that the State has constitutional authority to give a spouse unilaterally the ability to prohibit a wife from terminating her pregnancy." The court further observed that "inasmuch as it is the woman who physically bears the child and who is the more directly and immediately affected by the pregnancy, as between the two, the balance weighs in her favour." Earlier in *Skinner* Vs. *Oklahoma (1941) 86 L.Ed. 1655*, the American Supreme Court characterized the right to reproduce as one of the basic civil rights of man. In the same case, Justice Jackson spoke of the State interference with reproductive decisions as involving dignity and personality. See also the decisions in *Loving* vs. *Virginia (1967), 18 L. Ed. 2d. 1010* and *Zeblocki* vs. *Redhall (1978) 54L. Ed. 2d. 618*.

The above cases of the American Supreme Court clearly establish the proposition that the reproductive choice is fundamental to an individual's right to privacy. They uphold the individual's reproductive autonomy against the State intrusion and forbid the State from usurping that right without overwhelming social justification. That this right belongs even to a married woman is clear from Justice Brennan's opinion quoted above.

(11) Smt. Harvinder Kaur Vs. Harminder Singh Choudhary AIR 1984 Delhi 66

Avadh Behari Rohtagi J. This appeal raises an issue of great importance to well-being of the nation, as it goes to the very root of the marriage relationship. The husband petitioned for restitution of conjugal rights. The wife opposed. The Additional District Judge granted a decree of restitution of conjugal rights to the husband. From that decree the wife appeals to the court.

On appeal, counsel for the wife attacked the constitutional validity of Section 9 of the Hindu Marriage Act. I. issued notice to Attorney-General. He appeared and argued the case. This part of the judgement deals with the constitutional question. The rest is concerned with the facts of the case.

In the forefront of his arguments, counsel referred [him] to *T. Sareetha* Vs. *T. Venkata Subbaiah, AIR 1983 A.P. 356*. In that case P.A. Chaudhary J. held that Section 9 of the Hindu Marriage Act, 1955. (The Act) offends Articles 14 and 21 of the Constitutioin and therefore declared it null and void. It was a simple case in which the husband had filed an application against the wife for restitution of conjugal rights under Section 9 of the Act. The wife raised an objection to the jurisdiction of the Court. The Subordinate Judge held that Cuddapah Court had jurisdiction to try the petition. The wife went in revision to the High Court. Chaudhary J. in agreement with the Subordinate Judge, held that Cuddapah Court had jurisdiction to try the petition.

But the case is not important on this point. The chief point decided was about the constitutional validity of Section 9 of the Act.

The learned Judge held that the remedy of restitution of conjugal rights was "barbarous", "uncivilsed" and "an engine of oppression". The main reason for holding that Section 9 offended Article 21 of the Constitution was that a decree for restitution of conjugal rights was an order "to coerce through judicial process, the unwilling party to have sex against that person's consent and free will with the decree-holder." This, he held, was "degrading the human dignity and monstrous to human spirit." The learned judge took the view that the British Indian courts "thoughtlessly imposed that rule into our country and blindly enforced it among the Hindus and the Muslims. The origin of this uncivilised remedy in our ancient country is only recent and is wholly illegitimate. Section 9 had merely aped the British and mechanically re-enacted that legal provision of the British ecclesiastical origin."

RESTITUTION OF CONJUGAL RIGHTS

In (his) opinion this view is based on a misconception of the true nature of the remedy of restitution of conjugal rights. Section 9 reads as under:

"*Restitution of Conjugal rights*: When either the husband or the wife has, without reasonable excuse withdrawn from the society of the other, the aggrieved party may apply by petition to the District Court for restitution of conjugal truth of the statements made in such petition and that there is no legal ground why the application should not be granted, may decree restitution of conjugal rights accordingly.

Explanation: Where a question arises whether there has been reasonable excuse for withdrawal from the society, the burden of proving reasonable excuse shall be on the person who has withdrawn from the society."

Chaudhary J. thought that Section 9 imposes "sexual cohabitation between unwilling opposite sexual partners". He called it "forced sex," "coerced sex" and "forcible marital intercourse". He went on to hold that the State interference destroyed the "sexual autonomy" and "reproductive autonomy" of the individual's wife who keeping away from arrangement, cannot be forced without violating her rights to privacy, to bear a child by her husband, he said. A large number of decisions have been cited in support of the view.

This decision is the first of its kind to take this view. [He] respectfully dissent(s). The decree for restitution does nothing of the kind under Section 9 the court has power to make a decree of restitution of conjugal rights which is the remedy available to enforce the return of a spouse who has withdrawn from cohabitation. The decree if granted, orders the respondent to return within a period of one year to the aggrieved party. This period is specified in Section 13 (1-A) (ii) of the Act. "This remedy is aimed at preserving the marriage and not at disrupting it as in the case of divorce or judicial separation." As Tolstoy says in his *Law and Practice of Divorce* (6th Edition), p. 99:

> "The court cannot enforce sexual intercourse, but only cohabitation, and restitution of conjugal rights cannot be ordered where the respondent refuses sexual intercourse but continues to cohabit with the petitioner."
>
> [*See Jackson* Vs. *Jackson* (*1924*), *p. 19*]

In Halsbury's *Laws of England* (3rd Edition), Volume 12, page 284 it is said:

> "If (cohabitation) does not necessarily mean sexual intercourse, which the court cannot enforce, so that refusal of sexual intercourse by itself does not constitute refusal to cohabit."

In support of this proposition the high authority of Lord Stowell in *Forster* Vs. *Forster* (*1790*) *1 Hag Con 144*; *Orme* Vs. *Orme*, (*1824*) *2 Add 382*: *162 ER 335* and *Rowe* Vs. *Rowe* (*1865*) *34 LJP M&A III* have been cited:

One thing is clear from Lord Stowell's decision in *Forster* Vs. *Forster* and Halsbury's statement of law that the court does not and cannot enforce sexual intercourse. [He] accept(s) it as true that sexual relations constitute a most important attribute of the conception of marriage. But it is also true that they do not constitute its whole content, nor can the remaining aspects of the matrimonial construction be said to be of wholly unconstitutional or trivial character. Marriage has been described in these words:

> "Besides the procreation and education of children, marriage has for its object the mutual society, help and comfort, that the one ought to have of the other both in prosperity and adversity. Marriage is the most solemn engagement which one human being can contract with

another. It is contract formed with a view not only to the benefit of parties, to the the benefit of their common offspring and to the moral order of civilised society.

[Shelford on Marriage and Divorce (1841) p. 3 quoted in *Weatherley* Vs. *Weatherley* (1946) 2 AII ER 1 (11)]

COHABITATION: ITS MEANING

The object of the restitution decree is to bring about cohabitation between the estranged parties so that they can live together in the matrimonial home in amity. That is the privacy purpose. Cohabitation has been defined in these words:

"Cohabitation does not necessarily depend upon whether there is sexual intercourse between the husband and the wife. Cohabitation means living together as husband and wife and as I endeavoured to point out in *Evans* Vs. *Evans (1948) 1 KB 175*, cohabitation consists in the husband acting as a husband towards the wife and the wife acting as a wife towards the husband, the wife rendering house-wifely duties to the husband and the husband cherishing and supporting his wife as a husband should. Of course, sexual intercourse usually takes place between parties of moderate age if they are cohabiting and if there is sexual intercourse it is very strong evidence – in fact it may be conclusive evidence – that they are cohabiting; but it does not follow that because they do not have sexual intercourse they are not 'cohabiting'. Cohabiting as I have said, means the husband and wife living together as husband and wife."

[*Thomas* Vs. *Thomas (1948) 2 KB 294, per Lord Goddard C.J. at p. 297*]

"The cohabitation of two people as husband and wife means that they are living together as husband and wife, the wife rendering wifely services to her husband; the husband rendering husband-like service to his wife. They must live together not merely as two people living in one house, but as husband and wife."

[*Thomas* Vs. *Thomas (1948) 2 KB 294 per Lord Goddard C.J. at p. 297*].

"The cohabitation of two people as husband and wife means that they are living together as husband and wife, the wife rendering wifely services to her husband; the husband rendering husband-like service to his wife. They must live together not merely as two people living in one house, but as husband and wife."

[*Wheatley* Vs. *Wheatley (1950) 1 KB 39 per Lord Goddard CJ at p. 43*]

This is the true office of a restitution decree. Not that it compels sexual intercourse by "force of arms", as Chaudhary J. thought. Where either the husband or the wife has withdrawn from the society of the other party without just cause, the court orders the withdrawing party to return to the conjugal fold, so that the consortium is not broken.

Consortium: Its meaning

Consortium means "Companionship, love, affection comfort, mutual services, sexual intercourse. All these belong to the married state. Taken together they make up consortium." Consortium has been defined as a partnership or association; but in the matrimonial sense it implies much more than these rather cold words suggest. it involves a sharing of two lives, a sharing of joys and sorrows of each party of their successes and disappointments. In the fullest sense it implies a companionship between each of them; entertainment of mutual friends, sexual intercourse – all these elements which when combined, justify the old common law dictum that a man and his wife are one person.

[*Crabtree* Vs. *Crabtree (No. 2) (1964) Australian LR 820, per selby; J. at p. 821*]

Refusal of Sexual Intercourse:

From the definitions of cohabitation and consortium it appears that sexual intercourse is one of the elements that goes to make up the marriage. But it is not the ***summum bonum***. Sex is the refrain of *T. Sareetha's case (AIR 1983 Andh Pra. 356)*. As if marriage consists of nothing else except sex, chaudhary, J.'s overemphasis on sex is the fundamental fallacy in his reasoning. He seems to suggest that restitution decree has only one purpose, that is to compel the unwilling wife to "have sex with the husband. This view was discarded long ago. As early as 1924 Sir Henry Duke President in *Jackson* Vs. *Jackson (1924 p. 19) (Supra) at pages 23, 24*, said:

"Wanton refusal of one or other of the parties to a marriage to have sexual intercourse is no doubt a wrong

> thing. It is the international breach of one of the ties of marriage, but it does not produce, either separation or living apart ... Reflection upon the manifold duties of the married state must, [He] think(s), convince any reasonable mind that this refusal of itself by one of the parties, while the parties remain living together and discharging the other duties of the married stage cannot be said to amount to desertion. It is not abandonment, it is not living apart. If it is a refusal of a duty it does not purport to conclude the matrimonial relationship."

The remedy of restitution aims at cohabitation and consortium and not merely at sexual intercourse. To say that the restitution decree "subjects a person by the long arm of the law to a positive sex act is to take the grossest view of the marriage institution. The restitution decree does not enforce sexual intercourse. This can be proved by a simple illustration. A husband and wife are living under the same roof. But the wife does not allow the husband sexual intercourse with her because she thinks that it is a horrid and beastly thing. Will the court pass a restitution decree? The answer is 'No'. Since they are living together as one household, as one unit and not as two the law cannot go further and compel them to have sexual intercourse. The court has neither the means nor the capacity to enforce its decree in the marriage bed. It is most undesirable, save where we are clearly enjoined by statute so to do to seek to discover or reveal the secret intimacies of the marriage bed. If a question arises whether the marriage has been consumated, no doubt this may be necessary. It is not, (he) think(s), right that we should do so in a case such as the present. All that the court in a husband's petition under Section 9 does it to seek to enquire whether there is a "reasonable excuse" for the withdrawal by the wife from the society of the husband. It is a fallacy to think that the restitution of conjugal rights constitutes "the starkest form of governmental invasion of "marital privacy" as Chaudhary J. seems to think. The burden of proving reasonable excuse lies on the wife. A spouse is entitled to the other's society and if the law enforces this conjugal duty there is nothing wrong.

The leading idea of Section 9, to [his] mind, is to preserve the marriage. The outstanding fact is that the husband and wife are living apart and leading their own separate lives. The court seeks to enquire into this separation. The enquiry into the affairs of the matrimonial life is to be confined to this one fact – "Is there a just cause for the respondent to live apart and separate from the petitioning spouse?" Further delving into their matrimonial life is not necessary. If there is no rupture of marital relations and the parties are living together in the ordinary way of man and wife there is no need to resort to Sec. 9 of the Act. Section 9 is a means of saving the marriage. It can be that the erring spouse comes on the right path and a broken home is rebuilt. Section 9 in a sense is an extension of sub-section (2) and (3) of Secton 23 of the Act which encourages reconciliation by the court. The court is enjoined to make every endeavour to bring about a reconciliation between the parties. Section 9 is a concrete illustration of this. What the court seeks to do is to enquire into the causes which have led to the rupture of the marital relations and a refusal to share the matrimonial life. If there is no reasonable cause for living apart the court orders the withdrawing party to live together. It is the policy of the Act that the parties should live together. Living apart is the very antithesis of living together as society is the antithesis of separation. The policy of the Act is to assist in the maintenance of marriage other than those referred to a mere shell. Where there is a complete cessation of cohabitation and the parties are living apart Section 9 can properly be involved. This state of affairs is normally brought about by one spouse leaving the matrimonial home, so that they are no longer living under the same roof. They are living in a state of separation. They are living as two units rather than one. Two separate households are created. So they are treated as living apart unless they are living with each other in the same matrimonial home.

A difficult situation arises. The matrimonial relationship has been terminated though marriage is subsisting. The marriage is in name only and not in substance, in law and not in fact. The policy underlying the legislation is that it is not conducive to the public interest permanence by the bonds of a marriage, the duties of which have long ceased to be observed by either party and the purposes of which have immediately failed. Such a condition of marriage in law which is no marriage in fact leads only to immorality and unhappiness.

Germ of the Breakdown Theory:

The germ of the breakdown theory is to be found in a New Zealand case reported in 1921. Salmond J. in a passage which has now become classic enunciated the breakdown principle in these words:

"The legislature must, I think, be taken to have intended that separation for three years is to be accepted by this court as *prima facie* a good ground for divorce. When the matrimonial relation has for that period ceased to exist *de facto* it should, unless there are special reasons to the contrary cease to exist *de jure* also. In general it is not in the interests of the parties or in the interest of the public, that a man and woman should remain bound together as husband and wife in law when for a lengthy period they have ceased to be such in fact. In the case of such a separation the essential purpose of marriage have been frustrated, and its further continuance is in general not merely useless but mischievous."

(*Lodder* Vs. *Lodder* (1921), *New Zealand LR 876 at p. 877*, qoted in Seventy-first Report of Law Commission of India, pp. 11, 12].

The marriage has ceased to be a real union in the true sense because the spouses are withdrawn from each other. They are living apart. There is no cohabitation. Living apart and cohabitation are mutually exclusive opposites.

Where do we go from here? The marriage is on the rocks. If the rift between husband and wife is no more than the ordinary wear and tear of married life there should be no great difficulty in the parties coming together or living as ordinary husbad and wife. A restitution decree should be able to achieve this in some cases if not all. But if the differences are deep-seated and there is no resumption of cohabitation in spite of the decree of restitution, the only course open to the legislature is to end the marriage, because it cannot be mended. This is done by dissolving it by a decree of divorce. If the decree of restitution is not obeyed for the space of one year and the parties continue to live separately it is undoubtedly the best evidence of breakdown of marriage, and the passing of time, most reliable evidence that the marriage is finished. Section 13 (I-A) is a legislative recognition of this principle which was enunciated by Salmond J. as early as 1921 in *Lodder* Vs. *Lodder* (1921) *New Zealand LR 876* (*supra*).

Concept of Breakdown in Section 13 (*I-A*):

Section 13 (I-A)(ii) says that if the withdrawing spouse is disobedient to the decree of restitution of conjugal rights and the husband and wife continue to live separately as before each of them is entitled to a dissolution of marriage which has been a marriage in name only but in fact as empty legal shell. This law is based on the theory of irretrievable breakdown of marriage. The Indian Legislature introduced this theory although in part only, as early as 1964 when it inserted sub-section (I-A) by the Amending Act 44 of 1964 in the parent Act. In England this theory found favour with the Parliament in the Divorce Law Reforms Act, 1969. In the Matrimonial Act of 1973, the provision based on breakdown theory has been re-enacted. The Law Commission of India has recommended its adoption in its Seventy-first Report of 1978. But a foresighted legislature thought as early as in 1964 that the decree of restitution of conjugal rights will serve a useful purpose because it will give to the parties a cooling-off time of one year which was not only desirbale but essential. If the marriage cannot be saved even after passing the decree of restitution it must be dissolved. A factual separation gives an easily justiciable indication of breakdown. "Living apart" by itself spells breakdown. The breakdown is so patent.

The decree of restitution of conjugal rights acts as an index of connubial felicity. It is a sort of litmus paper. It shows a change of heart if the restitution decree is obeyed. If the decree is disobeyed it is an indicia that the parties have reached a stage of no return. The Act's professed object is to facilitate reconciliation in matrimonial cases. This it does by asking the withdrawing spouse to return to the matrimonial home and gives one year's time to do so. If the restitution decree is not obeyed the court dissolves the marriage on proof of non-compliance of the restitution decree.

There is no warrant in authority extending over 150 years in England from where we have borrowed this matrimonial remedy nor any in India before or after the passing of the Act, the assigning to this remedy of conjugal rights the meaning given by Chaudhary J. He has interpreted Section 9 in a sense clearly inconsistent with the law as expounded in England and India in a stream of authorities. As long as 1866 the Privacy Council in *Moonshee Buzloor Ruheem* Vs. *Shumsoonaissa Begum (1866-67)* 11 *Moo Ind App* 551 applied to this country the English remedy of restitution. The Indian Legislature in 1955 codified this remedy.

The dictum of Chaudhary J. that the restitution decree enforces "sexual cohabitation with an unwilling party" and "constitutes the grossest form of violation of individual's right to privacy" and "offends the inviolability of the body and the mind subjected to the decree and offends the integrity of such a person and invades the marital privacy and domestic intimacies of such a person" is the high water mark of his judicial pronouncement. With respect to the learned judge [he] cannot agree that this is what the restitution decree does. The cases referred to by him do not prove his proposition. *Jackson* Vs. *Jackson* (1924) p. 19 which was approved by the House of Lords in *Weatherley* Vs. *Weatherley (1947) 1 All ER 563* clearly shows that the object of the restitution decree is not to enforce sexual intercourse as the learned judge thought. The Court simply cannot enforce it. In the nature of things it is an impossible task.

Breakdown Theory in Section 13 (ii):

The theory of irretrievable breakdown is also the basis of sub-section (ii) of Section 13. That sub-sction says:

(ii) That in a suit under section 18 of the Hindu Adoption and Maintenance Act 1956 or in a proceeding under Section 125 of the Code of Criminal Procedure, 1973 (or under the corresponding Section 488 of the Code of Criminal Procedure, 1898), a decree or order as the case may be has been passed against the husband awarding maintenance to the wife notwithstanding that she was living apart and that since the passing of such decree or order, cohabitation between the parties has not been resumed for one year or upwards."

This sub-section was inserted by Act No. 68 of 1976.

This provision is akin to the provision of Section 13 (I-A) (i) which provides a ground for divorce on the basis of non-consumption of cohabitation for a period of one year or more after the decree for judicial separation. That ground is available to both, the husband and the wife, because the decree of judicial separtion can be passed in favour of the husband also under Section 10 of the Act. But the provision in Section 13 (ii) is made only in favour of the wife who has been awarded maintenance against the husband either under Section 18 of the Hindu Adoptions and Maintenance Act, 1956 or Section 125 of the Cr. P.C. 1973, or Section 488 Cr. P.C., 1898. This is another indicia of the breakdown of the marriage because living apart and an award of maintenance are strong indications that marriage has broken down beyond repair and there is no hope of the wife over returning to cohabitation with the husband.

More and more the legislature is moving towards the breakdown theory. But it has not completely broken away with the guilt theory which has dominated the law of divorce for 150 years. Section 13 (I-A) is based on the breakdown theory. Section 9 is based on fault theory. After having found fault with the withdrawing spouse and after giving her time of one year for reparation the legislature proceeds to dissolve the marriage because it has utterly broken down. The truth is that the legislature has not accepted the breakdown theory in its modern form as has been accepted in England and has now been recommended for adoption in India by the Law Commission in its Seventy-first Report of 1978. In England Parliament has decreed: "If the marriage has broken down irretrievably, let there be a divorce". It carries no stigma but only sympathy. It is a misfortune which befalls both. No longer is one guilty and the other innocent. No longer are there long contested divorce suits. Nearly every case goes uncontested. The parties come to an agreement, if any, they can, on the things that matter so much to them.

This is in consonance with the modern trend not to insist on the maintenance of a union which has utterly broken down after several years of continuous separation; it may fairly be surmised that the matrimonial life is beyond repair. The only alternative is the legal dissolution of marriage and not a restoration of the marriage bond. It has not been sufficiently realised at all hands that the maintenance of the fiction of a marriage by a legal tie will only drive one or the other or both spouses to sexual and other relations with outsiders clandestinely or under a social stigma rather than openly. Such a marriage serves no purpose except that it increases adultery, fornication and personal bitterness. [*Friedmann – Law in a Changing Society, 2d. Ed. (1959), p. 233*].

The truth is that the fault theory has utterly failed and has provided no solution to marriages which are on the rocks. In the guilt theory "Judges and Lawyers are sometimes reduced to the role of scavengers. The lawyers have to look for the expose, and the Judges are confronted with, the worst obscenities within a married life" (71st Report, p. 14). In the breakdown theory judges certify the death of marriage and lawyers attest the fact. The breakdown theory is a recognition of the defects and demerits of the guilt theory. The remedy of restitution of conjugal rights provided by Section 9 of the Act is based on the assumption that the spouses have a reciprocal right to the society, company or companionship of each other. If the assumption proves wrong divorce is the only "escape route out of a difficult situation."

Origin of the Remedy:

The remedy had its origin in ecclesiastical law of England. In the ecclesiastical courts before 1813 the sanction for enforcing restitution of conjugal rights was excommunication. In that year 6 months' imprisonment was substituted by the English Parliament. In 1884 payments took the place of imprisonment, but at the same time failure to comply was, by Section 5 of the Act of 1884, deemed to be a desertion. The Matrimonial Causes Act, 1965 altered the law. Disobedience to a decree of restitution enabled the petitioning spouse:

(1) To obtain a decree of judicial separation;

(2) To obtain an order for permanent alimony or periodical payments or, if the husband is a petitioner settlement of the wife's property.

In 1970 restitution was abolished.

In India the Code of Civil Procedure (O.21, Rules 32 and 33) has abolished imprisonment but has retained attachment of property. But Rule 33 confers a discretion on the court to refuse execution by attachment and to order periodical payments to be made by the judgement-debtor to the decree-holder. So, in the end there is only a financial sanction behind the restitution decree. Even if the court is bound to make a decree for restitution in a fit case it is no longer bound to enforce it as before by imprisonment or attachment.

There may be cases where though the parties are living under the same roof yet the marriage has completely broken down. In these days of housing shortage the spouses may be compelled to live under the same roof though they have no love for each other. The practical test applied in cases where the parties are still living under the same roof is usually whether one party continues to provide matrimonial services for the other, and whether there is sharing of domestic life. If there is family or communal life there is evidence of resumption of cohabitation. If there is estrangement including a refusal to have sexual intercourse this may be evidence of consortium having come to an end. Whether cohabitation or marital relationship has or has not been resumed is a question of fact and degree to be determined according to common sense principles. Some acts may be eloquent enough to serve as an indication of resumption of cohabitation and some of utter breakdown.

The Test of Resumption of Cohabitation:

It is true that there is a general outcry against this remedy in modern times. It has variously been described as "archaic", "primitive" or "a rehearsal before the main drama of divorce". But in the scheme of the Act the restitution decree is a stepping stone to the more serious step of divorce. It is a passage or passport to divorce. The Indian Legislature believes that there should not be a sudden break of the marriage tie. It believes in reconciliation. It believes that cooling-off period is not only desirable but essential. This is why it allows husband and wife time to come together to the conjugal fold. In the case of restitution decree it orders the withdrawing spouse to return to cohabitation. In the case of judicial separation it sees whether there has been resumption of cohabitation within a period of one year or not. Because in a decree for judicial separation it ceases to be obligatory for the parties to cohabit. But the underlying principle is the same. Section 9 is a provision designed to encourage reconciliation. The Act's professed object is to facilitate reconciliation in matrimonial causes. "Living apart by itself spells breakdown." That this is the theory of the Indian Legislature is clear from Section 13 (iii) of the Act. That sub-section provides for divorce by the wife on the ground that she is living apart and that since the passing of the order of maintenance in her favour there has been no resumption of cohabitation between the parties for one year or upwards. Whether it is a judicial separation or restitution or a maintenance order the legislature employs one single test: Has there been resumption of cohabitation between the parties during the space of one year? If not the answer is dissolution of marriage.

In short, cohabitation is the highest common factor in the material provisions. It is the essence of married life. Take away cohabitation and you take the bottom out of marriage. Resumption of cohabitation means restitution of conjugal rights. Non-resumption means the death of marriage. This is the legislative policy. This court neither approves nor condemns any legislative policy.

According to the Indian Legislature the marriage has not to be ended at once. The breakdown of marriage does not take place in one day. It is a process in which the spouses drift apart. First there is apathy, then indifference and then positive aversion. The consortium of husband and wife, the kind of associaiton which is only possible between husband and wife, ultimately comes to an end.

Divorce Structure:

The divorce structure contemplated in Section 13 (I-A) is based on Section 9 proceedings. If Section 9 is unconstitutional as Chaudhary J. has held, it must necessarily follow that Section 13 (I-A) (ii) is also constitutionally void. By a single stroke the learned judge has demolished the essential part of the divorce structure. Not only has he held Section 9 to be bad he has also, though indirectly, held that henceforth there will be no decree of restitution and no divorce under Section 13 (I-A) (ii). The function of the courts is to interpret and apply the law as enacted by the Legislature. "Courts are concerned only with power to enact statutes, not with their wisdom."

[Stone J. in *U.S.* vs. *Butler (1936) 297 USI*]

A Plea for Abolition:

[He is] aware that there is a body of opinion which favours the abolition of this remedy. The main argument of the abolutionists is that you can take the horse to water but you cannot make it drink. The withdrawing spouse cannot be compelled to cohabit even though a decree is passed against him or her. Some academics have strongly argued for its abolition. (See Article on Restitution of Conjugal Rights Under Hindu Law: A Plea for the Abolition of the Remedy, by R.K. Aggarwal, 1970, ***Journal of the Indian Law Institute***, page 257). But that is to be done by the Legislature and not by the courts. Others have argued for an improvement upon Section 9 and 13 (I-A). It has been suggested that after the passing of the decree of restitution and passing of a prescribed period of time within which cohabitation may be resumed there should be an automatic dissolution of marriage. If there is no return by the withdrawing spouse to cohabitation, it is suggested that there should be no need for fresh divorce proceedings.

(*See Civil Marriage Law: Perspective and Prospects – Indian Law Institute Publication of 1978*)

Professor Duncan Derett has argued for retention of the remedy. He says:

> "The practical utility of the remedy is little in contemporary England, but in India where spouses separate at times due to misunderstandings, failure of mutual communication; or the intrigues of relatives, the remedy of restitution is still of considerable value..."

[*Introduction to Modern Hindu Law (1963) p. 197*]

The Law Commission in their Fifty-ninth Report have not recommended its abolition. The Commission was aware that it had been abolished in England by Section 20 of the Matrimonial Proceedings Act, 1970. (See Footnote 7 at page 55 of the 59th Report).

A recent writer has suggested that "the opinion of Derett is more realistic and that the Hindu society is not mature enough to do away with the remedy. Its abolition would be like throwing away the baby with the bath-water." [R.C. Nagpal–*Modern Hindu Law* (1983) Edition, page 110]. [He] agree(s) with the view of Derett.

Section 9 is the only positive relief under the Act aiming at the prescription of the marriage. The mental make-up of the Anglo-Saxons is different from ours. The truth is that it is requisite that our marriage laws should conform to a logical coherence, that is a matter which the legislature must declare and provide. Time has come to recognise that matrimonial offences are in many cases merely symptomatic of the breakdown of the marriage and that there should also be a provision for divorce in cases where, quite apart from the commission of such offences, the marriage has broken down completely. Courts should be relieved of the difficult task of assigning where fault lay, an issue in matrimony offences too subtle for the average man to determine [*Rayden on Divorce, Vol. I (14th Edition) (1983) p. 311*]. But the remedy lies with the legislature. On this part of the case [his] conclusion is this. Dicta of eminent judges notably Lord Stowell, are all against the view that restitution decree compels the wife "to have sex" with an "unwilling party". No case has even said anything of the sort. None of the cases relied upon says anything of the sort.

Section 9 and Art. 14:

There remains the second argument that Section 9 offends Art. 14 of the Constitution which found favour with the learned Judge. He held that in the remedy of restitution there is inequality because "a suit for restitution by the wife is rare. A passage in Gupte's "Hindu Law in British India", p. 99, 2nd Edition attests to this fact." [He has] consulted Gupte's book. It is an old book of 1947 with a supplement of 1955. At page 929 (not p. 99, as the learned Judge says) the author says: "A suit for restitution by the wife is rare". This was true before the Hindu Marriage Act was enacted in 1955. Gupte was referring to old Hindu Law and not to the Act because the Act had not been passed by then. Previously under Act the decree-holder alone was entitled to issue for divorce. By the Amending Act 44 of 1964 "either party to a marriage" is allowed to present a petition on the ground given in Section 13 (I-A). Even the party found guilty in restitution proceedings is entitled to petition for divorce, under Section 13 (I-A) (ii). "The theory that one cannot take advantage of one's wrong has not been adhered to in the Hindu Marriage Act." (71st Report, p. 16). There is complete equality of the sexes here and equal protection of the laws. [He does] not see how Section 9 can be struck down as violative of Art. 14 of the Constitution.

Constitutional Law and Family Laws:

One general observation must be made. Introduction of Constitutional Law in the home is most inappropriate. It is like introducing a bull in a China shop. It will prove to be a ruthless destroyer of the marriage institution and all that it stands for. In the privacy of the home and the married life under Art. 21, not Art. 14, have any place. In a sensitive sphere which is at once most intimate and delicate the introduction of the cold principles of Constitutional Law will have the effect of weakening the marriage bond. That the restitution remedy was abolished in England in 1970 by Section 20 of the Matrimonial Proceedings and Properties Act, 1970 on the recommendation of the Law Commission headed by Justice Scarman is no ground to hold that it is unconstitutional in the Indian set-up.

In the home the consideration that really obtains is the natural love and affection which counts for so little in these cold courts. Constitutional Law principles find no place in the domestice code – Atkin L.J. in a famous judgement said:

> "The parties themselves are Advocates, Judges, Courts, Sheriff's Officer and Reporter. In respect of these promises each house is a domain into which the King's writ does not seek to run, and to which his officers do not seek to be admitted."
>
> [*Balfour* Vs. *Balfour* (*1919*) *2K.B. 571*].

This illustrates that the house of everyone is to him his castle, and fortress. The spouses can claim a kind of sacred protection behind the door of the family house which generally speaking, the civil authority may not penetrate. The introduction of Constitutional Law into the ordinary domestic relationship of husband and wife will strike at the very root of that relationship and will be a fruitful source of dissension and quarrelling. It will open the door to unlimited litigation in a relationship which should be obviously as far as possible protected from possibilities of that kind. The "domestic community" does not rest on contract scales with seals and sealing wax. Nor on Constitutional Law. It rests on that kind of moral cement which unites and produces "two-in-one-ship."

The learned judge has quoted men of letter like Havelock Ellis and Betrand Russel. It is well known that Betrand Russell had iconoclastic views on marriage and morals. For instance, he advocated that "adultery in itself should not, to my mind, be a ground for divorce unless people are restrained by inhibitions or strong moral scruples, It is very unlikely that they will go moral scruples. It is very unlikely that they will go through life without occasionally having strong impulses to adultery. But such impulses do not by any means necessarily imply that marriage no longer serves its purpose." (*Marriage and Morals* 1967, p. 116). The Indian Legislature has not followed Russell's views in this or in other respects. The fact is that the law of the land cannot be coextensive with the law of morals, nor can the civil consequences of marriage be identical with its religious consequences.

The learned Judge has called restitution a "barbarous remedy". He has quoted Lord Hershell in *Russel* Vs. *Russel (1897) AC 395*. But Lord Hershell was not saying this. What he was saying at pp. 455-56 was that reasonable excuse was not confined only to the grounds of divorce. It can as well be "something short of legal cruelty" which might constitute a reasonable excuse for refusing restitution. This is precisely what happened in India as the history of the Act would show. Section 9(2) as originally enacted provided that "Nothing shall be pleaded in answer to a petition for restitution of conjugal rights which still not be a ground for judicial separation or for nullity of marriage or for divorce." This created considerable difficulty. The Law Commission in its Fifty-ninth Report recommended its deletion. It is not possible for the party to plea a reasonable excuse which may not necessarily be a ground either for judicial separation or nullity or divorce. So the Act was amended and by Act No. 68 of 1976, Section 9(2) was deleted. This brought the law in conformity with the opinion of Lord Hershell. It will, therefore, appear that Lord Hershell's expression "barbarous" was used in a different context. One single sentence from his judgement does not empower the court to strike down Section 9 on the ground that it is "barbarous".

(12) *Wainright* Vs. *Stone 414 U.S. 21 (1973)*

In this case, two males, one convicted for "copulating *per os* and *per anum*", the other for copulating "*per anum*" attacked as unconstitutional the Florida Statute under which they had been tried. Speaking only to the claim that the law was *void* for vagueness the Supreme Court unanimously sustained the conviction.

Comment: Despite *Doe* and *Wainwright*, there has been a trend in American States either toward repealing or amending statutes prescribing homosexual relations between consenting adults or judicial interpretation excluding such conduct from statutory coverage. Enforcement of existing laws is haphazard, encouraging blackmail rather than adherence to particular moral standards. In July, 1975 the U.S. Civil Service Commission published a set of rules governing standards for hiring and promoting which were to apply equally to homosexuals and hetrosexuals. There is absence of evidence that homosexuals exert an adverse effect on society.

(13) *West German Constitutional Court: "Homosexual activity clearly offends against the moral code".*

HOMOSEXUALITY CASE — *6B VERF GE 389 (1957)*

Two male homosexuals brought a constitutional complaint alleging that Section 175 of the Penal Code violated equal protection of the law and also interfered with the free development of their personalities. Art. 2(1) of the Basic Law stipulates:

"Everyone shall have the right to the free development of his personality, in so far as he does not infringe the rights of others or offend against the constitutional order or the moral code."

Comment: The Penal Code of the Federal Republic has since been amended so that homosexuals relations between consenting adults is no longer a crime. Section 58 of the Canadian Criminal Code now exempts from punishment homosexual acts committed in private between consulting adults. The catalyst for much recent liberalising legislation in this field has been the famous Wolfendan Report to the British Parliament. (*The Commission on Homosexual Offences and Prostitution Report* (1957). The Irish, however, have not responded affirmatively; homosexuals relations are still serious crimes there.

(14) *West German Constitutional Court: "The Basic Law protects as an independent value the life which is developing in a mother's body."*

ABORTION REFORM LAW CASE : *39 B VERF GE 1 (1975)*

Since the German Empire first adopted it's Penal Code in 1871, Section 218 had forbidden all abortions. The only exception in case of a serious threat to the mother's life, was judicially created in 1927. Capping decades of discussion and months of acrimonious Parliamentary wrangling, the Bundestag in June 1974 overrode a suspensive veto by the Bundesrat to pass the highly controversial Fifth Penal Code Reform Bill that the ruling coalition of social democrats and Free Democrats had sponsored.

Except under specified circumstances, abortion after the 13th Day of pregnancy remained a crime, although the penalty for the mother's obtaining an abortion was reduced from five years in prison to one year, with no penalty for her unsuccessfully attempting an abortion. The exceptions under which abortions would not be punished were broad and divided the pregnancy into three intervals. Though the first twelve weeks, a woman and her doctor were free to decide on an abortion. Then, between twelve and twentytwo weeks, a woman and her doctor could opt for an abortion if –

(1) The continuation of the pregnancy would gradually jeopardize the mother's health or life, or

(2) There was strong reason to believe that the child would suffer from serious and irreparable defects if born. Abortion after twenty-two weeks remained illegal except where the mother's life was imperilled. In addition, the Bill made it a serious offence for a physician to perform an abortion at any time without advising the woman of the consequences of termination and counselling her about public and private institutions that could help ease problems in continuing a pregnancy or in caring for a child.

Judgement of the First Senate

How the law should handle termination of pregnancy has been

publicly discussed for decades. This phenomenon of social life raises manifold problems involving questions of biology, particularly human genetics, anthropology, medicine, psychology, social and political relations and finally ethics and moral theology. The legislator's task is to consider their diverse and interconnected arguments to integrate them with specific political considerations and practical experiences of legal life, and to decide how the legal order should respond. The Constitutional Court can examine legislative regulations only with respect to their compatibility with the Basic Law. The significance of this constitutional inquiry is evident if one keeps in mind that protection of human life is a central value of every legal order. A decision on standards and boundaries of legislative discretion requires an overall view of the system of Constitutional norms and order of values.

Art. 2, Section 2, Sent. I, of the Basic Law protects as an independent value the life which is developing in a mother's body. Interpretation of Art. 2, Sec. 2, Sent. 1, of the Basic Law must begin with its exact words: "Everyone shall have the right to life."

According to biological and psychological knowledge, human life exists from the fourteenth day after conception. This process of development continues without sharp breaks. Not even birth completes it. Therefore, the protection of Art. 2, Section 2, Sent. I, cannot depend on the "complete" human being after birth nor on the independently viable *nasciturus* (fetus). The right to life is granted to everyone who lives. One cannot make distinction between individual phases of developing life before birth or between unborn and born life. Everyone in the sense of Art. 2 includes every living person. "Everyone" includes the unborn human being.

The State's duty of protection is far-reaching. Of course, direct State interference in a developing life is outlawed; even further, the State must protect and promote this life, above all, defend it from unlawful interference by other persons. Human life is among the highest values in the Basic Law's order. It is the vital basis of human dignity and the precondition of all other basic rights.

The State's duty to protect developing life also extends to the matter. There is no question that the natural connection between the unborn life and the mother's life constitutes a special relationship. Pregnancy belongs to the private sphere of a woman whose protection the Basic Law guarantees through Art. 2, Section I, and Art. 1,

Section 1. If one considered the fetus only as a part of the material organism, termination of pregnancy would remain in the sphere of private life in which public interference is not allowed. But because fetus is an autonomous human being, under protection of the Constitution, termination of pregnancy has a social dimension which opens it to public regulations and demands regulations. Of course, the Basic Law also acknowledges and protects a woman's right to free development of her personality, which includes a general liberty of action and thereby also freedom to decide against parenthood. But this right is not guaranteed without limitations. The rights of others, the constitutional order, and the moral code all restrict it. The rights of woman can never allow interference in the protected legal sphere of others without a legitimizing reason, or permit destruction of life itself, especially if there exists by nature a special responsibility for this life. A compromise which guarantees both protection of the fetus as well as freedom of abortion to the pregnant woman is impossible because termination of pregnancy always means destruction of unborn life. Following Art. I Section I of the Basic Law, the decision cannot give priority to protection of the fetus over the woman's right of self-determination. Pregnancy, birth and raising a child can restrict her freedom. On the other hand, termination of pregnancy liquidates the unborn life.

The legal order cannot make a woman's self-determination the principle of its regulations. The state must, in principle, act in accordance with the mother's duty to carry out the pregnancy in principle. It must outlaw termination of pregnancy. This disapporval must be clearly expressed in the legal order. The false impression must be avoided that termination of pregnancy is something like a visit to a doctor to cure an illness, or even a legal alternative to birth control. Neither can the State dismiss its responsibility by acknowledging a "law-free State" and, refraining from upholding values, leave them to autonomous individual decisions.

The State's duty to protect developing life also exists in relation to the mother. But in this case, use of Criminal Law causes special problems arising from the unique status of the pregnant woman. In indiviudal cases, serious, even life-threatening conflicts can lead to burdens for the woman which sharply exceed those of a normal pregnancy. This raises questions of reasonable demand. Respect for unborn life can collide with the woman's right not to be forced to sacrifice her own life values. In such a situation, which in general also allows no clear moral evaluation, and in which a decision to terminate pregnancy has the equality of an honourable decision of conscience, the legislator must exercise restraint. The Court should construe as constitutional the legislator's decision not to punish the pregant woman in such a case.

It would seem especially unreasonable to demand continuation of pregnancy if termination is obviously needed to protect the pregnant woman "from a threat to her life or a threat of a serious impact on her health". In this case her own "right to life and to inviolability of her person" [Art. 2, Section 2, Sent. 1, of the Basic Law] would be at stake, a right one cannot expect her to sacrifice for the unborn life. Furthermore, the legislator can exempt from punishment other cases in which the burden is extraordinary. Included here would be eugenic criminological, and social emergency factors that might indicate a termination of pregnancy. The general social situation of the pregnant woman and her family can generate conflicts of such dimension that one cannot use Criminal Law to force her to undergo additional sacrifices. In regulating this type of case, the legislator must circumscribe the unpunishable deed

In all other cases, termination of pregnancy is a punishable offence, because destruction of a higher legal value is left to the free discretion of another person.

By not considering termination of pregnancy and not punishing those undertaken for reasons incompatible with the Basic Law's order of values, the legislator has failed his constitutional duty to protect the right to life. The individual person and his dignity form the centre of all its regulations.

(15) *Supreme Court of New Jersey.... "no external compelling interest of the State could compel Karen to endure the unendurable".*

IN RE. KAREN QUINLAN: 70 N.J. 10 (1976)

On April 15, 1975, for judicially undetermined reasons, Karen Quinlan then twenty-one years old, stopped breathing for two 15 minute periods. Given artificial respiration and rushed to a hospital, she remained deeply commatose, kept alive by a respirator, fed by a tube, and drained by a Catheter. An electroencephalogram showed some small brain activity, while essentially in a vegetative state, she did occasionally blink or cry out. In the judgement of attending physicians, Karen could maintain prolonged existence with the support of the life-sustaining apparatus; but there was no hope of her ever regaining any cognitive function.

After months of deliberation, prayer, and consultation with clergy, Karen's father, Joseph, a practising Catholic, decided to ask the doctors to withdraw the special equipment and allow her to live or die naturally. The physicians, however, refused to disconnect the appratus, contending that, under existing medical standards and practices, Karen was still alive and would quickly die if the machinery were withdrawn.

Mr. Quinlan then sought a judicial order appointing him guardian of Karen with express power to discontinue all extraordinary medical procedure. He also requested that the doctors and staff of the hospital be restrained from continuing the extraordinary treatment and that local officials be enjoined from interfering with or prosecuting for disconnecting the medical equipment. After an extensive hearing the trial judge denied Mr. Quinlan's requests, and he appealed to the State Supreme Court.

Opinion of the Court delivered by Hughes, C.J.

It is the issue of the constitutional right of privacy that has given us most concern.

We have no hesistancy in deciding that no external compelling interest of the State could compel Karen to endure the unendurable, only vegetate a few measurable months with no realistic possibility of returning to any semblance of cognitive or sapient life.

Although the Constitution does not explicitly mention a right of privacy, Supreme Court decisions have recognised that a right of personal privacy exists and that certain areas of privacy are guaranteed under the Constitution. The court has interdicted judicial intrusion into many aspects of personal decision, sometimes basing this restraint upon the conception of a limitation of a judicial interest and responsibility, such as with regard to contraception and its relationship to family life and decision.

The Court in *Griswold* found the unwritten constitutional right of privacy to exist in the penumbra of specific guarantees of the Bill of Rights "formed by emanations from those guarantees that help give them life and substance". Presumably this right is broad enough to encompass a patient's decision to decline medical treatment under certain circumstances, in much the same way, as it is broad enough to encompass a woman's decision to terminate pregnancy under certain conditions. [*Roe* Vs. *Wade*]

The claimed interests of the State in this case are essentially the presenation and sanctity of human life and defence of the right of the physician to administer medical treatment according to his best judgement. In this case the doctors say that removing Karen from the respirator will conflict with their professional judgement. The plaintiff answers that Karen's present treatment serves only a maintenance function that the respirator cannot cure or improve her condition but at best can only prolong her inevitable slow-deterioration and death; and that the interests of the patient, as seen by her surrogate, the guardian; must be evaluated by the Court as predominant, even in the face of an opinion contra by the present attending physicians. Plaintiff's distinction is significant. The nature of Karen's care and the realistic chances of her recovery are quite unlike those of the patients discussed in many of the cases where treatments were ordered. In many of those cases the medical procedure required (usually a transfusion) constituted a minimal bodily invasion and the chances of recovery and return to functioning life were very good. We think that the State's interest weakens and the individual's right to privacy grows as the degree of bodily invasion increases and the prognosis dims. Ultimately there comes a point at which the indiviudal's rights overcome the State interest. It is for that reason that we believe Karen's choice, if she were competent to make it, would be indicated by the law. Her prognosis is extremely poor. She will never resume cognitive life. And the bodily invasion is very great. She requires 24 hours intensive nursing care, antibiotics, the assistance of a respirator, a catheter and feeding tube.

Our affirmation of Karne's independent right of choice, however would ordinarily be based upon her competency to assert it. The sad truth, however, is that she is grossly incompetent and we cannot discern her supposed choice based on the testimony of her previous conversations with friends. Nevertheless, we have concluded that Karen's right of privacy may be asserted on her behalf by her guardian under the peculiar circumstances here present.

If a putative decision by Karen to permit this non-cognitive, vegetative existence to terminate by natural forces is regarded as a valuable incident of her right of privacy then it should not be discarded solely on the basis that her condition prevents her conscious exercise of the choice. The only practical way to prevent destruction of the right is to permit the guardian and family of Karen to render their best judgement, subject to the qualifications hereinafter stated, as to whether she would exercise it in these circumstances. If their conclusion is in the affirmative this decision should be accepted by a society the overwhelming majority of whose members would, we think, in similar circumstances exercise such a choice in the same way for themselves, or for those closest to them. It is for this reason that we determine that Karen's right of privacy may be asserted in her behalf, in this respect, by her guardian and family under the particular circumstances presented by this record.

The termination of treatment pursuant to the right of privacy is, within the limitations of this case, *ipso facto* lawful. A death resulting from such an act would not come within the scope of the homicide statutes prescribing only the unlawful killing of another. There is a real and in this case determinative distinction between the unlawful taking of the life of another and the ending of artificial life-support systems as a matter of self-determination.

We do not question the State's undoubted power to punish the taking of human life, but that power does not encompass individuals terminating medical treatment pursuant to their right of privacy. The constitutional protection extends to third parties whose action is necessary to effectuate the exercise of that right. Where the individuals themselves would not be subject to prosecution or the third parties are charged as accessories to an act which would not be a crime. And, under the circumstances of this case, these same principles would apply to and negate a valid prosecution for attempted suicide, were there still such a crime in this state.

(16) *Morgentaler* Vs. *The Queen*(1975) 20 C.C.C. (2d) 449
(C.J. Laskin of the Canadian Supreme Court)

The contention that a right of privacy, as an element of liberty, is protected against federal invasion is founded upon *Roe* vs. *Wade*. Yet that case did not recognise this as an absolute to the exclusion of a State interest to protect health or potential life. Rather, it sought to balance its recognitioin of the right to privacy (that is, the right to decide on an abortion) with the right, time-wise of the state to interfere.

(17) *Doe et al vs. Commonwealth's Attorney* : *403 F. Supp. 1199 (1975)*

(U.S. District Court for the Eastern Court of Virginia)

Two male homosexuals filed suit in a Federal District Court challenging the constitutionality of Section 18.1–212 of the Virginia Code, which makes it a crime, even for consenting adults acting in private, to engage in homosexual relations.

In *Griswold* vs. *Connecticut*, the court has most recently announced its views on the question here. Striking down a State statute forbiding the use of contraceptives, the ruling was put on the right of marital privacy and was also put on the sanctity of the home and family.

That *Griswold* is premised on the right of privacy and that homosexual intimacy is denunciable by the State is unequivocally demonstrated by Mr. Justice Goldberg in his concurrence in his adoption of Mr. Justice Harlan's dissenting statement in *Poe* Vs. *Ullman (1961)*.

Adultery, homosexuality and the like are sexual intimacies which the State forbids but the intimacy of husband and wife is necessarily an essential and accepted feature of the institution of marriage, an institution which the State not only must allow, but which always and in every age has fostered and protected. It is one thing when the State exerts its power either to forbid extra marital sexuality or to say who may marry, but it is quite another when, having acknowledged a marriage and the intimacies inherent in it, it undertakes to regulate by means of the Criminal Law the details of that intimacy.

Equally forceful is the succeeding paragraph of Justice Harlan:

In sum, even though the State has deterimined that the use of contraceptives is an iniquitous as any act of extra marital sexual immorality, the intrusion of the whole machinery of the Criminal Law into the very heart of marital privacy, requiring husband and wife to render account before a criminal tribunal of their uses of that intimacy is surely a very different thing indeed from punishing those who establish intimacies which the law has forbidden and which can have no claim to social protection.

Justice Harlan's words were authentically approved in *Griswold*.

On the plainfiff's effort presently to shield the practice of homosexuality from State incrimination by according it immunity when committed in private as against public exercise, the Justice said this:

Indeed to attempt a line between public behaviour and that which is purely consensual or solitary would be to withdraw from community concern a range of subjects with which every society in civilised times has found it necessary to deal. The laws regarding marriage which provide both when the sexual powers may be used and the legal and societal context in which children are born and brought up, as well as laws forbidding adultery, fornication and homosexual practices which express the negative of the proposition, confining sexuality to lawful marriage, form a pattern so deeply pressed into the substance of our social life that any constitutional doctrine in this area must build upon that basis.

Again:

Thus, I would not suggest that adultery, homosexuality, fornication and incest are immune from criminal inquiry, however privately practised. So much has been explicitly recognised in acknowledging the State's rightful concern for its people's moral welfare. But not to discriminate between what is involved in this case and either the traditional offences against good morals or crimes which, though they may be committed or concealed in the home, would entirely misconceive the argument that is being made.

Merhge, District Judge, Dissenting:

The Supreme Court has consistently held that the *Due Porcess* Clause of the Fourteenth Amendment protects the right of individuals to make personal choices, unfettered by arbitrary and purposeless restraints, in the private matters of marriage and procreation. *Roe* vs. *Wade....Griswold* Vs. *Connecticut* (Harlan J. concurring). I view those cases as standing for the principle that every individual has a right to be free fron unwarranted governmental intrusion into one's decisions of private matters of intimate concern.

A mature individual's choice of an adult sexual partner, in the privacy of his or her own home, would appear to me to be a decision of the utmost private and intimate concern. Private consensual sex acts between adults are matters, absent evidence that they are harmful, in which the State has no legitimate interest.

Merhge (D.J.) Dissenting:

To say, as the majority does, that the right of privacy is limited to matters of marital, home or family life is unwarranted under the law. Such a contention places a distinction in marital-nonmarital matters which is inconsistent with current Supreme Court opinions and is unsupportable.

In my view, *Griswold* applied the right of privacy to its particular factual situation. That the right of privacy is not limited to the facts of *Griswold* is demonstrated by later Supreme Court decisions. After *Griswold* by virtue of *Eisenstadt* Vs. *Baird* (1972), the legal viability of marital-normarital distinction in private sexual acts if not eliminated, was at the very least seriously impaired. In *Eisenstadt* the court declined to restrict the right of privacy in sexual matters to married couples:

> Yet the marital couple is not an independent entity with a mind and heart of its own, but an association of two individuals each with a separate intellectual and emotional make-up. If the right of privacy means anything, it is the right of the individual, married or single, to be free from unwarranted governmental intrusion into matters so fundamentally affecting a person as the decision whether to bear or beget a child.

In significantly diminishing the importance of the marital-nonmarital distinction, the Court to a great extent vitiated any implication that the State can forbid extra-marital sexuality.

Griswold in its context, applied the right of privacy in sexual matters to the marital relationship. *Eisenstadt* however, clearly demonstrates that the right of privacy in sexual relationships is not limited to the marital relationship. Both *Roe* and *Eisenstadt* cogently demonstrate that intimate personal decisions or private matters of substantial importance to the well-being of the individuals involved are protected by the *Due Process* Clause. The right to select consenting adult sexual partners must be considered within this category. The exercise of that right, whether hetrosexual or homosexual, should not be prescribed by State regulation absent compelling justification.

This approach does not unqualifiedly sanction personal whim. If the activity in question involves more than one participant, as in the instant case, each must be capable of consenting, and each must in fact consent to the conduct for the right of privacy to attach. For example, if one of the participants in homosexual contact is a minor, or force is used to coerce one of the participants to yield, the right will not attach. Similalry, the right of privacy cannot be extended to protect conduct that takes place in publicly frequented areas. However, if the right of privacy does apply to specific courses of conduct, legitimate State restriction on personal autonomy may be justified only under the compelling State interest test.

The defendants made no tender of any evidence which even impliedly demonstrated that homosexuality causes society any significant harm. No effort was made by the defendants to establish either a rational basis or a compelling State interest in the proscripction.

On the basis of this record one can only conclude that the sole basis of the proscription of homosexuality was what the majority refers to as the promotion of morality and decency. As salutary a legislative goal as this may be, I can find no authority for intrusion by the State into the private dwelling of a citizen whether the guarantee of personal privacy springs from the First, Fourth, Fifth, Ninth, the Penumbra of the Bill of Rights, or as I believe in the concept of liberty guaranteed by the first Section of the Fourteenth Amendment, the Supreme Court has made it clear that fundamental rights of such an intimate facet of an individual's life as sex, absent circumstances warranting intrusion by the State are to be respected. The issue centers not around morality or decency, but the constitutional right of privacy.

(18) *Irish Contraceptive Case*

MC GEE *VS.* ATTORNEY GENERAL AND REVENUE COMMISSIONERS
(1974) I.R. 284

Justice Walsh of the Irish Supreme Court: "It is a matter exclusively for the husband and wife to decide how many children they wish to have."

Mrs. Mary McGee a young married Catholic woman who was the mother of four children, had suffered such severe complications during each of her pregnancies that her physician advised her another pregnancy would entail serious hazards to her life. He prescribed a contraceptive that she had to order from England because the drug was not manufactured in Ireland. Her shipment of contraceptives was seized by revenue commissioners acting under

Section 17 (3) of the Criminal Law Amendment Act of 1935, which provides:

> Contraceptives shall be deemed to be included among the goods enumerated and described in the Table of Prohibitions and Restrictions Inwards contined in Section 42 of the Customs Consolidation Act, 1876, and the provisions of that Act (as amended or extended by subsequent Acts) relating to the importation of prohibited goods shall apply accordingly.

Natural rights or human rights are not created by law but the Constitution confirms their existence and gives them protection. The individual has natural and human rights over which the State has no authority and the family as the natural primary and fundamental unit group of society has rights as such which the State cannot control. At the same time, however, it is true, as the Constitution acknowledges that the State is the guardian of the common good and that the individual as a member of society, and the family, as a unit of society have duties and obligations to consider and respect the common good of that society. The view expressed by Mr. Justice O'Bryne in *Buckley and others* Vs. *The Attorney General* is that the power of the State to act for the protection of the common good or to decide what are the exigencies of the common good is not one which is peculiarly reserved for the legislative organ of government.

It is a matter exclusively for the husband and wife to decide how many children they wish to have. Husband and wife have a correlative right to have no children. What may be permissible to the husband and wife is not necessarily permissible to the State. For example, the husband and wife may mutually agree to practise either total or partial abstinence in their sexual relations. If the State were to attempt to intervene to compel such abstinence it would be an intolerable and unjustifiable intrusion into the privacy of the matrimonial bedroom. On the other hand, any action on the part of the husband and wife or of the State to limit family sizes by endangering or destroying human life must necessarily not only be an offence against the common good but also against the guaranteed personal rights of the human life in question.

The sexual life of a husband and wife is of necessity and by its nature an area of particular privacy. The question of whether the use of contraceptives by married couples within their marriage is or is not contrary to the moral code or codes to which they profess could not justify State intervention. Similarly the fact the use of contraceptives may offend against the moral code of the majority of the citizens of the State would not *per se* justify an intervention by the State to prohibit their use within marriage. The private morality of its citizens does not justify intervention by the State into the activities of those citizens unless and until the common good requires it.

If this right of marital privacy cannot be directly invaded by the State it follows that it cannot be frustrated by the State's taking measures to ensure that the exercise of that right is rendered impossible. The possibility of the state being justified cannot be excluded in a case where the public good requires it, as for example a dangeous fall in population threatening the life or the essential welfare of the State, to take such steps to ensure that in general that even if married couples could not be compelled to have children they could at least be hindered in State endeavours to avoid having them. That, however, is not the present case. Similarly, it is not impossible to envisage a situation where the availability of contraceptives to married people for use within marraige could be demonstrated to have led to or would probably lead to such an adverse effect on public morality so subversive of the common good as to justify State intervention. In such a case it would have to be demonstrated that all the other resources of the State had proved or were likely to prove incapable to avoid this subversion of the common good while contraceptives remained available for use within marriage.

Section 17 of the Act of 1935, in so far as it unreasonably restricts the availability of contraceptives for use within marriage is inconsistent with the provisions of Art. 41 of the Constitution for being an unjustified invasion of the privacy of husband and wife in their sexual relations with one another.

Not only has the State the rights but the State has the positive obligation to ensure by its laws as far as possible that there would be made available to married women in the condition of health of Mrs. McGee the means whereby a conception which was likely to put her life in jeopardy might be avoided.

The development of the constitutional law of the United States of America is ample proof of this. There is a Constitution which while not professing to be governed by the precepts of Christianity, also in the Ninth Amendment recognises the existence of rights other than those referred to expressly in the Constitution and its amendments. The views of the United States Supreme Court as reflected in the decisions interpreting that Constitution and in the development of their Constitutional law also appear firmly to reject legal positivism as a jurisprudential guide.

Budd. J.: Whilst "personal rights" are not set out specifically it is scarcely to be doubted that in our society the right to privacy is universally recognised and accepted with possibly the rarest of exceptions and the matter of marital relationship must rank as one of the most important of matters in the realm of privacy.

(19) *Rudul Shah* Vs. *State of Bihar* : *AIR 1983 SC 1086*

Article 21 which guarantees the right to life and liberty will be denuded of its significant content if the powers of the Supreme Court were limited to passing orders of release from illegal detention. One of the telling ways in which the violation of that right can reasonably be prevented and due compliance with the mandate of Article 21 secured, is to mulct its violaters in the payment of monetary compensation. Administrative sclerosis leading to flagrant infringements of fundamental rights cannot be corrected by any other method open to the judiciary to adopt. The right to compensation is some palliative for the unlawful acts of instrumentalities which act in the name of public interest and which present for their protection the powers of the State as a shield. Respect for the rights of individuals is the true bastion of democracy. Therefore, the State must repair the damage done by its officers to the petitioner's rights. It may have recourse against those officers.

In the instant case the petitioner was detained illegally in the prison for over fourteen years after his acquittal in a full dressed trial. He filed a *Habeas Corpus* petition in the Supreme Court for his release from illegal detention. He obtained that relief, his detention in the prison after his acquittal being wholly unjustified. He further contended that he was entitled to be compensated for his illegal detention and that the Supreme Court ought to pass an appropriate order for the payment of compensation in the *Habeas Corpus* petition itself.

(20) *Maneka Gandhi* Vs. *Union of India* : *AIR 1978 SC 597*

The petitioner was issued a passport on June 1, 1976 under the *Passport Act, 1967*. On the 4th July, 1977, the petitioner received a letter dated 2nd July, 1977 from the Regional Passport Officer intimating to her that it was decided by the Government of India to impound her passport under section 10(3) (c) of the Act "in public interest". The petitioner was required to surrender her passport within 7 days from the receipt of that letter. The petitioner immediately addressed a letter to the Regional Passport Officer requesting him to furnish a copy of the statement of reasons for making the orders as provided in Section 10 (5). A reply was sent by the Government of India, Ministry of External Affairs on 6th July, 1977 stating *inter alia* that the Government decided "in the interest of the general public" not to furnish her copy of the statement of reasons for the making of the order. The petitioner thereupon filed the present writ petition challenging action of the Government in impounding her passport and declining to give reasons for doing so. The Act was enacted on 24-4-1967 in view of the decision of the Court in *Satwant Singh Sawhney's case*. The position which obtained prior to the coming into force of the Act was that there was no law regulating the issue of passports for leaving the shores of India and going abroad. The issue of passport was entirely within the unguided and unchanneled discretion of the Executive. In *Satwant Singh's Case*, this Court held by a majority that the expression 'personal liberty' in Article 21 takes in the right of locomotion and travel abroad and under Article 21 no person can be deprived of his right to go abroad except according to the procedure established by law. This decision was accepted by the Parliament and the infirmity pointed out by it was set right by the enactment of the *Passport Act, 1967*. The Preamble of the Act shows that it was enacted to provide for the issue of passport and travel documents to regulate the departure from India of citizens of India and other persons and for incidental and ancillary matters. Section 3 provides that no person shall depart from or attempt to depart from India unless he holds in this behalf a valid passport or travel document. Section 5(1) provides for making of an application for issue of a passport or travel document for visiting foreign country. Sub-section (2) of Section 5 says that on receipt of such application the Passport Authority after making such enquiry, if any, as it may consider necessary, shall by order in writing, issue or refuse to issue the passport or travel document or make or refuse to make that passport or travel document endorsement in respect of one or more of the foreign countries specified in the application. Sub-section (3) requires the Passport Authority where it refuses to issue the passport or travel document or to make any endorsement to record in writing a brief statement of its reasons for making such order. Section 6(1) lays down the grounds on which the Passport Authority shall refuse to make an endorsement for visiting any foreign country and provides that on no other ground the endorsement shall be refused. Section 6(2) provides the grounds on which alone and on no other grounds the Passport Authority shall refuse to issue the passport or travel document for visiting any foreign country and amongst various grounds set out there the last is that in the opinion of the Central Government the issue of passport or travel document to the applicant will not be in the public interest. Sub-section (1) of Section 10 empowers the Passport Authority to vary or cancel the enforcement on a passport or travel document or to vary or cancel it on the conditions subject to which a passport or travel document has been issued having regard to *inter alia*, the provisions of Section 6(1) or any notification under Section 19. Sub-section (2) confers powers on the Passport Authority to vary or cancel the conditions of the passport or travel document and with the previous approval of the Central Government. Sub-section (3). provides that the Passport Authority may impound or cause to be impounded or revoke a passport or travel document on the grounds set out in clauses (a) to (h). The order impounding the passport in the present case was made by the Central Government under clause (c) which reads as follows:

> "(c) If the Passport Authority deems it necessary so to do in the interest of the sovereignty and integrity of India, the security of India, friendly relations of India with the foreign country, or in the interests of the general public."

Sub-Section (5) requires the Passport Authority impounding or revoking a passport or travel document or varying or cancelling an endorsement made upon it to record in writing a brief statement of the reasons for making such order and furnish to the holder of the passport or travel document on demand a copy of the same, unless, in any case, the Passport Authority is of the opinion that it will not be in the interest of the sovereignty and integrity of India, the security of India, friendly relations of India with any foreign country, or in the interest of the general public to furnish such a copy. The Central Government declined to furnish a copy of this statement of reasons for impounding the passport of the petitioner on the ground that it was not in the interest of the general public to furnish such copy to the petitioner.

The petitioner contended:

(1) The right to go abroad is part of "personal liberty" within the meaning of that expression as used in Art. 21 and no one can be deprived of this right except according to the procedure prescribed by law. There is no procedure prescribed by the Passport Act for impounding or revoking a passport. Even if some procedure can be traced in the said Act it is unreasonable and arbitrary inasmuch as it does not provide for giving an opportunity to the holder of the passport to be heard against the making of the order.

(2) Section 10 (3) (c) is violative of fundamental rights guaranteed under Articles 14, 19(1) (a) and (g) and 21.

(3) The impugned order is made in contravention of the rules of natural justice and is, therefore, *null and void*. The impugned order has effect of placing an unreasonable restriction on the right of free speech and expression guaranteed to the petitioner under Art. 19(1) (a) as also or the right to carry on the profession of a journalist conferred under Art. 19(1) (g).

(4) The impugned order could not consistently with Articles 19(1) (a) and (g) be passed on a mere information of the Central Government that the presence of the petitioner is likely to be required in connection with the proceedings before the Commission of Inquiry.

(5) In order that a passport may be impounded under Section 10(3)(c) public interest must actually exist in present and mere likelihood of public interest arising in future would be no ground for impounding the passport.

(6) It was not correct to say that the petitioner was likely to be required for giving evidence before the Shah Commission.

The respondents denied the contentions raised by the petitioner.

Beg C.J. (Concurring with Bhagwati J.):

(1) The right to travel and to go outside the country is included in the right to personal liberty.

Satwant Singh Sawheny Vs. *D. Ramanathnum Assistant Passport Officer, Government of India, New Delhi and others (1967) 3SCR 525* and *Kharak Singh* Vs. *State of U.P. and others (1964)* ISCR *332* relied on.

(2) Article 21 though framed as to appear as a shield operating negatively against executive encroachment over something covered by that shield, is the legal recognition of both the protection or the shield as well as of what it protects which lies beneath that shield.

A.K. Gopalan Vs. *State of Madras [1950] SCR 88 and Additional District Magistrate, Jabalpur* Vs. *S.S. Shukla (1976) Suppl. SCR 172 @ 327* referred to.

Haradhan Saha Vs. *The State of West Bengal and others (1975) ISCR 778, Shambhu Nath Sarkar* Vs. *State of West Bengal (1973) ISCR 856 and R.C. Cooper* Vs. *Union of India (1973) 3 SCR 530* referred to.

(3) The view that Articles 19 and 21 constitute watertight compartments has been rightly over-ruled. The doctrine that Articles 19 and 21 protect or regulate flows in different channels, was laid down in *A.K. Gopalan's Case* in a context which was very different from that in which that approach was displaced by the counter view that the Constitution must be read as an integral whole, with possible overlappings of the subject matter of what is sought to be protected by its various provisions, particularly by Articles relating to fundamental rights. The observations in *A.K. Gopalan's Case* that *due process* with regard to law relating to preventive detention are to be found in Art. 22 of the Constitution because it is a self contained code for laws. That observation was the real *ratio decidendi* of *Gopalan's Case*. Other observations relating to the separability of the subject matters of Arts. 21 and 19 were mere *obiter dicta*. This court has already held in *A.D.M. Jabalpur's Case* by reference to the decision from *Gopalan's Case* that the ambit of personal liberty protected by Art. 21 is wide and comprehensive. The question relating to either deprivation or restrictions of personal liberty concerning laws falling outside Art. 22 remain really unanswered by the *Gopalan's Case*. The field of *due process* for cases of preventive detention is fully covered by Art. 22 but other parts of that field not covered by Art. 22 are "unoccupied" by its specific provisions. In what may be called unoccupied portions of the vast sphere of personal liberty, the substantive as well as procedural laws made to cover them must satisfy the requirements of both Articles 14 and 19 of the Constitution.

Articles dealing with different fundamental rights contained in Part III of the Constitution do not represent entirely separate streams of rights which do not mingle at many points. They are all parts of an integrated scheme in the Constitution. Their waters must mix to constitute that grand flow unimpeded and impartial justice (social, economic and political), freedom (not only of thought, expression, belief, faith and worship, but also of association, movement, vocation or occupation as well as of acquisition and possession of reasonable property), or equality (of status and of opportunity, which imply absence unreasonable or unfair discrimination between individuals, groups and classes) and of fraternity (assuring dignity of the individual and the unity of the nation) which our Constitution visualises. Isolation of various aspects of human freedom for purposes of their protection is neither realistic nor beneficial but would defeat very objects of such protection.

Blackstone's theory of natural rights cannot be rejected as irrelevant. If we have advanced today towards higher civilisation and in a more enlightened era we cannot lay behind what at any rate was the meaning given to 'personal liberty' long ago by Blackstone. Both the rights of personal security and personal liberty recognised by what Blackstone termed "natural law" are embodied in Art. 21 of the Constitution.

A.D.M. Jabalpur Vs. *S.S. Shukla (1976) Supp. S.C.R. 172* relied on.

The natural law rights were meant to be converted into our constitutionally recognised fundamental rights so that they are to be found within it and not outside it. To take a contrary view would involve a conflict between natural law and our constitutional law. A divorce between natural law and our constitutional law would be disastrous. It would defeat one of the basic purposes of our Constitution.

The total effect and not the mere form of a restriction would determine which fundamental right is really involved in a particular case and whether a restriction upon its exercise is reasonably permissible on the facts and circumstances of that case.

If rights under Art. 19 are rights which inhere in Indian citizens, individuals carry these inherent fundamental constitutional rights with them wherever they go in so far as our law applies to them, because they are part of the Indian National just as Indian ships, flying the Indian flag are deemed in international to be floating parts of Indian territory. This analogy, however could not be pushed too far because Indian citizens, on foreign territory, are only entitled by virtue of their Indian nationality and passports to the protection of the Indian Republic and the assistance of the Diplomatic Missions abroad. They cannot claim to be governed abroad by their own constitutional or personal laws which do not operate outside India.

In order to apply the test contained in Arts. 14 and 19 of the Constitution we have to consider the objects for which the exercise of inherent rights recognised by Art. 21 of the Constitution are restricted as well as the procedure by which these restrictions are sought to be imposed, both substantive and procedural laws and actions taken under them will have to pass the tests imposed by Arts. 14 and 19 whenever facts justifying the invocation of either of these Articles may be disclosed, for example an international singer or dancer may well be able to complain of an unjustifiable restriction on professional activity by denial of a passport. In such a case, violation of both Arts. 21 and 19(1) (g) may be put forward making it necessary for the authorities concerned to justify the restriction imposed by showing satisfaction of tests of validity contemplated by each of these two Articles.

The tests of reason and justice cannot be abstract. They cannot be divorced from the needs of the nation. The tests have to be pragmatic otherwise they would cease to be reasonable. The discretion left to the authority to impound a passport in public interest cannot invalidate the law itself. We cannot, out of fear, that such power will be misused, refuse to permit Parliament to entrust even such power to executive authorities as may be absolutely necessary to carry out the purpose of a validly exercisable power. In matters such as grant, suspension, impounding or cancellation of passports, the possible dealing of an individual with nationals and authorities of other States have to be considered. The contemplated or possible activities abroad of the individual may have to be taken into account. There may be questions of national safety and welfare which transcend the importance of the individual's inherent right to go where he or she pleases to go. Therefore, the grant of wide discretionary power to the executive authorities cannot be considered as unreasonable yet there must be procedural safeguards to ensure that the power will not be used for purposes extraneous to the grant of the power. The procedural proprieties must be insisted upon.

A bare look at the provisions of Section 10(3) shows that each of the orders which could be passed under Section 10(3) (a) and (b) require a satisfaction of the passport authority on certain objective conditions which must exist in a case before it passes an order to impound a passport or a travel document. Impounding or revocation are placed side by side on the same footing in the provisions.

It is clear from the provisions of the Act that there is a statutory right also acquired, on fulfilment of the prescribed conditions by the holder of a passport, that it should continue to be effective for the specified period so long as no ground has come into existence for either its revocation or for impounding it which amounts to a suspension of it for the time being. It is true that in a proceeding under Art. 32, the Court is concerned only with the enforcement of fundamental constitutional rights and not with any statutory rights apart from fundamental rights. Article 21, however makes it clear that violation of all law whether statutory or of any other kind is itself an infringement of the guaranteed fundamental right.

The orders under Section 10(3) must be based upon some material even if that material concerns in some cases of reasonable suspicion arising from certain credible assertions made by reliable individuals. In an emergent situation, the impounding of a passport may become necessary without even giving an opportunity to be heard against such a step which could be reversed after an opportunity is given to the holder of the passport to show why the step was unnecessary. However, ordinarily no passport could be reasonably either impounded or revoked without a prior opportunity to its holder to show cause against the proposed action.

It is well-settled that even when there is no specific provision in a statute or rules made thereunder for showing cause against action reposed to be taken against an individual, which affects the right of that individual the duty to give reasonable opportunity to be heard will be implied from the nature of the function to be performed by the authority which has the power to take punitive or damaging action.

State of Orissa Vs. *Dr. (Miss) Binapani Devi and others* : *AIR* (1967) *SC 1269 @ 1271* relied on.

Cooper Vs. *Wandsworth Board of Works* : *(1863) 14 C.B. (N.S.) 180* quoted with approval.

An order impounding a passport must be made quasi-judicially. This was not done in the present case. It cannot be said that a good enough reason has been shown to exist for impounding the passport of the petitioner. The petitioner had no opportunity of showing that the ground for impounding it given in this court either does not exist or has no bearing on public interest or that the public interest can be better served in some other manner. The order should be quashed and the respondent should be directed to give an opportunity to the petitioner to show cause against any proposed action on such grounds as may be available.

There were no pressing grounds with regard to the petitioner that the immediate action of impounding her passport was called for. The cavaliar fashion in which the disclosure of any reason for impounding of her passport was denied to the petitioner despite the fact that the only reason said to exist is the possibility of her being called to give evidence before a Commission of Inquiry. Such a ground is not such as to be reasonably deemed to necessitate its concealment in public interest.

Even executive authorities when taking administrative action which involves any deprivation of or restriction on inherent fundamental rights of citizens must take care to see that justice is not only done but manifestly appears to be done. They have a duty to proceed in a way which is free from even the appearance of arbitrariness, unreasonableness or unfairness. They have to act in a manner which is patently impartial and meets the requirements of natural justice.

As the undertaking given by the Attorney General amounts to an offer to deal with the petitioner justly and fairly after informing her of any ground that may exist for impounding her passport, no further action by this Court is necessary.

The impugned order must be quashed and Passport Authorities be directed to return the passport to the petitioner. Petition allowed with costs.

Kailasam J. Dissenting:

The Preamble to the Constitution provides that the people of India have solemnly resolved to constitute India into a sovereign, socialist, secular and democratic republic and to secure to all its citizens, justice – social, economic and political –, liberty of thought, expression, belief, faith and worship, equality of status and of opportunity. Article 12 defines the State as including the Government and Parliament of India and the Government and the Legislature of each of the States and of local or other authorities within the territory of India or under the control of the Government of India. Article 13 provides that laws that are inconsistent with or in derogation of fundamental rights are to that extent *void*. Article 245 (2) provides that no law made by Parliament shall be deemed to be invalid on the ground that it would have extra territorial operation. In England Section 3 of the Statute of Westminister declares that Parliament has full power to make laws having extra territorial operation. The following are the principles to determine whether the provisions of a Constitution or a Statute have extra-territorial application:

(a) An Act unless it provides otherwise applies only to the country concerned.

(b) An Act of a legislature will bind the subject of the realm both within and without if that is the intention of the legislature, which must be gathered from the language of the Act in question.

(c) Legislature normally restricts operation of legislation to its own territories. However, on occasions legislation controlling the activities of its own citizens when they are abroad may be passed.

Nibayet vs. *Nibayet 48* : *L.J.P.I.* at *p.10* and *Queen* Vs. *Jameson and others – (1896) 2Q.B. Division 425 at 430* referred to.

(d) In the absence of an intention clearly expressed or to be inferred from its language, or from the object or subject-matter or history of the enactment, the presumption is that Parliament does not design its Statute to operate beyond the territorial limit of the country.

Governor General in Council Vs. *Raleigh Investment Co.Ltd.: AIR (31) [1944] Federal Court 51*, referred to.

Wallace Brothers and Co. Ltd. Vs. *Commissioner of Income-Tax, Bombay, Sind and Baluchistan* : *(1945) F.C.R 65 and Mohammed Mohy-ud-din* Vs. *The King Emperor (1946) F.C.R. 94* referred to.

The application of Article 14 is expressly limited to the territory of India. Articles 15, 16, 17, 18, 20 and 22 by their very nature are confined to the territory of India. Articles 23 to 28 are applicable only to the territory of India. At any rate, there is no intention in these Articles indicating extra-territorial application. So also Articles 29 and 30 which deal with cultural and educational rights are applicable only within the territory of India. Article 31 does not expressly or impliedly have any extra-territorial application. It is possible that the right conferred by Article 19 (1) (a) may have extra-territorial application. It is not likely, however, that the framers of the Constitution intended the right to assemble peaceably and without arms or to form associations or unions or to acquire, hold and dispose of property, or to practise any profession or to carry on any occupation, trade or business, to have any extra-territorial application for such rights would not be enforced by the State outside the Indian territory. The rights conferred under Article 19 are fundamental rights and Arts. 32 and 226 provide that these rights are guaranteed and can be enforced by the aggrieved person by approaching this Court or the High Courts. These rights cannot be protected by the State outside its territory and, therefore, there is a presumption that the Constitution makers would not have intended to guarantee any rights which the State cannot enforce.

Virendra Vs. *The State of Punjab and Another*: *(1958) SCR 308* referred to

It is most unlikely that before the declaration of human rights was promulgated the framers of the Constitution decided to decalre that the fundamental rights conferred on the citizens would be available even outside India. Even in the American Constitution there is no mention of right to freedom of speech or expression as being available outside America. The law made under Article 19(2) to 19(6) imposes restrictions on the exercise of right of freedom of speech and expression etc. The restrictions thus imposed normally would apply only within the territory of India unless the legislation expressly or by necessary implication provides for extra-territorial operation. In the Penal Code, Section 3 and 4 specifically provides that crimes committed by citizens of India outside India are punishable. In Article 19, however, there is no such provision expressly or by necessary implication. Secondly, a citizen cannot enforce his fundamental rights outside the territory of India even if it is taken that such rights are available outside the country. Therefore, the contention of the petitioners that by denying the passport the petitioner's fundamental rights guaranteed by Article 19 are infringed cannot be accepted.

The important question which arises is whether an Act passed under Article 21 should also satisfy requirements of Article 19. It has been decided by this court in *Gopalan's Case* that the punitive detention for offences under the Penal Code cannot be challenged on the ground that it infringes fundamental rights under Art. 19.

The rights guaranteed under Article 19(1) are subject to restrictions that may be placed by Articles 19(2) to 19(6). The right not to be deprived of life and personal liberty is subject to its deprivation by procedure established by law. In *Gopalan's Case* it was held that

Article 19 dealt with the rights of the citizens when he was free and would not apply to person who had ceased to be free and has been either under punitive or preventive detention. It was further held that Article 19 only applies where a legislation directly hit the rights enumerated in the Article and not where the loss of rights mentioned in the Article was a result of the operation of legislation relating to punitive or preventive detention. The aforesaid *ratio* of *Gopalan's Case* has been confirmed by this court in *Ram Singh* vs. *State of Delhi*. The view was again confirmed in *The State of Bihar* Vs. *Kameshwar Singh*.

Ram Singh Vs. *State of Delhi (1951) SCR 451* and *State of Bihar* Vs. *Kameshwar Singh (1952) SCR 889* relied on.

In *Express Newspapers* the test laid down was that there must be a direct or inevitable consequence of the measure enacted in the impugned Act and that it would not be possible to strike down the legislation as having that effect and operation.

Express Newspapers (P) Ltd. and another Vs. *The Union of India and others (1959) ISCR 135* referred to.

In *Hamdard Dawakhana's Case* it was held that it is not the form or incidental infringement that determines the constitutionality of a statute but the reality or the substance.

Hamdard Dawakhana (Wakf) Lal Kuan Vs. *Union of India (1960) 2 SCR 671 at page 691* and *Kochunni* Vs. *The State of Madras (1960) 3 SCR. 887* referred to, *Sakal Papers (P) Ltd. and others* Vs. *The Union of India (1962) 3 SCR 842* distinguished.

In *Sakal Paper's Case*, the court held that the order was *void* as it violated Article 19(1) (a) and was not saved by Article 19(2). In that case the impact of legislation under Article 21 on the rights guaranteed under Article 19(1) was not in issue.

Kharak Singh (1964) 1 SCR 332 relied on; *Bank Nationalisation (1970) 3 SCR 530 and Bennet Coleman (1973) 2 SCR 757* distinguished.

In *Bank Nationalisation Case* the Court was only considering the decisions that took the view that Articles 19(1) (f) and 31 (2) were mutually exclusive. The basis for the conclusion in *Bank Nationalisation Case* is that Articles 19 and 31 are parts of a single pattern and while Article 19(1) (f) enjoins the right to acquire, hold and dispose of property. Clause (5) of Article 19 authorises imposition of restrictions upon the right. There must be a reasonable restriction and Article 31 assures the right to property and grants protection against the exercise of the authority of the State and clause 5 of Article 19 and clauses (1) and (2) of Article 31 prescribe restrictions upon the said action, subject to which the right to property may be exercised. The case specifically over-ruled the view taken in *Gopalan's Case* that the approach and form of the State action alone need to be considered and the fact of loss of fundamental rights of the individual in general will be ignored. The entire discussion in ***Bank Nationalisation Case*** related to the inter-relation between Article 31(2) and Article 19(1) (f). Certain passing observations have been made about the liberty of persons. However, there is no justification for holding that the case is an authority for the proposition that legislation under Art. 21 should also satisfy all the fundamental rights guaranteed under Art. 19(1). That the decision in *Bank Nationalisation Case* so far as it relates to Articles 19(1) and 21 is in the nature of *obiter dicta*. The court had not applied its mind and decided the specific question. The observations were general and casual observations on a point not calling for decision and not obviously argued before it cannot be taken as an authority on the proposition in question. The Court cannot be said to have declared the law on the subject when no occasion arose for it to consider and decide the question. The judgement proceeded on some erroneous assumptions. It was assumed by the judgement that the majority of the Court in *Gopalan's Case* held that Article 22 being a complete code relating to preventive detention the validity of an order of detention must be determined directly according to the terms within the four corners of that Article. The said statement is not borne out from the record of the judgement in *Gopalan's Case*. If the *Obiter dicta* based on the wrong assumption is to be taken as correct position in law it would lead to strange results. If Articles 19(1) (a) to (c) and (g) are attracted in the case of deprivation of personal liberty under Article 21, a punitive detention for an offence committed under I.P.C., such as theft, cheating or assault would be illegal, for the reasonable restrictions in the interest of public order would not cover the said offences. There can be no distinction between the punitive detention and preventive detention. Observation in *Bank Nationalisation Case* that a legislation under Art. 21 should also satisfy the requirements of Article 19 cannot be taken as correct law.

Chiranjit Lal Chowdhari (1950) SCR 869, The State of West Bengal Vs. *Subodh Gopal (1954) SCR 587, State of Bombay* Vs.

Bhanji Manji (1953) 1 SCR 777, Dabu Barkya Thakur Vs. *State of Bombay (1961), 1SCR 128, Smt. Sitabati Debi and another* Vs. *State of West Bengal (1967) 2 SCR 940* and *K.K. Kochunni (1968) 3 SCR 887* referred to.

In *S.N. Sarkar's Case* also, the majority held that Article 22 was a self-contained code. The view taken in this case also suffers from the same infirmities referred to in the *Bank Nationalisation Case*. In *Khudi Ram's Case* also this court erroneously stated that *Gopalan's Case* has taken the view that Article 22 was a complete code.

In *Additional District Magistrate, Jabalpur*, Chief Justice Ray held that Article 21 is the rule of law regarding life and liberty and no other rule of law can have separate existence as a distinct right. Justice Beg observed that *Gopalan's Case* was merely cited in *Cooper's Case* for illustrating a line of reasoning which was held to be incorrect in determining validity of law. The question under consideration was whether Articles 19(1) (f) and 31(2) were mutually exclusive. The learned judge did not understand the *Cooper's Case* as holding that effect of deprivation of rights outside Article 21 will also have to be considered.

In *Bennet Coleman's Case*, the Court held that though Article 19(1) does not mention the freedom of press it is settled view of the Court that freedom of speech and expression includes freedom of press and circulation. In that case also the question whether Articles 21 and 19 are mutually exclusive did not arise for consideration. *Bennet Coleman's Case*, *Express Newspapers Case*, and *Sakal Newspapers Case* were all concerned with the right to freedom of the press which is held to form part of the freedom of speech and expression.

Commonwealth of Australia Vs. *Bank of New South Wales (1950) A.C. 235* referred to.

The *Passport Act* provides for issue of passports and travel document for regulating the departure from India of citizens of India and other reason. Since the said Act complies with the requirements of Article 21 *i.e.*, compliance with procedure established by law, its validity cannot be challenged. If incidentally the Act infringes on the rights of a citizen under Art. 19(1) of the Act, it cannot be found to be invalid. The pith and substance rule will have to be applied and unless the rights are directly affected, the challenge will fail.

The procedure established by law does not mean procedures

however fantastic and oppressive or arbitrary which in truth and reality is no procedure at all. Section 5 of the Act provides for applying for passports or travel documents etc. and the procedure for passing orders thereon. The authority can either grant passport or can refuse it. In case the authority refuses to grant it, it is required to record in writing a brief statement of his reasons which are to be furnished to the person concerned unless the authority for reasons specified in sub-section (3) refuses to furnish a copy. Section 6 provides that the refusal to give an enforsement shall be on one or other grounds mentioned in sub-sections (2) to (6). Section 10 enables the Passport Authority to vary or cancel the endorsement on a passport. Section 10(3) provides the reasons for which a passport may be impounded. Again reasons are required to be furnished to the person concerned on demand, except if the Passport Authority is of the opinion that it will not be in the interest of sovereignty and integrity of India, security of India, friendly relations of India with any foreign country or in the interest of the general public to furnish such a copy. Section 11 provides for an appeal except when the order is passed by the Central Government.

The legislature by making an express provision may deny a person the right to be heard. Rules of natural justice cannot be equated with the fundamental rights. Their aim is to secure justice and to prevent miscarriage of justice. They do not supplant the law but supplement it. If a statutory provision can be read consistently with the principles of natural justice the court should do so but if a statutory provision that specifically or by necessary implication excludes the application of any rules of natural justice, this court cannot ignore the mandate of the legislature or the statatory authority and read in the concerned provision the principles of natural justice. To a limited extent it may be necessary to revoke or to impound a passport without notice if there is real apprehension that the holder of the passport may leave the country if he becomes aware of any intention on the part of the Passport Authority or the Government to revoke or impound the passort but that itself would not justify denial of an opportunity to the holder of the passport to state his case before the final order is passed. The legislature has not by express provision excluded the right to be heard.

Purtabpur Vs. *Cane Commissioner, Bihar (1969) 2 SCR 807 and Schmidt* Vs. *Secretary of State, Home Affairs (1969) 2 ch. 149* referred to.

A passport may be impounded without notice but before any final order is passed the rule of *audi alternam partem*, would apply and the holder of the passport will have to be heard. The petitioner has a right to be heard before a final order under section 10(3) (e) is passed. Earlier, the courts had taken a view that the principle of natural justice is inapplicable to administrative orders. However, subsequently, there is a change in the judicial opinion. The frontier between judicial and quasi-judicial determination on the one hand and an executive or administrative determination on the other has become blurred. The rigid view that principles of natural justice apply only to judicial and quasi-judicial acts and not to administrative acts no longer holds the field. The court is not intended to sit in appeal over the decision of the Government. The decision of the Government under Section 10(3) (c) is subject to a limited judicial scrutiny.

H.K. (An infant) (1967) 2 Q.B. 617 at p. 630 Barium Chemicals Ltd. Vs. *Company Law Board (1966) Supp. SCR 311, Rohtas Industries Ltd.*, Vs. *S.D. Aggarwal (1969) 3 SCR 103 and U.P. Electric Co.* Vs. *State of U.P. (1969) 3 SCR 865* followed.

The provision empowering the Government not to disclose the reasons for impounding etc. is valid. The Government is bound to give opportunity to the holder of the passport before finally revoking it or impounding it. The cases in which the authority declines to furnish reasons for making an order would be extremely rare. In case where the Government itself passes an order it should be presumed that it would have made the order after careful scrutiny. If an order is passed by the Passport Authority an appeal is provided. In the present case, there is no reason in declining to furnish to the petitioner statement of reasons for impounding the passport.

In view of the statement of the Attorney General that the petitioner might make a representation in respect of the impounding of passport and that the representations would be dealt with expeditiously and that even if the impounding of the Passport is confirmed it will not exceed a period of six months, it is not necessary to go into the merits of the case any further.

(21) *Kharak Singh* Vs. *The State of U.P. and others (1964) 1 SCR 332*

In this case, this court had occasion to consider the validity of Regulation 236 of the U.P. Police Regulations which is in *pari materia* with Regulation 856 in *Govind's Case*. Here it was held by a majority that regulation 236 (b) providing for domiciliary visits was unconstitutional for the reason that it abridged the fundamental right of a person under Article 21 and since Regulation 236 (b) did not have the force of law, the regulation was declared bad. The other provisions of the regulation were held to be constitutional. The decision that the regulation in question there was not law was based upon a concession made on behalf of the State of U.P. that the U.P. Police Regulations were not framed under any of the provisions of the *Police Act*.

In this case the majority said that "personal liberty" in Article 21 is comprehensive to include all varieties of rights which go to make up the personal liberty of a man other than those dealt with in Article 19(1) (d). According to the court, while Article 19(1) (d) deals with the particular types of personal freedom, Article 21 takes in and deals with the residue. The court said:

"We have already extracted a passage from the judgement of Field J. in *Munn* Vs. *Illinois (1877) 94 U.S. 113, 142* where the learned judge painted out that life in the 5th and 14th Amendment of the U.S. Constitution corresponding to Art. 21 means not merely the right to the continuance of a person's animal existence, but a right to the possession of each of his organs–his arms and legs etc. We do not entertain any doubt that the word life in Art. 21 bears the same signification. Is then the word 'personal liberty' to be construed as excluding from its purview an invasion on the part of the police of the sanctity of a man's home and an intrusion into his personal security and his right to sleep which is the normal comfort and a dire necessity for human existence even as an animal? It might not be inappropriate to refer here to the words of the Preamble to the Constitution that it is designed to "assure the dignity of the individual" and therefore of the cherished human value as the means of ensuring his full development and evolution. We are referring to these objectives of the framers merely to draw attention to the concepts underlying the Constitution which would point to such vital words as "personal liberty" having to be construed in a reasonable manner and to be attributed that sense which would promote and achieve those objectives and by means to stretch the meaning of the phrase to square with any preconceived notions or doctrinaire constitutional theories.

The court then quoted a passage from the judgement of Frankfurter J. in *Wolf* Vs. *Colorado (1949) 338 U.S. 25* to the effect that the security of one's privacy against arbitrary intrusion by the police is basic to a free society and that the knock at the door, whether by day or night, as a prelude to a search, without authority of law but solely on the authority of the police, did not need the commentary of recent history to be condemned as inconsistent with the conception of human rights enshrined in the history and the basic constitutional documents of English-speaking peoples. The Court then said that at Common Law every man's house is his castle and that embodies an abiding principle transcending mere protection of property rights and expounds a concept of "personal liberty" which does not rest upon any element of feudalism or any theory of freedom which has ceased to exist. The Court ultimately came to the conclusion that regulation 236(b) which authorised domicillary visits was violative of Art. 21 and "as there is no law" on the basis of which the same could be justified, it must be struck down as "unconstitutional". The court was of the view that other provisions in regulation 236 were not bad as no right of privacy has been guaranteed by the Constitution.

Suba Rao, J. writing for the minority was of the opinion that the word liberty in Article 21 was comprehensive enough to include privacy also. He said that although it is true our Constitution does not expressly declare a right of privacy as a fundamental right, but the right is an essential ingredient of personal liberty, that in the last resort, a person's house where he lives with his family, is his "castle"; that nothing is more deleterious to a man's physical happiness and health than a calculated intereference with his privacy and that all the acts of surveillance under Regulation 236 infringe the fundamental right of the petitioner under Art. 21 of the Constitution. And, as regards Article 19(1) (d), he was of the view that that right also was violated. He said that the right under that Sub-Article is not mere freedom to move without physical obstruction and observed that movement under the scrutinizing gaze of the policemen cannot be free movement, that the freedom of movement in clause (d), therefore, must be a movement in a free country, *i.e.* in a country where he can do whatever he likes, speak to whomsoever he wants, meet people of his own choice without any apprehension, subject of course to the law of social control and that a person under the shadow of surveillance is essentially deprived of this freedom. He concluded by saying that surveillance by domicilary visits and other acts is an abridgement of the fundamental right guaranteed under Art. 19(1) (d) and under Art. 19(1) (a). He however did not specifically consider whether regulation

236 could be justified as a reasonable restriction in public interest falling within Art. 19(5).

(22) *Jane Roe* Vs. *Henry Wade 410 U.S. 113 (1973) (Mr. Justice Blackman)*

In this case an unmarried pregnant woman who, wished to terminate her pregnancy by abortion instituted an action in the United States District Court for the Northern District of Texas, seeking a declaratory judgement that Texas criminal abortion statutes, which prohibited abortions except with respect to those procured or attempted by medical advice for the purpose of saving the life of the mother, were unconstitutional. The Supreme Court said that although the Constitution of the U.S.A. does not explicitly mention any right of privacy, the United States Supreme Court recognises that a right of personal privacy, or a guarantee of certain areas or zones of privacy, does exist under the Constitution, and "that the roots of that right may be found in the First Amendment, in the Fourth and Fifth Amendments, in the penumbras of the Bill of Rights, in the Ninth Amendment, and in the concept of liberty guaranteed by the first Section of the Fourteenth Amendment and that the "right to privacy is not absolute".

The Constitution does not explicitly mention any right of privacy. In a line of decisions, however, the Court has recognised that a right of personal privacy, or a guarantee of certain areas or zones of privacy, does exist under the Constitution. In varying contexts the Court or individual justices have indeed found at least the roots of that right in the First Amendment (*Stanley* Vs. *Georgia*) in the Fourth and Fifth Amendments (*Terry* Vs. *Ohio, Katz* Vs. *United States*) in the penumbras of the Bill of Rights (*Griswold* Vs. *Connecticut*), in the Ninth Amendment (id. Goldberg J. concurring); or in the concept of liberty guaranteed by the first Section of the Fourteenth Amendment (*Meyer* Vs. *Nebraska*). These decisions make it clear that only personal rights that can be deemed "fundamental" or "implicit in the concept of ordered liberty" (*Palko* Vs. *Connecticut*) are included in this guarantee of personal privacy. They also make it clear that the right has some extension to activities relating to marriage (*Loving* Vs. *Virginia* ...procreation, *Eisenstadt* Vs. *Baird*....family relationships, *Prince* Vs. *Massachusetts*... and child rearing and education, *Pierce* Vs. *Society of Sisters...Meyer* Vs. *Nebraska, Skinner* Vs. *Oklahoma* – contraception).

The right of privacy whether it be found in the Fourteenth Amendment's concept of personal liberty and restrictions upon State action, in the Ninth Amendment's reservation of rights to the people, is broad enough to encompass a woman's decision whether or not to terminate her pregnancy. The detriment that the State would impose upon the pregnant woman by denying this choice altogether is, apparent. Specific and direct harm medically diagnosable even in early pregnancy may be involved. Maternity, or additional offsping may force upon the woman a distressful life and future; psychological harm may be imminent. Mental and physical health may be taxed by child care. There is also the distress, for all concerned, associated with the unwanted child, and there is the problem of bringing a child into a family already unable, psychologically or otherwise, to care for it. In other cases, the additional difficulties and continuing stigma of unwed motherhood may be involved. All these are factors the woman and her responsible physician necessarily will consider in consultation.

The Court's decisions recognising a right of privacy also acknowledge that some State regulation in areas protected by this right is appropriate. A State may properly assert important interests in safeguarding health, in maintaining medical standards and in protecting potential life. At some point in pregnancy, these respective interests become sufficiently compelling to sustain regulation of the factors that govern the abortion decision.

The right of personal privacy includes the abortion decision, but this right is not unqualified and must be considered against important State interests in regulation.

The pregnant woman cannot be isolated in her privacy. She carries an embryo and, later, a fetus. The situation therefore is inherently different from marital intimacy, or bedroom possession of obscene material, or marriage or procreation, or education. It is reasonable and appropriate for a State to decide that at some point in time another interest, that of health of the mother or that of potential human life, becomes significantly involved. The woman's privacy is no longer sole and any right of privacy, she possesses must be measured accordingly.

*

SUMMARY

(A) Introduction:

(1) In recent times however, the individual's space about him and over which he has a personal control has rapidly diminished. A good deal of Data stored in Government or private files or record is without the knowledge or consent of the individual or individuals. Data is partially stored due to one's own submission to questionnaires and personality texts: Westin described three topics which involve intrusions into privacy. He included what Geong Simmel called "self-invasion", or self-revelation so frequently resulting from inquiries of pollsters. A second topic is the intrusion because of curiosity, including pure gossip, but also with a generous measure of human and mechanical "peeping Toms". Third, he considers the heavy invasions into privacy by varying kinds of surveillance, such as surveillance by observation by extraction (a psychological method); and a newer method, which he calls "reproducibility of communication". The last could be labelled general "electronic surveillance", including the use of camera devices.

[Westin, Privacy and Freedom, Chapter 3].

(2) Since judges make many of these determinations in the last analysis, heavy reliance, has been made on selected cases which have come before the U.S. Supreme Court and other courts. The privacy object is to present the views of judges in particular instances as means of showing judicial attitudes toward privacy as a right and how and why and to what extent it is to be protected against governmental invasion or intrusion.

(3) The maximum protection to privacy which a free society can tolerate and should ensure and a balance between

individual rights and community interests, but with the balance tilted in favour of individual rights is strongly favoured. Agreement is easy with Professor Beaney's statement before the Special Inquiry on Invasion of Privacy, held by a House Sub-committee in 1965:

"You do not have to be vary intelligent to see that if this drift towards more and more intrusive action by private groups and organisations of all kinds and by Government is not checked in 20 or 30 years no one will bother asking questions about privacy, and we will take it for granted that we live a fishbowl and that we are not free men, but fish."

(4) Judicial pronouncements provide the basic resources for both the purposes and content of right to privacy.

(5) Right to Privacy has only recently begun to come into its own as a legal right. This changing status reflects a response to social need. As Watergate revelations of "enemy lists", national security wiretaps, and burglaries have dramatised in the United States. The technology of surveillance has increased in sophistication to include the microphone secreted in a cocktail olive; the "emotional stress evaluation" to probe our innermost emotions, the message carrying laser beams capable of piercing the thickest wall and transmitting information over the expanse of the continents. Technology, social needs and cultural and political circumstances all have a bearing on the legal status of privacy.

(6) If the existence of privacy safeguards depends upon the stimulus provided by some degree of threat then the legal responses should be greatest in the United States, merely as great in Britain and nearly non-existent in India, because the level of technological and economic development of India compared to the other two countries does not establish the conditions necessary for the legal safeguard of privacy rights. A casual student of Indian Law might conclude that the right of privacy is unknown except for a few isolated instances in that system. Nevertheless an alternative conclusion is in order.

(B) Definition of Right to Privacy:

(7) In Adam Carlyle Breckenridge's view in his book "The Right to Privacy" (November 1971) in 1st Chapter "A Most Comprehensive Right":

"Privacy is the rightful claim of the individual to determine the extent to which he wishes to share of himself with others and his control over the time, place and circumstances to communicate to others. It means his right to withdraw or to participate as he sees fit. It is also the indiviudal's right to control dissemination of information about himself; it is his own personal possession."

(8) Judge Cooley observed in his book–

[Thomas M. Cooley, A Treatise on the Law of Torts, 2nd ed. (Chicago: Callagham and Co. 1888), p. 29]

"Privacy is synonymous with the right to be let alone."

(9) Edward Shils, "Privacy: Its Constitution and Vicissitudes", Law and Contemporary Problems 31, No. 2 (Spring 1966), 281, has defined privacy as a "zero-relationship" between two or more persons in the sense that there is no interaction or communication between them, if they so choose.

(C) Development of Right to Privacy:

(10) It has been said that the modern claim to privacy has been based on "Science, the secularization of Government, and political democracy". Undoubtedly scientific advancement has made much of our personal privacy possible; but science has also taken its toll in making possible severe invasions into privacy. An example is the use of electronic devices to overhear and record what is said without the knowledge of those speaking. Individual differences in outlook and development of personality can be attributed in part at least to the separation of Church and State. And guarantees of basic freedoms and a respect for the dignity of man stem from the strengths of political democracy.

(11) Judicial development of the right to privacy has some of its roots in concurring and dissenting opinions. So what was "said" may be as important as what was "held" or "decided" in any particular case.

(12) The common law did not recognise any right to privacy. Apparently the courts in the United States did not consider privacy as a right to be protected until the eve of the twentieth century, since that time hundreds of cases have come before the courts to determine whether a privacy exists as a legal right and, if so, then to what extent and under what conditions.

The concern about privacy may be traced, in modern times in the famous article by Samuel D. Warren and Louis D. Brandeis which appeared in Harward Law Review, 1890, 4, No. 5 (December, 1890), 193 entitled "The Right to Privacy". It has been quoted or referred to in countless cases since that time. [One of the first references to the article in a higher court was in *Roberson* Vs. *Rochester Folding Box Co., 171 N.Y. 538 (1902)*]. The effect it had on decisions and opinions has been usually high so much so that the central theme expressed has been given constitutional sanction by the U.S. Supreme Court.

The "right to privacy", however, is not spelled out in the Constitution. The word "privacy" is not used at all. Judges, nonetheless, have considered the existence of a right to privacy since the first apparent case in 1891 in the Supreme Court of New York.

[*Schuyler* Vs. *Curtis, 15 N.Y. supp. 787* (1891)]

(Schuyler may be the first to recognise the Warren Brandeis Article). This case involved the issue whether private citizens had a right to erect a statue of a locally prominent woman over the objections of her family. It was claimed to violate privacy. In denying the claim, the court said: "It is true that there is no reported decision which goes to this extent in maintaining the right to privacy, and in that respect this is a novel case". Reference may also be made to the famous English Case of 1849 involving Prince Albert that it and other cases and the Warren Brandeis Article gave ".....clear recognition....of the principle that the right to which protection is given is the right to privacy". *Prince Albert* Vs. *Strange*, 1 Macn. & G. 25, in *Schuyler* Vs. *Curtis, 789*.

The first higher American Court to deal with the right to privacy was in *Roberson* Vs. *Rochester Folding Box* Co. (171, N.Y; 544), a New York appellate case decided in 1902. Speaking of the lower court decision, chief Justice Parker said:

....defendants had invaded what is called a "right of privacy"; in other words, the right to be let alone. Mention of such right is not to be found in Blackstone, Kent or any other of the great commentators upon the law; nor so far as the learning of counsel or courts in this case have been able to discover, does its existence seem to have been asserted prior to about the year. 1890, when it was presented with attractiveness, and no inconsiderable ability, in the Harward Law Review (Volume IV, Page 193).

The so-called "right of privacy" is, as the phrase suggests, founded upon the claim that a man has the right to pass through this world, if he wills without having his picture published, his business enterprises discussed, his successful experiments written up for the benefit of others, or his eccentricities commented upon either in hand-bills or newspapers; and, necessarily, that the things which may not be written and published of him, must not be spoken of him by his neighbours, whether the comment be favourable or otherwise.

Three years later a Georgia Court considered the question whether there was a right to privacy. The comment by Judge Cobb is of interest in tracing the development of a right to privacy because of his reference that the right is derived from natural law, a source for fundamental rights steadfastly denied by Justice Hugo Black. Judge Cobb said:

> The right of privacy has its foundations in the instincts of nature. It is recognised intuitively, consciousness being witness that can be called to establish its existence. Any person whose intellect is in a normal condition recognises at once that as to each individual member of society there are matters private and there are matters public so far as the individual is concerned. Each individual as instinctively resents any encroachment by the public upon his rights which are of a private nature as he does the withdrawal of those rights which are of a public nature. A right of privacy in matters purely private is therefore derived from natural law.

[*Pavesich* Vs. *New England Life Insurance 122 Ga. 190; 194 (1905)*]

(13) For Justice Hugo Black's dissents see for example –

(a) *Adamson* Vs. *California 322 U.S. 46, 75 (1947).*

(b) *Griswold* Vs. *Connecticut 381 U.S. 479, 511 (1965).*

Black has sternly insisted that any natural-law formula may not be employed to expand or contract the commands of the Bill of Rights. In 1966, the U.S. Supreme Court handed down its decision in *Osborn* Vs. U.S. 385 U.S. 323, 341, 342, 343. In his forceful dissent Justice Douglas summed up the fears and concerns held by many about the right to privacy:

> We are rapidly entering the age of no privacy, where everyone is open to surveillance at all times, where there are no secrets from the Government. The aggressive breaches of privacy by the Government increase with geometric proportions. Wiretapping and "bugging" run rampant, without effective judicial or legislative control.
>
> Secret observation booths in govt. offices and closed television circuits in industry, extending even to rest rooms, are common. Offices, conference rooms, hotel rooms and even bedrooms are "bugged for the convenience of government. Personality tests seek to ferret out a man's innermost thoughts.... Federal agents are often wired so that their conversations are either recorded on their persons or transmitted to tape recorders some blocks away.... They have broken and entered homes to obtain evidence... The dossiers on all citizens mount in number and increase in size. Now they are being put on computers so that by pressing one button all the miserable, the sick, the suspect, the unpopular the off-beat people of the nation can be instantly identified. These examples and many other demonstrate an alarming trend whereby the privacy and dignity of our citizens is being whittled away by sometimes imperceptible steps. Taken individually, each step may be of little consequence. But when viewed as a whole, there begins to emerge a society quite unlike any we have seen – a society in which government may intrude into the secret regions of a man's life at will.

During the 1967 and 1968 Sessions of the Congress, the *Omnibus Crime Control and Safe Streets Act* was debated and passed. It is a far-reaching piece of legislation which its supporters held was vital to the peace and security of the nation and which its critics roundly denounced as succumbing to the hysteria of the time.

(14) Senator Edward V. Long of Missouri during the debate on May 23, 1968 proposed an amendment to a bill which would recognise a right of privacy. It went as follows:

"The Constitution of the U.S. guarantees to all individuals a basic right of privacy. Accordingly the Congress endorses the requirement that what an individual seeks to preserve as private is to be protected, even in an area accessible to the public. The Congress supports the view that wherever a man may be, he is entitled to know that he will remain free from unreasonable searches and seizures."

(D) Scope and Extent of Right to Privacy:

(15) One writer recently observed that a wish to have privacy was closely associated with "increased value placed on private property", and those without property were liable to be also without privacy.

[Bruno Bettelheim, "*The Right to Privacy is a Myth*", Saturday Evening Post, July 27, 1968, pages 8, 9].

(16) One ultimately looks to the Bill of Rights of the U.S. Constitution and the interpretations given by the courts to determine the extent of one's rights to freedom of various sorts. The right to privacy, however, is not spelled out in the Constitution. The word "privacy" is not used at all. Judges nonetheless have considered the existence of a right to privacy.

(17) The primary object and purpose is to show how far government in the United States has gone in invading the right to personal privacy, and how far government has gone also to protect that right. It is to examine how government is prevented, in the words of Justice Brandeis from "obtaining" disclosure in court of what is whispered in the closet;" how government is restricted from intrusions into the privacy of the home and of the person; how the right to privacy is frequently in conflict with other claimed liberties and governmental power, and finally, to show how some intrusions of privacy have become accepted as necessary in the interest of public health, safety, morals and the general welfare.

(18) In one of its most controversial cases, the Supreme Court found unconstitutional a Texas abortion statute which,

like laws in force in most States, forbade procuring or attempting an abortion except "by medical advice for the purpose of saving the life of the mother". In *Roe* Vs. *Wade 410 U.S. 112 (1973)*, Justice Blackman said that the State regulation violated the *due process* clause of the Fourteenth Amendment which was found to protect the right of privacy against State action. The right of privacy was said to be the basis of a woman's qualified right to procure an abortion free from State interference during most of her pregnancy. As in the *Griswold Case*, the court appeared to go out of its way to reach the constitutional issue despite traditional theories of judicial restraint that usually preclude reaching of constitutional questions particularly when the State law is involved. While finding privacy to be a "fundamental right", Justice Blackman's decision for the court did not clarify the definitional basis of that right. In some ways, the decision seemed to narrow the scope of the right by cataloguing "certain areas or zones of privacy".

The list of areas in which the right of privacy was found to have some application included marriage –(*Loving* Vs. *Virginia*, 388 *U.S. 1, 12* (1967); procreation –*Skinner* Vs. *Oklahoma, 316 U.S. 535, 541-42 (1942)*; Contraception –*Eisenstadt* Vs. *Baird 405 U.S. 438, 453-54*; White concurring 460, 463-65, (1972); family relationship–*Prince* Vs. *Massachusetts 321, U.S. 158, 166 (1944);* cf. *United States* Vs. *Kahn 415 U.S. 143* (1974) and – Child Rearing and education – *Pierce* vs. *Society of Sisters), 268 U.S. 510, 535 (1925*), *Meyer* Vs. *Nebraska 262 U.S. 390, 399 (1923)*. Justice Blackman concluded that the "right of privacy" whether it be founded in the Fourteenth Amendment's concept of personal liberty and restrictions upon state action, as we feel it is, or, as the District Court determined in the Ninth Amendment's reservation of rights to the people, is broad enough to encompass a woman's decision whether or not to terminate her pregnancy. [*Roe* Vs. *Wade, 410 U.S. at 153 (1973)*]. Like written guarantees, privacy rights were found to be subject to limitation when they conflicted with a "compelling State interest". For the first trimester of pregnancy, the Court held the State can only regulate abortion procedures in a manner reasonably related to material health but must leave decisions relating to effectuation of an abortion to the woman and her physician. After that point the State interest increases as the potentiality of human life increases until, in the last trimester, it can limit abortions to those cases in which it is medically necessary in order to preserve the life or health of the mother.

(19) The cases in which the right of privacy has been controlling center predominantly in the area of contraception and abortion. If this trend continues, we may witness the limitation of constitutional privacy rights to mere marital privacy (thus providing little protection against governmental intrusion upon privacy interests not related to sex and family and not completely covered by other constitutional guarantees). The explanation for this development is to be found partly in judicial politics. *Roe* Vs. *Wade* and its companion case *Doe* Vs. *Bolton* demonstrate that the Supreme Court is divided over the question as to whether there is a constitutional Right of Privacy and, if it exists, what it means and from where it arises. Justice Stewart, in his concurring opinion in *Roe* suggested that the right of privacy developed in *Griswold* was merely a device to avoid admitting reliance on the *due process* clause of the Fourteenth Amendment and the "*Substantive due process doctrine* which Justice Douglas had said in 1963 "could not be used to substitute the Court's social and economic benefits for that of elected legislative bodies." If Justice Stewart is correct that there is no right of privacy apart from traditional constitutional guarantees, then protection from many forms of invasion of privacy will have to come from legislative action rather than from the courts relying on existing constitutional prohibitions. Four examples at the federal level reflect this aspect.

(i) First, the Privacy Act of 1974, worked enactment of the first comprehensive law to regulate use of records of personal information collected and maintained by the federal government. This landmark legislation, which gives citizens the right to see and copy most records about them stored by federal agencies and the right to challenge and correct any inaccurate information, also prohibits non-routine dissemination and disclosure of personally identifiable information, unless requested by or consented to by the file subject. Each federal agency is required to publish annual notices in the

Federal Register as to the existence and nature of personal records maintained by it including a description of categories of individuals on whom records are maintained, the routine uses and users of the systeḿ, and procedures concerning access to and for correction of such records.

The Privacy Act also established a Privacy Protection Study Commission, prohibited sale of mailing lists by federal agencies and prohibited denial of privileges or benefits by any government agency because of an individual's refusal to disclose his social security number, unless disclosure is specifically required by law or the system in question had been established prior to January 1, 1975 violations of the Act are punishable by criminal penalties or by civil suits brought against the agency involved by persons adversely affected by Act violations.

(ii) Second, Title 3 of the *Omnibus Crime Control and Safe Streets Act of 1968* broke new ground by specifying criminal and civil sanctions against persons who engage in unauthorised wiretapping or electronic surveillance. More important, the Act specifically advances privacy interests by prohibiting virtually all electronic surveillance activities conducted without court authroisation and under some degree of judicial control.

(iii) Third, *The Fair Credit Reporting Act of 1970* marked the first attempt by the Federal Government to control the accuracy of investigative reports made on millions of Americans each year by credit reporting agencies which the Act does not permit the report, subject to see the contents of the actual dossier compiled on them, it does require notice to be given to the subjects of such reports. This step is mandated when report forms part of the basis for insurance, credit or employment. Criminal and civil damages are available to report subjects when the credit agency fails to make a reasonable effort to purge inaccurate information from the file. Bills such as $2360, 93rd Congress have been introduced to require written authorisation from the subject before an investigative report is begun, and upon completion, to supply him with a copy of the report at the expense of the agency.

(iv) Fourth, concern for the detrimental effects that unwarranted dissemination of criminal records can have on an individual's reputation and rights led to enactment of a floor amendment to the *Crime Control Act of 1973*. Affected are all state law enforcement agencies, collecting, storing or disseminating criminal history information through support received from the *Law Enforcement Assistance Administration (LEAA)*. They must assure that the security and privacy of all information is adequately provided for and that information shall only be used for law enforcement and criminal justice and other lawful purposes. All LEAA research or statistical information identifiable to a specific private person is barred from use for any purpose other than that for which it was collected. Further, it is, immune from legal process, and cannot be used in any judicial or administrative proceeding without the consent of the person furnishing the information. In view of the increasing on LEAA, this new requirement is likely to mark the first significant protection for computerized criminal records.

(20) The rapid advances made by the Ninty-third Congress in the privacy area toward the end of its session indicate that Watergate, revelations of political surveillance by the F.B.I. and of possible misuse of tax returns by the Internal Revenue Service may have caused a consensus to form.

(21) In 1974 alone, more actions were taken to provide formal protection to Privacy than had been achieved in all of the prior history of the United States. In addition to the passage of the Privacy Act, Congress enacted the "Family Educational Rights" and Privacy Act of 1974, which would deny federal funds to any educational institution that prevented parental access to a child's school records or permitted the release of a student's records without parental consent to anyone but another school official or in compliance with a court order. Among over 300 other privacy bills introduced in the Ninty-third Congress relating to privacy, serious consideration was given to a Bill to establish rules on the use and dissemination of criminal records and a bill to prohibit military surveillance of civilian activities.

It is peculiarity of the American Policy-making process that the Supreme Court is able to open new avenues of reform by posting directional markers reading "legal rights and liberties". But the more substantial work of smoothing the way for citizens to make use of their rights is often left for legislative follow-up. Of course, executive action and administrative policy also play a role which citizens expect to be constructive. Unfortunately, that has not always been the case.

These politically motivated invasions of privacy and related scandals have damaged public trust and confidence in Government. The "Bill of Complaints" against Watergate style abuses has generated significant demands for a more secure right to privacy. Popularly esteemed rights and liberties also grow out of deeply felt complaints against very specific executive abuses.

(22) India is far behind both Britain and the United States in active judicial enforcement or even public discussion, of privacy laws. The lack of demands for judicial enforcement of the laws safeguarding privacy, and the further lack of public debate on the threat to the right of privacy, may mislead a casual observer to believe that there are no laws safeguarding this human right in India. Nevertheless research in Indian law on the subject reveals propositions which are somewhat startling.

Consider the following examples which in each instance are more demanding than American and British law:

(a) One, Section 509 of the Indian Penal Code of 1860 specifically makes it a crime to intrude upon the privacy of a woman intending to insult her modesty.

(b) Two, in the case of *In re Ratnamala AIR 1962 Mad. 31, (35)*, the court ruled legally inexcusable the behaviour of a police officer (accompanied by witnesses to observe a raid on a brothel). They proceeded to the bedroom of a girl and pushed open the door, as the court observed, "...without even the civility of a knock or warning to her to prepare for the intrusion". Thus, even a prostitute is entitled to elementary decencies.

(c) Three, the fact that a man can command the view of the interior of his neighbour's house does not entitle him to gaze at his neighbour's home at all times. Elaborate easement legislation covers this situation.

(d) Fourth, case law shows that a police officer searching a dwelling without a warrant must take precautions. Prior to the search, he should record reasons why the search cannot be made after obtaining a warrant and state what he expects to find as a result of the search. Strict compliance with this law is necessary to insure against humiliation and reckless searches in disregard of citizens' rights (*State of Rajasthan* Vs. *Rehman AIR 1960 S.C. 210*).

A listing of several such safeguards propositions taken from Indian law (surpassing in some respects Western parallels) supports the conclusion that in the body of Indian law there exists a No. of safeguards which enforce the right of privacy of the individual (see *Mohd. Hussain Saheb* Vs. *Chartered Bank AIR 1964 (1) Mad. 1012*, for discussion of secrecy in Bankings; *Indian Evidence Act, 1872*, Secs. 121 to 129, 132 on privileged communications; Sections 24, 25, 26, 29 on confessions, Section 33 of the *Special Marriage Act,* 1959; Section 53 of the *Indian Divorce Act, 1869* (*in camera* proceedings), Sections 16, 95, 127-A, 128, *Representation of Peoples Act (Secrecy of Ballot*).

For almost a century Indian Criminal Law has embodied some of the modern constitutional safeguards which the United States Supreme Court did not apply as national safeguards until the 1960s. For example, *Miranda* Vs. *Arizona*, decided by the American Supreme Court in 1966, is less stringent in some regards than the *Indian Evidence Act of 1872*. The latter prohibits the admissibility of any confession of guilt made to a police officer, "unless it be made in the immediate presence of a magistrate." Compare *Miranda* Vs. *Arizona, 384 U.S. 436 (1966)* with the following:

(1) Indian Evidence Act, 1872, Section 25. No confession made by any person while he is in the custody of a police officer, unless it be made in the immediate presence of a magistrate, shall be proved as against such person.

(2) Section 164 (3) of the Code of Criminal Procedure, 1898, dealing with the procedure for recording confession by magistrate provides: *164(3)* A magistrate shall before regarding any such confession, explain to the person making it that he is not bound to make a confession and that if he does so it may be used as evidence against him and no magistrate shall record any such confession unless, upon questioning the person making it, he has reason to believe that it has made voluntarily; and when he records any confession, he shall make a memorandum at the foot of such record to the following effect:

> "I have explained to (Name) that he is not bound to make a confession and that if he does so any confession he may make may be used as evidence against him and I believe that his confession was voluntarily made. It was taken in my presence, and hearing, and was read over to

> the person making it and admitted by him to be correct, and it contained a full and true account of the statement made by him."

Moreover, under Indian Law, even an accused person has the privilege of protection of privacy against an arbitrary search. According to Section 165 of the Code of Criminal Procedure, the power of an officer to conduct a search is limited to quests pursuant to the investigation of an offence (*Shreenath Prasad* Vs. *State of Bihar, AIR 1966 SC 1577*).

While conducting a search, the officer must enlist two respectable residents of the locality to join him as witnesses. To protect a citizen's privacy, magistrates must comply with the conditions for warranting a search according to Section 94 of the Code. These conditions are mandatory and not merely directory (See the *New Swadeshi Mills of Ahemedabad* Vs. *S.K. Rattan AIR 1968 Gujarat 117*).

Prior to issuing a warrant, the magistrate should examine the informant under oath, and take upon himself the responsibility of considering the weight of the information preparatory to issuing an order of search. [*Laurenco Rocha* Vs. *Euclidas Joao Rodrigues, AIR 1968 Goa 48*). The law of searches and seizures, restrictions on the admissibility of evidence procured by improper means, and related rules, act as strong bastions in defence of individual privacy.

From the Indian point of view, the problems for further present-day development of the law of privacy grow out of factors assoicated with the nature of the courts and the nature of debate over public policy, one reason why Indian law, especially the law of torts, is slow to develop can be traced to the exorbitant expenses associated with litigation. This discourages speculative actions and offended parties often simply refrain from making demands on the judicial system to meet the needs of changing times. A plaintiff tends to go to court only if there is established law to grant him redress. Since the scope for development of law through adjudication is narrow, the judicial function becomes mechanical on the view that cases that do arise are covered by precedent. Developments in Indian Law tend to arise out of petitions for constitutionally provided writs, criminal cases, and through legislation. A second inhibition on contemporary development of privacy protection lies in the fact that it has not been isolated by influential spokesmen and policy makers as an agent subject for debate and policy reform.

(E) Effects of Right to Privacy:

(23) Privacy as a basic human right touches upon fundamental needs and values associated with man's gregarious nature. Certainly the level of technological and economic development creates pressures to protect these privacy values through legal enforcement techniques. But even in the absence of such development, the value of and the basic human right to privacy may prevail irrespective of legal recognition. On the other hand, active claims for legal enforcement of the right seem to have a very direct relationship to the degree of threat posed to its survival. Certainly this relationship holds at the level of legal development, and it supports the thesis that human rights such as privacy, although recognised by laws, are enforced only when the danger to underlying values is perceived. The values, themselves, may also be shared and implied in cultural norms, but often they are not articulated as legal norms until threatened.

(F) Importance and Significance of Right to Privacy:

(24) More than forty years ago in his famous dissenting opinion, U.S. Supreme Court Justice Brandeis wrote this about privacy:

The makers of our Constitution undertook to secure conditions favourable to the pursuit of happiness....They conferred, as against the Government, the right to be let alone the most comprehensive of rights and the right most valued by civilised man.

[*Olmstead* Vs. *U.S. 277 U.S. 438, 478 (1928)*]

(25) Man lives in a community of others, and he also has the need to participate and communicate. When this double faceted aspect of privacy is coupled with the recognised power of government to function for the public good, there is ample reason for much of the recent concern about invasions and intrusions into individual privacy.

(26) Shils says that the respect for privacy has its roots in the "values of modern liberalism" [See his "Social Inquiry and the Autonomy of the Individual" in Daniel Leamex, ed.; The Human Meaning of the Social Sciences (New York: Meridian Books, Inc., 1959), p. 120].

(27) For all of the public character of social life, it will turn out that the heart of personal freedom, creativity, rests in privacy. And the significance of privacy is its creative contribution to the public.

(G) Case Law on Right to Privacy:

(28) Sooner or later it becomes the business is of the judges to determine the metes and bounds of individual privacy claims. Thus, it is to the decisions and opinions of judges, that we must turn to find the status of claims to any right of individual privacy.

(29) Most of the States have recognised varying degrees of privacy through Statutes or court decisions. A few have not. The Supreme Court of Nebraska, for example, said in a 1955 case that "....if such a right is deemed necessary or desirable, such right should be provided for by action of our legislature and not by judicial limitation on the part of the courts".

[*Branson* Vs. *Ranks Army Store, 161, Nebr. 519, 525*]

(30) Roscoe Pound said that if privacy was not given protection in law there was technically no legal right to privacy.

[*Harward Law Review, 28, No. 4 (Feb. 1915), 343, 363*]

(H) Right to Life under the Constitution of India:

(31) The right to life of a human being is as old as mankind. The nature creates the life and right to it is essentially natural. When the process of civilisation began, a human being became conscious of his rights, particularly his right to exist. Law, international and municipal, both have duly recognised this fundamental right of a human being on which rests all other rights. A human has a right to pursue against the State, if his basic rights are infringed by it. Similarly, under international law, every convention on human rights gives a distinct place to the right to life as also the offshoots of this right, like the right to liberty. The issue of human rights has crossed the bounds of nations and has evoked a vigorous international dialogue.

(32) The Universal Declaration of Human Rights, 1948 embodied

the right to life explicitly. Art. 3 states that "everyone has the right to life, liberty and security of person. The Geneva Convention also deplored the killing of human beings and declared it to be the crime liable to punishment (Convention on the Prevention and Punishment of the crime of Genocide, 1948 adopted on 9th December, 1948 and came into force on 12th Jan. 1951). This Convention very firmly advocated the preciousness of human life and vehemently condemned any attempt to extinguish it.

The Charter of the United Nations also crystallised the inalienable rights of all members of human family. The Charter reaffirmed faith in fundamental human rights in the dignity and worth of human person. The Charter also expressed the resolve of the United Nations "To promote social progress and better standard of life".

(*United Nations Charter,* see Preamble and Arts. 1, 13, 15, 55, 56, 62, 68 and 76)

The European Convention for the protection of human rights also states that "every one's right to life shall be protected by law" and that no one shall be deprived intentionally of his life except in the execution of a lawful scheme by the court (Art. 2 of *European Convention for the Protection of Human Rights and Fundamental Freedoms, 1950*).

It is clear, therefore, that the right to life is placed at the summit of all other basic rights of a human being. Under international laws too, the reason is that it is ultimately a human being who is the subject of international law, may be not directly but vicariously. The municipal laws also place the fundamental right to life above all other fundamental rights. The right to life is therefore, recognised and protected both from within and without.

(33) The fundamental rights in England have to be traced back to the days of the *Magna Carta* (*Magna Carta* contains Preamble and 63 clauses). The *Magna Carta* was not a Charter of the rights of the people or the common man. It was instead the Charter of concessions wrested from King John, in 1215. This Charter also protected the right to life of a human being. The Charter was followed by the Petition of Rights and Bill of Rights (The Petition of Rights, 1627, The Bill of Rights, 1688). It is essentially the French Revolution and American Constitution which influenced

the formal enunciation of fundamental rights in most of the modern Constitutions of the world, including the Constitution of India.

(34) The declaration of fundamental human rights has almost become the normal feature of Constitution making particularly in the post-World War I, period. The Indian Constitution also has enshrined these basic rights in Part III. (F. Rs. under Part III of the Constitution are contained in Arts. 12 to 35). The right to life has been specifically guaranteed under Art. 21. However, we may hasten to add that Art. 21 is not the sole repository of right to life. It is pertinent here to refer to the Draft Constitution as also the Constituent Assembly debates. The Draft Art. 15 (the 5th Amendment and 14th Amendment of American Constitution are the source from which substantial part of Draft Art. 15 was derived). The Draft Art. 15 (which corresponds to Art. 21 of the Constitution) as originally passed by the Constitution Assembly provided:

> "No person shall be deprived or his life of liberty without *due process of law*, nor shall any person be denied equality before the law or the equal protection of the laws within the territory of India."

The Equality provision of the Draft Art. was transferred to the present Art. 14 of the Constitution. But, in the first part of Draft Art. 15 the Drafting Committee brought about two changes. Firstly, the word "liberty" was prefixed by the word "personal". Secondly, the expression "except according to the procedure established by law" was substituted for the words "without due process of law". The first change transformed the word liberty into personal liberty, making it a rather narrow concept. Liberty will include property also as in the American Constitution, personal liberty was strictly meant to be the liberty of one's personality only. The reason as to why the expression liberty was restricted in scope was that the other aspects of liberty were specifically dealt with in other fundamental rights like Art. 19. Moreover, it would have been unwise to leave open an interpretation which would include in the word "liberty", the freedoms which had been denied to non-citizens in Art. 13 (now Art. 19).

(35) The Draft Art. 15 was essentially on the pattern of the 5th and the 14th Amendment of the American Constitution.

(5th Amendment of U.S. Constitution states that "no person shall be...deprived of life, liberty or property without due process of law..." The 14th Amendment further declares liberty or property without due process of law.") Another alteration made in this Article is regarding the phrase "without due process of law". These words were substituted by the expression "except according to the procedure established by law". This change meant that legislature has to be the ultimate protector of individual liberty instead of the judiciary. This expression curtailed the power of judicial scrutiny to a large extent. The moot question was: Should the final power be given to the judiciary to protect individual liberty, or should the legislature have the last word as to the extent of individual freedom ? There is no doubt that the Constituent Assembly in this regard preferred to vast powers in the legislature rather in the judiciary.

(36) The elimination of "due process" was substantially influenced by B.N. Rau (Sir B.N. Rau was appointed as Constitutional Advisor in 1946). He believed that the substantive interpretation of "due process" might interfere with legislation for social purposes. The majority view in the Constituent Assembly was that the power of judicial review was undemocratic. How could a few judges sitting in courts disapprove a legislation brought about by the representative of people?

(37) The expression "except according to procedure established by law" is taken, it seems from Japanese Constitution. However, the rules of natural justice are not read into this expression in the Japanese Constitution. Kania C.J. in *Gopalan Case* observed:

The phrase "procedure established by law" seems to be borrowed from Art. 31 of the Japanese Constitution ...It is not shown that the world law means "*just*" in the Japanese Constitution. By adopting the phrase "procedure established by law," the Constitution gave the legislature the final word to determine law (*A.K. Gopalan* Vs. *State of Madras AIR 1950 S.C. 27*).

(38) It is clear, that the framers of the Indian Constitution deliberately avoided the expression "due process" in

Art. 21. They wanted to make the provision more specific and less controversial.

(39) Right means a claim, an entitlement and right to life signifies a claim to one's life. The right to life is presupposed by every other right of a human self and that is what makes it a fundamental of all fundamental rights.

(40) The claim to one's life is inherent in every man by virtue of the law of nature. This right being fundamental as also natural is necessary for the existence of society as well. This view is lucidly presented by Julius Stone when he states:

The life of individual in society is one thing, and not two. Any claim made by a member of society has the respect both of his own continuance as an individual, and of the continuance of the society in which he is an individual.

[Julius Stone; Social Dimensions of Law and Justice at 1999 (1966)]

(41) The right to life undoubtedly is an initial claim and all other claims emanate from this basic claim.

(42) The right to life is not only important but also necessary. The right to life is paramount, basic and fundamental and is so undoubtedly. The right to life does not only mean the right to exist but also mean a right to exert. The right to life which is primarily a natural right has been given a place in all the Constitutions of the world invariably.

(43) Indian Constitution is an amalgam of many Constitutions *i.e.* Constitutions of America, Britain and Japan. It should not surprise anyone, therefore that the main provisions of the Constitution of India guaranteeing the right to life has been lifted from the American and the Japanese Constitutions. It may be added here that what we have borrowed is the form or the style of expression and not the right itself. The right to life is not something that Constitution create or even confers. The Constitution only recognises this inalienable and indispensable right. The Constitutional provision is therefore only of evidentiary value. The main provision of the Constitution of India which declares the right to life is Art. 21.

(44) Art. 21 is the filterate of the mixture of 5th and 14th Amendments of American Constitution plus Art. 31 of the Japanese Constitution. To appreciate the Constitutional provisions *vis-a-vis* the right to life, it is necessary to mention other provisions which embody the right to life as understood in a social, economic and political sense. All fundamental rights in the Part III of the Constitution of India are only different facets of the right to life.

(45) In India Art. 21 has not only survived but has also widened in scope and content by judicial interpretation. It is interesting to record the following statement of Allan Glandhill:

In some of the older countries, the rights to life and liberty receive more effective protection from constitutional conventions than they do in countries with Constitutions elaborating the rights.

[*Alan Glandhill*, "Life and Liberty in first ten years of republican India". 2 JI LI 241 at 266 (1959-60)].

He however, admits that:

The degree of personal liberty enjoyed by the average Indian is not remarkably less than that enjoyed by a citizen of any other Parliamentary democracy.

(46) The right to "life" as envisaged by 5th and 14th Amendments of the U.S. Constitution was examined in *Munn's Case* [*Munn* Vs. *Illinois 94 U.S. 113* (1877)]. The Indian Supreme Court quoted Justice Field's minority judgement as having significantly observed:

That "life" in 5th and 14th Amendment of U.S. Constitution....means not merely the right to the continuance of a person's animal existence, but a right to the possession of each of his organs, his arms and legs etc.

[*Kharak Singh* vs. *State of U.P., AIR 1963 SC 1295* at 1302. See also *Martin Shapiro and Douglas S. Hobbs*, American Constitutional Law Cases and Analysis at 142 (1978)].

(47) Art. 21 embodies a very crucial right and it is the duty of courts to expound the true meaning of the concept of life mentioned in it. After all the Constitution of India is not a self executing document: one cannot help agreeing with Bernard Schwartz when he states:

"A Constitution is, in practice, what the courts say it is. The Indian Constitution like other organic instruments, would lose much of its practical efficacy if its terms were to be read by the courts in decinating spirit."

[Bernard Schwartz "*A Comparative View of Gopalan Case*": ILR at 276 (1950).]

(48) It is true that fundamental right to life as envisaged by Indian Constitution is worthwhile only if Courts adequately safeguard it. If the courts shun from playing the role, they have to, then we are afraid that the right to life may become ***redunant*** and unmeaning. The words of the Preamble to the Constitution of India that it is designed to assure the dignity of the individual and hence of those cherished human values as the means of ensuring his full development and evolution.

(49) Justice Bhagwati's interpretation of word "life" further substantiates the earlier contention that the right to life presupposes all other rights. In *Kharak Singh's Case*, the S.C. favoured the *Gopalan's* strict construction, but it is appropriate to advert to Justice Ayyangar's statement in this case which runs thus:

Personal liberty is used in the Article as a compendious term to include within itself all the varieties of rights which go to make up the "personal liberties" of Art. 19 (1). In other words while Art. 19(1) deals with particular species or attributes of that freedom "personal liberty" in Art. 21 takes in and comprises the residue.

Justice Suba Rao who was in the minority in this case went a step further and declared:

Further, the right to personal liberty takes in not only a right to be free from restrictions placed on his movements but also free from encroachments on his private life. It is true that our Constitution does not expressly declare a right to privacy as a fundamental right, but the said right is an essential ingredient of personal liberty.

(50) The memorable minority opinion of Suba Rao J. was reaffirmed by Justice Mathew in *Govind's Case*, in which he maintained that right to privacy was also an aspect of personal liberty under Art. 21. The minority judgement of Suba Rao J. in *Kharak Singh's Case* was

reiterated by him in *Satwant Singh's Case (Satwant Singh Sawhney* Vs. *A.P.O., New Delhi AIR 1967 SC 1836)*, now in majority, wherein wide sweep was attributed to the concept of personal liberty in Art. 21. In *Maneka Gandhi's Case*, Justice Bhagwati very aptly described the concept as follows:

"The expression personal liberty in Art. 21 is of the widest amplitude and it covers a variety of rights which go to men and some of them have been raised to the status of distinct fundamental rights and given additional protection under Art. 19. The judges have been really doing a great service to humanity by enlarging the scope of Art. 21 of the Constitution with a view to realising the basic human right *i.e.*, the right to life."

*

BIBLIOGRAPHY

A Comparative view of Gopalan Case ILR at 276 (1950): Bernard Shwartz.

"A Definition of Privacy" quoted in "Philosophy and Public Affairs" (1975) Vol. 4 No. 4, p. 295-314: Richard B. Parker.

American Constitutional Law, p. 921: Prof. Tribe.

American Constitutional Law, Cases and Analysis (1978): Dougles S. Hobbs and Martin Sharpio.

A New Conception of Human Rights: Carl Wellman.

Assault on Privacy, 71: Miller, A.R.

Attack on Privacy: Raines J.C.

California Law Review Vol. 64, p. 1447 : Gary L. Bostwick.

Cases in Civil Liberties (1976): Robert F. Cushman.

Constitutional Protection to Personal Liberty : U.N. Gupta.

Constitutional Law of India, A Critical Commentary (1979) : H.M. Seervai.

Constitutionalism in the Emergent States (1973) : B.C. Nwabueza.

Constitutional Sources of the Penumbral Right to Privacy, Villanova Law Review, Vol. 19 (1974), p. 6 : R.H. Clark.

Comparative Constitutional Law Cases and Commentaries (St. Martin's Press, New York) : Walter F. Murphy & Joseph Tohenhaus.

Computers and Privacy (1969), 67 Michigan L.R. 1091 at 1176.7 : Miller.

Cower's Individual Liberty and the Law (Tagore Law Lectures, 1977) : Zelman Cower.

Democracy, Equality and Freedom (1978) : V.K. Mathew and Upendra Baxi (ed.).

Freedom and Protection: The Bill of Rights : Andrew D. Weinberger

Freedom of Expression with particular reference to freedom of the media : Justice H.R. Khanna.

Freedom of Information and the Protection of Privacy in the Protection of Liberty : I.N. Stevens & D.C. Yardley.

Human Dignity, The Internationalisation of Human Rights (1979) : Alice H. Henkin.

Human Rights – Ideas and Ideologies : Edited by Eugene Kamenka & Alice Erhson Tay.

Harward Law Review, 28, No. 4 (Feb. 1915) : 343. 363 : Roscoe Pound.

Human Rights in the Modern World (1979) : R.S. Aggarwal.

Human Rights and International Cooperation (1969) : Nagendra Singh.

International Right to Privacy Conference, 1967 : Stockholm.

International Protection of Human Rights (1968) : John Cary.

Indian Constitution: Trends and Issues (1978) : Rajiv Dhavan, Alice Jacob (ed.).

37 Law and Contemporary Social Problems : Meannis.

Law and Contemporary Problems: The Historical and Constitutional Context of the Proposal–Canadian Charter of Rights and Freedoms (44) (1981), 169 : Walters Tarnopolsky.

Law and Contemporary Problems: The Privacy of Govt. Employees, p. 413 : William A. Crench.

Law and Contemporary Problems, Privacy in Tort Law: Were Warren and Brandeis Wrong (p. 326) : Herry Kalven Jr.

Law and Contemporary Problems, p. 342: The Files, Legal Controls over the Accuracy and Accessibility of Stored Personal Data : Kenneth L. Karst.

Law and Contemporary Problems, p. 377: Privacy in Welfare Public Assistance and Juvenile Justice : Joel F. Handley and Margret K. Rosenheim.

Law of Torts, 9th Edition, p. 501 : Winfield & Jolowicz.

Legislative History of the Privacy Act of 1974, September, 1976, Source Book on Privacy : U.S. Government Printing House, 1976.

Liberty and Law, Tagore Law Lecture : Zelmeck Cohon.

"Life and Liberty in First Ten Years of Republican India" 2JJLJ 241 at 266 (1959-60) : Alan Gledhill.

Michigan Law Review (May, June 1975) Project : Increasing Protection of Citizen Privacy.

Natural Law and Natural Rights (1966) : John Finnis.

Our Fundamental Rights–their nature and extent as judicially determined (1968) : D.N. Banerjee.

One Dimensional Man (1964) : Herbert Marcuse.

Privacy, Atherton Press, New York, 1979 : Pennack Roland J. & Chapnson J.

Privacy and Freedom, New York, Athenem, 1967 : A.P. Westin.
"Privacy: Its Constitution and Vicissitudes", Law and Contemporary Problems, 31, No. 2 (Spring 1966), p. 281 : Edward Shils.
Privacy and the Press, The Law, the Mass Media and the First Amendment : Pember D.R.
Personal Liberty: Meaning and Scope, 1950–1975 (9) J.C. P.S. 1975, p. 423 : Vinod Sethi.
Philosophical Views on the Value of Privacy (319) : Glenn Negley.
Privacy and Autonomy: Columbia Law Review (74), 1974 (1410) : Lewis Menkin.
Privacy and Human Rights (ed.), p. 176 : A.H. Robertson.
Privacy and the Law – A Philosophical Prelude, Law and Contemporary Problems, Vol. 31, 1966, p. 272 : M.R. Konvitz.
Privacy as a Public Issue: Vidura, June Issue, 1981 (p. 157): G. Mishra.
Public's Right to Know: The Supreme Court and the First Amendment : David M.O'Brien.
Right to Privacy, The H.W. Wilson Company, New York, 1976 : Edited by Grant S. McClellan.
Right to Privacy, 1973 : William Seuern.
Right to Privacy: Jagdish Swaroop.
Redefining Privacy, 12 Harv. Civ. Rights., Civil Liberties Review, p. 233 : Tom Gaiety.
Right to Life under the Constitution of India: Zaffar Ahmad.
"The Right to Privacy is a Myth", Saturday Evening Post, July 27, 1968, pages 8, 9 : Bruno Bettelheim.
The Right to Privacy (November 1971) in 1st chapter – A Most Comprehensive Right, Lincoln University of Nebraska Press : Adam Carlyle, Breckenridge.
"Right to Privacy" in "Human Rights in the United Kingdom", Pamphlet, 162, 1978 : Central Office of Information Reference.
Right to Freedom of Movement of Individuals under the Constitution of India : B. Errabi.
Right to Personal Liberty and the Rule of Law : Ramesh K. Keswani.
Right to Personal Liberty in interpretation of Art. 21 : Vijay Kumar Shali.
The Right to be Let Alone: A Fundamental Right, 1977, Vol. (17) IA, p. 80 : F.S. Nariman.
Right to Know Symposium held in Faculty of Law, University of Delhi on 9th December, 1981 : P.K. Tripathi.

The Right to Privacy 1980 (4), Harv. L. Rev. 193 : Warren and Brandeis.

The Right to be Let Alone (1979) 4 SCC I (Journal Section) : K.K. Mathew.

The Right to Privacy and American Law : William M. Beaney.

Science, Privacy and Freedom – Issues and Proposals, 66 Columbia L. Rev. 1003 : Westin

Society's Interest in the Privacy of the Individual (Chapter 2) in Modern Constitutional Law, Volume I. The Individual and the Government : Chester J. Antieau.

Social Dimensions of Law and Justice at 199 (1966) : Julius Stone.

Social Inquiry and the Autonomy of the Individual: The Human Meaning of the Social Sciences (New York. Meriolin Books Inc. 1959), p. 120 : Daniel Leamex (ed.).

The Framing of Indian Constitution (1967) : Shiva B. Rao.

Torture and the Right to Human Dignity (1981), 4 SCC 31 : Paras Diwan.

Treatise on the Law of Torts, 2nd Ed. Chicago, Callaghan & Co. 1888, p. 29 : Judge Cooley.

Was Due Process Due – A Critical Study of the Protection of Reasonableness in Art. 21 since Maneka Gandhi (1983) I SCCI : Solil Paul.

With Liberty and Justice For All (1968) : Harold V. Knight.

Your Right to Know : Whalen.

LIST OF CASES

1. A.K. Roy *Vs.*Union of India (1981) 1 SCC 274
2. Abortion Reform Law Cases 39 B Verf GEI (1975)
3. Agnello *Vs.* United States (1925) 269 U.S. 20
4. Alderman *Vs.* United States 394 U.S. 165
5. Amalgamated Society of Engineers *Vs.* Adelado Steamship Co. Ltd.
6. Bachan Singh *Vs.* State of Punjab (1980) 2 SCC 684
7. Bell *Vs.* Marylad 378 U.S. 226 (1964)
8. Beham Khursid *Vs.* Bombay State AIR 1965 SC 123
9. Berger *Vs.* United States
10. Berger *Vs.* New York 388 U.S. 31 (1967)
11. Boyd *Vs.* United States 116 U.S. 616 (1886)
12. Bread *Vs.* Alexandria (1951) 341 U.S. 622
13. Breithaupt *Vs.* Abram (1957), 352 U.S. 432
14. Buckley *Vs.* Attorney General
15. Buck *Vs.* Bell (1929) 274 U.S. 200
16. Camera *Vs.* Municipal Court 387 U.S. 523 (1967)
17. Cantwell *Vs.* Connecticut 310 U.S. 296 (1940)
18. Carey *Vs.* Population Services International 431 U.S. 678 (1977) at 685
19. Charles Sobhraj *Vs.* Supdt. Central Jail, Tihar, AIR 1978 SC 1514
20. Chiml *Vs.* California 395 U.S. 752 (1969)
21. Coolidge *Vs.* New Hampshire (343) U.S. 451
22. Davis *Vs.* Berry (1914) D.C. Iowa 262 F. 687
23. Davis *Vs.* United States 328 U.S. 582 (1946)
24. D'Emden *Vs.* Peddar
25. District of Columbia in Ackerley *Vs.* Ley 420 F 2d. 1336 (1969)

26. Dit Law *Vs.* Shultz (1974)
27. D.B. Mohan Patraik *Vs.* State of A.P. (1975) 3 SCC 185
28. Doe Vs. Bolton
29. Doe et al *Vs.* Commonwealth's Attorney 403 F. Supp. 199 (1975)
30. Donalive *Vs.* Warner Bros. Pictures Inc. (1952) CA 10 Utah 194 F 2d. 6
31. Eastland *Vs.* United States Serviceman's Fund
32. Eisenstadt *Vs.* Baird 405 U.S. 438, 453-54
33. Express Newspapers (P) Ltd. *Vs.* Union of India (1959) SCR 12
34. Francis Corlie Mullin *Vs.* Delhi Administration (1981) I SCC 608
35. Frank *Vs.* Maryland 359 U.S. 360 (1959)
36. Getman *Vs.* NLRB (1971)
37. Gitlow *Vs.* New York
38. Goldman *Vs.* United States (1942) 316 U.S. 129
39. Govind *Vs.* State of M.P. (1975) (3) SCR 946
40. Griswold *Vs.* Connecticut, 381 U.S. 479
41. Harvinder Kaur *Vs.* Harminder Singh AIR 1984 Delhi 66
42. Hoffa *Vs.* United States 385 U.S. 293 (1966)
43. Hogan *Vs.* The Queen
44. Homosexuality Case 6B Vexf. GE 389 (1957)
45. Hussainara Khatoon *Vs.* State of Bihar (1980) ISCC 81
46. Inder Singh *Vs.* State (Delhi Administration) AIR 1978 SC 107
47. In *re* O' Leighlei's (1960) I.R. 93
48. In *re* Karen Quinlan 70 N.J. 10 (1976)
49. In *re* Ratnawala AIR 1962 Mad. 31 (35)
50. Irvine *Vs.* California 374 U.S. 128 (1954)
51. Jane Roe *Vs.* Henry Wade, 410 U.S. 113
52. Johnson *Vs.* United States (1948) 333 US 10
53. Jolly George Verghese *Vs.* Bank of Cochin AIR 1980 S.C. 470

54. Jones *Vs*. United States (1958) 357 U.S. 493
55. Kastigar *Vs*. United States 406 U.S. 441 (1972)
56. Katz *Vs*. United States (1967) 389 U.S. 347
57. Keshwananda Bharati Case AIR 1973 SC 1461
58. Kharak Singh *Vs*. State of U.P. AIR 1963 SC 1295
59. King *Vs*. The Queen (1969) 1 A.C. 304
60. Kishore Singh *Vs*. State of Rajasthan AIR 1981 SC 625
61. Laird *Vs*. Tatum 408 US 1 (1972)
62. Lanza *Vs*. New York 370 U.S. 139 (1962)
63. Lee *Vs*. United States 343 U.S. 747 (1952)
64. Lopez *Vs*. United States (1963)
65. Loving *Vs*. Virginia 388 U.S. 1, 12 (1967)
66. Lourenco Rocha *Vs*. Euclidas Joao Rodrigues AIR 1968 Goa 48
67. Malak Singh *Vs*. State of Punjab AIR 1981 SC 760
68. Maneka Gandhi *Vs*. Union of India (1979) 1 SCC 248
69. Mapp *Vs*. Ohio 367 U.S. 643 (1961)
70. Martin *Vs*. Struthers (1943) 319 U.S. 141
71. Maryland Drydock Co. *Vs*. NLRB (1950 CAA) 183F 2d. 538
72. Mcgee *Vs*. Attorney General & Revenue Commissioners (1974) I.R. 284
73. Memod *Vs*. Mitchell
74. Meyer *Vs*. Nebraska 262 U.S. 390, 399 (1923)
75. Miranda *Vs*. Arizona 384 U.S. 436 (1966)
76. Minerva Mills Ltd. *Vs*. Union of India AIR 1980 SC 1789 at 1811
77. Mohd. Hussain Saheb *Vs*. Chartered Bank AIR 1964 (1 Mad. 1012)
78. Monroe *Vs*. Pope 365 U.S. 167 (1961)
79. Morgentaler *Vs*. The Queen (1975) 20 C.C.C. (2d) 449
80. M.P. Sharma *Vs*. Satish Chandra (1954) SCR 1077
81. Munn *Vs*. Illinois 94 U.S. 13 (1877)
82. NAACP *Vs*. Alabama, 357 U.S. 449 (1958)
83. NAACP Vs. Button 371 U.S. 415 (1963)

84. Nardone *Vs*. United States 302 U.S. 379 (1937)
85. Near *Vs*. Minnesota 283 U.S. 679 (1931)
86. New York Times Company Vs. Sullivan 376 U.S. 254 (1964)
87. Nixon *Vs*. Sirica (1973)
88. Olmstead *Vs*. United States 277 U.S. 438 (1928)
89. Osborn *Vs*. U.S. 385 U.S. 323, 1966
90. Paverich *Vs*. New England Life Insurance Co. 122 G.A. 190 (1905)
91. Pierce *Vs*. Society of Sisters 268 U.S. 510, 535 (1925)
92. Planned Parenthood of Missori *Vs*. Danforth (1976-49 L Ed. 2d. 788)
93. Poe *Vs*. Ullman 367 U.S. 497
94. Prince *Vs*. Massachusetts 321, U.S. 158, 166 (1944)
95. Privacy of Communications Case 30 B Verf GEI (1970)
96. Public Utility Commission *Vs*. Pollock 343 U.S. 451
97. Quinn *Vs*. Ryan
98. Ramesh Thapar *Vs*. State of Madras (1950) SCR 594
99. Redrup *Vs*. New York (1967) 386 U.S. 767
100. Reid *Vs*. Covert 354 U.S.I 1957
101. Regina *Vs*. Drybones
102. Robles *Vs*. Environmental Protection Agency 484 F 2d. 843
103. Rochin *Vs*. California (1952) 342 U.S. 165
104. Roop Lal Makker *Vs*. Jagdish Singh AIR 1978 NOC Delhi 255
105. Rose *Vs*. Department of the Air Force (1974)
106. Rudal Shah *Vs*. State of Bihar AIR 1983 SC 1086
107. Rural Housing Alliance *Vs*. Department of Agriculture (1974)
108. Sampat Prakash *Vs*. State of Jammu & Kashmir (1969) 2 SCR 547
109. Satwant Singh Sawhney *Vs*. APO New Delhi AIR 1967 SC 1836
110. Schwartz *Vs*. Texas 344 U.S. 199 (1952)
111. Schemerber *Vs*. California (1966) 384 U.S. 757

112. Seekalz *Vs*. United States (389) U.S. 347
113. Silverman *Vs*. United States (1961) 365 U.S. 505
114. Sheonath Prasad Vs. State of Bihar AIR 1966 SC 1577
115. Sharma *Vs*. Satish (1954) SCR 107
116. Slaughter House Cases 83 U.S. (1873)
117. Skinner *Vs*. Oklahoma (1942) 316 U.S. 535
118. Smith *Vs*. Wayre Probate Judge (1925) 231 Mich. 409
119. South West Case 1 B Venf. GE 14 (1951)
120. State (Coughlan) *Vs*. Minister for Justice (1967) I.R. 106
121. State (O'Haa) *Vs*. Governor of the Central Mental Hospital (1971)
122. State of Bombay *Vs*. Katni Kalu (1962) 3 SCR 10
123. State of Rajasthan *Vs*. Rehman AIR 1960 SC 210
124. State of Maharashtra *Vs*. Prabhakar (1966) ISCR 702
125. Stanley *Vs*. Georgia 394 U.S. 557 (1969)
126. Sunil Batra *Vs*. Delhi Administration (1978) 4 SCC 494
127. Sweety *Vs*. New Hampshire
128. Terry *Vs*. Ohio 392 U.S.I (1968)
129. Time Inc. *Vs*. Hill (1967) 385 US. 377
130. The New Swadeshi Mills of Ahmedabad *Vs*. S.K. Rattan AIR 1968 Gujarat 117
131. The State (Quinn) *Vs*. Ryan (1965) I.R. 70
132. T. Sareetha *Vs*. T. Venkata Subbiah AIR 1983 A.P. 356
133. Tuchinsky *Vs*. Selective Service System (1969)
134. United States *Vs*. Burn
135. United States *Vs*. Giordnno 416 U.S. 505 (1974)
136. United States *Vs*. Kohn 415 U.S. 143 (1974)
137. United States *Vs*. Nixon 418 U.S. 683
138. United States *Vs*. United States District Court 407 U.S. 297 (1972)
139. Victoria Park Racing Co. *Vs*. Taylor (1937) 58 C.L.R. 479
140. Waden *Vs*. Hoyden 387 U.S. 294 (1967)
141. Wainwright *Vs*. Stone 414 U.S. 21 (1973)
142. Weeks *Vs*. United States 232 U.S. 383 (1914)

143. Wilson *Vs*. United States 221 U.S. 361 (1911)
144. Winc Hobby USA Inc. *Vs*. United States Bureau of Alcohol, Tobacco and Firearms, 1973
145. Wilson *Vs*. United States 221 U.S. 361 (1911)
146. Wolf *Vs*. Colorado (1949) 338 U.S. 25
147. Wyman *Vs*. James 400 U.S. 309 (1971)
148. Zeblocki *Vs*. Redhall (1978) 54 L.Ed. 2d. 618
149. Zicarelli *Vs*. State Commissioner of Investigations, 406 U.S. 472 (1972)

LIST OF DOCUMENTS

1. Constituent Assembly Debates, Vol. VII & IX
2. Constitutions of Congo, Czechoslovakia, Zambia
3. International Covenant on Civil and Political Rights, 1966
4. Convention for Protection of Human Rights & Fundamental Freedom, 1950
5. The Report of the Indian Commission, 1930
6. The Report of the Joint Committee of Indian Constitutional Reform, 1934
7. United Nations Declaration of Human Rights, 1948
8. American Convention on Human Rights, 1969
9. European Convention on Human Rights, 1950
10. International Covenant on Economic, Social and Cultural Rights, 1966
11. Montreal Statement of the Assembly for Human Rights, 1968
12. The Younger Committee Report, 1972

INDEX